PHENOMENAL

WORLD

REMOTE VIEWING, ASTRAL TRAVEL, APPARITIONS, EXTRATERRESTRIALS, LUCID DREAMS AND OTHER FORMS OF INTELLIGENT CONTACT IN THE MAGICAL KINGDOM OF MIND-AT-LARGE

by Joan d'Arc

THE BOOK TREE
ESCONDIDO, CALIFORNIA

Phenomenal World: Remote Viewing, Astral Travel, Apparitions, Extraterrestrials, Lucid Dreams and Other Forms of Intelligent Contact in the Magical Kingdom of Mind-at-Large
ISBN 1-58509-128-6

THIS IS VOLUME TWO IN THIS SERIES:

VOLUME ONE: Space Travelers and the Genesis of the Human Form
ISBN 1-58509-127-8

LAYOUT AND DESIGN
Tedd St. Rain

COVER ART:

M57, The Ring Nebula, Hubble Space Telescope (January 1999)

Printed on Acid-Free Paper

Published by
The Book Tree
Post Office Box 724
Escondido, CA 92033

We provide controversial and educational products to help awaken the public to new ideas and information that would not be available otherwise. We carry over 1000 Books, Booklets, Audio, Video, and other products on AIDS, Alchemy, Aliens, Alternative Medicine, Ancient America, Ancient Astronauts, Ancient Civilizations, Ancient Mysteries, Ancient Religion and Worship, Angels, Anthropology, Anti-Gravity, Archaeology, Area 51, Assyria, Astrology, Atlantis, Babylonia, Biowarfare, Townsend Brown, Chemical Warfare, Christianity, CIA, Cold Fusion, Colloidal Silver, Comparative Religions, Conspiracies, Crop Circles, The Dead Sea Scrolls, The Drug War, Early History, Electromagnetics, Electro-Gravity, ELFs, Egypt, EMAG Smog, ET Archaeology, Extraterrestrials, Fascism, Michael Faraday, Fatima, The Federal Reserve, Fluoride, Flying Saucers, Forfeiture Laws, Free Energy, Freemasonry, Global Manipulation, The Gnostics, God, Gravity, The Great Pyramid, Gyroscopic Anti-Gravity, Healing EMAG, Health Issues, Hinduism, Hollow Earth, Human Origins, Implantable Microchips, Jehovah, Jesus, Jordan Maxwell, John Keely, Lemuria, Lost Cities, Lost Continents, Magic, Masonry, Mercury Poisoning, Metaphysics, Microwaves, Mind Control, MK-Ultra, Monetary Systems, Mythology, NWO, Occultism, OKC, Paganism, Pesticide Pollution, Personal Growth, The Philadelphia Experiement, Philosophy, Population Control, Powerlines, Prophecy, Psychic Research, Pyramids, Rare Books, Religion, Religious Controversy, Roswell, Walter Russell, Scalar Waves, SDI, John Searle, Secret Societies, Sex Worship, Sitchin Studies, Smart Cards, Joseph Smith, Solar Power, Sovereignty, Space Travel, Spirituality, Stonehenge, Sumeria, Sun Myths, Symbolism, Tachyon Fields, Templars, Tesla, Theology, Time Travel, The Treasury, UFOs, Underground Bases, World Control, The World Grid, Zero Point Energy, and much more. Call **1 (800) 700-TREE** for our *FREE BOOK TREE CATALOG* or visit our website at www.thebooktree.com for more information.

TABLE OF CONTENTS

ACKNOWLEDGEMENTS

Grateful acknowledgements to the iconoclasts: David Abram, David Bohm, Trevor Constable, Michael Cremo, Bob Dobbs, Amit Goswami, Martin Gray, William Gray, Nick Herbert, L. Ron Hubbard, David Icke, L. Kin, Thomas Kuhn, Paul Laffoley, Gregory Little, John Mack, Harold McGowan, Joseph Chilton Pearce, Dean Radin, Israel Regardie, Dan Russell, Elisabet Sahtouris, Jack Sarfatti, Ingo Swann, Michael Talbot, Charles Tart, Colin Wilson, Fred Alan Wolf; and to those iconoclasts on whose shoulders they stand, the philosophers: G.I. Gurdjieff, P.D. Ouspensky, Edmund Husserl, Maurice Merleau-Ponty, Martin Heidegger, Rupert Sheldrake, and Jean Paul Sartre; the occultists: Alice Bailey, Annie Besant, Helena Blavatsky, Max Heindel, C.W. Leadbetter; and the inventors: Wilhelm Reich, Nikola Tesla and Marcel Vogel.

Special gratitude to artist Paul Laffoley for reading my manuscript and providing the encouragement to pursue this research, and for making the provocative assertion which avalanched into this book: that "Magic is the wave of the future." Gratis to my publisher, The Book Tree, for giving these works a fighting chance.

This book is dedicated to mind control victims and ritually-abused children, whose pain should remain our pain and whose battle should remain our battle until human beings learn to create only free energy and white magic.

Volume one in this series, *Space Travelers and the Genesis of the Human Form*, (ISBN 1-58509-127-8, available from The Book Tree) leaves off where this book picks up.

INTRODUCTION

Phenomenal World is Volume II of an investigation into the materialist scientific world view and how that mindset informs us that physically measurable phenomena are all that exist. *Phenomenal World* illustrates that the nature of human existence is to be stuck in a historical freeze frame which imposes the captivating belief system that the reality currently presenting itself from 'out there' represents the ultimate truth. But if quantum physics is correct, this reality is more like a shimmering holographic mirage teetering from moment to moment on the cusp of panoramic potential, and we, the participants, are holding it all in place by an agreement known as 'consensus reality.'

This investigation began with Volume I, the book *Space Travelers and the Genesis of the Human Form*, which explores the possibility that the earth and human consciousness is a 'construct.' In Volume I, the author explored the Space Travel Argument Against the Existence of ETI. This argument is shown to be dependent on three factors: (1) the persistent imposition of Earth-centered technological constraints (specifically, rocket technology and radio signals) implying an anthropocentric 'you can't get here from there'attitude; (2) mathematical logic deduced from the faulty linear notions of Darwinian evolution, which only serve to put the 'cart before the horse'; and (3) a circular and untestable hypothesis which essentially states 'they aren't here because they aren't here.'

In Volume I, the author also illustrated that Darwinian evolution is actually not an empirically predictable or testable scientific paradigm, but is a highly touted philosophy of Western materialism. The author deduced that Darwinian evolution is a circular argument which serves to keep Earth humans earthbound, since it keeps us from potentially adding up 2+2 with regard to our true ancestry from the "sky" rather than from the "water." Furthermore, the author illustrated that ancient anthropomorphic artifacts on Mars and the Moon may be evidence of "Game Wardens" in our own solar system; suggesting that the Earth is a controlled DNA repository for the ongoing creation and dissemination of life forms, including humans. It is in this sense that the world of our perception, the phenomenal world, can be considered a 'construct.'

Volume II of this continued investigation, *Phenomenal World*, revisits the Science of Experience propounded by the existentialist and phenomenological philosophers Husserl, Merleau-Ponty, Heidegger, Sartre and others as a basis for understanding the role of such 'constructs' in the development of a shared personal world view. We are reminded in these pages that 'reality'is a provision of social consensus; reality is 'brought to you by' an historically-bound scientific construct. Our modern reality construct is the materialist world view. In this sense, the second book is an introduction to the first book, but, at the same time, it completes the message of the first book; that message being: *all is not as it seems.*

Research into psychic phenomena has a long and distinguished history of which we are largely unaware due to our current materialist bias which sees the individual, isolated brain as the source and control center of intelligent communication. There is a large body of research into psychic phenomena which cannot be sufficiently covered here, and which the reader is encouraged to examine if sufficiently interested. Arguments against the existence of a psychic force or human 'X-Factor' have generally been based on the inability to locate, measure, quantify or qualify an energy or medium capable of carrying 'thought' emanations across time and space: a 'nonlocal' causal connection. However, because this unknown factor or energy is not recognized by mainstream science, and most experimental research in this area has a tendency to be 'non-repeatable,' should we automatically deny the existence of a 'nonlocal' psychic force capable of distance communication and influence?

After publication of *Space Travelers* in 2000 I received feedback from all points of view. As the co-publisher since 1992 of the well known conspiracy magazine *Paranoia: The Conspiracy Reader*, and as a well known author in the conspiracy genre, I received many questions regarding the ultimate 'conspiracy;' that of the totalitarian invasion of the human soul by non-human entities. The ultimate question on everybody's lips seemed to be 'is there a conspiracy or cover-up concerning the 'true'nature of reality?'

One might suspect that in order for there to be a conspiracy in this regard, at least some human beings would have to have information that the general populace doesn't have with regard to the true nature of reality. In this case, this assumption might be suspect, since no human being could actually *know* the answer to the ultimate question: 'what is reality?' Yet, on the other hand, could there be a conspiracy or cover-up by persons who *think* they know the true nature of reality, or who believe they hold a defining or at least controlling key, or who *carry on as though* they can *manipulate* reality to their own ends? Also, could there be a cover-up by non-human entities who feel it is in the best interest of Earth humans to be unaware of the existence of other human types in the universe, and/or could certain elite world leaders have convinced such Visitors that this is necessary to avoid societal chaos? Furthermore, might the Earth and all life upon it in the three-dimensional world be an experimental construct? Or, conversely, might the nature of three-dimensional reality be simply an illusion, as ancient religious doctrines teach? *Phenomenal World* explores all these possibilities.

Due to space considerations, it is not possible in this work to include a sizable overview of the mind control literature, although it will touch upon some of the basics, and the reader is urged to explore the pertinent information contained in the bibliography and suggested reading list. In this regard, this book is meant to complement works in the mind control genre, and to contribute information pertaining to how the development of mind control programming is related to both magical systems and to developments in theoretical physics. It goes without saying but must be noted nonetheless that the vast military/corporate intelligence apparatus is not only well aware of these relations but has manipulated and funded physics research toward this end since World War II.

As this book illustrates, the information management of these two elements—magic and physics—have created a totalitarian regime comprising a modern day secret society of sorts. This information is kept secret in order to keep power in the hands of the few; for, as we must readily admit, knowledge IS power, and the more secretive the nature of the knowledge, the more powerful it is.

The aim of this book is to explore the principles of magic and physics in order to get to the bottom of the intelligence community's fascination with psychic phenomena—i.e., the 'supernatural'—including the reasons for UFO secrecy and what that might have to do with issues of mind control and psychological warfare. The fact that new developments in physics are being utilized to manipulate, control and contain human consciousness can no longer be denied. It is the purpose of these heinous machinations and their trials on planetary citizens that is beyond human ability to comprehend. This is directly due to the fact that the information pertaining to current developments in theoretical physics is in the ownership of the hands of an elite faction of society—a global military intelligence 'Beast' which can be considered, for all practical purposes, a secret society.

This information is also kept hidden under the pernicious cover of the outmoded scientific paradigm of materialist cause and effect. This hegemony essentially comprises a cover-up of the potential for cause on the material plane to be effected from another platform: the unseen dimensions of space-time. What this means is that the purpose we are all looking for, the inexplicable reason for the tortures and power-plays of a covert mind control apparatus, may be a hidden effect of fourth dimensional phenomena, the very existence of which the materialist mindset miscomprehends as a matter of course and, therefore, fully denies.

This point of view necessarily opens up a can of worms regarding the nature of 'evil.' What is evil? Can evil planetary machinations be simply chalked up to 'greed' on the part of an elite global faction? Are concepts of class, money, power and greed enough to explain the drive toward total Earth population control? Or does there quite simply have to be more to it than that? Is evil on a grand scale something that can be attributed to unseen, perhaps inter-dimensional, forces? Does the tail wag the dog?

These are questions for which, perhaps, there is no readily identifiable answer, but, as we embark on our odyssey into the 21st Century, a shift toward open discussion of the following concepts may become inevitable: Who is pulling the invisible strings? Is magic simply hocus-pocus, or is there more to it? Have magicians and occultists actually been in contact with entities, intelligences or powers from higher dimensions? Is there a telepathic war of the worlds being fought on planet Earth for planetary bounty, i.e., souls and/or human 'containers' in which to put them? Unfortunately, these are questions we no longer have the luxury of placing in a category with other ideas attributable to fringe fundamentalist theological politics.

The other problem that necessarily arises in connection with this exploration is the concept of good vs. evil. Since human beings are accustomed to equate concepts of good and evil to behaviors and actions, it is difficult to shed this programming, particularly as it regards an unbiased appraisal of the concepts of magic and the occult (occult meaning 'hidden knowledge').

This book attempts to keep an open mind about subject matter which may normally elicit an emotional reaction from those with certain religious leanings. However, I am not an occultist and I do not claim to have detailed knowledge of any secret magical rituals. I have simply tried to expose the very general attitudes and teachings of certain schools of both Eastern and Western esoteric knowledge, and how these concepts are related to a physics of consciousness which has been under study by the intelligence community over the past forty plus years. We must also be aware, with regard to the intelligence/national defense community's interest in physics and UFO propulsion, that this interest is two-fold.

The most obvious question physics has to answer regarding UFOs might come under the heading 'mode of travel,' or how do they get here? What type of science and technology might be utilized by an advanced spacefaring ETI and how can developments in theoretical physics help us to achieve the same spacefaring status? However, we must realize that — going beyond the obvious — the presence of UFOs in our skies has forced a reappraisal of the nature of time, space and reality. Therefore, a perhaps less obvious question which arises might be: What kind of world allows visitors from time and what would be the implications of this paradigm-shattering news on human beings accustomed to cause and effect linear explanations for events occurring in the material world?

This analysis carries us back to the infamous Brookings Report of 1961, wherein our government was advised by a think tank called the Brookings Institute that human beings could not handle this type of information. This book explores the idea that the potential threat of such a dangerous paradigm shift causing chaos to Earth's social institutions (i.e. science, religion and other dogma) is at the bottom of the intelligence community's interest in UFO phenomena, and is also one of the main reasons for UFO secrecy in general.

Phenomenal World explores the correlations between physics, magic and existential philosophy. Yet, readers must realize that in order to fully explore this enigma, we must delve into the sometimes 'dark' abyss of obscure occult/arcane knowledge: of that which is considered 'supernatural' within our current materialist scientific confines. As this book will illustrate, the supernatural becomes a natural matter when you utilize a Science of Experience, a science which returns to full and complete trust of the sensory experience of the human being, to that which 'seems' to be real according to the qualities of sensations, rather than that which is 'proven' to be real according to scientifically accepted quantitative measurements.

Phenomenal World explores the human experience of such things as out-of-body experience, remote viewing, lucid dreaming, the LSD experience, psychic-machine interface, spirit manifestation and ETI contact, and will also attempt to understand why the intelligence community might be interested in such 'supernatural' phenomena. Why are U.S. intelligence agencies interested in such things as LSD, remote viewing, lucid dreaming and mind control technology? What is the connection between arcane/occult precepts, the 'new' physics of consciousness and the vast intelligence apparatus? *Phenomenal World* digs into these connections to find the common denominator: occult mind control.

From P.D. Ouspensky's *Tertium Organum*, this book borrows the following proposition:

> We may say—not as a supposition but as a definite affirmation—that the world of physical phenomena represents as it were a section of another world, which also exists *here*, and the events of which take place *here*, but invisibly to us. Nothing is more miraculous and supernatural than life. ... We have every right to regard the visible phenomenal world as a section of some other world, infinitely more complex, which at a given moment is manifesting itself for us in the first one.

> The phenomenal aspect of the world is limited and finite, embracing those properties of a given thing which we can generally know as phenomena; the *noumenal* aspect of the world is unlimited. ... This world of *noumena* is infinite and incomprehensible for us, just as the three-dimensional world in all variety of its functions is incomprehensible for the two-dimensional being. The nearest approximation to 'truth' possible for man is contained in the formulation: *each thing has an infinite variety of meanings, and to know all these meanings is impossible.* In other words, truth as we understand it, i.e. the finite definition, is possible only in a finite series of phenomena. In an infinite series it is bound somewhere to become is own opposite.

> We must remember that the world as we know it does not represent anything stable. It must change with the slightest change in the forms of our perception. Phenomena which appear to us totally unrelated may be seen by another, wider consciousness as parts of one whole. Phenomena which appear to us completely identical may look totally different. ... And everything together may form one whole, but in a category quite incomprehensible to us. Therefore, side by side with our view of things, another view is possible—a view as it were from another world, from 'over there', from 'that which lies on the other side.'

> But 'over there' signifies not another place, but another method of perception, a new understanding. And we shall begin to look not from *here* but from *over there* if we regard a phenomenon not as something isolated, but in conjunction with all the chains intersecting in it.

The phenomenal world is truly a remarkable place, and even more so if we attempt to see it without the prejudices and practicalities we have learned to impose upon it. What is the meaning of mankind's existence, with the phenomenal world as background and human existence as foreground? Is it, as Sartre insists, there for our own ends, to make of it an existential and meaningful challenge? What is our relationship with everything we see, as well as everything we don't see? *Phenomenal World* attempts to answer these questions from the point of view of strange 'unexplainable' phenomena, and how these events may be explainable if we look at them from 'over there.'

—Joan d'Arc

CHAPTER ONE

A SCIENCE OF EXPERIENCE:

PHENOMENOLOGY AND "STRANGE" PHENOMENA

Suddenly my feet are feet of mud
It all goes slo-mo,
I don't know why I'm crying
Am I suspended in Gaffa?

Kate Bush

Now, it was an ordinary day, Sir. I love being in the Bush, I love the smell of the animals, the smell of the trees, the sound of the birds. I was just thinking, and all of a sudden I was aware of a strange silence all around me. This lasted a few moments when all around me there was a blue smoke, a sort of vapor which obscured the landscape. I could no longer see the trees, hear the birds, or feel the heat of the sun. I was standing there looking stupid and feeling even stupider, when I was suddenly in a place made of iron, looking like a water tank lying on its side. I'm inside this thing, the thing has a floor, and I'm lying on a table, Sir, looking like a working table and around it was a blue stuff like a plastic curtain. I had no clothes on. I said, 'I want to get off this table.' It made no sense. Why was I lying here? Where was 'here'?

Then through the curtain I saw these dolls looking at me, like tribal dolls, you know, they looked stupid, with faces like white clay and those eyes which are like nothing on Earth. What scared me so was that they were alive. They were coming from somewhere. They were coming towards me, but the way they walked was ridiculous. They walked as if they had no bones, like chickens with broken legs. They were coming, but not saying anything, and I was just lying there like a stupid, thinking where am I? Am I in the hospital? Am I dead? What's going on? And what is this terrible stink? There was light but not like electric lights. They came all around me, about six of them, all wearing a kind of silvery gray, crinkley, shiny uniform. They were about two and a half feet tall.

This alien abduction story was reported by a 73-year old South African medicine man and artist named Credo Mutwa. Mutwa is a scholar and historian, and is the author of several books on the history of the Zulu tribe; among them: *My People: Writings of a Zulu Witchdoctor* and *Indaba, My Children.*

This profoundly disturbing experience occurred during the 1970s while Mr. Mutwa was working for a mining company in the African Bush. While on a South African public television program called Agenda in late November of 1994, Harvard psychiatrist, Dr. John Mack, interviewed the shaman, who had appeared on the program to talk about his experiences with what he calls "shapeshifting" entities. His sculptures of the abducting entities remarkably resemble the image of the alien "gray." Dr. Mack has shown this videotaped interview with the shaman during public talks before audiences interested in these phenomena.

Let us return to this profoundly existential happening. The shaman reports: "Their eyes were like plastic, no mouth, no lips, just a little cut, like a razor cut pierced on an angry body." When you look into the eyes, Credo reports, you see no detail, "just an empty eternity, a void, no expression." Using his own native expressions, as well as comparisons from his native culture, Credo depicts humanoids with no hair and no ears, and with an extra joint on their fingers. He describes the skin as "reptilian, like human but with no hair." They moved like "flowing water, like a ballerina, very slowly." Credo's body was almost completely paralyzed; and he could not speak. The entities were not holding him and had not tied him down, but somehow he could not move anything but his eyes.

Credo explains that one of the entities was different, and that he "felt strongly" from the beginning that she was a woman. She was bigger than the others but, he felt, she was not the leader. Later, he recounts, "this mendina (spelled phonetically), the female, came up to me." He recalls certain abnormalities about her physical nature. Speaking "as an artist for many years" he insists, "her arms were too short for her body, she looked even more like a doll than those other creatures looked like dolls. Her skin looked as if it was polished."

We can imagine the incredible chill Credo experienced when the "mendina" put her hands on his face. He explains, "this was a living hand, but this creature felt utterly unnatural. She was not warm like a human being. She felt like a dead body." Although the skin of this entity appeared lifelike, there seemed to be "no beating of blood in the veins." Then, he recounts, she climbed on him "like a crazy Zulu girl" and had sexual intercourse with him. She moved "like a machine" and there was no "woman's smell." Then Credo explains, embarrassed, "I ejaculated too much" and another creature put something over him to collect the sperm. He recounts, "I was very ashamed and my man-thing was burning, as if put in scalding water."

When he returned from this first abduction experience, Credo reports that he smelled like "rotting fish," although he had not been near a river. In addition, his skin was covered with a "gray dust." He wandered lost in the Bush until he saw human footprints and came to a small village where people recognized him as the man who had been missing for three days. He recalls, "every dog was so excited it came and pulled me down." Credo claims he was elated to see his fellow human beings, but apparently the feeling wasn't mutual. The people who found him could only grimace in disgust. They wanted to know why he smelled so bad.

In immense pain all over his body, Credo fell to the ground and was transported to a house by wheelbarrow. He tells Dr. Mack: "Sir, I have had many experiences in my life," including being attacked by lions and crocodiles. But, he adds, "my experience with the mendina was something else." Credo has continued to have abduction experiences throughout his life, as relayed in his book *Indaba My Children*.

At a meeting of the Mutual UFO Network (MUFON) in Rhode Island in 1995, Dr. Mack stated that he is hopeful that such cross-cultural field studies will eventually help to support the reality of the visitor contact experience, since UFO debunkers rationalize that a psychological preoccupation with modern aerospace culture is behind the upsurge of reports of this nature. Mack argues that the international cases he has investigated, among them the South African shaman and several young girls who had a contact experience in a school yard in Zimbabwe, are "relatively independent of western cultural influence," and "maintain structures of the third world realm." He believes these studies might eventually establish the reality of this bizarre and scientifically unexplainable experience, and perhaps find "that place where everybody agrees this is real."

Identifying Flying Objects

Thousands of books have been written on the subject of flying saucers and the phenomenon of alien abductions since pilot Kenneth Arnold first gave the discs their appropriate name as they flew in formation over Mount Ranier in 1947. These books describe in detail an array of activities involving the observance of futuristic 'chariots in the sky' and the off-beat behavior of the occupants thereof.

From the beginning of the UFO enigma it is clear that good faith attempts have been made to apply objective scientific analysis to its study. Thus, the remarkable reports came to be categorized with regard to, among other criteria, an approximate measurement of the distance which the purported object appeared to be from the witness. Those categories define a sighting of a craft within 500 feet as a close encounter of the first kind (CE-I), a sighting of a craft which leaves physical evidence, such as radar readings, landing marks or scorched Earth, as a close encounter of the second kind (CE-II), and a sighting of a craft together with the sighting of occupants (either inside or out and about) as a close encounter of the third kind (CE-III). These three designations, which may be familiar to some readers, were established in the early days of UFO research by J. Allen Hynek, and are based on primarily visual, and to a lesser degree auditory, stimuli, along with hard evidence such as radar readings, scorched Earth areas and high radiation counts where landings have occurred.

The 1950s contactees, like George Adamski, Howard Menger and others claimed to be in contact with a group of benevolent and, it has been noted, rather Aryan-looking 'space brothers' who passed along messages containing dire warnings of future Earth calamity. Such contactee and 'channeled' information has since crept into the UFO literature to become a faith-based metaphysics of the universe. Many of the early contactees eventually confessed to be frauds, making legitimate researchers from then on understandably hesitant to go anywhere near occupant-related claims. Fraudulent reports from New Age channelers and contactees began to tarnish the reputation of legitimate UFO research, and tended to confound reports made by more credible witnesses. In short, it became difficult to separate the bogus claims from those appearing to contain authentic elements.

Every so often, however, occupant motifs that did not fit the contactee mold piqued the interest of UFO researchers. The early contactees, as it turned out, had actually contributed something important to the picture, since they gave researchers an idea of how an *imaginary occupant* might look, or what he might say or do. As Dr. David Jacobs of Temple University suggested at a talk before an Omega Communications UFO Conference in 1988, the bogus reports became a useful template for the qualities of "fraudulence," so that these could be used as a gauge for comparison against potentially authentic reports. Thus, as is evident by the careful demeanor of researchers looking to maintain some semblance of credibility, it had become even more necessary to bring the tools of scientific inquiry to a field of research which, like other parapsychological studies, was apt to be preyed upon by hoaxers.

CE-IV: A Complete Sensory Experience

Researchers began to realize that the new claims being reported in the 1960s and 70s were immensely different from George Adamski's joy rides in flying saucers. On the contrary, the new developments seemed to take an even more bizarre turn for which a new designation, CE-IV, was created. The fourth designation was added when the *taking* of Earth people against their will by the occupants of these craft was first reported in New Hampshire in the early 1960s by Betty and Barney Hill.

A CE-IV experience is characterized by all or most of the following elements: levitating or walking through closed doors or windows; being pulled up as if by a magnet into a hovering UFO; body paralysis and inability to speak; intense fear; telepathic communication with alien beings through their eyes involving transfer of various types of information; physical examinations, often excruciatingly painful, including attention to genital and gynecological examination; group abductee situations involving observation of other abductees in the room; reproductive sexual encounter with alien being or human abductee; painful removal of fetus at about three months' gestation; and later meetings with offspring of those unions for purposes of physical contact.

With regard to reproductive exams, it is reported that males are forced to ejaculate semen by means of masturbation, induction of sexual imagery, by the use of a special instrument, or by introduction of a "female" alien entity. Conversly, female alien abductees are reportedly impregnated by donor sperm without actual sex. This is allegedly followed by the painful extraction of the fetus, which occurs at about 3-month's gestation, followed by the showing of fetuses in tubes of watery substance and, later, the showing of hybrid children and requests by the aliens to hold or touch them. However, there is some disagreement on the subject of sex with aliens. Michelle LaVigne writes, in *The Alien Abduction Survival Guide*, that some experiencers claim that ETs have no sex organs, yet she recalls having sex with them. She was told by one ET that, although they lack the proper sex organ, they can create a very real facsimile of the sex act.

In the U.S., UFO "waves" have occurred in 1947, 1952, 1965-66 and 1973, as well as smaller, less defined waves during 1987-1988. Reportedly, another increase in sightings occurred between 1993 and 1997. Between these UFO waves, local "flaps" occurred in Pine Bush, New York; Fyffe, Alabama; Gulf Breeze, Florida; and LaGrange, Georgia. It has been noted that UFO sightings fall off between these waves. However, reported alien abductions do not seem to fall off as do UFO sightings. They are seemingly a completely different phenomenon.

Abduction events are followed by memory erasure or masking of memories, which often includes the memory of seeing animals, such as deer, with large eyes. There is often an unaccountable lapse of time of two or more hours. There is often pain in the ears, or nosebleeds or sinus problems, indicating that an implant has been inserted into the frontal lobe area of the brain. It is suggested that these implants serve the same purpose as the injectable microchips humans would use to track animals in the wild.

Podiatrist Dr. Roger K. Leir, in his book *The Aliens and the Scalpel*, documents eight surgeries on reported alien abductees in order to remove reputed alien implants. Leir's team has concluded that some individuals with reported abduction histories do have artificially manufactured objects in their bodies, and these objects are of "a demonstrably extraterrestrial origin." His team reports that metallurgical analysis indicates that the composition of the objects removed from these patients reportedly includes metals whose isotopic ratios are not from Earth. In addition, the form of these objects, according to Leir's team, are not naturally occurring shapes. Rather, the forms are consistent with what would be expected from a precision engineered or manufactured artifact. In an article which appeared in *MUFON UFO Journal*, April, 1996, entitled "In Search of Hard Evidence," Dr. Leir describes the first three objects which he surgically removed. The largest object, he writes, was wrapped in a very tight membrane, and appeared to be triangular or star-shaped. The other two resembled small cantaloupe seeds. The objects were wrapped in a very dense, tough gray membrane which was reportedly strong enough to prevent removal with a sharp scalpel. The objects appeared to be magnetic and clung to the blade. After the membranes were removed, a black, shiny metallic core was revealed.

Of course, this new 'hard' evidence is completely different from the evidence that had been previously garnered regarding alien abduction reports. Up until now, a close encounter of the fourth kind has implicated a fundamentally distinct happening, which encompasses the subjective phenomenal/sensory experience of the witness. Some have even suggested perhaps what we are dealing with here is a possible 'sixth sense.' For instance, note that the shaman's first realization that something was amiss was a type of sensory deprivation; he suddenly could "no longer see the trees, hear the birds, or feel the heat of the sun" and sensed that he was "in a place made of iron" like a "water tank on its side." Recall that he could smell a "terrible stink" and could see and feel some kind of strange lighting all around him. He discerned a void, like "an empty eternity" when he looked into the eyes of the entities, and during his sexual encounter he noted there was "no beating of blood in the veins" and "no woman's smell."

Unfortunately, the objective analysis of subjective perceptual phenomena is ambiguous at best, and is at the heart of the question of whether such 'abductions' are occurring at all. Yet, an important point to consider with respect to the ostensibly 'value-free' analyses which are the ideal of scientific rationalism is that they do, after all, have to be interpreted in the "ambiguous realm of everyday life."

As David Abram points out in *The Spell of the Sensuous*, our "spontaneous experience of the world, charged with subjective, emotional and intuitive content, remains the vital ground of all objectivity ... and yet this ground goes largely unnoticed or unacknowledged in scientific culture." He laments that this rather static realm of direct experience has come to be seen as a "secondary, derivative dimension," or simply a "*consequence* of events unfolding in the *realer* world of quantifiable facts." The living person has thus become "an epiphenomenon of the anatomized corpse": that dead mechanical world which we humans have cleverly set about to map. The fact that living, sensing subjects are required to conceptualize, measure and dissect this reality is "brushed aside as inconsequential."

Nonetheless, the scheme of things being as they are, some type of objective guidelines for the study of this novelty in human experience had to be painstakingly carved out from scratch. Of what utility could our current materialist scientific paradigm be with regard to these seemingly immaterial happenings? What type of *specialist* could assist people who had reportedly been *taken* by flying saucer people? Was the experience real in a physical sense, or was it happening, as John Mack wonders, somewhere in the "hazy outer boundaries of the gross physical world?" What does this experience tell us about the nature of physical reality, when the seeming suggestion is that what we *see* is actually held up against a background of movements and causes that we *don't see*?

In addition, how could we avoid the pitfall of interpreting these visitations as a modern mental aberration? It is clear that in the entire history of human civilization, no area of human experience has carried such dire importance to the ruling power structure, and such dire consequences to human liberty, than that sacred realm where 'angels' or 'demons' speak to humans. Tight controls have always been kept by elite practitioners of Church, State and Patriarchy over the transmission lines to 'God,' or the realm beyond our senses. Their controls have included defining the *illness* (after acquiring the requisite sanction) using various labels such as 'demon possession' or 'schizophrenia,' and effecting the requisite *cure* (after acquiring the requisite force) by cutting out the 'demon seed' with burnings, lobotomies, electric shock, behavior modifiers and other psychic tortures. In all these 'treatments' the message is the implicit ownership of those transmission lines.

In order to avoid repetition of our historical mistakes, it is important that these claims are studied with due care and the persons making these claims are treated with utmost dignity. In response to various 'debunker' attitudes, I would respond simply that human society has absolutely nothing to lose and everything to gain by maintaining a humane posture in addressing the Otherworld contact dilemma.

Two People Looking Together at Something

How do human beings 'know' anything? Is knowledge intuitive? How do humans tackle novel problems? How does novel information reach the human mind? Does it enter from the 'outside' or the 'inside'? These questions will be addressed throughout this book by examining the alternative ways in which humans have 'come to know' various articles of faith. This study requires us to permit an exogamous route on the path to human know-how, including information imparted through lucid dreams, remote viewing, out-of-body travel, near death experience and other contacts with the world outside our material enclave, or what Aldous Huxley termed in *Doors of Perception,* "Mind-at-Large."

What *tools* would a *specialist* use to study the novel claim of alien abduction? And, importantly, how would one go about it without losing the respect of one's peers? In Dr. Mack's experience, the respectability part of the equation was the first to go. While Mack's peers in respectable academia and psychiatry scrambled to come up with logical explanations for very illogical goings-on, Mack scrambled to disentangle himself from a fine mess. He states that his dabblings in this area were utterly naive. He truly believed that his peers would sit up and take notice! They sure did.

Mack's peers tried to oust him from his post at Harvard, but eventually his tenured position prevailed. He has now added anthropology and documentary filmmaking to his existential toolbox in an attempt to counter the academic assertion that abduction accounts are the psychological projections of a sophisticated Western world obsessed with futuristic technology. This idea was originally propounded by neo-Freudian psychologist Carl Jung in his 1958 book *Flying Saucers: A Modern Myth of Things Seen in the Skies.*

If, like Dr. Mack, one believes that expanding knowledge of the boundaries of existence is more important than traveling down a road already well trampled, there is no question of allegiance. Bravely, Mack has tried to come up with some novel ways of looking at these phenomena which, interestingly, turn out to be suggestions made by the early phenomenologists! As he suggested at a MUFON meeting in Rhode Island in 1995, trust is established on a professional level with the witness "by entering into their world, by meeting with them ... by opening your psyche!" He explains that as soon as you do that, you have "reduced that gulf, that distance, that dualism, that 'I-Am-The-Observer/You-Are-The-Observed' which is asked for in traditional science." You are then involved in what he calls *intersubjectivity*: that is, "two people looking together at something." While he acknowledges that it may be "kind of messy scientifically," Mack believes it is really the only way to learn about the inner experience of another human being.

Importantly, Mack suggests that persons who object to this intersubjective methodology are, in essence, judging that "human experience is not a valid source of information about the universe." To disavow that information because the source is "questionable," Mack laments, is a violation of scientific method. After the information is allowed in, one may apply scientific rationale, but to rule out the information and the people with the information in advance, he warns, "is ideology, not science." These are extremely powerful sentiments which were long ago addressed by phenomenologists and existentialists. An overview of this body of work is in order.

Phenomenology: Does the Earth Move?

Philosopher Edmund Husserl believed that in order to maintain its meaningfulness and integrity, the quantitative sciences developed by man should acknowledge that its roots are in the same qualitative sensory world which it studies and measures, and that as an expression of this world of shared sensory qualities it must be guided by this world. It was hoped that a new Science of Experience would someday "articulate the ground of the other sciences," and re-establish lived experience as a basis of scientific method. Husserl spoke of the phenomenal world, the world of subjective experience, as being pure transcendental consciousness.

Husserl hoped to isolate this qualitative dimension of experience from the quantitative world of material 'facts' in order to protect it from "being colonized by those technological methods of inquiry." Yet this insistence upon the mental character of phenomenal reality, writes David Abram in *The Spell of the Sensuous,* "led critics to attack Husserl's method as inherently solipsistic." In other words, this point of view only succeeds in isolating man inside of his own mind. How could Husserl move man into the reality of the world without giving up his idea of transcendental mind?

Abram relays an account of Husserl's long struggle to connect man's internal reality with his external fixtures, whereupon he came upon a "singularly important structure within the phenomenal field" which resolved this conundrum. That structure was the human body. The body is "that mysterious and multifaceted phenomenon that seems always to accompany one's awareness." As Husserl came to realize, the body is the location of "one's awareness within the field of appearances." But there are other bodies within this field; other "forms that move and gesture in a fashion similar to one's own." The difference is that my own body is experienced from within and the other bodies are experienced from without; I can move around these other bodies but I cannot (at least under normal conditions) move out of my own body or view it from the outside.

Despite this difference, Husserl believed that there was an inescapable affiliation between these other bodies viewed from the outside and my own body experienced from within. Husserl recognized that an embodied subject recognizes other bodies as other centers of experience, as other subjects, via "empathy." Therefore, to counter the charge of solipsism in his theory, Husserl postured that the field of appearances is inhabited by *multiple subjects* in an empathic communion.

So then, *intersubjectivity*, according to Husserl, results from the shared perceptions of various subjects or bodies which are located in the same world of experience. Intersubjective experience consists of subjective phenomena which are not the isolated perceptions of one individual, such as fantasies or daydreams, and, thus, cannot be altered at will since they are reinforced by the shared experience of other beings. In *Essays in Existentialism*, we learn that existentialist Jean Paul Sartre also utilized the concept of *intersubjectivity*, which he held as "the world in which *man decides* what he is and what others are."

This observation that 'man decides' implies a consensus or agreement between subjects. Interestingly, as David Abram points out, an actually value-free *objectivity* may be an unrealizable ideal since it can be phenomenologically understood as the striving for consensus between subjects: *intersubjectivity* or, in Mack's words, "two people looking together at something." Thus, the scientific ideal of *objectivity* may more closely describe an act of *intersubjective* engagement, wherein those subjects involved come to an unspoken agreement on the parameters of a *temporary* window on their personal, subjective realities. So, rather than being a measure of an actual ulterior Truth 'out there' in the solid world of 'facts,' *objectivity* may simply be a temporary agreement between subjects: *intersubjectivity*. Or, to re-coin a phrase made popular by the *X-Files* television series, the Truth is not *out there*.

From a phenomenological point of view, the conventional *contrast* between subject and object can be seen as a contrast between subjective and intersubjective phenomena, or different interpretations within the subjective fields of multiple witnesses. The desirable *decrease* of that contrast, commonly called *objec-tivity*, is seen simply as the wish to *increase* intersubjective agreement. In this instance, the term 'agreement' should be understood as a tacit assumption involving the medium of culture. As Joseph Chilton Pearce writes in *Crack in the Cosmic Egg*, "agreement is a common exclusion of alternate possibilities. Agreement is the cement of social structure."

Phenomenology, then, can be seen as a philosophical tradition which calls into serious question Galileo and Descartes' assumption of an objective reality. Edmund Husserl proposed that the real world, that which our sciences strive to label and understand, is not purely a fixed object *out there*, but is part of a reciprocal interaction with consciousness through a matrix of perceptions, sensations and experiences; or, as Husserl proposed, "a silent conversation that I carry on with things." The human being, however, experiences the world as a solid and stable object which we can count on to exhibit its unchanging 'laws.' This experienced stability, he stressed, is sustained by our constant encounter with other 'centers of experience' similarly embodied. It is just this encounter with other perceivers which "assures me that there is more to any thing, or to the world, than I myself can perceive at any moment." As Abram writes, "the mutual inscription of others in my experience, and (as I must assume) of myself in their experiences, effects the interweaving of our individual phenomenal fields into a single, ever-shifting fabric, a single phenomenal 'reality'." Thus, multiple subjects maintain the structure of reality by *agreement*, which has been called "the cement of social structure."

Husserl called the intersubjective world the *Lebenswelt*, or 'life-world.' The life-world is the world of immediately-lived and organically-perceived experience prior to our thoughts about it; it is reality as it engages us before analytical processes take it apart. The *Lebenswelt* is a collective dimension, since it is shared with others, yet it is also an ambiguous dimension due to our particular situation in it. It is present on the periphery of all our thoughts and activities, yet we are not wholly aware of our participation in it. Husserl proposed that the life-world had various layers of diverse cultural acquisitions, under which was a more unitary life-world possessed by all humans.

Husserl wrote about this deepest of life-worlds in notes dated 1934. In these investigations he attempted to define a concept of *space* as it is experienced in the life-world. Husserl noted that there was a profound schism between our scientific beliefs and our spontaneous sensory experience of space. He wrote that phenomenologically "all bodies (including our own) are first located relative to the ground of the Earth," and that, due to our groundedness on Earth, the Earth does not appear to us to be *in* space, but rather to *provide* space. To our most immediate sensory experience, Husserl maintained, the concepts of 'motion' and 'rest' can only have meaning in the context of a motionless Earth base. We do not perceive ourselves as being on a spinning planet. Hence, our bodily experience of being in motion or at rest are relative to the absolute rest of our Earth-based *Lebenswelt*. Husserl took his Science of Experience to the limit. On the envelope in which these notes were found was written the words: "Overthrow of Copernican Theory ... The original ark, Earth, does not move."

Husserl believed that scientific objectivism (so-called positivism) had led to "an almost total eclipse" of the life-world in the modern era and that we had nearly completely forgotten "this living dimension in which all of our endeavors are rooted." In short, he regretted that Western science and technology had estranged mankind from direct human experience, and he was sure that the ensuing impoverishment of language would lead to the obliteration of the life-world entirely. So, we see that George Orwell wasn't the first to note that confining language could confine thought. Yet, on the other hand, language is always confined, and we still manage to communicate without knowing very much about how we are doing it. As Bob Dobbs has noted in *Phatic Communion*: "Language is an artificial intelligence. It gives us a grasp of the world; it gives us a way of looking at the world, but it is not the whole of intelligence. To exceed your grasp is what we do when we speak because you can't pin down what you're talking about in the essential bit, yet you're talking and using it. So we are making something out of nothing."

It is evident that the inescapable materialist scientific apparatus has succeeded wonderfully in confining our definition of reality within the scope of acceptable parameters of agreement. It is the purpose of this book, along with my previous work *Space Travelers and the Genesis of the Human Form*, to alert its readers to these insidious materialist paradigms which have a powerful claim on the definition of reality.

The Primacy of Perception

Taking up Husserl's work, philosopher Maurice Merleau-Ponty believed it was the obligation of philosophy to return to the *primacy of perception*; to "that world which precedes knowledge, of which knowledge always speaks, and in relation to which every scientific schematization is an abstract and derivative sign-language." His philosophy was founded in the investigation of the primordial structures of perception which, he reminds us, "come before and pervade the entire range of scientific reflection." Thus, we read in *Existential Philosophers*, while other philosophies have defined the world as that which is *actively discovered by science*, in Merleau-Ponty's thinking the need to assess perception by using the tools of science is an unnecessary tautology.

Typical of philosophical tradition, however, Merleau-Ponty was stuck in an historical-intellectual situation which he felt was full of misconceptions and contradictions regarding the relation between consciousness and nature/mind and body. This, it would appear, hasn't changed. Merleau-Ponty performed an intensive study of materialist science, experimental psychology and behaviorist "reflex theories" in order to judge whether this science was internally consistent. He concluded that behaviorism had made its task easier by rejecting the notion of consciousness altogether and accounting only for 'behavior' observed from the outside. He argued that it was impossible to explain the interior by the exterior.

In addition, Merleau-Ponty argued that sensory perception is only a fragment of perception, taking place within a field of perceptual activity which is largely outside of conscious awareness. While objective science can adequately record some of these phenomenal/sensory experiences, they do not constitute the entire range of perceptual experience. Furthermore, he argued, since the mind was viewed as simply a passive recording device to these extreme mechanists, there could be no *meaning* derived from sensory data passively received. Therefore, to Merleau-Ponty, such scientific discovery was moot.

Merleau-Ponty began with Husserl's posture that the "world is not a given place in which experience occurs, but is that toward which one is turned in experience." Merleau-Ponty wrote in the preface to his book *Phenomenology of Perception*:

> The whole universe of science is built upon the lived world, and if we want to subject science itself to rigorous scrutiny and arrive at a precise assessment of its meaning and scope, we must begin by reawakening the basic experience of the world of which science is the second-order expression.

As the authors of *The Spell of the Sensuous* explain, Merleau-Ponty felt that philosophy should take the world in its totality and watch the *process* through which the world takes shape; that is, "the *way* the world makes itself evident to awareness; or the *way* things first arise in our direct, sensorial experience." Merleau-Ponty stressed that "in order to see the world, we must break our familiar acceptance of it."

Merleau-Ponty concluded that "one is led to examine consciousness on its own naive terms," and the result of his work in the study of perception is considered a "victory for subjectivity." His book, the *Phenomenology of Perception*, is a theory of experience and a presentation of phenomenological method as a tool which, rather than relying on argument, relies on intuition and, rather than attempting to prove, attempts to evoke, uncover, or show. Thus, phenomenology, as a Science of Experience, looks to simply pay attention to and become familiar with the rhythms, textures and diversity of subjective experience, rather than to capture or control it and define it by unrealizable 'objective' methods.

The Essence of Human: A Being-in-the-World

Existentialist philosopher Martin Heidegger, in his book *Being and Time,* stressed that the *meaning* of an object is its *essence,* which is "brought out into the open when we interpret successfully what the object is." In the perceptual process of acquiring knowledge about an *object,* it is isolated out of the "stream of experience" and held up to that which it is *not.* Reality is distinguished and ordered and made meaningful when it is broken down *logically* and factual (*ontic*) knowledge is deduced from it.

Heidegger's metaphysical inquiry into the essence of consciousness was *teleological* (concerned with design or purpose in nature as the final cause) as opposed to mechanistic. Heidegger was concerned that *traditional* ontology studied the *structures* that constitute the objects of study without questioning the *meaning* of the encounter. He was interested in meeting this deficiency by studying the structure of the *relationship* itself.

In an examination which goes beyond what is merely apparent, phenomenology is "the exhibition of the structures constitutive of *beings.*" Phenomenology looks beyond what is familiar to the "meaning of the ground of the investigated beings;" to discover the essence, nature, or meaning of "Being." Heidegger stressed that phenomenology isn't concerned with making new discoveries, but with "freeing our vision from obstructions so as to see in the familiar the concealed meaning."

What does it *mean* to be a human being? Man is a "being-in-the-world," Heidegger states, but he is not something which just *happens* to be in the world, rather, he is "something whose *essence* is to be in the world." Further, it is impossible to give any meaning to the notion of "a self which does not find itself in some world." In *Existential Philosophers,* we learn that Heidegger identified man as the relation holding between subject and object; the "gap which separates and at the same time unites subject and object." He deduced that man is not a substance, or a subject, but is a *relation*; essentially a "being dwelling in and familiar with the world," who, as such, "stands over against the world while at the same time tied to it." The essence of human *is* contact and communication. Thus, we might deduce from this, all extraordinary Contact experiences describe the world and should be included in any so-called scientific study of the world.

Heidegger stressed that our first and foremost encounter with the world is not as a detached observer but as a "being-in-the-world." Importantly, along with landscape and history as structures of man's understanding of his situation, he is a "being-with-others." Man is not an isolated being who establishes relationships with other equally isolated beings. The community of man is not something which he has to establish, but is "given to man as part of his own being."

Also given to man as part of his existential being is the gift of language; that tool by which he *communes* with others. Evolutionists have invented lots of theories about how language "evolved" as part of mankind's adaptive cultural package, but phenomenologists have argued against such simplistic explanations. In addition, language presents an important philosophical problem since, being grounded in perception, it is essentially confined by perception. Let us now address the problems presented by language as mankind attempts to dialogue with and about the cosmos.

The Psychological Power of the External World

Language is centered in *temporality,* in mankind's linear space-time perceptual constructs. It is a way of describing the world and his relationships in it and with it. But language may not reflect a true cosmic reality. At a Rhode Island MUFON public meeting, John Mack induced the audience to think about language, the words we take for granted and which need to be reconsidered;

words like *real*, and *dreaming*, or *inside* and *outside*. He reminded us that, by consensus, these words "constitute the psychological power of our external world," since they are "distinctions we make in language which may *not* be distinctions that constitute *proof* of the way the cosmos is organized."

Therefore, when an observer is able to describe what is going on inside of a hovering space craft while standing on the ground, we need to suspend our judgment of this person as mistaken or dreaming. Perhaps there is a long-lost sensory apparatus which is awakened in mankind by these mysterious, mostly nocturnal visits which allows us to be ostensibly in two places at once, standing in one locale and 'remote viewing' another. Likewise, a witness might claim to have stepped out of a spaceship to find that he or she is inside an even larger spaceship or, may report that the exterior dimensions of the ship did not conform spatially to the perceived size of the interior.

But in order to even begin to understand these perceptual experiences, or share in them, or adapt ourselves to their possibility, we must adjust our ideas of the concrete boundaries of the "external world." Quantum and post-quantum physics and idealist theories have come a long way in describing the world inside our heads which may very well create the world outside our heads. Of course, we have the alternate choice of allowing the reigning materialist science, that body of knowledge which enforces those boundaries, to allow what *we think we know* of the world to further define the world. Are we condemned to repeat this mistake *ad infinitum*?

Inventor Joseph Newman contends that the teaching of science from grammar school through college consists entirely of the memorization of accepted principles. He laments that there is little or no time for creative thinking, and claims that this system is very detrimental to the progress of science. In his book, *The Energy Machine of Joseph Newman*, he reminds us that "because a subject matter is taught in accordance with a given line of thought at that instant in time does not make it fact." It is important to hold the perspective that science is a body of knowledge which historically ebbs and flows, and should not be allowed to be used as a political tool to obscure the true nature of reality.

Stephen Schwartz of MIT has stated that "the time and space framework so crucial to the Grand Material world-view is by no means as absolute a construct as most scientists believe." Since the Enlightenment, science has utilized mechanical explanations of reality in order to perform its reductionist routines, breaking down physical reality into components. Science has effectively marginalized alternative ways of knowing our world by stating that anything that cannot be analyzed and broken down in this manner is simply not comprehensible and, therefore, does not exist. As Charles Emmons writes in *At the Threshold*, "normal science is mainly about certainty, and the marginalization of other views of reality through debunking."

In his article entitled "Six Studies of Out-of-Body Experience," published in the *Journal of Near Death Studies* (1997), Dr. Charles Tart of the Institute for Transpersonal Psychology refers to this perversion of genuine science as "scientism," the dogmatic commitment to a materialist philosophy which attempts to explain away the spiritual rather than to actually examine what it might be. Dr. Tart opines that, "since scientism never recognizes itself as a belief system, but always thinks of itself as true science, the confusion is pernicious." As a long-time researcher of alternative states of consciousness, Tart believes a scientist should be committed to observe things carefully and honestly, and then devise theories and explanations about what those observations mean without *ad hoc* rationalizations. Tart suggests that those who ritually practice "scientism" have an emotional attachment to a materialist worldview, a belief which in itself should be subjected to continual testing and modification.

Martin Heidegger lamented that the detached, objective view demanded by traditional science and philosophy "isolates things from the living context in which they normally appear," and reduces the object to a "brute fact confronting me." Knowledge, then, becomes "*of* a thing" which suggests distance and disengagement, and separates the discovered from the *act* of discovery. Having split understanding from its object, Heidegger suggests, both are regarded as "beings-at-hand." This type of truth is merely a *correspondence* between the two rather than the expression of an *experience* which reveals *meaning*. Heidegger felt that true discoveries are made in the context of human existence being essentially *understanding*. The existential structure of human existence (*Dasein* in German) is as the "clearing of Being;" the place where Being reveals itself.

John Mack also laments the scientific tradition whereby we strive to be objective by maintaining a "maximum separation between the observer and the observed," and working toward an ideal whereby "we can measure what we're doing from a distance and other people can come up with the same measurements separately." These rules have always worked, he explains, for "phenomena that can be established as being in the gross physical world." But here we have stumbled upon a novel and complex situation where these objective criteria do not apply. It would seem that we are being confronted with phenomena which Mack is not alone in suspecting might come from a higher dimension of space-time and manifest in the 3-D world. And our initial knee-jerk reaction is denial.

Worlds Within Worlds

We must remind ourselves that the real anomaly here is not these notorious Otherworldly visitations, but, rather, the Western world's scientific denial that unseen or 'invisible' phenomena may exist. As Keith Thompson writes in *Angels and Aliens*, the true anomaly is "modern Western culture's project—unparalleled in history—of placing entire dimensions of reality off limits, thereby forcing these dimensions to 'return with a vengeance' in various forms, including UFOs."

What we call 'reality' is a limited perceptual case file stored in our memory banks, which consists only of information perceptible to us within a limited spectrum of sensory experience. Therefore, in a sense, true reality is in the fringes or margins of our limited view, since much of it falls off the 'edge' of our visible spectrum. Under normal environmental and psychic conditions, we simply don't have the functioning apparatus to sense the borders of the phenomenal world. You might say, this ultra reality, what P.D. Ouspensky calls the *noumenal world*, is also beyond the spectrum of our limited imagination as well, since we perceive our world through the filtered lens of what we already "know" or think we know.

As P.D. Ouspensky explains in *Tertium Organum*, the necessity of our being stuck in a three-dimensional universe may merely be based on our limited sense apparatus, which is incapable of perceiving or imagining a form containing more than three perpendicular lines. We can measure space in three independent directions only: length, breadth and height. Our geometry knows only three lines which can lie simultaneously at right angles to one another and are not parallel in relation to each other. This is what is meant by 3-D. As Ouspensky explains, "either by virtue of some mysterious quality of the universe, or because of the limitations of our mental apparatus, we cannot visualize more than three perpendiculars." Yet, he argues, we must assume that since space is infinite it has an infinity of dimensions; that is, an infinite number of lines which can lie perpendicular to one another without being parallel. Since we are incapable of imagining this, Ouspensky notes, "if these properties of space are created by certain attributes of our own, then it follows that the limitation is also in ourselves." As Ouspensky remarked in *Tertium Organum* (p. 137):

> There is no side of life which does not reveal to us an infinity of the
> new and the unexpected if we approach it with the knowledge that it

is not exhausted by its visible side, that behind this visible side there lies a whole world of the invisible, a whole world of new and incomprehensible forces and relations. The knowledge of the existence of the invisible world is the first key to it.

Yet, when Ouspensky remarks that we cannot "visualize" more than three perpendiculars, perhaps other senses aside from vision are required to sense the upper dimensions. After all, we are vision-based beings; and therein may lie our limitation. What about qualities like sound, smell, color, light, tone, pulse, vibration, tactility, telepathy or affinity? Might certain combinations of sensory qualities, or other unimaginable sensory qualities, extend the borders of our universe?

As a matter of fact, a spectrum of energies encompassing gravity, magnetic fields and infrasonic sound known as the "superspectrum" was hypothesized by early UFO researcher, John Keel, as the source of paranormal manifestation. These extradimensional phenomena, he posited, exist outside of our space-time continuum and are unaffected by the natural laws of our world. Infrared lenses and film often catch these phantoms on the edges of reality. To make transitions between our world and their own, Keel suggested, UFOs utilize the electromagnetic light spectrum, altering vibrational and tonal frequencies in order to appear as a solid object. This hypothesis is actually based on ancient information contained in magical systems we will be looking at shortly.

In his classic UFO study, *The Cosmic Pulse of Life*, Trevor James Constable posits that UFOs are both physical metallic ships *and* biologically alive critters. Mead Layne, founder of Borderland Science, along with other experimental ufologists, also held similar theories. Constable's theories are neo-Reichian, meaning that he follows the scientific principles discovered by Wilhelm Reich, which assert the existence of a primordial, biological substrate energy called Orgone, or chemical "ether." Constable claims that he first began taking pictures of spaceships in 1957 using infrared film. In many cases, rather than capturing pictures of physical spaceships in the atmosphere above Earth, his team recorded the existence of plasmoidal living organisms sometimes forty to fifty feet in diameter.

In an interview with Constable in issue 5 of *Paranoia: The Conspiracy Reader*, he explained to me that infrared film extends the range of the human eye far beyond what the eye itself will register. The plasmoids, which have been captured on film by researchers in Italy, Romania and Australia, are not from anywhere else, he explains, but are what we might call the upper dimension of our physical world. Constable refers to them as macrobacteria, and explains that they constitute the counterpart at the upper border of physical nature of the microbes that infest the sub-sensible realms. Constable explains that he is not arguing against the existence of real, physical spaceships, but that both phenomena exist simultaneously.

Geobiologist Dr. Elisabet Sahtouris, before the 1995 "When Cosmic Cultures Meet" conference, stated that "the universe is composed of ten or more dimensions, known to most cultures, while the western scientific worldview limits itself to four." This limitation, she asserted, necessarily obscures most of the existing universe. Other-dimensional or other-planetary experiences are not as strange to people in cultures outside of our Western scientific culture. On the contrary, some cultures have a long history of connectedness with an interdimensional "web of beings" in constant communication with humans.

When phenomena of other dimensions intrude upon the three-dimensional world, Sahtouris explained, they are seen as magical, miraculous, fearful or dangerous, or they are simply denied. Just as in the two-dimensional hypothetical world of "Flatland," she explained, where there is no way to fathom the passing of a three-dimensional ball through that world, four-dimensional phenomena are inexplicable to those who live in our three-dimensional world. Thus, just as in

Flatland, when interdimensional visitors appear in our skies and disappear just as suddenly, we find it difficult to accept them as real. Perhaps the cognitive area where we keep such denials should be referred to as "Outland" for, we must realize, a system is *outlandish* only to opposing systems.

Sahtouris believes that it would not be possible to travel the vast distances between planets using 3-D ships and 3-D fuels. The only way intelligent inhabitants of the universe would be able to traverse the cosmos is by entering and exiting other dimensions which have no space-time limitations. In addition, she propounded, these entities would be likely to communicate over interstellar distances by utilizing other dimensions, and they would communicate telepathically or by some interdimensional technology. It is unlikely, she suggested, contrary to the hopes of SETI scientists and the late Carl Sagan, that they would communicate using signals discernible to our very primitive radio telescopes.

If we have made no room for the possibility of other-dimensional experience in our consensus-reality, it follows that these experiences become figments of our imagination. Outland is the only *place* we have conceptually made for them. Language, in turn, reflects and enforces this attitude. As John Mack has asserted, distinctions made in language may not constitute proof of the way the cosmos is organized.

Philosopher Martin Heidegger also realized that because the vehicle of language is finite, it limits man's world in that "being reveals itself in language in such a way that this revelation is at the same time a concealment." He believed that language presents a *danger* because it reveals the surface and conceals the depth; its essential danger is "superficiality." Heidegger warned that all "inauthentic modes of existence" develop their "peculiar grammars," which provide rules for determining how a certain word should be used and in so doing "silence its claim." He wrote that "inauthentic existence demands clichés to guard man against the shock of having to encounter reality."

Joseph Chilton Pearce writes in *Crack in the Cosmic Egg* that an education in the sciences enforces thinking which "determines the ideas that will be accepted to begin with, the new ideas most likely to occur to mind, and the phenomena accepted as factual." Our ideal of distance and disengagement has, it would seem, 'separated the discovered from the act of discovery,' and, since language reflects the belief systems of a culture, the 'peculiar grammars'of our science have followed along to 'silence the claim' of the universe. Science, as the Old Guard, indeed serves to guard against the shock of having to encounter unfettered reality by boxing us into a fixed concretion reminiscent of Flatland, and silencing the claim of anything that doesn't fit into the box.

Perhaps it is in our best interests to suspend our materialist scientific conventions as we explore the extrasensory, the extraordinary, the exogenous, and the excluded, whether these stimuli are coming from *inside* or *outside* our heads. It has become painfully clear that scientific materialism has no tools to measure or prove the existence or non-existence of contact/visitor-related phenomena. As James Hurtak suggested at the "When Cosmic Cultures Meet" conference, the scientific method must be "expanded to handle experiential situations of contact that may come from sources representing a whole new spectrum of multiple realities that fall outside our scientific measurement."

An interview with top scientists throughout Europe and America has suggested that scientists are beginning to admit the possibility of a non-physical dimension to the universe. *Science Digest* reported that "from Berkeley to Paris and from London to Princeton, prominent scientists from fields as diverse as neurophysiology and quantum physics are admitting they believe in the possibility of immortal human spirit and divine creation." (HPF)

In his 1985 book *The Wonder of Being Human*, Sir John Eccles wrote that "the universe is no longer composed of 'matter and void' but now must make (spaceless) room for (massless) entities." Even as far back as 1937, Sir Arthur

Eddington noted in *Science and the Unseen World* that "to imagine conscious-ness ruled by the laws of physics and chemistry is as preposterous as the sug-gestion that a nation could be ruled by the laws of grammar." Arthur Koestler declared in a lecture that "the 19th Century clockwork model of the universe is in shambles and, since matter itself has dematerialized, materialism can no longer claim to be a scientific philosophy." (HPF)

In its stead, Nick Herbert proposes in *Elemental Mind*, future science will have to acknowledge "a kind of 'quantum animism' in which mind permeates the world at every level," as a fundamental force in cooperation with matter. As Herbert points out, there is no scientific way to measure the presence or absence of awareness in matter. Therefore, the common assumption that matter is "dead," or that stars, rocks or atoms do not possess consciousness, has no sci-entific basis. As Ouspensky has noted in *Tertium Organum*,

> We recognize as animate beings only those possessing a mind acces-sible to our observation in the three-dimensional section of the world; i.e. beings whose mind is analogous to ours.... Consequently, every-thing that lives, thinks and feels in a manner not completely analo-gous to ours is bound to appear to us dead and mechanical.

On the contrary, Ouspensky writes, if life and intelligence constitute the world, then intelligence must exist in all of life. There can be nothing dead or mechanical in Nature. Yet, when we say that there is 'mind'in nature, this is not the same type of mind as that possessed by a human. Man's mind is logical. Yet, there is no reason whatever to suppose that in the *noumenal world*, which Ouspensky considered the 'world of causes,'relations can be logical from man's point of view. On the contrary, everything logical can only be phenomenal, and can only be at home in man's mind. Whereas, everything in the *noumenal world* is bound to appear to man's mind as a logical absurdity, as in Alice's Wonderland.

At its best, wrote psychologist Abraham Maslow, science should be com-pletely open and should exclude nothing. It should have "no entrance require-ments." With idealist science, Amit Goswami writes in *The Self-Aware Universe*, there are no entrance requirements which might exclude the subjec-tive or objective, nor spirit or matter. Thus, Goswami writes, with idealist sci-ence we are able to "integrate the deep dichotomies of our thought." Let's talk about what might constitute such an animal as Idealist Science.

CHAPTER TWO

UNIVERSE AND MIND: MODELS OF CONSCIOUSNESS

> To imagine consciousness ruled by the
> laws of physics and chemistry is as prepos -
> terous as the suggestion that a nation
> could be ruled by the laws of grammar.
>
> Sir Arthur Eddington,
> *Science and the Unseen World*

A good place to begin this chapter is with the statement that neither the belief that matter is alive (animism) nor the belief that matter is dead (material-ism) have been proven scientifically. The "real status of the inner life of 'inani-mate' objects," writes Nick Herbert in *Elemental Mind*, "awaits for its resolu-tion a deeper kind of science than we currently possess." This brings us to the question: 'what is mind?'

Mind is viewed in varying contexts by various cultures. Predominant scien-tific theories on the nature of the mind work with the premise that it is an "emer-gent feature" of certain complex biological systems, or that it is the "software" controlling the brain's hardware. Nick Herbert instead proposes that mind is a "fundamental process deeply embedded in nature."

Seen in this light, mind is an elemental constituent of the natural world which interacts with matter at the quantum level. How it interacts is the subject of countless experiments and hypotheses. Herbert proposes that the behavior of matter at the quantum level "affords the opportunity for mind to manifest itself in the material world." Along with other elementary particles and forces identi-fied as constituting the physical world, Herbert posits that "mind must be con-sidered an equally basic constituent of the natural world." In the same manner that medieval philosophers underestimated the size of the physical world, he suggests, modern science may be "vastly underestimating the quantity of con-sciousness in the universe."

We currently hardly understand 'ordinary' consciousness, so how can we expect to approach an understanding of its 'variations,' such as telepathy, out-of-body experience, remote viewing, lucid dreaming, the LSD experience, hyp-nosis or, perhaps even, alien abduction? Where does extraordinary information come from? Is there a 'nonlocal' connection between the human mind and the world of subjects/objects? Does Nature 'speak' to mankind? Does information travel via a 'subconscious' conduit? Is there an outer connection—some sort of invisible strings—beyond our sensory awareness? To delve into possible answers to these questions, it's helpful to have a basic map of the philosophical models of consciousness and its relationship to the world 'out there.'

Models of Consciousness

Since meat bodies like ours are at present the only vehicles which we rec-ognize as having an "inner life," and because of our tendency to split things into oppositions, philosophers of all time have divided the world into a "mind/mat-ter problem." Thus, they have divided the phenomenal/sensory world into two components—mind and matter, or subject and object—and have had a barrel of fun for hundreds of years postulating the relationships that are possible between them. Basically, they have come up with *dualism* and *monism*.

The dualistic model maintains that mind and matter are different *essences* operating under different *laws*. This model allows for a sentient essence which animates the body and survives its death. But this *essence* sounds too much like a spirit, which is an inoperable force in the meat market of materialist science.

Herbert proposes that dualism is not illogical or irrational, but that it is simply profoundly unfashionable at this time. On the other hand, P.D. Ouspensky notes the incorrectness of dualistic theories which accept 'spirit' and 'matter' as different principles, co-existing but independent of one another. Ouspensky notes in *Tertium Organum* (p. 118):

> There can be no greater mistake than to regard the world as divided into phenomena and noumena—to take phenomena and noumena as separate from one another, existing independently one from another and as capable of being perceived apart from one another. This is complete philosophical illiteracy, which manifests itself most clearly in dualistic spiritualistic theories. The division of phenomena and noumena exists only in our perception. The 'phenomenal world' is merely our incorrect representation of the world.

As Nick Herbert explains, there are three kinds of dualism. In *epiphenome - nalism*, matter is the real substance of the world and mind is a by-product; subject to the motion of matter. In *animism*, every material motion has an invisible spiritual cause; matter is subordinate to mind. In *interactionalism*, mind and matter mutually influence one another.

There are also three kinds of monism. In *materialism*, matter is all there is; mind is one of matter's possible attributes having no special status. Mind is simply a particular mechanical motion of matter. Importantly, Herbert clarifies that materialism as a scientific hypothesis is separate from atheistic materialism, or the active un-belief in God, soul, afterlife or other "spiritual" concepts, and an "unreasonable faith in reason itself."

Two types of materialism are *reductive* and *emergent*. Reductive materialists believe that virtually any mechanical motion results in some kind of 'inner experience.' This thinking perhaps resembles animism in its willingness to believe that everything has an 'inner life,' but its concept of *aliveness* is a purely mechanical property. Emergent materialists also believe that consciousness is a wholly mechanical property of matter, but that only complex systems containing special mechanisms have the capacity to possess it. Such materialists would believe that machines can be built which would equal the quality of inner experience of the human being. This is the dominant mindset of the present scientific community, which has, incidentally, been seriously working on psychotronics, cybernetics and artificial intelligence. (But we will get to that later.)

Idealism is the second type of monist viewpoint where mind is the fundamental substance of the world and the existence of a material world is 'inferred' from evidence presented to our sense organs. The material world is, to an idealist, like a film being projected from a mental projection booth.

Neutral monism, the third type of monist view, attempts to strike a balance between the extreme claims of materialism and idealism, taking the theoretical stance that a single substance or action possesses shared attributes, such as the "electromagnetic" field. The unification of two physical forces into one is a trend in today's physics. As Herbert explains, neutral monism sees matter and mind as interdependent, but suggests that a purely physical account of the world must be factually wrong with regard to consciousness.

The Spiritual Sky

As we will see when we come to the theories of Gregory Little, the electromagnetic theory of UFO manifestation is both popular and quite unpopular among researchers today. This is due to the fact that it is difficult for believers in physical metallic spaceships, who are seeking solid evidence of visitation from other planetary systems, to include an idealist interpretation into their scientific investigations. Thus we have researchers laboring under the false presumption that the physical planetary spheres are all that exist.

If we visit the medieval spiritual sky, however, we find that the celestial realms were composed of a different material than those found in the Earth's sphere. As Margaret Wertheim writes in *The Pearly Gates of Cyberspace: A History of Space from Dante to the Internet*, an essential feature of the medieval cosmology was that the domain of the planets and stars was of a different quality than man's terrestrial domain. As she writes:

> On earth, everything was mortal and mutable, subject to death and decay, but according to medieval understanding the celestial realm was immutable and eternal. In the terrestrial realm everything was said to be composed of the four material elements – earth, air, fire, and water – but things in the celestial domain were supposedly made of the fifth essence, or quintessence, sometimes known as the "ether."

Medieval scholars believed that as one proceeded out from the Earth sphere, each celestial sphere became more pure and "ethereal" by virtue of its increasing proximity to the Supreme Being; as Wertheim calls it, "a graduated scale of increasing purity and grace." The medieval cosmological scheme, she writes, was like "a great metaphysical onion." Yet, she writes, for Dante and his contemporaries, the physical world was but a reflection of the true underlying "realm of soul," and it was into this primary reality that Dante would venture both below Earth to the Gates of Hell and into the celestial sphere to Heaven.

Since an unimpeded soul moves naturally to God, Dante finds that with the weight of his sins gone he easily rises to the celestial domain. The beings that greet Dante in this domain are "glowing forms of light." The realm of pure spirit defies description. In this realm, we find that we have reached the limits of time and space, as well as the limits of language. Yet, in Dante's world view, in the realm of Purgatory earthly space-time was intact. As Wertheim explains, "the two spaces were bound together in the same temporal matrix." Indeed, according to medieval theology, "the boundary between the land of the living and the second kingdom of the afterlife was surprisingly permeable." Thus, Purgatory established a bond between the two worlds which served as a bridge between physical space and spiritual space. It is notable that this spatial hierarchy seems to describe the 4th dimension: that 'space' which we sense as being 'next door' to our material enclave, or just one toke over the line.

If we step back even further, to the exceedingly ancient religious philosophies of India, we find again the proposition that various planetary systems may exist in various dimensions. Therefore, planetary systems are both manifest and unmanifest. According to the *Bhagavad-gita*, the spiritual sky, or *brahmajyoti*, contains innumerable spiritual planets; far more numerous than all the universes of the material world. The spiritual world represents three-fourths of creation, and the other one-fourth consists of innumerable material universes like ours. Each material universe has millions of planets, but all of these universes together comprise only one-fourth of the whole of creation. The *Bhagavad-gita* gives human beings "the opportunity to leave this material world and to go to that eternal existence in the eternal abode of the Lord."

According to the *Bhagavad-gita*, material nature is a display of only *one of the energies* of the Supreme Lord. The Lord has innumerable types of energies, which are inconceivable to the human mind. The first is the superior, or internal potency of the Lord, which is transcendental. The second is the marginal energy, which lies between the spiritual and the material. The third energy, matter, is in the mode of ignorance. Material energy is also from God. At death, we can either leave this material world or remain here. Therefore, human beings are considered *marginal* beings.

In the eternal sky there is no need of sun or moon, nor of fire or electricity, because the spiritual sky is already illuminated by the *brahmajyoti*, the rays of the Supreme Lord. The *Bhagavad-gita* teaches that living entities can travel from one planet to another without mechanical means. For anyone who wants to go to another planet, even the highest planet, *Brahmaloka*, the *Bhagavad-gita* contains a simple formula. This includes the practice of worshipping the particular demigod of the particular planet. According to *Bhagavad-gita*, those whose minds are distorted by material desires surrender to demigods and follow the particular rules and regulations of worship according to their own natures. According to *Bhagavad-gita As It Is:*

> I [Krsna] am seated in everyone's heart as the Supersoul. As soon as one desires to worship demigods, I make his faith steady so that he can devote himself to that particular deity. Endowed with such faith, he seeks favors of that demigod and obtains his desires but in actuality these benefits are bestowed by Me alone. Men of small intelligence worship the demigods, and their fruits are limited and temporary. Those who worship the demigods go to the planets of the demigods, but My devotees reach My supreme abode.

Incidentally, this latter teaching is echoed in Christian beliefs which assert that the Egyptian and Babylonian worship of the planets, including the one we are walking on, is a sinful, 'pagan' preoccupation. Perhaps this Vedic account is the true source of this teaching; and is indeed a much more 'choice' oriented directive, involving a hierarchy of celestial beings associated with the planets. Of course, Christians believe Genesis to be the oldest book in the world, and argue against the presumption that its origin lies in much more ancient world sources.

City of Nine Gates: An Idealist Model

At a 1996 Tucson, Arizona conference entitled "Toward a Science of Consciousness, " Michael Cremo presented a model for mind/body dualism obtained from ancient Vedic texts. Cremo is a research associate of the Bhaktivedanta Institute in Los Angeles. His presentation can be found in an on-line article entitled "The City of Nine Gates: A Complex Model for Mind/Body Dualism from India's Bhagavata Purana." In this article Cremo asks: "Is there a conscious self that is distinct from the physical mechanism of the body? Is there a mind that is distinct from the brain?" As Cremo suggests, the philosophy of dualism as a solution to the "mind/body problem" has been hampered of late by "the impoverished analogical and allegorical resources of Western thought." But it's time once again to return our thoughts to these ideas.

As Cremo explains, mind/brain dualism is usually identified with Rene Descartes, who posited the existence of matter extended in space and mind existing outside of space. Problematically, Cartesian dualism is characterized by a largely unexplained interaction between the rather separate operations of mind and matter. As an alternative, Cremo presents an ancient tale which explains the interaction between mind and matter in allegorical terms. "The City of Nine Gates" is an allegorical tale found in a Sanskrit text from India called the *Bhagavata Purana*. The sophistication and explanatory power of this tale, explains Cremo, is a challenge to the materialist mindset. As noted earlier, there are three types of dualism: In *epiphenomenalism*, matter is the real substance of the world and mind is subject to the motion of matter. In *animism*, every material motion has an invisible spiritual cause; matter is subordinate to mind. In *interactionalism*, mind and matter mutually influence one another. Although Cremo doesn't clarify, the type of dualism being considered here appears to be *animistic dualism*.

As Cremo explains, the central character in the allegory of the City of Nine Gates is a King named Puranjana. In Sanskrit, this word means "one who enjoys in a body." As this tale tells, King Puranjana originally existed as a spirit soul in a purely spiritual realm in relationship with a supreme conscious being. Cremo points out that materialists who oppose the idea of a transcendental realm must consider the transcendental nature of their own creation myth, the Big Bang, which essentially comprises an unexplainable force or source which was there 'in the beginning.' This Western material cosmology essentially describes an unfathomable "expansion" from which the features of time and space, the material universe, mysteriously arise. As Cremo notes, "This transcendental reality, existing beyond time, space, and matter is called the quantum mechanical vacuum, and is pictured as a pure energy field in which particles appear and instantly disappear. From this sea of virtual particles, some go through a process of expansion that keeps them in existence. According to many cosmologists, our universe is one such expansion."

As Cremo aptly illustrates, "both the Bhagavata Purana and the Big Bang cosmology of modern science have an eternal transcendental existence from which our universe of matter, with its features of time and space, arises. Once this is admitted, we can then decide which version of ultimate reality has the most explanatory power, when applied to the variegated reality of our experience." As Cremo explains:

> According to the Bhagavata Purana, both matter and the souls in the material world are energies of God, and as such both have a single spiritual source. The Bhagavata Purana philosophy is thus both dualist and monist, simultaneously. The interactions of matter and the soul in the material world are mediated by the Supersoul, who exists inside each material atom and also accompanies each spirit soul. By the arrangement of Supersoul, impressions of material experience can be channeled to the soul. How this takes place is the subject of the allegory of Puranjana.

As Cremo notes, this philosophy is both dualist and monist simultaneously. Animistic dualism and idealist monism both see matter as animated by 'spirit.' It's easy to confuse animistic dualism and idealist monism, but the difference is made obvious once you consider Ouspensky's point that you can't separate noumenal from phenomenal existence. Yet, the philosophy of dualism essentially proposes that mind and matter are different essences operating under different laws. In idealist monism, mind is the fundamental substance of the world, and all else is 'inferred' by the senses, while animistic dualism asserts that every motion of matter has a cause arising from the subsensible or invisible realm of Mind-at-Large. As Ouspensky argues, mind is what animates matter but the two cannot be separated, at least in the three-dimensional world. As he writes, "There can be no greater mistake than to take phenomena and noumena as separate from one another, existing independently one from another and as capable of being perceived apart from one another."

Let's see how the allegory of the Nine Gates handles this conundrum. Upon leaving the spiritual world in the company of an "unknown friend, the Supersoul," Puranjana, who represents the conscious self, wanders through the material world to find enjoyment; or, to find, in Cremo's words, "a suitable kind of body to inhabit." Puranjana tries on many kinds of bodies on many planets, suggesting that there are souls inhabiting various forms of life with different kinds of bodies. (In contrast, Cremo points out, Cartesian dualism held that only humans have souls. For Descartes, animals were simply "automatons" with no souls.)

Eventually, Puranjana comes to a place called Nava Dvara Pura, the City of Nine Gates. As Cremo explains, the City of Nine Gates represents the human male body, with its nine openings: two eyes, two nostrils, two ears, mouth, anus and the genital opening. Puranjana becomes attracted to a woman who becomes his Queen. The Queen represents intelligence. According to the Bhagavata Purana philosophy, "intelligence is a subtle material energy with discriminatory capabilities; those manifested by artificial intelligence machines." Importantly, as Cremo notes, the attraction between King Puranjana and the Queen is "the root of embodied consciousness," in the sense that his nonmaterial capabilities (his "superpowers" or the Vedic *siddhis*) become dormant when he comes into his relationship with the Queen, or intelligence. This relationship, which results in the dormancy or unawareness of superpower potential, essentially describes the nature of human existence. As Cremo explains:

> The Queen (the subtle material element called intelligence) allows Puranjana (the conscious self) to enjoy the City of Nine Gates (the

gross physical body). Employing a computer analogy, we might say Puranjana represents the user, the City of Nine Gates represents the computer hardware, and the Queen represents the software that allows the user to interface with the hardware and use it for practical purposes.

The five knowledge-acquiring senses are the senses of sight, smell, taste, hearing, and touch. The five working senses are those of walking, grasping, speaking, reproduction, and evacuation. All ten senses are grouped around the mind. The ten senses are considered servants of the mind. Each of these servants has hundreds of wives. The wives are desires for material experience, and the senses act under their pressure.

According to this system, the 'senses' are different from the physical sense organs. The senses are part of the invisible subtle material covering of the soul, along with the mind and intelligence. The physical organs of sensation (the eyes, nose, tongue, ears, skin, legs, arms, mouth, genitals, and anus) are part of the gross physical body that is visible to the eyes. In this allegory, the senses are the Queen's attendants. The senses serve the Queen (who represents intelligence) by bringing information and conducting activity. Taken together as a dynamic system, they make up an energetic matrix of intelligence and sensory capabilities. This energetic matrix comes together to "manufacture a sense of self," with which the King (the conscious self) "becomes entranced and falsely identifies." Thus, this sense of self is based on "illusory identification."

To understand the nature of this illusory identification, Cremo explains, we need to readjust the familiar mind/body dualism to a "triad" which incorporates a nonmaterial conscious self, a subtle material body of "mind and intelligence," and a physical body composed of gross matter. In this triadic model, Mind is at the center of the subtle senses, which are in turn connected to the physical sense organs, but are quite different from them.

In the Bhagavata Purana model, the integrating function of the senses is performed by "mind," a subtle element which receives sensory input from the subtle senses grouped around it. However, Cremo concludes, the mind is not "conscious." This concept of Mind might be better understood as similar to computer software which integrates audio and visual input into an integrated display. In this model, material intelligence directs the consciousness of the living entity to a sort of "integrated display of sense data." Thus, as Cremo concludes, "Intelligence, as a subtle material energy, is not itself conscious, but it mimics the behavior of consciousness [presumably by resonating at a sympathetic frequency?]. It thus attracts the attention of the conscious self, causing the self to identify with it, just as we identify with the image of an actor on a movie screen."

As Michael Cremo deduces from the Vedic tale of City of Nine Gates, the mind/body dualistic conundrum can be explained by the concept of a "triad" incorporating (1) a nonmaterial conscious self, (2) a subtle material body formed of mind and intelligence, and (3) a physical body composed of gross matter. Thus, this tale seems to incorporate a dualistic theme which views the various materials comprising consciousness as different essences operating under different laws, but which are able to come together to create a living, thinking being; or, to "manufacture a sense of self."

Incidentally, in an allegorical sense, this very same triad—the King, the Queen, and the Supersoul—should be familiar to Christians as "the Father, the Son and the Holy Ghost." This triad is essentially an allegory of the human existential situation, which has been widely utilized to describe a recognizable phenomenon of human experience: how the body is animated by "mind." In the world of psychology, Freudians will recognize this triadic tale as Ego, Id and Superego, and Jungians will recognize it as Conscious, Unconscious and Superconscious. This triad essentially describes a hierarchical relationship of material awareness, from completely material to transcendental and immaterial, with dormant transcendental awareness being descriptive of the nature of human existence.

Newton's Deterministic Universe

The Newtonian, or Cartesian, worldview effectively separated "mind" from "matter." During this scientific era (error), we took apart the world to see how it ticks, and we were never able to piece the holistic pattern back together again. Ancient teachings such as the above were eventually forgotten and replaced with the modern world view. Those readers who would like to follow the course of the deconstruction of ancient knowledge can read, among other works, *Shamanism and the Drug Propaganda, The Christ Conspiracy, Hamlet's Mill* (see bibliography), and other books on the history of science or the history of mythology. Regardless of how this occurred, the ancient worldview which taught that reality is a huge fabric of connected wholeness and order was lost in the Newtonian shuffle.

It has been observed that the Newtonian worldview was a determined universe. The motion of every atom of matter was, in principle, absolutely determined for all of past and future time. The forces of matter are determined by the position and motion of the particular matter being observed. If we know the laws governing these forces, we can then compute the entire history of the universe. In this pre-determined cause and effect universe, Mind is reduced to a series of internal (physical) reactions to external stimuli, making the human being "a machine within a machine."

In such a universe, writes Graham Martin in *Shadows in the Cave*, consciousness becomes "a pointless luxury." Newton's deterministic universe logically leads to an absurdist philosophy, for what is the point of a machine possessing consciousness? Furthermore, is it not an act of cruelty to trap a conscious awareness inside of a machine or a clock and to taunt him with the ideal of freedom? Since all of our actions would be governed by unchanging laws of causality, then free will and responsibility would not exist in such a world. If we had the impression of being able to change our circumstances, you might say we would be terribly misguided.

As Allan Combs and Mark Holland point out in *Synchronicity: Science, Myth, and the Trickster*, the world of Newtonian physics was easy to grasp: it was that of a "great celestial machine – a cosmic clock – running effortlessly and eternally." Then, Einstein's theory of relativity added a fourth dimension – time – to our world. And, if this wasn't difficult enough to grasp, quantum theory then proceeded to give us "absolutely nothing to hang an optical hat on." This is why, the authors suggest, quantum physics, even though it's decades old, is not widely taught, and therefore, not widely known or understood. As Harold McGowan has also pointed out: "living in a world of fields seems to be very different from living in a world which operates like a mechanism. Our philosophic viewpoints and our language are still based on a mechanistic conception of the universe, to the extent that they are based on anything scientific at all."

As it turns out, quantum physics added an element of uncertainty to the behavior of atomic particles. The assumption of cause and effect was shattered when, according to quantum physics, elementary particles (neutrons, positrons, neutrinos and quarks) escaped mechanical causality by being completely unpredictable.

According to Nick Herbert in *Elemental Mind*, quantum theory has been "flawlessly successful" in describing the world at all levels, and in passing every test that has been devised. Unfortunately, scientists and philosophers have been unable to clearly deduce from mathematical theory what is *really going on* when certain *behavior* is *observed*. These are two very important concepts to physicists and, as it turns out, to philosophers as well. To measure behavior at the quantum level, the observer must look at the atom and describe it as having certain "values" for the "attributes he specifically chooses to look at," such as position, momentum, spin, etc. Physicists discovered that in the micro world we cannot accurately measure both the *momentum* and the *location* of an elementary particle. We can only accurately measure one or the other. This measurable degree of uncertainty is known as Planck's constant, after its discoverer Max Plancke.

Looking at this another way, the physicist is required to observe the atom, look away for a moment, and observe it a second time. As Herbert explains, if the physicist attempts to describe the atom as "a tiny object possessing definite attributes at all times," he will not be able to correctly predict what attributes it will have on his second observation. Yet, if a physicist attempts to describe the unobserved atom in the peculiar quantum context of "a *wave of possibilities*," he will consistently obtain perfect results upon his second observation.

Thus, the physicist is forced to describe the unobserved atom as a *possibil - ity wave* rather than as an actual object, by a mathematical formula called a *wave function*. In its mathematical representation, the atom *seems* to be in many possible places at the same time. Although the wave's amplitude is largest where the atom was last sighted, the wave function is spread out over space. Thus the wave function represents only the *possibility* of the atom being in one particular place rather than its actual presence. So, Herbert explains, according to quantum physics, mathematically the world exists not as solid actuality but as "shimmering waves of possibility."

It's not as important to fathom the details of these physics experiments as it is to realize the impact these ideas will have on our scientific world view once they settle in for the long haul. In fact, they do seem to be settling in, slowly but surely. As it turns out, our notion of the solidity and substantiality of matter is based on our sensory interpretation of the world. The early phenomenologists 'sensed' this, and the mystics of various Eastern traditions 'meditated' on this, but 'objective' Western science didn't actually 'observe' these phenomena until fairly recently. Common sense should tell us that once ancient knowledge starts to bite us on the ass, the Ourobouros has arrived. Pay attention to how history repeats itself.

Recall Husserl's quirky insistence on the truth of primal perception, that the Earth does not move because there is no perception of such movement. Recall also Husserl's proposal that the interweaving of the perceptual modes of multiple witnesses creates a unified phenomenal reality, ministering to more than I, as one witness with a singular point of view, can possibly achieve. Although you and I together witness a unified field which we accept as a constant, eternal state of truth (i.e., the sky is blue), the world of solid, motionless objects is a sensory illusion.

According to Graham Martin in *Shadows in the Cave*, microscopic electrons within the atom are not composed of matter, but rather of "waves of or in probability," and matter somehow "emerges" from these immaterial probability fields. In addition, there are *virtual particles*, which appear out of nowhere and instantaneously vanish in a "ceaseless flicker of activity, full of the ghost of half existent possibilities, the mayflies of reality."

As Nick Herbert explains in *Elemental Mind*, atoms are continually vibrating at a particular frequency which depends upon the atom's energy content. When the atom is *observed*, it stops vibrating and objectifies one of its many possibilities, ceasing its "fuzzy dance" and "freezing" into a tiny object with observable attributes. When the observer looks away, the atom dissolves back into its "pool of possibilities;" an observer-induced collapse of the wave function called the *quantum jump*. Is this change in *mode of being* an actuality or is it a mathematical fiction? The answer is unknown, but the short answer is that the physicist *must* imagine the atom in an either/or situation; as "wavelike possibility" when not observed, and as "one particle-like actuality" when observed.

Let's explain this another way. As Nicholas Mann and Marcia Sutton explain in *Giants of Gaia*, a particle is in a constant state of formation and dissolution; "continually oscillating between energy and matter, between manifest and unmanifest, between the implicate order of the whole and its own explicate order." Attempts to measure this quantum state are conditioned by the observer, who is in turn conditioned by the quantum level. Thus, quantum theory establishes a "two-way flow between the previously considered separate orders of mind and matter," and on a deeper, formative level, "both mind and matter are the explicate forms which emerge out of a common generative order."

Rather than a universe of vast empty space, the modern world view shows that space is full of impermanent matter, which Martin describes in *Shadows in the Cave* as "many species of observable phantoms existing only for the briefest fraction of time." The materialist universe is gone for good, he writes, and in its place is a universe which is "more like an insubstantial pageant than a solid object," or, as Sir James Jeans noted in *The Mysterious Universe*, "more like a great thought than a great machine." Consciousness "appears to pluck reality out of probability" and "becomes an actor, or an interactor, in the universe." It has also been posited that consciousness selects from a range of available possibilities the "kind of reality it wants—but not the detail of that reality."

The universe is now seen as more than simply a machine; the idea of causality between separate entities has had to make way for a much more mysterious interconnectedness between things. Leading quantum physicists are postulating the presence of *intelligence* within the interrelationships *between* things, that is, in the way that information is perceived and processed by a *mind*.

In an infinite universe, by definition, everything is possible, even though all possibilities are not equally probable. Such a universe also has an "obliging nature" and is "reflexive," in that it "has the capacity to positively respond to any theory about it." It can, according to the authors of *Giants of Gaia*, "provide proof for any cosmological scheme, scientific or mystical, foisted upon it." Such 'proof' does not constitute the truth about the nature of the universe, but reveals the process by which our own minds create the parameters and schema we are looking for in the first place.

As a matter of fact, humans have a tendency to perceive only what can be incorporated into an established frame of reference, and tend to perceptually block out anything that does not fit into a preconceived notion of the physical world. Aldous Huxley suggested in *Doors of Perception* that normal consciousness has been funneled through a "reducing valve" of sorts, consisting of brain, nervous system and sensory organs, which protects the perceiver from sensory overload. This isn't much different from saying, as the City of Nine Gates tells us, that transcendental awareness becomes dormant in relationship with material intelligence or physical brain/mind. Our reducing valve, Joseph Chilton Pearce writes, may be "designed to simplify, select, focus and make real a specific event out of a continuum of possible events." Thus, Pearce has pointed out, the only reality available in our material universe may be a "homemade one."

Time and the Fourth Dimension

Nowhere has the implied presence of the fourth dimension been so compellingly explained as in P.D. Ouspensky's 1920 work, *Tertium Organum*. In his explanation of 3-D space, Ouspensky begins with the question: is the 'appearance' of three spatial dimensions a property of the material world (out there) or a property of human perception? Is the world of three dimensions, in Pearce's words, a "homemade one"? If it can be proven that 3-D space is a property of our own cognition and not a property of the world per se, we can go on to admit that upper dimensions exist but are merely out of the range of our physical sense organs. Lets see how Ouspensky comes around to proof of this likelihood.

Ouspensky begins with the fact that what we actually see in the world is an individual (and shared) perspective, not the world as it is. In this sense, we distort the world with our sense apparatus; as he puts it, "mentally we continually correct what the eye sees." This we know to be true. The capacity for this continual correction of what we see implies conceptual reasoning. Without this capacity for conceptual alignment of perception, our world would have quite a different appearance. What we would see, Ouspensky charges, is lots of nonexistent movements. Why is this so?

Ouspensky gives an example. When we ride past a house, we see the house from various angles. We see the various surfaces of the house, but not all of them, and not all at once. First we might see one side, then the edge, then the front side, then the other side, of a three-dimensional object. But, did the house turn? Well, it appeared to, but we made a perceptual correction using conceptual information which already exists in the mind. We already hold in mind the three-dimensional concept of a house. But for an animal, indeed the house does turn. When you take your dog out for a walk, what does it see? It sees only what is before it at each instant. It has no concept of time. The dog sees time as movement: the continual movement of surfaces as they appear before it. It cannot hold a three-dimensional concept in its mind. It only sees the surfaces of things.

What does a dog see when it goes for a car ride? It sees a world of objects in motion; it sees trees appear suddenly, move and vanish, it sees a building *turn its sides toward it*. In other words, it sees movement where there isn't movement to us, because we compensate for this perception by using our knowledge of 3-D conceptual forms to correct our vision. As Ouspensky asks: "How many illusions would we see if we were unable mentally to unravel the causes which produce them, and were to regard everything as existing exactly as we see it?"

According to Ouspensky, animals live in a two-dimensional world which consists of a series of continually moving surfaces having the appearance of the continual animation of objects. Indeed, he explains, the world appears also as a 'surface' to human beings, but we make conceptual compensations. Animals, however, are less able to make these corrections, and must accept everything as it appears. While humans can take a perceptual measurement of an object in three dimensions—length, breadth and height—an animal cannot hold in mind any concept that would measure a 3-D object. It forgets the properties of the first object when it encounters a third object; i.e. it cannot hold more than two properties in mind. Yet, the memory of properties of objects they have seen, along with odors and instinctual information, helps them find their way in the world.

Importantly, Ouspensky proposes that animals constantly *sense* the third dimension even though they can't see it. As he explains, they sense the 3-D world as something *transient*, in the same way that humans sense *time*. As he explains, all objects to animals are moving, *which means the third dimension of solids is manifested as motion*. Actual movement is seen as something transient, or "a change in the state of the object." An angle will be perceived as a turning, and the surface seen before will be regarded as gone, vanished, or, if the animal could reason thus, as belonging to the past. What this means is that angles and surfaces (as phenomena) which the animal has not yet seen do not exist. Anything that has appeared in the past, or has not yet appeared, has no real existence. Out of sight, out of mind. As Ouspensky writes (*Tertium Organum*, p. 84):

> For a horse, the corner of a house past which it runs every day is a phenomenon which recurs in certain circumstances, but which still takes place only in time; it is not a spatial and constant property of the house. For the animal an angle must be a time-phenomenon, instead of being a space-phenomenon as it is for us. Thus we see that the animal will perceive the properties of our third dimension as movements and will refer these properties to time, to the past or future, or to the present; i.e. to the moment of transition of the future into the past.

Having explained that the two dimensional world of the higher animals is part of the human three-dimensional world sans conceptual space-time modifications, Ouspensky goes on to explain that the lower animals in this world see it in one dimension. A lower animal, such as a snail, moves in one line, from the unpleasant toward the pleasant. It has only sensation, no perception of surface. This one line constitutes the whole of its world. All sensations entering from the outside appear from potentiality to become actuality. Only one line exists in the present; all the rest lies in *time*. A snail is a one-dimensional being which exists in our three-dimensional world.

The most important thing to understand, as Ouspensky sees it, is that to a higher animal such as a dog or a horse, *space appears as a surface and every - thing else lies in time*. Thus a higher animal *extracts one more dimension out of time*. For instance, Ouspensky explains, the world of a snail lies in one dimension, and for this one-dimensional entity our second and third dimensions lie "in time." The world of a dog or similar higher animal lies in two dimensions, and our third dimension lies "in time." A lower animal may observe phenomena, but for them these perceptions are "recurring" and not "permanent." As Ouspensky maintains, in the psychology of perception of the lower animal, "a new sun will rise every day."

The concept of time, according to Ouspensky, is a composite of two ideas: the idea of space and the idea of movement in space. Regarding time, Ouspensky makes the following remark: "Contact with a certain space, of which we are but dimly aware, provokes in us the sensation of movement in that space, and all taken together, i.e. the dim awareness of a certain space and the sensation of movement in that space, we call time." Rather than the observation of motion arising from outside of us, or in nature, this definition of time purports that the sensation of motion arises from the "time-sense" which we possess as part of our thinking apparatus, and can also be thought of as "imperfect space sense." This can also be thought of as the limit or boundary of space-sense which we are capable of possessing before it melts into "time." In other words, where space-sense ends, time sense begins. Time sense is the sense of successive moments; time sense is the boundary or surface of our space-sense. As Ouspensky points out, the laws of this universe may be the "surface tensions of a higher universe."

Ouspensky defines space-sense as "the faculty of representation in forms." Every living being feels as "space" only that which it is capable of understanding with its built-in "space sense," and everything "imperfectly felt is referred to time." That which is referred to time is that which one is incapable of representing to itself as form, everything felt as "ever-flowing, inconstant, and so unstable that no forms can represent it."

As an example of what might be meant by this, Immanuel Kant, in his *Critique of Pure Reason*, asserted that "time and space are forms of intuition." Intuitive knowledge is based on impressions which are beyond experiential knowledge; ideas which come to mind without an obvious relation to other thoughts. Kant believed that intuition is *a priori* knowledge, immanent wisdom which comprises the nature of the human being and is a condition of human existence. Intuition is dependent upon sensory phenomena in order to be expressed, however, it exists outside of such experience. So we might suppose that "space-sense" constitutes an information conduit; potential ideation hovering on the edge of Mind-at-Large, waiting to take up space in matter as a vibrating phantom thought form. As we mull over a problem, we know it will resolve itself in "time." In "time," we have the resolution of problems. Thus, intuition as a major source of novel information and problem-solving can be thought of as, in Ouspensky's words, the "surface tension" of a higher universe; something "imperfectly felt" which we can only refer to "time."

It's important to note here that all activity of life is a form of information processing. As Tom Etter explains in "Psi, Influence and Link Theory" (www.boundaryinstitute.org), causality is closely related to the arrow of time. He writes:

> There is a parallel between our problem with time's arrow and the ancients' problem with up and down. For the pre-scientific mind, up and down are intrinsic to space itself, which is why the round Earth had such a hard time gaining credence, despite the overwhelming evidence in its favor. The practical needs of long distance navigation finally triumphed over instinctive prejudice, but up and down still remained a mystery until Newton realized that the arrow here is not a property of space at all, but rather a relationship between massive bodies. There is an analogous solution to the problem of time's arrow; it is really not a property of time (or of space-time) at all, but rather a relationship between bodies of information.

> As with Newton's gravity, the strong directional arrow of time characterizes the situation of small informational bodies in the neighborhood of a much larger informational body. Such *bodies* are actually *events*. When these events are more nearly equal in size, the situation becomes more complex, and the simple arrow of time gives way to a multi-event relationship, just as the arrow of up and down among the satellites of Jupiter gives way to a multi-body relationship. Though the breakdown of an absolute distinction between past and future is baffling to common sense, it is quite harmonious with the larger picture of the universe that has emerged from physics.

Returning to Ouspensky's marvelous ideas, he notes that in its relationship to the world of phenomena, an animal is analogous to the make believe person we have imagined lives in Flatland. The three-dimensional world, to an animal, appears as a flat plane through which objects move in various directions. As Ouspensky explains, "two subjects, living side by side but possessing different mental apparatuses, must live in different worlds." Ouspensky deduces from these observations that the world's three-dimensionality is not its own property, but is a property of human perception and human consciousness. He concludes that by proving the existence of a lower space-sense existing within our own sphere of material space-time, we have proved as well the possibility of a higher space-sense existing within our own sphere of material space-time. In addition, Ouspensky asserted the following (*Tertium Organum*, p. 88):

> If a fourth unit of thinking were to become formed in the human, there would appear a fourth characteristic of the world; i.e. a fourth direction or perpendicular.... The surrounding objects as well as ourselves would then reveal the properties of a fourth dimension which we had not noticed before, or which we had previously regarded as individual properties of objects (or their motion), just as animals regard the extension of objects in the third dimension as motion.

Does this mean that our inner thoughts, emotions, ideas, intuitive hunches, dreams, visions, and so forth, which have "motion" and appear to move "in time," may be the result of a "higher space sense" existing within our own sphere of material space-time? Does this mean that novel ideas, inventions and solutions come to us via some 'outside' information conduit of which we are unaware? As Albert Einstein once stated, "The intellect has little to do on the road to discovery. There comes a leap in consciousness, call it Intuition or what you will, the solution comes to you and you don't know how or why." Movement equals information. All activity of life is information processing. This is the cosmic dance. As Tom Etter has suggested, time is a relationship between bodies of information. As he states, "the strong directional arrow of time characterizes the situation of small informational bodies in the neighborhood of a much larger informational body. Such *bodies* are actually *events*." They are huge informational events beyond our perception and comprehension. We can only perceive them as time.

Just as animals perceive 3-D motionless angles, curves, and surfaces as movements, or time phenomena, might the human being also perceive as time phenomena (movement) the angles, curves, and surfaces of the fourth dimension? As Charles Fort once noted: "All seeming things are not things at all; if all things are intercontinuous then they are only a projection from something else." Ouspensky adds: "maybe what appears to us as movements are in reality the motionless sides and angles of some kind of things existing outside us, things about which we know nothing. Maybe our consciousness, incapable of grasping these things by means of sense organs, and representing them to itself in their entirety, as they are—and grasping only the separate moments of its contact with them, builds up the illusion of motion, imagining that something moves outside it, i.e. that it is the 'things' that move."

If this is so, then what we think of as 'motion,'Ouspensky suggests, may in reality be derivative of some 'thing' beyond our grasp, and may arise in our mind at its contact with objects located in a higher dimension which we cannot fully comprehend. In this sense, our relationship to time, or the fourth dimension, is exactly the same as that of a dog to objects in the 3-D world. As Ouspensky explains, "time gradually comes as though arising out of nothing, and disappears into nothing;" or "everything imperfectly felt is referred to time." As Ouspensky concludes with regard to the presence of the fourth dimension:

> The sensation of motion is the consciousness of the transition from space to time, i.e. from a clear sense of space to an obscured one. And, on this basis, we can arrive at a real recognition of the fact that we perceive as sensations and project into the external world as phenomena the motionless angles and curves of the fourth dimension.

> Is it necessary or possible to assume, on this basis, that no motion of any kind exists in the world, that the world is static and constant and that it appears to us to be moving and evolving simply because we look at it through the narrow slit of our sense-perception? ... If the world is a Great Something, possessing self-consciousness, then we are the rays of this consciousness, conscious of ourselves but unconscious of the whole. If there is no motion, if it is nothing but illusion, then we must seek further for the source of this illusion.

Quantum Theories of the Universe

Now, to return to quantum theory, the ten million dollar question is what is an atom actually doing when nobody is looking at it? The twenty million dollar question is what goes on during a quantum jump when someone does look at it? How does consciousness interact with matter? Because of this new way of looking at the world, physicists have come up with various theories about the universe, some of which give the cosmic mode-of-being some rather bizarre attributes. Let's have a look at some quantum theories outlined by Nick Herbert in *Elemental Mind*.

Atoms Are Not Real. Niels Bohr posits that "only phenomena are real;" atoms are not so real. The atomic world can never be pictured by human beings because the mode of existence of an atom is of a type that cannot be grasped by humans.

The Perceiver is the Creator. No phenomenon is 'real' until it is observed; nothing actually exists except as the perception of a being who is the perceiver. The observer makes a "record" and crystallizes a possibility into actuality.

Quantum Entanglement. Once two quantum systems have interacted, their possibility waves become entangled in such a way that an action on one causes a change in the other. Bell's Theorem proves that non-local quantum entanglements are present mathematically as well as actually; once any two atoms have interacted they remain intimately connected, suggesting a quantum wholeness to the universe.

Many Worlds. A Many Worlds Universe theory proposes that unobserved atoms actually are in many places at the same time, each located in a different universe. This theory proposed by Hugh Everett, posits that everything that can possibly happen does happen! In this scenario, the cosmos might be thought of as being made up of "strands of spaghetti in space-time," with each strand being a different possible sub-universe. The observer in this universe finds himself actually in the universe he has chosen to observe. This interpretation would suggest that the world is immensely larger than it would appear to our senses, and that human consciousness is an "inadequate tool" for perceiving the world as it really is. The parallel universe model has become popular among some quantum theorists, as well as science fiction writers.

Quantum Logic. If the expression of an atom's attributes is not possible using ordinary language, perhaps a new language is needed. Mathematical logic is the codification of the rules of reason in an artificially constructed symbolic language invented by George Boole in the mid-nineteenth century. This yes/no systems logic, so-called "Boolean logic," forms the basis for the mechanical reasoning of computers. Quantum logic, however, is a non-Boolean approach, still in its infancy, which involves new grammatical rules for other choices and combinations of choices, for instance, involving the words, *and*, *or* and *not*. Problematically, if we accept quantum logic as the way the world really works, the every day world ceases to make sense.

Neo-realism. Reviving the original realist approach, neo-realism posits that quantum entities are particles which always have definite positions whether observed or not. The problem is that "the behavior of ordinary particles is just not crazy enough to explain the quantum facts." The neo-realist approach adds something to explain that crazy behavior: all of the world's "quantum strangeness" is attributed to a *pilot wave* which acts on each particle. A private pilot wave guides its particle by supplying and updating information about the universe and, problematical to the theory, must transmit these signals faster than the speed of light. Physicists are generally uneasy about the postulation of such unobservable entities which travel fast than light.

The Duplex World of Werner Heisenberg. In this view, the unobserved world is merely semi-real and achieves full reality status only at the instance of observation. Nothing ever really happens in the quantum world; it does not consist of actual events but of "unrealized tendencies for action." These tendencies are continually growing, merging, disappearing and moving according to quantum laws of motion discovered by Heisenberg. Events in the atomic world remain suspended in this realm of "quantum potentia" as long as they remain unobserved. During observation, one quantum possibility is "singled out, abandons its half-real, shadowy sisters, and surfaces in our ordinary world as an actual event." Our world sets limits, however, on "how far pools of potentia are permitted to spread." Importantly, since certain facts have become actual, not everything is equally possible in the quantum world. There is an interplay which controls what is and what is not possible.

Consciousness Creates Reality. The world according to John von Neumann is entirely quantum-possibility, where events hesitate on the brink of actuality. Rather than yes or no, von Neumann's "Hilbert Space" is a world of "maybes." But something was needed in this theory to "collapse the wave function," and turn the fuzzy possibilities into actual reality. The process that von Neumann looked for mathematically had to be an actual process, but not a physical process. Searching for such an "actually existing non-physical entity that could collapse the wave function," von Neumann concluded that the only known entity to fit this task was consciousness, or "mind."

Overlapping Worlds. Other prominent physicists have suggested that the entry of information into the consciousness of the observer is the fundamental step in the establishment of reality. Niels Bohr's Copenhagen Interpretation hypothesizes that "the state of a photon travelling towards a polarizer is a superposition of two worlds;" one photon's polarization being vertical and the other being horizontal. When the photon reaches the polarizer, one of these two worlds emerges as the true reality and the other is obliterated. In another proposition, when the photon reaches the polarizer, the universe splits in two; one being vertical and one being horizontal. According to this theory, the universe is continually splitting up into near-identical versions of itself.

Retrocausality

What if the "guiding purposes" are not simply "teleological" but are influences from the future? As Dean Radin writes in an online article entitled "Evidence suggestive of a retrocausal effect in the human nervous system," (www.boundaryinstitute.org):

> Common sense maintains that causality can flow only from past to future. But in spite of common sense, a growing number of scientists – mainly physicists – are seriously considering the possibility of genuine time-reversed effects. The scholarly literature contains over a hundred articles proposing ways in which retrocausality may be consistent with known physics. These articles are not found in fringe sources, but in mainstream journals like *Physical Review, Science, Foundations of Physics*, and *American Scientist*.

In another article entitled "Time reversed human experience: Experimental evidence and implications," Radin discusses four classes of experimental evidence for time reversed effects in human experience. The implications of these experiments is that all scientific disciplines may be vulnerable to time-reversed influences, that is, influence from the future.

Radin writes that "ordinary notions of causality may be viewed as a caricature of what is actually a set of highly complex, entangled relationships." There is substantial evidence, Radin reports, for the presence of "genuinely acausal experiences." In this context however "acausal" means "time-reversed, cause–effect relationships." As Radin also explains, retrocausality is presumed to manifest only in "exotic domains," and is considered "irrelevant" to human experience. However, while some exotic physical realms may well be outside the scope of human experience, some are not. How would "exotic" quantum events, such as time-loops, reversals, symmetries and acausal correlations, manifest in human perception? As Radin explains, such "exotic" correlations would emerge as precognition, déjà vu, synchronicity, or similar intuitive hunches. Radin argues that evidence strongly suggests that time-reversals do occur at the human scale, both consciously and unconsciously, and that "these phenomena are more pervasive in human experience than previously thought."

However, it is important to note that the future does not necessarily change the past. As Radin explains, time reversed effects appear to "probabilistically influence past events that were disposed to being influenced," and further, "the same influence cannot change what actually did occur, nor can it change events that are not susceptible to probabilistic influence."

Maverick physicist Jack Sarfatti has speculated that the UFO may indeed represent "intelligent messages back from the future in deliberate response to messages that the late Carl Sagan sent to the stars years ago in Voyager and Aricebo." Sarfatti asserts that remote viewing and precognition are not explainable with quantum physics theories. He writes that remote viewing and precognition violate the causal postulate of classical special relativity, as well as the quantum randomness postulate included in Shimony's "passion at a distance." According to Sarfatti, any theory of 'quantum mind' forbids remote viewing, forbids "presponse" or "subjective temporal antedating" and similar phenomena. Sarfatti believes that quantum theory is not a large enough theory to accommodate this data. Sarfatti's post-quantum theory predicts a critical complexity of a billion billion electron qubits to generate a conscious experience of approximately one second. Sarfatti's post-quantum time loop theory suggests that the future "co-creates" the present with the past in a globally self-consistent fashion. The future cannot change the present, but it co-creates a globally self-consistent loop in time. (This is not a many worlds theory, since global self consistency presupposes a single universe.) As Sarfatti explained in an e-mail on 6/12/00:

> We have a critical complexity of a billion billion electron qubits to generate a conscious moment in the range of 1 second. This comes from balancing the quantum action of mind moving matter in configuration space against the post-quantum reaction of matter moving mind. The latter is not possible in 20_{th} Century quantum physics, which is the low-complexity limiting case of the really new 21st Century post-quantum physics. This balancing act is made possible by the $1/N^2$ coherence factor for N nonlocally entangled qubits forming a macroscopically quantum phase coherent network or "hologram" (Bohm-Pribram) made possible by the "enslavement" (Haken's "Synergetics") (see http://stardrive.org/Jack/Synergy.pdf and http://stardrive.org/Lilly/) of the N qubits by a coherent near ELF electric field like Crick's 40 Hz brain clock field. The power needed to erase one conscious moment to make room for the next one forming William James's "stream of consciousness" is only 5 milliwatts per Hz of conscious channel bandwidth.

The Nature of Movement

David Bohm writes of the nature of thought and *movement* that whenever one *thinks* of anything, it seems to be apprehended as *static*, or as a *series of stationary images* much like still photographs. Writing in *Wholeness and the Implicate Order*, Bohm notes that a thought seems to be a frozen moment of time. But the actual experience of movement in real time is quite different. Therefore, what is the nature of thought as compared to actual movement in the present? Is thought a "stream of consciousness," or is it really quite distilled as images or snapshots? What is the relationship between consciousness and reality? Does thinking merely supply a picture of reality, or does it grasp the essence of actual living movement? As Bohm writes:

> In my scientific and philosophical work, my main concern has been with understanding the nature of reality in general and of consciousness in particular as a coherent whole, which is never static or complete, but is an unending process of movement and unfoldment.

The idea that the thinker is independent from that which is thought about is a culmination of the Western scientific tradition. We are taught that the brain is the locale of thought, but how can we really maintain that the ebb and flow of consciousness contains two separate realms: the thinker and the thought about? It has been necessary, Bohm points out, for man to divvy-up pieces of his world in order to manage it in a practical sense. But, in the end, he laments, this propensity to divide, as a way of thinking about things, has culminated in a destructive apparatus. As Bohm notes in his Introduction to *Wholeness and the Implicate Order*:

> When this mode of thought is applied broadly to man's notion of himself and the whole world (his self-world view), then man ceases to regard the resulting divisions as merely useful or convenient and begins to see and experience himself and his world as actually constituted of separate existent fragments. Being guided by a fragmentary self-world view, man then acts in such a way as to try to break himself and the world up, so that all seems to correspond to his way of thinking. Thus, he obtains an apparent proof of the correctness of his fragmentary self-world view, though he overlooks the fact that it is he himself, acting according to his mode of thought, who has brought about the fragmentation that now seems to have an autonomous existence.

We hearken to the myths of an early "golden age," Bohm also noted, before the split between man and nature, between subject and object, had occurred. Yet, how is mankind to be considered "human" without this essential self-awareness which comprises the subject-object split? As Amit Goswami has pointed out in *The Self-Aware Universe*, it is the appearance of the manifest world which leads to the experience of self, or the split between subject and object. In physics terms, he explains, "subject and object manifest simultaneously in the initial collapse of the quantum state of the brain-mind." Ironically, without the world of manifestation, there can be no self which is capable of the perception that it is separate from the world of objects. We are what we are, with no apologies.

The wholeness we seek only arises in fleeting moments: the "aha" experience, whole brain synchrony, or hemispheric synchronization, which are achieved through meditative states. True, this whole brain state was no doubt easier to achieve in some "golden age," or still today by those immersed in Eastern esoteric traditions which never compartmentalized their thought processes in the first place. But, short of joining a monastery, we can only do the best we can with what we've got. Human perception is very much a product of cultural history.

David Bohm looked for a "consistent account of consciousness," which would afford mankind a non-fragmentary world view, which would be appropriate for its time, and which, he believed, was "essential for harmony in the individual and in society as a whole." He claimed that the world needed to catch up with quantum physics concepts which are beginning to show that the world is connected in an underlying holistic order; what he called an "implicate order." This new approach would have to revolutionize language and knowledge systems; and would need to encompass the who, what, when, where, how and why of the structure of reality. In essence, we needed to start over. Since, as Bohm explained, this structure was essentially comprised of "movement," he called this non-linear, non-fragmentary, non-stationary world view: "holomovement."

The Holographic Model

According to Michael Talbot in *The Holographic Universe*, there is evidence to suggest that our world and everything in it is a "holographic" projection from another level of reality beyond material space-time. As a matter of fact, physicist David Bohm and neurophysiologist Karl Pribram arrived at their holographic theoretical models independently, from two very different disciplinary approaches. The history of this development in itself makes for a fascinating case load on the side of the holographic model, or holomovement.

In their decades of research into paranormal phenomena, both of these scientists discovered that the holographic model was able to make sense of a wide range of phenomena which had previously lain outside the range of scientific study. Talbot argues that the holographic model can account for extraordinary human perceptual phenomena, such as telepathy, psychokinesis, precognition, near death experience, out-of-body travel, remote viewing, lucid dreams, synchronicity, Marian apparitions, UFOs, shamanistic healing, hands-on healing, stigmata, the human aura, hypnosis, trance states, pre-cognition and retro-cognition, and virtually all paranormal and mystical human experience. How does the holographic model accomplish all of this?

Karl Pribram's studies in neurophysiology have shown that memories are not localized in a certain area of the brain, but are dispersed throughout the brain. His research also discovered that the brain is capable of storing a staggering amount of information in a small storage area. Holograms possess the capacity for enormous information storage. The holographic model explains the ability to recognize familiar objects and people, and the ability to transfer and apply knowledge, information and skills to other areas.

Pribram hypothesized a holographic model which would explain how the brain is able to convince us that inner processes are actually located outside the body; that our inner experiences project an external reality. Remember Husserl's view that the "world is not a given place in which experience occurs, but is that toward which one is turned in experience." This is tricky lingo, and it has to be pondered a little while in silence before it comes to you. Studies following Pribram's initial predictions about the holographic nature of memory and perception have corroborated his hypothesis that the mind works "holographically." But it wasn't until he read the work of physicist David Bohm that he realized the entire universe may be a hologram. Bohm's well known work in quantum physics convinced Pribram that the universe operated as a kind of giant, flowing hologram.

Bohm's 1980 pioneering work, *Wholeness and the Implicate Order*, introduced his radical theory of the holographic universe. Bohm suggested that the "implicate" order is a deeper level of reality which contains the potential for enfoldment, and the "explicate" order is our familiar material level of existence which has already unfolded. The universe, he suggested, is essentially the result of an interplay between these levels of reality, a continual process of unfolding. Because it is in constant flux, Bohm referred to the universe not as merely a hologram, but as "holomovement." Bohm also suggested that this deep and organized order in the universe explains why reality becomes nonlocal at the subquantum level. As will be discussed shortly, information is distributed in this holographic matrix in a 'nonlocal' fashion.

Bohm also tore the fabric of conventional quantum physics by asserting that it is essentially meaningless to separate physical aspects of reality into its minutest of parts in order to study how they interact. He suggested that everything in the universe was part of a continuum, and that subatomic particles are not separate entities unto themselves. Ultimately, he suggested, even the implicate and explicate orders blend into each other.

Bohm's holomovement model suggests that consciousness and matter cannot be separated, but that the observer IS the observed. His theory suggests that consciousness is a subtle form of matter, and that the basis for a relationship between consciousness and matter lies in the deeper layer of "implicate order." He suggests that consciousness is present in various degrees of enfoldment in all matter, and that even subatomic particles contain properties that are "mindlike." This would agree with Ouspensky's argument that the noumenal and phenomenal are inseparable. Like Ouspensky, Bohm warned that dividing the universe into living and non-living, animate and inanimate, is a mistake. He insisted that life and intelligence is present in *all matter* as "holomovement."

Just as every portion of the universe enfolds the whole, we learn from Bohm, every cell in our bodies is a mini blueprint for the cosmos. The synthesis of Bohm and Pribram's theories, Talbot suggests in *The Holographic Universe*, is the following:

> Our brains mathematically construct objective reality by interpreting frequencies that are ultimately projections from another dimension, a deeper order of existence that is beyond both space and time. The brain is a hologram enfolded in a holographic universe.

As Pribram posits, the waves and frequencies that are out there in space-time only appear as a concrete reality because our holographic brain takes this cosmically generated holographic "blur" of frequencies and converts it into a solid objective reality. The brain constructs an image of a world and projects it "out there." Yet, to view the holographic mind or brain as separate from the holographic universe is incorrect. We are not *looking* at a hologram, we are part of the hologram. In this sense, it might be suggested that human consciousness even constructs space and time.

Studies which have utilized mental imagery techniques in healing diseases like cancer and leukemia also suggest that the brain operates holographically. Talbot quotes Bohm in *The Holographic Universe* (p. 84):

Every action starts from an intention in the implicate order. The imagination is already the creation of the form; it already has the intention and the germs of all the movements needed to carry it out. And it affects the body, so that as creation takes place from the subtler levels of the implicate order, it goes through them until it manifests in the explicate.

Talbot reports that the "placebo effect" is another phenomenon which suggests that the mind controls the "body holographic." Further, studies of stigmata, bleeding wounds which arise after intense meditative states or mystical experiences, suggest that these wounds are produced by auto-suggestion. The holographic model can explain the phenomenon of stigmata, as well as the miraculous regeneration of wounds, and the laying on of hands in healing and shamanic ceremonies.

According to the holographic model, matter is kind of a "habit" we wear, and it is shaped from the implicate order. The laws of physics governing the universe can also be viewed as "habits" which are embedded in the "holomovement." Yet, these habits can be transcended or momentarily suspended by actions arising via intentions in the implicate order. In a holographic universe, Talbot explains, time and space are illusory; they are merely habitual modes of perception. This implies the laws of physics are not set in stone. They are only as fixed as the other habits we employ in order to hold our holomovement in place, or to fixate our concrete reality. As discussed earlier, reality is a social veneer which we agree to hold in place by mutual consensus.

This would also imply that altered states of consciousness are required to make changes in the implicate order. Prayer, meditation, imagery and intent are necessary to contact this level of consciousness. As William Gray writes in *Magical Ritual Methods*, "Magic is not unlike judo or karate which needs quality rather than quantity of energy, applied with exact precision of impact and intent." The dynamic interplay between the body's energy field, mental images, and the physical body explains why concentrated visualization techniques, meditation, and prayer can heal the body. Prayer and meditation can cause healing images to be impressed upon the body's energy field to effect physical healing. The energy field is a "blueprint" that guides and molds the physical body. Although western medicine cannot explain this apparent relationship, the holographic model can.

The phenomenon of retrocognition suggests that the past is active in the present within the implicate order. If, as Bohm suggests, the source of consciousness is in the implicate, the holographic record of the past also exists in the explicate order. A "shift in focus" is all that is required to access records of the "past." If past events are recorded in the "cosmic airwaves," Talbot suggests, ripe for the picking by human consciousness, can this explain ghosts and hauntings? After all, an apparition seems to be nothing more than a 3-D hologram of a person or scene from the past. Perhaps these "hauntings" are not the product of earthbound spirit forms, but are accidental pluckings from the holographic continuum, or holomovement. Along these lines, anthropologist Evens-Wentz, as quoted by Talbot in *The Holographic Universe* (p. 204), has suggested:

> Nature herself has a memory. There is some indefinable psychic element in the earth's atmosphere upon which all human and physical actions or phenomena are photographed or impressed. Under certain inexplicable conditions, normal persons who are not seers may observe Nature's mental records like pictures cast upon a screen, often like moving pictures.

In this regard, the phenomenon of "life review" which is reportedly contained in the near death experience may also be seen as a hologram. This experience has been reported as a "vivid, wrap-around, three-dimensional replay" of a person's entire life. Rosicrucians believe that every event in a person's life is instilled on an "atom" and is available for total recall at the moment of death or in "near death experience" (NDE). As Talbot explains, many NDEers have reported instantaneous, panoramic and total recall of their entire life span, right down to trivial details involving moral actions, which also included the vicarious feelings of other people who were hurt by their actions. In addition, NDEers have noted the sense that they themselves were composed of color and sound, and that each person in this realm has his own frequency in the light and sound range. It is reported that there is beautiful music and color in the ND dimension.

The following chapter explores various esoteric doctrines regarding the stuff thoughts are made of, and how thoughts can be considered a type of energy graffiti permanently inscribed on nature's walls.

CHAPTER THREE
THOUGHTRONS AND THOUGHT FORMS:
IS THOUGHT A PARTICLE OR WAVE?

Each man travels through space enclosed within a case of his own building, sur-rounded by a mass of the forms created by his habitual thoughts.

Besant and Leadbeater

Thought-forms

Mystics of Tibet referred to the stuff of thoughts as *tsal*, and believed that every mental action produced waves of thought energy. They believed that the entire universe is created and animated by the collective thought energy of all of its various inhabitants. New Age philosophy has its roots in these ideas. As an example, the Theosophist tradition holds that all sorts of different physical particles occupy space, and these exist as worlds within worlds. The inner worlds consist of matter of different densities and orders of vibration or move-ment (i.e. time). For instance, if a jar is filled with marbles, is it really filled? Can't you pour sand into the jar to further occupy the space? Is it filled now? Can't you now pour water into the jar to further occupy the space? If these dif-ferent particles of matter exist in the material world, how many different types of subtle or elemental matter exist in a form not visible to our senses? According to ancient traditions, thought is one of these particles of matter.

In their book *Thought-forms*, Annie Besant and C.W. Leadbeater wrote that thoughts are forms in mental matter; radiating vibrations created by the energy of the mind. Certain mystics claim the ability to see the shapes and colors of these forms hovering in the air around human beings. In their pioneering Theosophist work, Besant and Leadbeater analyzed the qualities of human thought-forms which signify their meaning in terms of their color, shape and form. Such thought waves are capable of affecting the thought of others to the extent that they cause similar types of thoughts as those of the sender. In this way, they write, "the thinker is in the same position as the speaker." Besant and Leadbeater wrote the following regarding thought-forms:

> Each man travels through space enclosed within a case of his own building, surrounded by a mass of the forms created by his habitual thoughts. Through this medium he looks out upon the world and nat-urally sees everything tinged with its predominant colors, and all rates of vibration which reach him from without are more or less modified by its rate. Thus until the man learns complete control of thought and feeling, he sees nothing as it really is, since all his observations must be made through this medium, which distorts and colors everything like badly-made glass.

> If the thought-form be neither definitely personal nor specially aimed at someone else, it simply floats detached in the atmosphere, all the time radiating vibrations similar to those originally sent forth by its creator. ... What it produces in the mind-body which it influences is not merely a thought of an order similar to that which gave it birth; it is actually the same thought. The radiation may affect thousands and stir up in them thoughts on the same level as the original, and yet it may happen that no one of them will be identical with the original; the thought-form can affect only very few, but in those cases it will repro-duce exactly the initiatory idea.

This is how, for instance, the "consciousness of a nation" comes to share the same ideology. According to Theosophists, certain "national ways of thinking" result from the continual reproduction of similar thoughts arising from the history and customs of a nation. According to this view, centuries of similar thoughts profoundly influence the minds of all the people born into that nation, and this is the "national vibration rate" through which impressions from other nations are modified. One nation can never quite fully understand the other due to the influence of these subtle thought-forms. Annie Besant wrote in *Thought Power* that we are all continually affecting each other by these waves of thought, and that "what is called public opinion is largely created in this way."

The pioneering studies discussed by Michael Talbot suggest that consciousness is not located in the brain, but is a "plasmic holographic energy field" that permeates and surrounds the physical body. Is this hologram built of thought waves or thought particles? In a holographic universe, Talbot, Bohm, Carl Jung and others have suggested, the concept of "location" is an illusion; everything is nonlocal, including consciousness. Although consciousness seems to be localized somewhere inside the skull, it can at times appear to be localized elsewhere, as in the case of out-of-body experience. The nonlocal aspect of consciousness is also suggested by dreams, where location and space are completely illusory and shifting.

In addition, as Talbot explains, the OBE body is a kind of hologram that can take on any shape or guise, just as the dream persona is capable of shapeshifting. He reports that, once they get their bearings in this strange habitat, seasoned OBE travelers find that they can see in all directions without turning their heads. Talbot suggests that our "thought habits" create our OBE forms. There is some indication that in out-of-body experiences we reproduce the body we are used to, and even put clothes on it. But some out-of-body travelers have reported being in other types of bodies, or have even described their "vehicle" as a vibrational pattern very much like a hologram.

These ideas suggest that thought is a vibrational wave or plasma form. Here we have an example of modern science coming around to ancient ideas. As I've said elsewhere and will say again because it's true, human knowledge has a way of biting itself on the ass. But in this case, it is apparent why it does so. Because thought begets similar thought. Why is that? Perhaps the Akashic records are the source of thought-forms from which we borrow our collective ideas; and a hologram is a helpful way to understand how this might work.

As Talbot has suggested, although all thoughts can affect the subtle energetic levels of the holographic universe, it is especially the emotionally powerful and transformational thoughts and events that are potent enough to manifest a series of synchronous coincidences in the matrix of physical reality. William Tiller suggests that the universe itself began as a subtle energy field or a divine thought-form, which functioned as a template influencing gradually denser and denser levels of cosmic energy until it eventually coalesced into a hologram of a physical universe. This means each of us is a mini-universe. Modern author David Icke describes a very similar notion when he writes:

> Our physical reality is a creation of the thoughts we hold onto, past and present. These create an energy-pattern within us which is then cast around us in the form of a magnetic cape or aura. This attracts us to a reality in terms of people, places and events which exactly reflects our own self-created pattern, how we see ourselves. The key to this reality is thought.

As another example, other ancient mystical traditions, including the Rosicrucians, taught that subtle energies permeate dense matter, and called this realm the Thought World. The Rosicrucians claim that the original source of this information was the Egyptians and, perhaps earlier, the Sumerians, and even earlier, the Atlanteans. The most subtle essence, Mind, is the "home world of the human spirit." Rosicrucian philosopher Max Heindel has noted that these gradations of matter are not distributed as distinct layers but, rather, the more subtle, invisible grades permeate and are part of the visible world. This is reminiscent of Bohm's implicate and explicate order. As Bohm suggests, consciousness is a subtle form of matter which is present in varying degrees of enfoldment (or potential) in all matter. It's remarkable how Western science is finally catching up with ancient wisdom.

The Rosicrucian portrayal of the visible and invisible hierarchy of worlds is described by Max Heindel in *The Rosicrucian Mysteries*. He writes that the earth and the other planets of our solar system are composed of three kinds of matter. The densest matter, which is our visible earth, is as "the center of the ball as the yolk is the center of an egg." Around that nucleus, "a finer grade of matter is disposed in relation to the central mass as the white of the egg is disposed outside the yolk." This second kind of invisible substance permeates solid, visible matter to the very center. Outside both of these commingling grades of matter there is "a still finer layer corresponding to the shell of the egg, except that this layer is the most subtle of the three grades of matter and interpenetrates the two inner layers."

The central mass of this cosmic egg is the visible world, "composed of solids, liquids, and gases, which constitute the earth, its atmosphere, and the ether." The second layer of matter is the Desire World. Heindel writes that all forms are impelled into motion by feelings, emotions and desires, which comprise the Desire World. The outermost layer is the World of Thought. The most subtle essence, which comprises the third layer, is Mind: the "home world of the human spirit." Heindel is careful to note that these gradations of matter are not distributed as distinct layers but, as Ouspensky also argues, the more subtle, invisible grades permeate and are part of the visible world. These subtle essences give mankind the ability to move about in his world, to think, to work, to love, and to create, and to wonder about the world that is his home.

Aha! Mind is Meaning

Martin Heidegger lamented that Aristotle had classified the world into a collection of mere facts which had emptied the world of meaning. To Heidegger, human existence is not a fact, but a *relation*, a *gap*, an *in-between*. It is a place of *disclosure*. It is a rift in which meaning is able to disclose itself. Can we apply the terms *subjective* and *objective* to this kind of phenomenological analysis? After all, subject and object are just a pair of opposites traditionally discussed in ontology and, as it turns out, in physics as well. As the phenomenologists have posited, there is *me* and there is *not me*; but is there something in between that space? What is happening when we close the closet door? Is the light on or off? The question drives us crazy, so we take apart the universe to find out.

The nature of being lies in movement; movement toward and movement away: the cosmic dance. All activity of life is a form of information processing. It has also been shown that the *act of looking* is one of the *determinants* in the particular *reality event* at hand. For example, a count of the word *look* thus far in this book might reveal that the human gaze, the existentially human act of "wanting to know" or "looking into something," is structurally part of our lingua-communication with the world or being-in-the-world. This act of studying an object or, better yet, *movement toward knowing*, is what constitutes this cosmic dance. We might conclude that if the cosmic dance is an act of *looking*, then problems in knowledge arise when we are *incorrectly looking*; not looking *in the wrong place*, but looking *with preconceived notions* (i.e. looking with the closet door closed).

Might we be *overlooking* what constitutes the space between the *looker* and the *looked at*? What is in the space between; the space where something happens only when we are *looking*? The space between is "Mind," and mind is alive and well as both a process and an elemental constituent of the universe. The mind holds *terra intermedia*, the middle ground, in a vast "Glass Bead Game" of cosmic proportion. Mind is Meaning.

As Joseph Chilton Pearce notes, human beings cannot examine the process of their own *mirroring* of the universe by standing outside of it because mind is part of this process. As Graham Martin suggests in *Shadows in the Cave*, "matter is the mode of being that the world appears to have when observed by a mind." This would appear to be in sync with Heidegger's sentiment that man is not a *substance*, but a *relation*, and that the *disclosure* between subject and object is *consciousness*. The scientific observation that *mind* fills in the gap, then, seems to be in agreement with the hypothesis posed by Heidegger and other phenomenologists that *meaning* lies *a priori* within the subject. And, as physicist David Bohm argues, the observer IS the observed!

So, we see that quantum physics revelations coincide with Merleau-Ponty's idea that the world is not a *place* in which experience occurs but is "that toward which one is turned in experience," and that perception is more than sense impressions but is already, beforehand, *charged* with *meaning*. Jean Paul Sartre suggests that a person must *impose* himself upon the world in order to see his relatedness and therefore his *meaning*; and, wouldn't you know it, Mind is seen as *synthesis* or *resolution* (a process not a thing). To the phenomenologists, mind is *disclosure* and *meaning*; the *place* where the sharp edges of polarity melt away. Meditation on the *object* has ultimately disclosed that the space between subject and object is *Mind*. New physics revelations are essentially telling us that the world of our perception is not really an object! It has also disclosed the paradox that there *is* no space between; or, subject and object are one and the space between is the intersubjective realm. This is the place where we agree to play a game; the game of creating what happens in the next move of the holomovement. As quantum physics is telling us, we're holding it all up.

We Are All Animists

David Abram suggests in *The Spell of the Sensuous* that, despite the cultural artifacts surrounding us, the world before we set our sciences out to measure it is not an inert object but is "a living field, an open and dynamic landscape subject to its own moods and metamorphoses." He stresses that our most immediate experience of things constitutes a "reciprocal encounter of tension, communication, and commingling" in which the thing or phenomenon becomes "our interlocutor," drawing us into relation.

Interestingly, Abrams explains that in this act of encounter it is necessary for human beings to isolate or objectify the phenomenon presenting itself by "mentally absenting ourselves from this relation." In effect, we repress our sensuous involvement with objects and block our perceptual reciprocity with that being. (As Bob Dobbs has similarly noted, the blocking of the intimate qualities of ESP, necessary to preserve individual identity, is always communicated when human beings interact.) Abrams ascertains that to define another being as an inert or passive object is to deny its ability to actively engage our senses. Prior to all our verbal reflections, Abram writes, at the level of our spontaneous and sensory engagement of the world, *we are all animists*.

Psi researcher Engr Ivan Doskocil would tend to agree. Writing in "Coincidental States in Psychotronics," he suggests that every person has an apparatus that enables him to detect the state of other people. As Doskocil explains, in every day communication with the world, man unconsciously projects himself into some 'other' or some object in his environment and imitates the other's behavior; sympathetically reproducing another person's motions, expressions, intonation and meaning. This is called "empathy." Interestingly, according to Soviet psychotherapist Levi, "empathy" is a certain type of "mental echo," and is the basic element of social psychology. Doskocil equates this "mental echo" with Carl Jung's concept of archetypes. He suggests that in everyday communication human beings are attempting to mentally imitate an unconscious archetype. We will very shortly attempt to 'define' just what an archetype is.

So, where are we at this point? Well, according to a synthesis of objective and subjective findings which can be quoted from a multitude of sources, we've arrived at the revelation that although there *appears* to be a *subject* and *object*, there may not *really* be such or, to put it another way, there may not be a sharp distinction between the two. Although all appearances would say that subject and object have definite edges, it is apparent that the only way reality can possibly *have any appearance at all* is by dulling those edges; by the knower and the known agreeing to temporarily participate in each other's being. Therefore, the disclosure, the movement toward knowing, gives birth to the world we see, which is in effect the *only world*. For, as Pearce writes in *Crack in the Cosmic Egg*, "stripping off the acquired interests of our worldview does not lead to a *true* universe... there is no other world for us; we would immediately have to weave another equally arbitrary garb. There is no going naked in the world."

If anything, we are led to conclude that there are a heck of a lot of more interesting ways of looking at what it means to be human than by the old 'matter causes mind' materialist paradigm. Interestingly, this observation would *appear* to agree with the Indian philosophy which distinguishes not between *mind* and *matter*, but between *consciousness* and *appearance*. Is reality an illusion in which we actively participate? As the *Bhagavad-gita* suggests, consciousness is eternal and transcendent, while material existence is caught in a tangled hierarchy of illusion and ignorance.

It is important to note that the various ultra-dimensional reality paradigms explained here would allow what we now consider to be the *supernatural* to become a *natural* matter. Such revisions to future science books would allow certain ultra-events into our physical locale; if not touchable, at least communicable in terms beyond little-green-men asides. The ability to discuss these ultra-possibilities out of the shadow of such banter will be a large leap for mankind.

Rupert Sheldrake has stated this a different way in *A New Science of Life*. He writes, "if the mechanistic theory states that all phenomena are capable of being explained in terms of the known laws of physics, it might well be wrong. ... If on the other hand the mechanistic theory states that living organisms obey *both known and unknown laws of nature*, then it would be irrefutable." In practice, however, the mechanistic theory of life is not viewed as a rigorously defined, refutable scientific theory. Instead, Sheldrake writes, it justifies "a conservative method which works within an established framework which simply does not and cannot include causal factors as yet unrecognized by physics."

Rupert Sheldrake's hypothesis of formative causation is also pertinent here. In his 1981 book *A New Science of Life*, Sheldrake postulates an invisible matrix or organizing field which regulates the structure, growth and behavior of all living things. These fields serve as patterns which guide the forms and behaviors of all life forms across time. When any one thing forms a new behavior at any level of its existence, it will formatively influence other things or entities of its kind, like an update to its template. Sheldrake believes these forms are "non-energetic," but only in terms of the kinds of energy known to current mainstream science. They are a completely different energy form; an intelligent energy matrix. Sheldrake's ideas bring back in from the margins the Lamarckian concept of an intelligently guided evolutionary process, as I argued in Volume 1 of this book, *Space Travelers and the Genesis of the Human Form*.

The mechanistic approach asserts that every effect must have a 'known cause' in the material world. But as we will see, quantum and post-quantum physics paradigms assert that nonlocal consciousness, or Mind-at-Large, does not operate within "local" causal parameters but, rather, operates through a common information conduit called "nonlocal consciousness."

Non-Local Consciousness

Nonlocal consciousness is consciousness that does not appear to reside in the brain. A nonlocal event is "acausal," in that it does not comprise a linear message transfer (i.e. corresponding to "linear time"), but appears to be a shared message arising in a common nonlocal realm of consciousness. It might be simpler to state that consciousness seems to reside not between the ears, but elsewhere. This implies that information transfer, in the form of ideas, symbols or messages that come to mind, arise from a collective Mind-at-Large rather than a place within the physical brain. A message or information unit which seemingly occurs at profoundly meaningful junctures was coined a "synchronicity" by world renowned psychologist Carl Jung. Jung described synchronicity as "meaningful coincidences that occur without a cause except perhaps a common cause in the transcendent domain."

As Ouspensky has suggested, this "domain" or "cause" could be the 4th dimension. As Dean Radin has pointed out, this "cause" or nonlocal domain could also be what we think of as the "future," since this domain is a non-linear shared information network. As Radin has pointed out, "ordinary notions of causality may be viewed as a caricature of what is actually a set of highly complex, entangled relationships." Thus, the concept of "acausal" may also indicate the possibility of "time-reversed, cause←effect relationships." Radin's research has shown that such time-reversals do occur at the human scale and may be common experiences.

The concept of synchronicity implies a wholeness and relatedness between seemingly unrelated events, or causally unconnected happenings in physical space-time. Experiments in nonlocality suggest that Jung was on to something. As Jung noted:

> Since psyche and matter are contained in one and the same world and, moreover, are in continuous contact with one another and ultimately rest on irrepresentable, transcendent factors, it is not only possible but fairly probable that psyche and matter are two different aspects of one and the same thing.

As Goswami explains in *The Self Aware Universe*, Jung also had a name for the transcendent realm of consciousness where synchronous events occur: the *collective unconscious*. Unfortunately, the Freudian terminology he used distracts from the idea of a transpersonal and collective domain operating from a nonlocal source, but this is nonetheless what he appears to be describing. The term 'unconscious' may refer only to our basic unawareness of this group mind. If we were to describe Jung's collective unconscious in quantum terms, Goswami suggests, we might say that "our nonlocal consciousness collapses the wave of a quantum object and chooses the result of the collapse when we observe it, but we are normally unaware of the nonlocality of the collapse and of the choice."

What we have come to understand as the 'unconscious' in Freudian terms may be something for which there is actually consciousness but not awareness. In the philosophy of idealism, consciousness is "the ground of being." Consciousness is "omnipresent, even when we are in an unconscious state." From this viewpoint, Goswami suggests, it is our "conscious self that is unconscious of some things most of the time and of everything when we are in a dreamless sleep." Conversely, the "unconscious seems to be conscious of all things all of the time."

We can further clarify then that nonlocal consciousness does not constitute causal relationships within causal parameters but, rather, "operates through us; or more properly, it *is* us, only subtly veiled." Goswami also posits that this seeming 'veil' can be penetrated. The essential component of nonlocal consciousness is "creative discontinuity," which means our creativity must break with the known or with 'continuous' repetitive cycles. By discontinuing repetitive behaviors or responses, we make a *quantum jump out of the system*. This, Goswami argues, is what is needed for consciousness to see itself. In creativity, we constantly, "take leaps that catapult us out of the context of our past experiences," and we must "exercise the freedom to be open to a new context." It is in this respect that we, as discussed earlier, are perhaps *incorrectly looking*, that is, with preconceived notions of what we will find, in effect, looking with the closet door closed.

Important to an idealist interpretation of quantum physics is the idea of *meaning*. Goswami writes that the concepts of nonlocal consciousness and non-local quantum collapse make the universe less comprehensible to the material-ist scientist, but more meaningful from an idealist perspective. The universe finally makes sense to those of us who are interested in an explanation for var-ious "paranormal" experiences like telepathy, out-of-body experience, remote viewing, psychokinesis, clairvoyance, and other forays into the mystical realm.

The Anthropic Principle

Goswami asks an extremely anthropomorphic question which turns out to be important to the question of the existence of intelligent extraterrestrial life. He asks: "How has the Cosmos existed for the past fifteen billion years if for the bulk of this time there were no conscious observers to do any collapsing of wave functions?" His answer, he thinks, is "very simple." He explains: "the Cosmos never stays in fixed form." Past universes, he writes, cannot be seen as paintings on canvas which unravel in linear fashion, which is precisely the materialist picture. Goswami proposes, instead, that "the universe exists as formless potentia in myriad possible branches in the transcendent domain and becomes manifest only when observed by conscious beings." He further clari-fies that these "self-referential observations plot the universe's causal history, rejecting the myriad parallel alternatives that never find their way to material reality."

Goswami suggests that this interpretation may also explain how life evolved from prebiotic matter through "beneficial mutations" leading to humans. He clarifies, "once we recognize that biological mutation is a quantum event, we realize that the universe bifurcates in every such event in the transcendent domain, becoming many branches, until in one of the branches there is a sen-tient being that can look with awareness and complete a quantum measure-ment." He suggests that, at this point "the causal pathway leading to that sen-tient being collapses into space-time reality."

Goswami proposes that the time is right for a strong Anthropic Principle— the idea that conscious observers are necessary to bring the material universe into being. He also notes that it is time to recognize the archetypal nature of mankind's creation myths—that the cosmos was created for our sake—and he suggests that such myths are compatible with quantum physics. Goswami adds: "we are the center of the universe because we are its meaning," and that perhaps "the universe that collapsed into physical space-time reality is the one with the possibility of the evolution of the greatest number of intelligent, self-aware beings."

As I have explained in *Space Travelers and the Genesis of the Human Form*, the Anthropic Principle is based on a biological argument: the minimum time required for the evolution of "intelligent observers." A billion years is required for the evolution of intelligence; therefore, a star must have been sta-ble for at least that long. The Anthropic Timescale Argument predicates that the types of processes allowed in the universe must be of such an age that "slow evolutionary processes will have had time to produce intelligent beings from non-living matter." (Barrow, 159)

The Space Travel Argument Against the Existence of Extraterrestrial Intelligent Life (ETI) is based on the Anthropic Principle: the mathematical assumption that a "communicating species" would evolve in less than 5 billion years and would eventually begin interstellar travel. This argument contends that "since 1 billion years is quite short in comparison with the age of the Galaxy, it follows from the absence of ETI in our Solar System that such space-travelling ETI apparently do not exist, and have never existed in our Galaxy."

Pondering how consciousness "arose in the universe," this peculiar Western viewpoint—the Anthropic Principle—refuses the primacy of consciousness, and instead assumes causality—an endless chain of causes—in the universe. The Anthropic Principle assumes the evolution of intelligence from non-organic matter, and extrapolates the time required for the evolution of "conscious observers" based on the presumed localized, one-of-a-kind anomaly of Earth-based human evolution. This assumption is then applied as a cosmic constant.

This peculiar view is the mistaken result of materialist scientific dogma, and is quite contrary to the ancient world view that matter cannot generate consciousness. According to the teachings of the *Bhagavad-gita,* consciousness is reflected in the material world, but it does not depend upon matter for its existence. According to these ancient teachings, consciousness is transcendental and is not generated by association with matter. The *Bhagavad-gita* rejects the theory that any material combination can generate consciousness. Instead, *Bhagavad-gita,* teaches that conscious entities in the material sphere are in a conditioned state due to "contamination" by contact with matter. According to *Bhagavad-gita,* it is "false ego" that consciousness is the product of matter.

Since we mistakenly think of the human mind as limited to the Earth-sphere and to the material world, we tend to think of ourselves as the only intelligent observers, and we presume that since we evolved purely by accident on this lone oasis, we understand our physics to be telling us that our own 'local' consciousness itself must have created the rest of it. As the authors of *Giants of Gaia* have noted, the universe has an "obliging nature," and one of its most enigmatic properties is that it can "provide proof for any cosmological scheme, scientific or mystical, foisted upon it." Yet, does this 'proof' actually describe the ultimate nature of reality?

There may be an even simpler answer to the question of how the Cosmos existed with no conscious observers (i.e. Earth humans): that we are *not* the first or the only conscious observers and we are *not* alone in the universe! In the first place, this assumption denies the plausible existence of much older intelligent human civilizations in the Universe. Furthermore, God as Eternal Mind is the first and the last Conscious Observer: the Alpha and the Omega. Goswami, like other scientists, is still seeing the Earth as a closed system and consciousness as an Earth-based local anomaly, and, as an atheist, is removing God as the prime conscious observer from the scene.

In short, the Anthropic view is dependent upon the Darwinian paradigm of the evolution of consciousness on Earth, which is a linear chain-of-cause view. Problematically, Goswami's seemingly 'nonlocal'theory is still hinged on a local event: the *myth* of the *accidental* evolution of Earth-based consciousness. As I have argued in *Space Travelers*, Darwinian evolution cannot prove the Earth-based uniqueness or singularity of the human form, since it is itself an anthropocentric and Earth-centered philosophy of the Western materialist mindset. In *Space Travelers,* I have argued that Darwinian evolution is a tautology: a self-contained system of circular proofs which are always true in a self-contained system of circular proofs. I have also argued that utilizing this hypothesis to prove we are alone in the universe is illogical. For, a circular dilemma confounds the popular use of the evolution argument against the co-existence of the humanoid form in the Cosmos, since we do not actually *know* that we are the only humanoids in the universe, nor do we *know* the genesis of the humanoid form. We are simply extrapolating an earthbound premise from an Earth-centric theory.

Reality Management and the Ego-Self

It would appear that quantum physics is now rediscovering what we knew in ancient times. In *The Self-Aware Universe*, Goswami writes that the "self of our self-reference" is part of a "tangled hierarchy." He describes consciousness as "consciousness of the Being that is beyond the subject-object split." This is the source of consciousness in the universe. The concept that self-consciousness arises from this "tangled hierarchy" has appeared throughout many cultures, and is represented by the Ouroboros: a snake biting its own tail.

Goswami further elucidates this principle. He writes that "the appearance of the world of manifestation" leads to the experience of self, or the split between subject and object. In physics terms, this means that "subject and object manifest simultaneously in the initial collapse of the quantum state of the brain-mind." The important thing to realize is that without the world of manifestation, there could be no self which is capable of the perception that it is separate from the world of objects. He explains, before this quantum collapse, the subject is "not differentiated from the archetypes of objects of experience—physical or mental." The quantum collapse is what brings about the split between subject and object, leading to awareness of self, or "quantum self." Yet, self-reference is circular, since we could just as well say that "awareness of the quantum self brings about the quantum collapse."

In either case, the "unity of the subject" persists. For, says mathematician G. Spencer Brown, the world seems to be constructed "in order (and in such a way as to be able) to see itself." This Anthropic view suggests that the universe sees itself through human consciousness. (Note, however, that since Earth-based human consciousness is the only type of consciousness we know about, this may just 'appear' to be true.) In the human, the universe splits itself into subject and object, that which sees and that which is seen. The unity of the subject as an experienced phenomenon becomes evident through a pattern of experiential identity, or the "ego" self. We experience the same ego day after day, and count on it waking up and greeting the same world every day.

But, how does the ego-identity arise? The identity of the self is located in past experience and memory. Goswami suggests that the brain-mind is a "dual quantum system/measuring apparatus." It is "the place where the self-reference of the entire universe happens." Goswami stresses that the brain's measuring apparatus makes a *memory* of every quantum collapse, every instance of observation, every experience. If the same or similar stimulus plays, the brain replays the old memory. The replay becomes secondary to the quantum system.

Once a task has been learned, it is highly likely that the corresponding memory will trigger a conditioned response. However, with a new experience, the brain-mind has the potential for a creative and novel response. Despite the fact that 'unconditioned' quantum responses are always available, learned 'programs'accumulate and dominate our behavior. When the creative potency of the quantum component is not engaged, Goswami writes, "the tangled hierarchy of the interacting components of the brain-mind," in effect, kicks down to a lower hierarchy. We become possessed by individual identity or ego: the limited, "classical self."

This lower hierarchy, or classical self, is also described in Vedic teachings. According to *Bhagavad-gita*, all humans are in difficulty due to "material entanglement." At a higher level, consciousness is eternal and transcendent, but we are put into this material position which is referred to as *asat*, or unreal. The living entity determines to act in one way, then becomes entangled in his own actions and reactions, and achieves only frustration. When he gives up one body for another, the reactions of his past activities remain with him, determining his next birth. According to *Bhagavad-gita*, the effects of karma may be old, but cannot be eternal. However, we do not know which activities will release us from our material entanglements.

According to quantum physics as well, true consciousness, or "quantum self," is at the transcendent level. As a truly non-local consciousness we operate from outside the system. But we are entangled in the lower hierarchy of consciousness, where the ego, or classical self, frantically repeats the same actions and reactions. Yet, at a level above this material entanglement, as Goswami notes, the "nonlocal, creative potency of consciousness and the versatility of the quantum mind never completely disappear." They are, as he asserts, the "quantum modality of the self."

From within the material enclave, unable to see the hierarchical nature of the system in which we are tangled, says Goswami, we "claim free-will to mask our assumed limitedness," which has arisen simply by our acceptance of the learned programs we act out. The ego may be described as simply "stored information about past states of consciousness recalled into consciousness." Consciousness then sees its own reflection in the mirror of memory, but always with a little time lag. Goswami sees this reaction time as that time lag between the collapse of a space-time event (onset of quantum modality) and the experience of the ego in the "classical mode."

Meditation practices are intended to eliminate the time lag which makes it difficult to be aware of our quantum self, and to experience pure mental states accessible at the quantum level of operation. Meditation reduces the time lag by creating whole brain synchrony, and puts us directly in touch with pure mental states. Exalted experiences occur when this time lag is reduced. A theory which may explain the physics of these events was introduced in a rare 1973 book. An elementary particle called the "thoughtron" was proposed by Harold McGowan to be the fundamental particle in communication between matter and mind: "the umbilical between the abstract and the concrete."

The Thoughtron Theory of Life and Matter

Harold McGowan proposed, in *The Thoughtron Theory of Life and Matter*, that a system of charged particles is controlled by elementary particles which he called "thoughtrons," which are coded instructions conceived by thought. He suggested that these minute particles laid out the configurations of eltrons and partons in various combinations to form electrons, protons and neutrons, which control the activities of the brain, nervous system and body.

If we someday are able to isolate a quark or a parton, McGowan proposed, we would be looking at a particle of smaller mass and wavelength, influenced by an even smaller particle which travels at the speed of thought. This particle, the thoughtron, travels at great speed caused by the intention of thought, which directs "infinite waves of an infinite number of thoughtrons to form nexions." Nexions, he proposed, form larger and larger particles which slow down in speed to become visible. Thus, he proposed, thoughtrons are the bridge between the visible and invisible worlds.

A thought, McGowan proposed, is composed of basic matter. Nothing can exist in the material world which is not composed of material *of this world*. McGowan proposed that the thoughtron is the basic particle of creation from non-physical to physical matter making abstract desire a reality. This elementary particle is directed by the same source that created the thought. Since this particle is simultaneously the messenger, the message, and the matter, it would "communicate the plan and furnish the material resulting in a realization of the desire of the creator." It would be, McGowan proposed, "the umbilical between the abstract and the concrete."

According to McGowan's theory, the physical universe is a concrete expression of the abstract realm or thought world. Since matter is designed by thought, ideas originate in the substrate realms, and are brought into being when they are desired into realization. If a thought is desired to come into being, thoughtrons are the particles which bring that idea into fruition in the material world so that, ultimately, a physical personality can act on that thought by physical exertion. Therefore, McGowan wrote, thought is the source of all matter and all life, as it conceives and carries out ideas by using a certain system it laid out originally: a physical system of projection of infinitrons into thoughtrons.

McGowan proposed that thoughtrons are both a wave and a particle, and that they are the elementary constituents of electrons, protons, and neutrons of the atom. Since matter is controlled by the movement of electrons through the nervous system, it would be expected that something even smaller controls these particles. McGowan suggested that thoughtrons comprise this elementary control station. The details of this system were elucidated in the following passage:

> The personality transmits orders to the brain according to its thoughts by concentrating thoughtrons at a nerve synapse. The thoughtrons are collections of infinitrons strung together in a pattern of various particles to form a code of instructions. As the concentration of thoughtrons increases, a pressure is built at a synapse causing them, by induction, to jump the gap to another neuron which leads to a proper location in the brain. The coded instructions in the thoughtrons then choose the proper neurons to connect with and transmit their data.

If or when discovered, McGowan proposed, the thoughtron will be found to be "the messenger, the message, and the matter to bring a thought into being—to make a desire become a concrete thing." McGowan proposed that the thoughtron will be found to be the bridge between two worlds, the visible and invisible; the medium that joins the mental and physical worlds. In the Appendix to his book, McGowan's "Manifesto" described his thoughtron theory in the following manner:

> Infinity is thought. Infinitrons are the smallest particles of matter having the smallest wavelength and the highest frequency which issue from infinity. Thought by its control of infinitrons is the source of all energy and the terminal of all energy. Thought created the physical laws. Thought designed the universe. Thought uses infinitrons to form and control matter. Thought by its intention, manifests all things by a process of particles which evolve from infinitrons.

> Thought projects infinite waves of infinite numbers of infinitrons instantaneously to evolve and make its conceptions a reality. The junctions of these waves of infinitrons form less than an infinite number of secondary particles, called thoughtrons. Thought, by its intention, projects waves of infinitrons that produce succeedingly larger particles traveling at succeedingly slower speeds until, at the nexuses of the waves and resonances, electrons traveling at speeds up to 186,300 miles per second are formed. Larger formations at slower speeds are also formed.

> Thought, by its intention, causes particles to have the various frequencies and resonances necessary to make each desired conception a reality. The DNA molecule which has within it the plan for its actions and reactions to result in a specified organism is an example of how these particles, as messengers, messages, and material, are organized to carry out thought's intention.

> Thought, by a system of waves and variable frequencies and resonances, projects infinitrons into thoughtrons, which by the evolution of particles, result in the partons, electrons, protons, and neutrons, which structure the atoms, which form the elements, that compose all the compounds that form life and matter.

> Thought is the starting point for the being of everything, animate and inanimate, physical and psychical. Thought produces subthoughts which are life thoughtrons, also called personalities or life units. When life thoughtrons animate systems of organized material, we call them organisms. Life thoughtrons can also think and make ideas a

reality but on a lesser scale than original thought. Life thoughtrons evolve from a blank mind to full awareness of their capabilities to think and make their desires a reality.

Some life thoughtrons have developed into an organism called man, in which individuals have developed various levels of awareness of their capabilities to think and act. Man is aware of his awareness, but life units on a lower level, and probably all animals lower than primates, are only aware.

As each personality develops its own mind and becomes fully aware of its capabilities to produce thoughts and make them realities, it completes its cycle as a subthought or life thoughtron and progresses back to original thought.

Progression—Infinity is everywhere—eternally. Thought is everywhere—eternally. Infinity and thought are synonymous. Thought conceives ideas and records them in a system of particles which it transduces from infinity. Ideas are configurations of thoughtrons located in space. Thoughtrons are the plans for matter and life. Matter is created by thoughtrons directing elpartons and atoms, etc. Life is evolved by thoughtrons directing particles and DNAmolecules. DNA molecules direct atoms to form organisms to support life.

(McGowan, 143-145)

As discussed earlier, Besant and Leadbeater have suggested that different types of thoughts have a corresponding color, form and intensity. This has been borne out in reputable psychic research performed in the Soviet Union. As Ostrander and Schroeder write in their infamous book *Psychic Discoveries Behind the Iron Curtain*, important clinical research studies indicate that telepathy—whatever it is—seems to involve the physical body. Extrasensory information has been shown to effect subtle changes in the body, including an affect on blood volume, enzymes and brain waves, as well as on polygraph readings. As a matter of fact, Soviet researchers discovered that quite often telepathic information is picked up by the body without conscious awareness. By using acupuncture to measure bioplasmic energy, Soviet studies suggested that the bioplasmic energy body picks up the telepathic message (thought command) and reflects it in the body. It was suggested by researchers that a bioplasmic energy body—the so-called 'astral body'—is both the "medium" and the "message."

From this deduction, Soviet researchers wondered whether different thoughts have different intensities, or whether different thoughts took different routes on the acupuncture maps of the body. The main route that psychic information takes, according to ancient Indian philosophy, is through the pituitary and pineal glands. It is possible, therefore, that psychic force can be stimulated with acupuncture. Is telepathy and bioplasmic energy one and the same force? Can we give this concept another name: i.e., thought form?

Lucid Dreaming and the Temperature of Thoughts

Lucid dreams are another conduit by which we can actively use thought forms to connect to ultradimensional realms. If thought forms have different qualities and intensities, this means that "temperature" could be another one of those qualities which we have not yet considered. Artist and lucid dreamer Paul Laffoley, author of *The Phenomenology of Revelation*, has suggested that temperature may be another sensory conduit included in humanity's medicine bag by which contact can be made with the other sides of things we don't normally sense. In an interview published in *Paranoia* magazine, he discussed thought forms and lucid dreaming:

Lucid dreaming is the ability to become aware, during a dream, that you are dreaming, and to do two things: one, take control of the dream, and two, take back a message.

In 1903, D. W. Leadbeater put forth the idea that you could see thought forms in people's auras ... forms that had an emotional translation.... In lucid dreaming you are creating a condition where you can turn up the heat or cold to whatever degree you want and it will actually be connected to the object you are dreaming about. You also have to train yourself so that you can go into lucid dreaming without any interface between a normal blackout and waking up into a regular dream, which is dealing with the past. When you dream, you are dealing with the subconscious past and you have a lot of baggage, which tends to negate any kind of energy or control which you have over this process.

When you go directly from the waking state into the lucid dream state you overcome the subconscious so that you are not using archetypes, or any of the baggage that psychology has lain on us. This is like using the energy directly as you would during the waking state, only you have access to systems and instrumentality that is limitless. It's only limited by what we can think of in the same way that our existence as humans has only been limited by what we can think of. It's totally dependent on our own creativity.

I want to use lucid dreaming in a methodical way, almost a scientific way. People use it to decode astral projection, to go on journeys. I think it has much more interesting consequences if seen as an instrument, and it thus produces a whole new genre of inventions which go beyond the traditional notion of psychotronics, which are defined as mind-matter interactive devices. But how consciousness and mass become continuous was never explained; it has just been assumed that there isn't any interface situation. There is no use of different aspects of this along the spectrum; it's either on or off.

But if we find that the process is literally true that mass and consciousness are continuous, then you can tap it at different points and achieve different results. So here is where you have consciousness and mass, with lucid dreaming as the mid-point. So it has the ability of consciousness to use the will, but also makes consciousness have mechanical aspects as well. You have invariants. You can engineer your next step and achieve a particular result.

Interestingly, as Laffoley has suggested, perhaps "temperature" (as he says, "turn up the heat or cold to be connected to the object you are dreaming about") is another facet in the interface between mass and consciousness. If atoms are vibrating at a specific rate, this vibratory rate corresponds to a specific temperature as well as frequency. Temperature certainly may be considered another sensory projection into ultradimensional space, along with light, sound, color, etc., but may be one which we have quite a bit more control over. If practiced and controlled, lucid dreaming can become an important instrument in the acquisition of knowledge. As Laffoley has explained, lucid dreaming is superior to an LSD trip because you can "slow it down" to any speed of knowledge acquisition you want, whereas LSD's velocity was usually greater than the absorption power of the average mind. In the lucid dream state you are able to control the velocity of information entering from another dimension. This requires absolute control over heat and cold: the temperature of the information coming in (i.e. thought form) has to be in sync with your own temperature, or vibratory rate. Once you learn to control this, you're in business. Also, if we give it some 'thought' we could come up with many more potential senses contained in the medicine bag of humanity.

There is a lot to think about here, since an elementary particle which McGowan called the thoughtron is surmised to be at once the message, the messenger, and the material that erects the bridge between the mental and physical worlds. As physicists have suggested, microscopic electrons within the atom are not composed of matter, but of "probability waves," and matter somehow emerges from immaterial probability fields. This umbilical, or bridge, as Ostrander and Schroeder write, connects "the world of 'plasma,' of the shifting 'tissue' of the universe connecting all to all." What this means is that mass and consciousness are not discontinuous; rather, consciousness animates all things. For instance, Kirlian photography, invented in the Soviet Union, has captured a "whirling universe" inside a lump of radium, and "whole galaxies of light" in living things and in humans. The body double of living organisms has been witnessed in modern, sophisticated Kirlian-based electronic equipment. Kirlian photography has also captured the bioplasmic body as it leaves a dead plant or animal.

Yet, it is interesting that *some* scientists are able to entertain these fascinating ideas, while education and language are largely stuck in a linear, materialist framework. There is obviously a time lag between the observation of data which do not fit into the larger scheme and the subsequent overhaul of an unacceptable paradigm. As Ouspensky has noted in *Tertium Organum*:

> The present state of our 'science' would be of great psychological interest to an unbiased observer. In all the domains of scientific knowledge there is a great accumulation of facts disrupting the harmony of the accepted systems. And these systems are able to exist only through the heroic efforts of scientists who strive to shut their eyes to the long series of new facts which threaten to engulf everything in an irresistible flood. ... Deep down a physicist may feel the real worthlessness of both old and new scientific theories, but he is afraid to be left hanging in mid-air with nothing but a negation. He has no system to take the place of one whose falsity he already feels; he is afraid to make a leap into the void.

As Ouspensky has noted, "science has come to an impasse from which there is no way out, and it is only a matter of time before it is openly admitted that its main tendencies have led it completely astray." We might expect that someday soon the idealist paradigm will get a fair hearing. But when can we expect these ideas to settle in, and what kind of philosophical battles can we expect on the road to extraordinary science: the Science of Experience?

Extraordinary Science

Scientific paradigm overhauls occur very slowly according to Thomas Kuhn in *The Structure of Scientific Revolutions*. This is because of the established route which science is in the habit of taking. As Kuhn explains, a paradigm is an accepted model or pattern which "functions by permitting the replication of examples, any one of which could in principle serve to replace it." Upon close examination, however, normal science seems to be "an attempt to force nature into the preformed and relatively inflexible box that the paradigm supplies." Kuhn writes: "cumulative acquisition of novelty is not only rare but improbable in principle." He further clarifies that the aim of normal science is not to elicit new kinds of phenomena; nor is it to invent new theories. On the contrary, those phenomena or results that do not "fit into the box are often not seen at all."

Scientists are generally intolerant of new theories, Kuhn notes. Instead, the trend in normal scientific research is directed to "the articulation of those phenomena and theories that the paradigm already supplies." Normal science actually works to increase the extent of the match between factual data and the paradigm's predictions, and in further articulating the paradigm itself. Yet, Kuhn explains, few people realize how much "mop-up work" is required by a scientific paradigm.

What constitutes "new science"? Well, within the scientific powerhouse, it's just a linguistic perception. But in the scientific margins, it necessitates a completely new bag of tricks. As Franklin Ellsworth Clarke has noted in his article "Charles Hoy Fort: Bibliomancer Extraordinaire," (www.borderland.com), "new science" is the following:

Those who follow the media science performers acquire some hopeful ideal, while gradually cultivating an emotional investment. The promise of a new science and a new world is the compelling aria from which sensitive hearts draw warmth in the vacuum. The sensitive followers find their heroic media speakers losing credibility when, after betraying their true prejudices and predispositions, fall short of their own promise. Young minds know that, while voicing the need for new science, the media science personalities remain completely ensnared in a deteriorating and failed scientific method. And they *instinctively know that the method is the problem.* [emphasis added]

The modern scientific 'big lie' is that it is forging new frontiers in our worldview. Nothing could be further from the truth. This perverse perspective is only a clever promotions attempt to stave off the extreme criticism harbored by science grant committees. The promise of a 'new' science refers potential patrons to a possible 'new world.' This new world will be theirs if the monies are given. We who are consigned to watch the science show from the shadows take notice of the repetitive pattern. We note, with bored familiarity, the recalcitrant scientific advocates. Those who maintain their theatrical poise, who cry out the most for 'new perspectives,' are always the very ones whose power policies destroy every opportunity toward that professed goal. And so we observe the sad plight of science professionals who are locked in a prisonhouse of perceptions, ruled by the highly enforced dictates and well policed precepts of a few science hierarchs.

Kuhn defines a scientific revolution as a "non-cumulative developmental episode" whereby an older paradigm is replaced in whole or in part by an "incompatible new one." Such scientific revolutions begin with a growing sense that "an existing paradigm has ceased to function adequately in the exploration of an aspect of nature." The emergence of new theories is usually preceded by a period of "pronounced professional insecurity," since it involves large-scale paradigm destruction and major shifts in problem-solving techniques of normal science. Scientists generally do not quickly renounce a paradigm in crisis and immediately begin looking for alternatives. They do not, Kuhn says, "treat anomalies as counter instances, though in the vocabulary of science that is what they are." Kuhn clarifies that once it has achieved the status of a paradigm, a scientific theory "is declared invalid only if an alternative candidate is available to take its place."

Rather than falsifying the theory outright when confronted with anomalous findings, Kuhn explains, scientists generally "will devise numerous articulations and *ad hoc* modifications of their theory in order to eliminate any apparent conflict." This is the way science works. Scientists do not reject paradigms when faced with anomalies or counter-instances essentially because "they could not do so and still remain scientists." Research performed in the absence of a paradigm isn't considered science. (I might add that scientism performed in the absence of any possible testing or predictive paradigm is called Darwinian evolution.) As Kuhn clarifies: "to reject one paradigm without simultaneously substituting another is to reject science itself." The normal response to crisis will be to loosen the rules of normal puzzle-solving in ways that ultimately permit a new paradigm to emerge.

Catastrophic Theory Quick and Dirty

As an example, catastrophic theory has gone through such a slow painstaking paradigm shift in the last few decades. Let's look at how this has happened. In *Catastrophism, Neocatastrophism and Evolution,* Trevor Palmer writes that the prevailing views of the evolution of life on Earth have changed significantly in the past few decades. The Modern Synthesis of neo-Darwinism, which incorporated developments in genetics into traditional Darwinism, and touted the triumph of gradualism and uniformitarianism, seemed completely secure in 1959, he writes. Yet, over the ensuing decades, it became clear that the fossil record revealed rather abrupt transitions.

In earlier times, Palmer explains, catastrophism and evolution were mutually exclusive explanations for the fossil record. But after the evidence began to accumulate during the second half of the nineteenth century, he writes, the fossil record could not be explained by the Earth-centered model of catastrophism, which linked such extinctions to global geological upheavals. As a result of distortions propagated by Lyell and others, he writes, "generations were led to believe that the views of the catastrophists owed more to preconceived ideas than to observation, whereas the theories of the uniformitarians were all derived by logical deduction from observed data." This myth became widely accepted, Palmer explains, along with the opinion that catastrophists relied on "supernatural explanations" as the cause of historical planetary catastrophes.

When the French chemist, Lavoisier, investigated rumors of a stone which had fallen from the sky near Luce in 1768, he concluded it could not have happened. It took over a hundred years, but the beginning of the 20th century saw the establishment of the extraterrestrial origin of meteorites. But, not until the 1960s was it generally accepted that impacts had caused large craters on Earth. Those who argued that this had anything to do with evolution were derided, even though the fossil record told the story of mass extinction. Palmer explains that the theory of a supernova explosion was largely ignored, the theory that macromutations might account for the origin of new species provoked derision, and Velikovsky was ridiculed for his theory that the Earth had come into near collisions with planetary-sized bodies.

During this time, evolutionary biologists came up with gradualist theories, such as plate tectonics and continental drift, to explain mass extinctions. In the 1970s, the Modern Synthesis challenged the gradualistic view of evolution by asserting the theory of "punctuated equilibrium." With regard to hominid species, they claimed, it was apparent that new species appeared rather rapidly, and the disappearance of species was quite abrupt. Furthermore, they asserted that all of this took place against a background of major environmental changes. To some extent, Palmer writes, this record can be explained by continental drift, but it cannot be ruled out that catastrophist mechanisms may have been involved in both vulcanism and plate tectonics.

Since 1980, Palmer explains, neocatastrophism has made remarkable advances. Today, extraterrestrial impacts are regarded as plausible agents of evolutionary change. Palmer writes that catastrophic events, involving collisions between cosmic bodies, have occurred throughout the history of the Solar System. He writes that the Earth has suffered many impacts, some large enough to cause widespread devastation. He asserts that "ignorance of this extraterrestrial dimension by nineteenth century catastrophists and uniformitarians alike contributed to the demise of catastrophism."

The above is an example of how articulations and *ad hoc* modifications make room for "anomalies" which do not fit into the scientism box. Kuhn explains that such "mopping-up operations" are what constitute normal science. By loosening the rules of normal puzzle-solving, these "divergent articulations," or "*ad hoc* adjustments" *must* find a way to return the "anomaly" back to the fold.

Archie Roy, Professor of Astronomy at Glasgow University, has put these observations another way. He explains that it is not unknown for the response to a new idea to progress from "this man is nuts," through "we'll really have to look at the problem just to dismiss it," to "of course I've always known that this was the case." With regard to the re-emerging acceptance of the theory of catastrophism, Trevor Palmer asserts that "something of a revolution in academic thought has taken place, but as with other paradigm shifts in the scientific world, there are those who deny that it has happened."

With regard to this process of vilification/acceptance of anomalous findings in scientific circles, Charles Fort, collector of all things strange, has noted in *The Book of the Damned*:

> The new is the obviously preposterous: it becomes the established and disguisedly preposterous; it is displaced, after a while, and is again seen to be the preposterous ... all progress is from the outrageous to the academic or sanctified, and back to the outrageous—modified, however, by a trend of higher and higher approximation to the impreposterous.

Kuhn suggests that early attacks on the problem will follow the paradigm rules closely (i.e., "this man is nuts"), however, eventually more of the attacks upon it will involve some minor (or not so minor) articulations of the paradigm (i.e., "we'll really have to look at the problem just to dismiss it"). Eventually, problem solving will stray from the structure of the original paradigm enough to be unacceptable (i.e., "of course I've always known that this was the case").

Explicit recognition of the breakdown of a scientific paradigm is extremely rare, but this is not to say the crisis has not been recognized. Kuhn writes: "all crises begin with the blurring of a paradigm and the consequent loosening of the rules for normal research." In any case, these "divergent articulations" or "*ad hoc* adjustments" *must* find a way to return the "anomaly" back to the fold, to the realm of the sanctified, as Fort suggests, "by a trend of higher and higher approximation to the impreposterous."

The next chapter looks at some biological, bioplasmic, and neurophysiological theories of how the "supernatural" might appear to manifest in the natural world.

CHAPTER FOUR
THE ANIMISTIC COSMOS

Man feels isolated in the cosmos because he is no longer involved in nature and has lost his emotional unconscious identity with natural phenomena ... no voices speak to man from stones, plants and animals, nor does he speak to them believing they can hear.

Carl Jung

The winter 1999-2000 issue of the biblical creationist magazine *Creation: Ex Nihilo* features an interview with a young missionary family who are with OMF International. This interview, entitled "People who 'walk backwards into the future,'" focuses on the Tigwas people situated in the southern Philippines on the island of Mindanao. The Tigwas are described in this article as "a tribe of about 10,000 animists who are part of the Manobo people." As the missionaries explain "animism is the belief that animals, plants and inanimate objects are inhabited by spirits. The Tigwas' lives are ruled by fear of evil spirits (demons)."

As this article explains, the Tigwas people worship the spirits of rocks, trees and rivers, and have direct contact with the spirit world. Furthermore, as animists, the Tigwas people are "constantly looking back into their history to their origins to see where they came from and how they fit into the world in which they live." This is important to animistic people, the article explains, because "the way they behave today is very much dependent on what they believe happened in their past." The Tigwas people want to ensure that "what they do now will not offend the spirits of their ancestors or the demons that are part of their daily life." The Tigwas consult shamans, or witchdoctors, on various occasions, and especially after calamities, in order to find out how they have offended these animistic spirits and how to appease them.

As this interview also explains, "demons are often mentioned in the Bible, mainly in the Gospels, as causing some physical and mental disorders, possessing human beings, and opposing the work of God." The missionaries believe that the key to evangelizing animistic peoples lies with the Book of Genesis, since their creation cosmology is a "remnant" of the Genesis account. The Tigwas believe there was a time when God the Creator was in communication with the people on Earth, but something went wrong. Some sort of conflict caused the Creator to be removed from their daily life. For reaching animistic tribes, this article explains, it is important to begin with the Book of Genesis and then clarify for them what occurred after that, since "their origin beliefs have been corrupted." The missionaries tell the Tigwas about Adam and Eve, and the coming of evil into the world, and they explain where Satan and the evil spirits fit into the picture, and then they present "God's solution."

What the Gospel offers to the Tigwas, according to these missionaries, is freedom from the oppression and dictatorial demands of evil spirits who have controlled every part of their lives for thousands of years. As this article explains, "Westerners struggle with the idea of the spirit world interacting with the physical, but the Tigwas don't separate the physical from the spiritual." The missionaries will be further researching the origins stories of the Tigwas in order to find more remnants from Genesis, especially regarding the Flood and the dispersion of the people at Babel. By showing the Tigwas their "true link" with the past and where their story ends, the aim is to pick up where the story leaves off ... "with God's son, who came to Earth and died for them on the cross."

This article illustrates not only that Christian missionaries continue to work under the false assumption that their own human-tainted doctrine is pristine and aboriginal, but it also shows that they do not consider the Tigwas'belief in evil spirits at all incorrect. As a matter of fact, they believe that evil animistic spirits do work evil deeds, and they present a solution to the madness and chaos which these evil spirits cause. As they assert, "we teach the believers to memorize appropriate verses of Scripture, and to quote these to see the power of God at work against the demons." Related to this is the belief among fundamentalist Christians that notions of "Gaian animism"—i.e. that the Earth is alive, are "Satanic." This probably stems from the assumption that it is a sin to worship the planets, stars and sun as demigods (Romans 1:25 states those who worship the creation rather than the Creator are foolish). It appears that *some* Christians hold the point of view that "nature worship" or "earth worship" is a "pagan" enterprise and a crime against God, or at least their anthropomorphized image of God. This attitude or fear seems to carry over in their attitude toward animal rights and environmental concerns, and is a truly baffling state of affairs.

Power Places

Since very ancient times people have been attracted to certain sites all over the world which command reverence and awe, writes Martin Gray in his illustrated book *Places of Peace and Power*. These "power places" can be located in or near "sacred" mountains, natural springs, caverns, or open forest areas. Some are man-made ceremonial structures, such as pyramids, stone rings, temples, mosques, shrines, and cathedrals. Some places are ancient, and some have only recently become pilgrimage centers. Utilizing both modern and legendary accounts of extraordinary events which have occurred at these sites, Gray has mapped out a large number of these places, and has traveled extensively to visit and take pictures.

Sacred sites, Gray writes, somehow contain "the power to heal the body, enlighten the mind, increase creativity, develop psychic abilities, and awaken the soul to a knowing of its true purpose in life." Is there an esoteric secret behind these places of reverent worship of the divine in nature? What is it about these locations that causes pilgrims to venture long distances to obtain the sacred gifts offered? To answer these questions, Gray writes, we must do something that anthropologists almost never do. We've got to talk about a living God and of the "sacred" as personal experience. Gray quotes from anthropologist Colin Turnbull in *The Anthropology of Pilgrimage*:

> We have tended to avoid, in our study of religious systems, what is central to all religion: the power of Faith, the sense of the Sacred, the perception of Spirit. In just the same way that it is not comfortable or seemingly appropriate, in 'polite'society, to discuss God in the living room, so among polite anthropologists it is too often considered improper and inappropriate, if not irrelevant, to discuss Spirit and Faith, Beauty and Goodness, which are dismissed as though they had no substantive reality or application. It is still less acceptable to attempt to capture such qualities and report on them from the point of view of personal experience....

In our cultural anthropology courses we are admonished to put Western objective science on the back burner, but never out of sight. We learn to accept other belief systems as valid, but this acceptance remains at a distance. We are admonished to bring a cool, calm, collected objectivity to field work, while accepting another point of view as valid. But this so-called "validity" is not a full acceptance of another's world view. There is no room for the spirit world in this mindset. Something is missing.

As Gray writes, what has been lost from the western viewpoint is "the ability to communicate with living, nonhuman entities, of which the Earth is the oldest and wisest." He suggests that this communication apparatus already exists, and only needs to be re-discovered. The Earth is alive and we can talk to it! And this isn't just something quaint that we read about in anthropology field studies. We will never fully understand this level of communication from the standpoint of materialist "objective" science. As Gray quotes from Carl Jung in *Man and His Symbols*:

> As scientific understanding has grown, so our world has become dehumanized. Man feels himself isolated in the cosmos because he is no longer involved in nature and has lost his emotional unconscious identity with natural phenomena ... no voices now speak to man from stones, plants and animals, nor does he speak to them believing they can hear. His contact with nature has gone, and with it the profound emotional energy that this connection supplied ... primitive man was much more governed by his instincts than are his "rational" modern descendants, who have learned to "control" themselves. In this civilizing process, we have increasingly divided our consciousness from the deeper instinctive strata of the human psyche, and even ultimately from the somatic (bodily felt and known) basis of psychic phenomenon.

Gray explains that while meditating at various power places over the Earth, he has actually received telepathic communiqués from earth spirits which came in as "distinct voices speaking in my mind or as visions of stunning visual clarity." Gray claims that his mind was a "receiver" of these words and pictures which seemed to be telepathically transmitted. He believes these messages were not the result of his own linear thought process, and that they occurred due to his visits to a large number of power places as well as his attitude of approach with an open heart and mind.

What is the subject matter of these visionary communications? Initially, Gray claims, they were concerned with teaching him about the power places themselves, and how they should be used by human beings. He was told that different power places have different "types" of energies and have different influences. For instance, some affect men and others affect women. He was also told that the knowledge of sacred sites was encoded in ancient mythology and legends about the sites.

In other sites, which he calls Oracular power places, Gray received prophetic types of information regarding the future. Certain places have the ability to induce prophetic visions. This has happened to many people after visiting sacred places in Egypt. Gray writes, "after visiting many of these places I became aware that the power or presence of the sites somehow awakened and catalyzed the psychic ability of precognition." This information was at times inspiring, and at other times frightening, he explains. Some of the visionary information imparted to Martin Gray over his years of pilgrimage to sacred sites are essentially of an environmental nature. He writes:

> With effort, I tried to listen with an open mind, free of preconceived ideas about what was and was not possible. Sometimes it was necessary to remind myself that I wasn't the only person who had ever spoken about a living Earth or who had sensed the charged energies at particular places. People all over the world, in hundreds of different cultures and spanning many thousands of years, had found and venerated these sites, as evidenced by their great pilgrimage temples. Certainly all of those people over all of those years couldn't all be wrong. I couldn't ignore the fact that many of the greatest religious figures of human history had considered certain places to be special. Moses experienced divine revelation upon Mount Sinai, Mohammed upon Mount Hara, Christ in a cave at Quarantana, and Buddha beneath the Bodhi Tree.

Sacred Geometry, Geodesy and Geography

Many of the world's great sacred structures were also designed and built using harmonious mathematical proportions called "sacred geometry." Gray writes that his photographs are also composed according to these proportions. Therefore, the pictures themselves can invoke an image in the mind, and can also be used as oracles. Since he carried the conscious intent throughout his pilgrimages that the photographs themselves should function as "magical picture beams," Gray believes that by the power of the reader's intention and imagination the photographs may actually *become* the sites. Gray quotes from Peter Lamborn Wilson, in *The Caravan of Summer*:

> In ordinary pilgrimage, the traveler receives *baraka* [spiritual energy] *from* a place, but the dervish reverses the flow and brings *baraka to* a place. The Sufi may think of himself or herself as a permanent pilgrim—but to the ordinary stay-at-home people of the mundane world, the Sufi is a kind of perambulatory shrine.

Gray hopes that his book, *Places of Peace and Power*, will serve as a portable shrine which he is able to bring to the reader. He claims that the visionary material which was imparted to him on the sacred mountains of Japan and Korea was concerned with "the consciousness of the Earth, the nature of power places, and the relationship between power places and human beings." The content of the vision concerned the purpose of his pilgrimage to the sacred power places. What should he do with the information he had gleaned from his extensive travels? This is where Gray learned that the power places on the Earth are similar to the acupuncture points on the human body, and that a human being with a loving heart can function something like an acupuncture needle for the Earth.

What is the actual nature of the sacred sites? What makes them sacred? What is common to all of them? After sixteen years of visiting these sacred sites, Martin Gray has identified the primary factors which contribute to the power of these sites. He writes:

> I believe that these various factors function—independently and together—to create, perpetuate, and amplify a presence or field of energy that saturates and surrounds the sacred sites. This energy field, or *power of place*, may be defined as a nonmaterial region of influence extending in space and continuing in time.

This nonmaterial region of influence is basically electromagnetic in nature. It is an invisible field of energy which permeates the area of the sacred site. This energy field is responsible for extraordinary phenomena which have been known to occur at these sites. Simply by walking into the vicinity of a sacred site one enters into its energy field. And this occurs with or without awareness of the presence of the energy fields. However, one's experience may be different if one approaches with an attitude of openness and intent.

Research has shown that many ancient sacred sites are located directly upon or in close proximity to areas exhibiting various geophysical phenomena, such as tectonic fault lines. Gray writes that energy-monitoring studies have revealed that many of these sites contain unusual geophysical energy anomalies. But, he asks, how did prehistoric people know this? He answers that perhaps ancient peoples used other parts of the brain that allowed them to sense the energy fields of the sacred sites. In addition, were ancient peoples more in tune with the life force of nature?

According to Martin Gray, sacred geography is the geographic locating of sacred places according to various mythological, symbolic, astrological, geodesical and shamanistic factors. One example Gray provides is the "landscape mandalas" of Japanese Shingon Buddhism. The mandalas are small geometric arrangements, drawn on paper, cloth, wood or metal, of symbols which represent the abodes of the deities. Mandalas are used in meditation by Hindus and

Buddhists. But the particular type of landscape mandalas in Shingon Buddhism are projected over a geographical area, and are symbolic representations of the residence of the Buddha. Gray explains:

> The mandalas were projected upon a number of pre-Buddhist (Shinto) and Buddhist sacred mountains, and the practice of monks and pilgrims was to travel from peak to peak, venerating the buddhas and bodhisattvas residing on them. Just as a meditator would "enter" a painted mandala through visual concentration upon it, a pilgrim to the landscape mandalas of the Kii peninsula would enter the mountains, thereby entering the realm of the Buddha. The passage through the landscape mandalas was made according to a specific and circuitous route. Ascents of the sacred mountains were conceived of as metaphorical ascents through the world of enlightenment, with each stage in the long walking pilgrimage representing a stage in the process through the realms of existence conceived of by Buddhism.

Astrology has also been the basis of sacred geographies found in other parts of the world. Writing in *Sacred Geography of the Ancient Greeks*, Jean Richer says:

> The evidence of the monuments shows in an undeniable way, but not yet clearly perceived, that during more than two thousand years, the Phoenicians, the Hittites, the ancient Greeks, and then the Etruscans, the Carthaginians, and the Romans, had patiently woven a fabric of correspondences between the sky, especially the apparent course of the sun through the zodiac, the inhabited earth, and the cities built by humanity.

Gray writes that the architects of these vast terrestrial zodiacs made their landscape "a living image of the heavens." Diagrams of huge astrological zodiacs were overlaid on the mainland and islands of Greece. The central points were located at sacred sites on the island of Delos, Athens, and in Egypt at the oracles of Delphi and Siwa. The knowledge of how people originally used the landscape zodiacs has been long forgotten, but the places themselves still exist.

The early Egyptians were masters of the lost science of geodesy, a mathematical science concerned with measuring the Earth and locating points on its surface. As Martin Gray explains, the primary longitudinal meridian of predynastic Egypt was laid out to bisect the country precisely in half. Cities and ceremonial centers were then constructed at precise distances from this sacred meridian. Within the temples a stone marker called an *omphalos* was marked with these meridians and parallels, as well as the direction and distance to other sacred sites. As Paul Devereux explains:

> The formation of matter from energy and the natural motions of the universe, from molecular vibration to the growth of organic forms to the motions of planets, stars, and galaxies are all governed by geometrical configurations of force. This geometry of nature is the essence of the sacred geometry used in the design and construction of so many of the world's ancient sacred shrines. These shrines encode ratios of creation and thereby mirror the universe. Certain shapes found in ancient temples, developed and designed according to the mathematical constants of sacred geometry, actually gather, concentrate and radiate specific modes of vibration. ... Certain shapes resonate to cosmic frequencies too fine to be registered on the electromagnetic spectrum. The fineness of the vibration is the key to their powerful effect.

Tectonic Strain Theory

What do geodesy and sacred sites have to do with ghosts and UFOs? Let's discuss the theories of three important researchers hailing from different countries who make the "electromagnetic theory" of UFO manifestation their starting point and then veer off in different directions. Following is a discussion of the theories of Canada's Dr. Michael Persinger, England's Albert Budden, and America's Dr. Gregory Little.

Tectonic Strain theory begins with the work of Michael Persinger and Paul Devereux. In a series of articles in professional journals, which can be found in any large university library, neuropsychologist/bio-chemical researcher Dr. Michael Persinger of Laurentian University in Ottawa, Canada has put forth the theory that reports of "luminous displays" (UFOs), apparitions, out-of-body experience, religious/mystical phenomena, poltergeists, telepathy, and other 'strange phenomena' are related to tectonic strain, that is, seismic activity connected with earthquakes and deep strata earth shifting. Persinger hypothesizes that the source of "strange" phenomena are transient, localized geophysical forces. He speculates that electromagnetic forces produced by geophysical pressures cause the unusual surface level movement of objects and create magnetic effects on the human nervous system.

Yet, an "unidentified flying object" can be described in many ways. As will be discussed later, one should be cautious of the concept of "luminous displays" being lumped in with observations that are clearly descriptive of man-made artifacts or "ships" that are capable of transporting humans or humanoid beings. Problematically, Persinger's scientific observations make no clear delineation between such descriptions and observations. We will certainly get to this point shortly.

Unlike most university professors, Dr. Persinger has specifically addressed the cosmic visitor experience in his research. His findings are that the specific trigger for the cosmic visitor experience involves direct exposure to tectonic strain fields. People whose houses are built over fault lines may be exposed to displays of these intense fields. Electrical stimulation of the temporal lobes generates electrochemical changes which could promote the Visitor experience. He has found in his research that "exposure to low intensity, extremely low frequency (ELF) brain frequency fields evoke partial amnesia, exacerbate vestibular images, and alter suggestibility." (Budden, 212)

In *Earth Lights Revelation: UFOs and Mystery Lightform Phenomena*, Paul Devereux presents evidence that Unidentified Atmospheric Phenomena (UAP), which include ball-lightning and "earthlights," are produced at fault lines in geological strata. Budden admits that "the precise geophysical mechanism for their production" is still under investigation. The typically witnessed large ball of orange light has been known to irradiate witnesses in close proximity, causing thermal or sunburn effects. Budden believes that these earthlight phenomena cause altered states of consciousness by altering electrical emissions from the witness's system.

Bord and Bord (1983) suggest that Persinger's hypothesis is a non-threatening interpretation, in that it avoids introduction of an exterior intelligence. It is noted that Ufologists who believe in "extraterrestrials" generally don't like this theory, and it is of course unpopular with people who believe that religious/mystical experiences are much more than electrochemical brain processes.

Electro-Staging

Albert Budden takes Dr. Persinger's findings quite a bit further in *UFOs, Psychic Close Encounters: The Electromagnetic Indictment*. Utilizing Persinger's Tectonic Strain Theory, Budden hypothesizes that the human Close Encounter (CE) experience is a "staged" drama produced by the human mind in altered states of consciousness. Further, his research has shown that UFO-related events have physical aspects which are similiar to poltergeist-related events. Budden believes that the psychic theory of UFOs has been ignored by UFO researchers because their mistaken understanding of psychic events is that they can have no physical aspects.

Believers in hard, physical spaceships cannot fit the psychic theory into their belief system because it does not explain concrete evidence like physical ground traces, radar, photos, military jet chases and multiple witnessing. So, how does Budden explain them? He doesn't. In the introduction to his book Budden states: "I used to believe in aliens." He also states: "The intelligence behind the phenomenon knows the power of pictures and primarily expresses itself in imagery. This intelligence, in its quest to manipulate belief and establish an identity for itself in the social world, constantly uses the language of imagery..."

We've also heard this directly from Martin Gray, who explains that he received telepathic communiqués from earth spirits, which come in as "distinct voices speaking in my mind or as visions of stunning visual clarity." Gray claims that he became a "receiver" of words and pictures, which seemed to be telepathically transmitted. But what was the source of these communications? Did they come from his own mind or did they come from another world or dimension of existence? Or is there no need for this dichotomy at all?

Budden's Electro-Staging Hypothesis (ESH) posits that the activity of the human unconscious in combination with various natural and artificial energies, studied and correlated by Persinger and others, produces "staged realities." He states: "suitably irradiated witnesses are able to produce hallucinations that seem totally real to them, apparitions that have selective and temporary physical aspects about them, and physical 'constructions'which have a transient existence."

The ESH extends identification of seismic/tectonic fields to artificially-produced fields, that is, electro-pollution caused by electronic communications systems such as are found on military bases. Problematically, this extension defines the poltergeist-UFO phenomena as a modern occurrence, which is a spurious assertion according to historical descriptions such as those reported in Jacques Vallee's *Passport to Magonia*, Mark Davenport's *Visitors From Time*, and biblical interpretations such as Schellhorn's *Extraterrestrials in Biblical Prophesy*, or even the ages-old poltergeist accounts which are numerous in Budden's book. Jacques Vallee has noted that the modern UFO era actually began in the late nineteenth century. Thus, historical claims would seem to be a problem for the electrical overload hypothesis.

The ESH posits that long term effects on persons living in a house over a fault line, combined with other artificial EM field effects such as powerful radio transmission lines, will produce a hypersensitivity to electrical energy. Furthermore, Budden proposes, such people become "overloaded" and "actually emit fields of some coherent intensity themselves." Other sources of electromagnetic radiation are seismic (earthquake) activity, VDU screens, radio and television transmission lines, ham radio transmissions, microwave repeaters, radar installations, hospital technology, domestic appliances and house wiring. Budden theorizes that people who become hypersensitive to electric emissions become saturated with electricity and can become ill in the presence of even low fields, such as fluorescent lighting.

Budden claims that when people react allergically they themselves emit fields and can affect electrical equipment such as street lights and household appliances. This emission of electromagnetic fields by hypersensitive 'allergic' individuals acts as a "carrier wave" for psychic effects, including psychokinesis, visions, apparitions, aliens and UFOs. This "carrier wave" affects other people around them, inducing multiple witnessing of "high strangeness" occurrences. Budden attributes the high rates of allergic conditions, a Twentieth Century disease, to "electropollution." He insists that persons exposed to natural earth fields for a prolonged period of time can also end up with "electrical allergy." Let's explore electromagnetic theories of archetypal phenomena a little closer.

CHAPTER FIVE
ARCHETYPES AND ELECTROMAGNETIC SPECTRUM MANIFESTATION

The government knows there are intelligent intrusions from the EM spectrum and they have quietly and systematically been studying it, while publicly all the furor is over crashed and recovered discs and aliens.

Dr. Gregory Little

Research in psychic phenomena has a long and distinguished history of which we are largely unaware due to our current materialist bias which sees the individual, isolated brain as the control center of intelligent communication. There is a large body of research into psychic phenomena which cannot be sufficiently covered here and which the reader is encouraged to examine. Arguments against the existence of a psychic force or human 'X-Factor' have generally been based on the inability to locate, measure, quantify or qualify an energy or medium capable of carrying 'thought' emanations across time and space. However, because this unknown factor or energy is not recognized by mainstream science, and most experimental research in this area has a tendency to be 'non-repeatable,'should we automatically deny the existence of a psychic force capable of distance communication and influence?

One of these areas of research is called electromagnetic (EM) theory. As Dr. Gregory Little explains in *Grand Illusions: the Spectral Reality of Sexual UFO Abductions*, we exist in an 'electromagnetic sea' which defines physical matter; it is the glue that holds the physical world together. Our visual senses only pick up about 5% of the electromagnetic energy spectrum, the upper end of which is ultraviolet light, x-rays, and cosmic rays and the lower end of which is infrared radiation, radio and television bandwidths and Extremely Low Frequency (ELF) radiation. The EM Theory of UFO manifestation hypothesizes that UFO and other paranormal manifestations are intelligent energy forms existing in the ultraviolet or infrared ends of the spectrum where they cannot be seen. They become visible by altering their vibrational frequency so that they vibrate in the range of visible light. This can also be seen as a 'mode of travel'theory explaining UFO propulsion as electromagnetic in nature. In other words, it doesn't mean UFOs aren't physical space ships. We have to try to move away from this dichotomy which so easily invades our thinking and forces us to reject electromagnetic theories off hand.

Dr. Little's theories are based on the research of Dr. Michael Persinger, whom we discussed earlier. Persinger's work can be found in scholarly journals in large university research libraries along with other scientific research into paranormal phenomena going back to the 1940s. Persinger hypothesizes that close encounter or near death experiences can be triggered by magnetic frequency disruption on the temporal lobe and other parts of the brain.

Dr. Little believes the EM spectrum is the 'spirit' world or the world of archetypes. The archetypes are known from ancient and occult sources as divine and spiritual sort of templates, or subtle memory containers, which give birth to each living form and guide it's equilibrium in the material world. Max Heindel writes in *The Rosicrucian Cosmo-Conception* that the archetypes are not merely models of the forms we see about us, but are "creative archetypes which fashion the forms of the Physical World in their own likeness(es), and work together to form a certain species, each archetype giving part of itself to build the required form." Thus, in full opposition to Darwinian theory, this ancient doctrine would suggest that earth species are *immutable* and they do *not* change over time. There is a separate guiding archetype for each form. (see *Space Travelers and the Genesis of the Human Form*)

It is difficult to talk about archetypes without realizing that these descriptions usually fall short of conveying what archetypes are. As June Singer writes in *Boundaries of the Soul*, it is impossible to provide an exact definition of the archetype, and the best we can do is 'talk around it.'The archetype is, in effect, a 'profound riddle'which can only express itself in metaphorical language. It is a part of the human mind which cannot be grasped by the human mind, unless the mind is very still. And once you grasp the feeling of what the archetype is, there are no words to describe it. The archetype lies behind and beyond personal experience. It is the 'background' of human experience. Ironically, the very ground of mankind's thought processes lie in unfamiliar and uncharted territory.

According to Jung, the archetypes are both "systems of readiness for action," as well as "images and emotions." Jung felt that the archetypes are inherited with the brain structure, and are its psychic aspect. Jung noted that the archetypes are the images by which the psyche is attached to nature, or, by which "its link with the *earth* and the world appears at its most tangible." This definition is actually quite helpful. In this particular definition, we come to understand that the archetypes are a connecting link between psyche and *earth*, a union or bridge between mind and matter. While the archetype is part of the brain structure, it is that part of the brain structure which is constantly building and maintaining the bridge between psyche and matter, keeping familiar territory familiar. How far is this concept from the idea of nature spirits? Let's explore.

Israel Regardie describes the archetype as "nodal points which act as termini or power stations through which the root-life stream flows and is diluted or transmuted so as to be assimilable or available to a lower form of life." The primordial archetypes, he explains, are "psychic forms into which repeated ancestral experiences have moulded the typically human mode of apprehension." The archetypes are forces of nature, and also comprise what is meant by Gods, Archangels and Angels. The Archangels important to magical systems are Raphael, Gabriel, Auriel, and Michael.

As William Gray writes, in magical ritual one is not dealing with inanimate lumps of matter, but with living energies capable of autoreaction upon each other. Magical ritual is the art of taking one piece of consciousness and "stretching it" so that it extends beyond the limits of the sensory world. It must then be "picked up," or "amplified," or "channeled," by Intelligences operating through the Inner Dimensions. Without the cooperation of "Inner contacts" which pick up the energy and extend it beyond their usual "point of neutrality," the magical practitioner would not be successful in making contact. Likewise, if we ourselves are unable to pick up the energies coming back toward us, and translate their expression on the material level, we will not be successful in making contact. This is also a helpful description of what archetypes are.

Beings Without Borders

Our current scientific understanding of the universe cannot explain such a thing as a collective realm, archetypal experience, or Carl Jung's concept of 'synchronicity,' as a place where our collective knowledge is stored. But the holographic model discussed in detail in Chapter Two can. Do humans, at some deep level, share the same consciousness? Are we "beings without borders"?

Carl Jung referred to an archetypal group mind that is so ancient that it was as if all humans have "the memory of a two million year old man lurking in the depths of our unconscious minds." In this sense, Jung's idea of the archetype can be explained by the holographic model. Images contributed by the participants of the hologram will tend to build on certain types of transpersonal experience, and a model or template of that type of experience will eventually be created. Carl Jung's idea of synchronicity as an "acausal connecting principle" is also evidence for Bohm's holographic implicate order. In the implicate order, time is not sequential, there is no temporal space, and there is no division between consciousness and matter.

According to Bohm, the apparent distinction between mind and matter is an 'artifact' which arises after the unfoldment of the implicate into the explicate order. Carl Jung's concept of synchronicity, then, can be seen as 'flaws in the fabric of reality,' or momentary breakthroughs of an underlying implicate order. The same might be said of the seemingly repetitive loop experience which we call *Deja vu*.

Carl Jung's theory of psychic projection borrows from Freud in its assertion that the human unconscious requires a reduction in tension or stress and seeks to balance the anxiety of the world. This is accomplished by the release of psychic energy, or the "psychic projection" of the archetypes which symbolize the particular balance which the person seeks. In this case, the archetypes are 'symbolic'of thought processes; they are modes of dealing with mental stress which are projected onto the world by the human psyche. As discussed, however, it is difficult to define what the archetype really is.

Dr. Little agrees that something like psychic projection can frequently be ascribed to high weirdness events, and he agrees that such archetypes do exist, but he disagrees that all strange phenomena are generated from the minds of the witnesses. As he asks in *People of the Web*: "If the phenomena feed on the energies of the people witnessing it, how could it have gotten its start?" He believes the phenomena have their own source separate from the witness, and that they are the 'archetypes' from a different dimension, the spirit world, which have taken on a temporary solid form in the third dimension.

Dr. Persinger believes that a release of geomagnetic energy can create an apparition, complete with its effects on witnesses, by creating a charged plasma. The plasma itself releases strong magnetic forces that alter brain chemistry in the areas of the brain associated with mystical experience. Incorporating the theories of Persinger, but splitting with him after a time, Dr. Little believes that this charged plasma is itself a manifestation from the spirit world, as opposed to a psychological or psychic projection stemming from a need for anxiety reduction. As he explains:

> The archetypes are powerful electromagnetic energy forces that interact with us by altering brain chemistry. When they enter our physical realm from the ultraviolet end of the spectrum, they are essentially a plasma, but a plasma with an intelligence and purpose.

He explains that this powerful electromagnetic field, or plasma, alters brain chemistry and trips off biochemical reactions. As the archetypal forces enter physical reality by slowing down their energy vibration, anyone in the proximity begins to be biologically influenced through the magnetite in the brain. As Dr. Little explains, ionic flow in the neurons is altered, and the brain's neurochemical 'dominoes' begin to tumble. This sequence of events "carries the person off in the direction that represents the underlying meaning of the particular archetype that appears."

Dr. Little explains that the earth is an incredibly powerful geoelectrical generator and earthlings are immersed in constant waves of electromagnetic forces. As he explains, "the center of the planet is molten metal that probably generates the magnetic field as the planet whirs around in its approximate 1,000 mph daily spin. Friction on its surface causes a variety of static electricity forces as well as a bizarre interlocking web of other electrical forces." Essentially, humans are electric beings.

To a very real extent, Dr. Little explains, humans are trapped by our own biochemistry, and events that happen in the brain often just "take us along for the ride." Some facets of human experience are like "being tied to a wild horse that takes us where it wants to go." The existential strangeness of the human condition in this regard is also emphasized by Budden when he states: "the brain is a vast memory bank where the conscious self feels like a visitor with only a limited number of access codes."

Thus, "electromagnetic spectrum manifestation" is Dr. Little's explanation for hauntings, visions, near death experiences, shamanic powers, sexual UFO abduction, incubus and succubus reports and various strange phenomena appearances and disappearances on earth. In an interview with environmental researcher Remy Chevalier, published in *Paranoia: The Conspiracy Reader*, Dr. Little explained first of all that the EM spectrum is not speculation but scientific fact, and he likens the universe to an electromagnetic sea. As he explained, human perception lies within a very narrow frequency band, corresponding to about 5% of the entire electromagnetic energy spectrum. At the upper end of the spectrum are the ultraviolet light, X-rays, and cosmic rays, and at the lower end are infrared radiation, communication waves, and ELF radiation.

Little speculates that paranormal manifestations are intelligent energy forms from the ultraviolet or infrared end of the light spectrum which intrude into the visible area of the spectrum. These intelligent energy forms become visible and take on a sort of solidity by altering their vibrational frequency either up or down so that they vibrate in the range of visible light. The geomagnetic web that encompasses earth is traversed by these intelligent energy forms. The EM spectrum is what the ancients called the spirit world.

In contrast to the idea that such intelligent energy forms actually exist, Albert Budden, whose theory we will discuss in more detail shortly, believes that the human unconscious harnesses electromagnetic conditions to 'produce' the hallucination of a structured or metallic spaceship by incorporating real aerial electrical field effects such as ball lightning with imagery and symbolism from the unconscious mind.

Archetypes and Brain Chemistry

Dr. Little's theory incorporates Carl Jung's ideas about archetypes. Jung called archetypes "psychoid factors" and believed that they were able to bridge the gap between the energy world and the physical world. Jung's archetypes consist of "pure nature," by which it is supposed he meant pure energy, existing normally in the unseen ultraviolet end of the spectrum. In his 1984 book, *The Archetype Experience*, Dr. Little was mainly concerned with how archetypes interact with humans either through their own volition in UFO appearances or abduction scenarios, and in other ways where people deliberately attempt to enter their realm through magical rituals.

Dr. Little's alien abduction theory suggests that archetypes have appeared to humankind throughout history. In the days of Thomas Aquinas it was commonly believed that demons were crossbreeding with humans, and that the incubus or succubus desiring to have sex with the human adjusts its shape to the one which 'lowers resistance.' Dr. Little suggests that these entities are energy forces from another reality which coincides with our physical reality. This other reality is not another dimension, but a different vibrational frequency which we call the 'spirit world.'

For many years it was not known how or why electromagnetic fields alter brain chemistry and human experience; that is, until the 1992 discovery of the substance called magnetite, which is found in quantity in human brain cells. What does magnetite have to do with the appearance of strange phenomena? As Dr. Little writes in *Grand Illusions*:

> Magnetite is found in the brain of the homing pigeon and has been
> believed since the mid-1970s to be the explanation for the pigeon's
> ability to navigate from anywhere. The substance is like an internal

compass for animals, but it apparently does much more. Quite simply, magnetite aligns itself to the field of whatever electromagnetic or geomagnetic force that the person is in. This alignment of magnetite subtly alters the ionic flow in the brain's cells and thus can increase the flow of neurotransmitters in some brain areas while decreasing the flow in other areas.

Dr. Little takes Carl Jung's basic concept of the archetype quite a bit further, giving them a 'life' of their own and hypothesizing a biological interplay between two worlds. On the subject of archetypes and brain chemistry, Dr. Little explains:

> The archetypes are powerful electromagnetic energy forces that interact with us by altering brain chemistry. When they enter our physical realm from the ultraviolet end of the electromagnetic spectrum, they are essentially a plasma, but a plasma with an intelligence and purpose. ... But the archetypes don't alter our brain chemistry through their own deliberation or thought. They simply appear in reality and the powerful electromagnetic field that surrounds them does the rest. Once the biochemistry is tripped, it's like a set of prearranged dominoes starts tipping each other over.

So where does human biochemistry play ball with the electromagnetic spectrum, or vice versa? In *Grand Illusions*, Dr. Little explains the rules of the game:

> Archetypal forces alter magnetite's alignment in the brain of anyone within proximity of them when they enter our physical reality. As they come into reality by slowing down their energy vibration, they begin throwing off powerful electromagnetic waves in a frequency that is tuned to that of the magnetite in the brain... while at the same time, the magnetite in the percipient's brain aligns toward the suddenly appearing powerful electromagnetic field. Ionic flow in the neurons immediately alters, and the brain's neurochemical dominoes begin to tumble in sequence, carrying the person off in the direction that represents the underlying meaning of the particular archetype that appears.

> Archetypes can emerge into reality either by beginning as a small charged ball of light that rapidly changes color and shape into the form they assume, or they can literally appear to "rip a hole" in the fabric of reality that surrounds us. Archetypes that emerge through rips in reality give witnesses the impression that everything around us is a curtain. Witnesses say that it seems a curtain is pulled up exposing aliens behind it. Some have witnessed the air just split open like a painting and from the exposed hole in reality out step the aliens. The alien forms are trickster forms that have plagued all societies for all time. They assume a shape that adjusts to the unconscious cultural expectations of the abductee.

Electrostaging

Consider the following scenario proffered by Albert Budden in *UFOs, Psychic Close Encounters*. A strange, very rigid entity in a space suit and helmet is seen on a farm in Middleton, Massachusetts over the course of a few days. A large rock is also noticed, which on closer inspection by the family is a landed spaceship with bulbous portholes and a textured surface. The bizarre craft simply vanishes after a few days. Budden's explanation for this turn of events gets to the heart of his Electrostaging Hypothesis (ESH). As it turns out, poltergeist phenomena in general are extremely active in this former witch hunt capital, near Salem, which lies on a major fault line.

Budden explains that whatever causes poltergeists is intrinsically involved in many UFO-related events. UFO abductees would argue on the side of the realism of the event and various physical traces left behind. What is possible in this common ground between the two? And how can these psychic processes create tangible and bizarre vehicles that 'pale' anything Buckminster Fuller could dream up? Using a range of poltergeist case studies, Budden shows that poltergeist disruptions include the ability to fling objects into the air, rearrange objects in a room, make objects appear and disappear (called 'apports'), disorganize, reorganize and generally create chaos out of order within specific confines, such as a "haunted house." Budden's research into psychokinesis (the ability of the mind to move objects) provides a strong indication that magnetic phenomena are at work.

Budden believes poltergeist activity is a mixture of both "person-mediated and direct field phenomena;" in other words, such activity can be produced by either psychokinesis (PK) or environmental stimuli of natural or artificial origin. He explains that earthlight phenomena (BOL) (which Budden proffers are related to UFO phenomena) and geophysical fields below a poltergeist-active house, may be related, since they both originate from tectonic strain in the strata. However it is not clear how Budden goes about proving his assumption that earthlight phenomena and other reported unidentified flying objects are the same phenomena!

As Greg Long has pointed out in his book, *Examining the Earthlight Theory*, there is no classification system incorporated into Persinger's identification of "luminous phenomena" (LP). Therefore, Long asks, are "naturally-occurring" 'IFOs' (Identified Flying Objects) contaminating Persinger's analysis? What is actually being measured by correlating "anomalous events" with tectonic strain release? Greg Long asks: "Of the total body of UFO reports [utilized in Persinger's studies], could some be descriptions of a rare, unrecognized natural phenomenon [LP] and others accurate records of classic extraterrestrial spacecraft?" Long stresses that to be correctly utilized within a scientific hypothesis, these baseline UFO reports should really be divided into discrete classes of objects, rather than being lumped as "luminous phenomena." Thus, the term "UFO" has been poorly defined, and this poor definition contaminates the results of the test.

Of all the descriptions of unidentified flying objects in the data gathered at the Yakima Reservation, concludes Long, the most consistent is the "ball of light" and, more specifically, the "orange ball of light." Such objects have been reported in widely separated geographical areas in the U.S., including the Uintah Basin in Utah and the Piedmont area of Missouri. Along with the reports at Yakima, these areas also experienced earthquakes during the sighting times of the orange balls of light.

In addition, Persinger has deduced that tectonic strain is the cause of the manifestations at all three places. However, Long disagrees. He points out that in the Yakima study, Persinger and Derr were looking at seismic activity within 100 miles of the Reservation, the Missouri study included quakes as far away as 250 miles, and in a study in Manitoba, Canada, Persinger looked at quakes which occurred 775 miles away. Can all of these widely disparate measurements be considered correlates? It appears that statistical correlations between luminous phenomena and tectonic strain are being made with no rule concerning the distance between the two correlates.

Apparently, there is no concern for the size of the tremor either. Persinger would have us believe that the energy released from a mild tremor registering at 1 or 2 can produce a plasma above the ground. Long asks: "even if electromagnetic radiation from a weak quake could pass through the hard intervening barriers of rock from great depths, how can the plasma be formed and sustained in the atmosphere, beyond appearing as a momentary flash of light?" He also asks: why is it that in each window area studied by Persinger and Derr, miscellaneous aerial objects show up as well, that is, objects other than orange balls of light? In addition, why is the presence of "unidentified" humanoids reported? How do you explain strange craft, auditory phenomena and abduction reports in the same areas?

Chris Rutkowski also questions the scientific basis of the Tectonic Strain Hypothesis (TSH). He explains that in theory it should be possible to verify whether UFOs are caused by underground strain fields. However, while strained rock certainly exists, the "strain fields," the mechanism itself, is a mystery. Even Persinger and Derr admit that there is no direct evidence to support the existence of strain fields. Since these fields are the foundation of the TSH, Rutkowski questions how the TSH can support an undefined mechanism. It may, he suggests, be easier to admit that UFOs are caused by extra- or ultra-terrestrials.

What Does the Government Know?

Electromagnetic energy manifestation is not a new idea and some early government reports apparently reached this conclusion about UFO manifestation. Dr. Little opines that EM theory fell into the "dark corridors of government," and if there exists a cover-up of UFO phenomena, EM spectrum manifestation is likely to be the reality being so painstakingly covered up. He asserts that the government knows there are intelligent intrusions from the EM spectrum and they have quietly and systematically been studying it, "while publicly all the furor is over crashed and recovered discs and aliens." Dr. Little maintains that over the past two decades scientific evidence has illustrated that EM spectrum theory appears to be the solution to UFO-related phenomena. Personal experience has led Dr. Little to validate the theory. He states: "research is one thing; having the other realm intrude into your world is another." Indeed, if UFOs are intelligent energy intrusions from the EM spectrum, what does this say about the stability of our 'stable illusion'? Is it falling apart at the seams?

In his on-line article entitled "Reflections on MJ-12," Dan T. Smith says this another way. (see, www.clark.net/pub/dansmith) Smith writes:

> MJ12 has only one official function. That is to report to the President. Each President is allowed at least one report. Along with this report there is some sort of briefing book. The report to the President is not upbeat, not even up tempo. It is not something that any politician would want to wave in front of the voters. The good news is that UFOs are just an illusion. The bad news is: *so is everything else*, including all of the cherished illusions near and dear to the electorate. … Depending on how you look at this report you might get the impression that by comparison the Big Bang cosmology of scientific materialism is downright cozy, or that paleo-Darwinian survivalism might not be such a bad idea after all, not when you consider what is coming 'round the mountain. When the revelation comes, the voters will unanimously demand a cover-up. UFO investigators will develop new and intense interests in stamp collecting and bird watching.

According to Dr. Robert Becker, author of *The Body Electric*, several thousand scientists have been independently working in electromagnetic field theory. Dr. Little maintains a listing from the Harvard Genetics Department of about 3,000 references to articles investigating EM and frequency vibrations on behavior, physiology and brain chemistry and he, claims, "it's clear that there are several separate, but interrelated, goals in this research." Little claims that the most important findings probably "never see the light of day and are communicated directly to the agency paying the grant." There are probably less than 100 scientists doing exactly what Persinger is doing, Little claims, but they are sponsored by government grants and published in very specialized professional journals in medicine, physics, acoustics and geophysics.

Electromagnetic theories, however, are not especially popular in mainstream ufology. Could this be due to an extensive government coverup of EM spectrum theory, as Dr. Little charges, in addition to a largely unknown or misunderstood physics of reality? As Little maintains, few people in ufology would ever see this research and most wouldn't understand the significance of it. Yet, the significance may lie in what Dan Smith has to say above: that reality is a construct of sorts, a 'stable illusion' which the participants themselves are holding up.

Does this also mean there are no 'real' or solid material ships travelling from other planetary systems? As Trevor Constable has noted, UFOs are both man-made artifacts *and* biological phenomena. In his classic UFO study, *The Cosmic Pulse of Life*, Constable shows that UFOs are both physical, metallic ships *and* what he calls "plasmoids," which are visible in the infrared spectrum and become evident on infrared film. As Constable suggests, perhaps they are able to shift between both of these manifestations. This can be translated a few different ways. One is that perhaps EM theory is simply a 'mode of travel' or 'mode of appearance' explanation for the same phenomena. These phenomena may be better described as both biology and artifact, a technology belonging to a very advanced high-tech civilization. On the other hand, EM Theory essentially describes a world in which such intelligent energy manifestations are possible as a bizarre world which in itself can only be described as an engineered 'construct' or as an 'illusion' created by its inhabitants.

Poltergeists and Pillow Tricks

Albert Budden tries to put together a theory that lumps UFO phenomena with spirits and apparitions. Yet, many argue that due to the physical aspects of the alien scenario this assumption is troubling. Budden explains that due to electromagnetic stimulation of the brain, the Unconscious Intelligence (UI), rather than acting on the nervous system of the witness, "reorganizes the external environment," which he terms "stage management" or "electrostaging." Electrostaging is essentially an organizational ability of the perceiver of which he or she is unaware. Budden proposes that Recurrent Spontaneous Psychokinesis (RSPK) has the potential to produce a cast of phantom actors, including aliens from space. Budden explains that these structured spaceships could "arrive and depart in the same manner as all apports, and it would be part of the staged reality of an encounter with Visitors from another world."

Budden is essentially saying that humans are capable of using the powers of psychokinesis (mind moving matter) to stir things up in the environment. For instance, consider an extremely bizarre ghost story relayed by Budden. The family of Reverend Phelps in Stratford, Connecticut, returned from church one Sunday to find the door wide open and their home in disarray. That afternoon, the family went out again, but the Reverend stayed home to keep watch. He reported that nothing disturbed him. But when the family returned, furniture had been scattered, and in the main bedroom, "a night gown and chemise had been laid out on the bed, with the arms folded across the breast, and a pair of stockings placed to make it look like a corpse laid out for burial." In another room, elaborate dummies had been constructed out of clothing and cushions, and were arranged in "attitudes of extreme devotion" with Bibles placed in front of them. The next day, objects began to fly in the air. The poltergeist continued to perform these complex "designer tableaux" oddities within minutes, a feat which would have taken several persons several hours to complete.

What is Budden's explanation? According to Budden's theory, unbeknownst to him and with his UI in charge, the Reverend's psyche, utilizing kinetic energy, flew around the room and fussed with the furniture while everyone was gone. But who had performed the pillow tricks during the earlier haunting he describes, when no one was at home? Underneath all the fancy lingo lies a theory lacking in credibility.

The idea of the "cyclic effect of the signal link" is Budden's attempt to explain how people seem to jump out of their skin to effectuate these occurrences. Here's the cycle: (1) the UAP (unidentified atmospheric phenomena) enters the ambient strain field, (2) ES (psychic) individual enters strain field, (3) ES witness reacts "allergically" to the field, (4) ES witness emits personal field, (5) UAP field and ES witness' field "signal link" through the medium of the ambient strain field, (6) physiology of ES witness affects UAP by electromagnetic upstroke or 'signal link' according to stage management of the encounter, in this case to act hypnotically, (7) increased personal emission from ES witness, linking back to (5) reinforcement of signal link.

The signal link provides a mechanism by which the unconscious interacts with aerial electrical phenomena, and by which "the unconscious contents of the human mind enters the arena of the ET mythology." Budden suggests that "the witness superimposes and subjectively transforms a mundane object—star, moon, plane—into an exotic craft." Furthermore, Budden suggests, the psychic witness creates an illusion for others to witness, thus explaining multiple witness sightings.

Budden's theory suggests that the psychokinetic properties of the first percipient trips off the brain chemistry of the other percipients in the vicinity and, importantly, that the "shared hallucination" has a beginning point in one person's psyche. Conversely, Dr. Little disagrees that all strange phenomena could be generated from the minds of witnesses. As he notes, if the phenomena feed on the energies of the witnesses, how did it get its start? He believes the phenomena are a source separate from the witnesses, and that they are the 'archetypes' from a different dimension which have taken temporary form in the third dimension. Another explanation might be provided by holographic theory. As Talbot suggests in *The Holographic Universe*:

> Our brains mathematically construct objective reality by interpreting frequencies that are ultimately projections from another dimension, a deeper order of existence that is beyond both space and time. The brain is a hologram enfolded in a holographic universe.

As Pribram posits, the waves and frequencies that are out there in space-time only appear as a concrete reality because our holographic brain takes this cosmically generated holographic "blur" of frequencies and converts it into a solid objective reality. As he qualifies, we are not *looking* at a hologram, we are part of the hologram.

Why should it be less disturbing to consider that humans are driven by an 'unconscious' hidden persona? In what sense is this argument preferable over the possibility that there is 'something' in some sense 'out there?' Psychology as a discipline has always been comfortable with the pretext of the monster within, but its adherents forget to mention in their wild theories that none of these imagined internal mechanisms has been proven to exist. What is the external "signal link" that switches on the collective unconscious mythology to which ETs belong? It is this switch mechanism that Budden's theory, no matter how hard it tries, still fails to explain. As Chris Rutkowski has pointed out, there is no evidence to support the existence of "strain fields" and the Tectonic Strain Hypothesis (TSH) essentially supports an undefined mechanism.

PsychoKinesia: Cerebral Exhibitionism

In his book *Flying Saucers, A Modern Myth of Things Seen in the Skies*, Carl Jung wrote: "It is difficult to form any correct idea of these objects, because they behave not like bodies but like weightless thoughts." Jung hypothesized three alternatives to the UFO enigma:

> In the first case an objectively real, physical process forms the basis for an accompanying myth; in the second case an archetype creates the corresponding vision; to these two causal relationships we must add a third possibility, namely that of a synchronistic, i.e. acausal, meaningful coincidence.

Jung admitted, "as a psychologist, I am not qualified to contribute anything useful to the question of the physical reality of UFOs. I can concern myself only with their undoubted psychic aspect." Yet, he alluded to a "third possibility" which seems to suggest that UFOs possibly come from another dimension of space-time, i.e. that they are an "acausal meaningful coincidence." Are they visits from the future? Or are they holographic images created by the participants of an unfolding 'holomovement' we refer to as 'reality'?

But there is a problem here. Some UFOs which are seen from a distance in more elusive form, such as large balls of light (BOL) which can change size and shape, and can appear and disappear, can sometimes be explained (IFOs—Identified Flying Objects). But what about instances where physical craft are seen at close range? How can a physical hovering or landed spacecraft, which cannot be explained as vortex phenomena, a whirlwind or BOL, but a real craft witnessed by several people, come to be designated as "psychic phenomena"? Even Carl Jung admitted he was unqualified to comment on the undeniable physical aspect of UFO phenomena. Budden's theory is equally unqualified and cannot explain the physical aspects of this enigma.

Perhaps Budden's hypothesis should not be called a "psychic" theory, but rather a "psychological" theory, specifically, neo-Freudian. Consider that *psy-che* is the Greek word for "soul," which modern psychiatry describes as "the mind," or "mental processes." Psychic means "beyond natural or known physical processes," or "apparently sensitive to forces beyond the physical world." Budden's mechanistic theory contains an allowance for the concept of 'within' but not for 'beyond.' It is a psychological theory. Or perhaps it is a "psychedelic" theory, given that the word comes from the root word "psyche" (the human soul) and the Greek root *delein*—"to make manifest," and means "of or causing extreme changes in the conscious mind, as hallucinations, delusions, intensification of awareness and sensory perception."

The root word *kinesis* is Greek for "motion" or "movement," therefore psychokinesis describes the ability of the mind to move matter. Interestingly, psychokinesia means "violent cerebral action due to defective inhibition." Therefore, in Budden's theory, does the condition of electromagnetic system overload cause "cerebral exhibitionism," or psychokinesia? But if there is no 'other world' which 'Alice' can visit or be visited from, that is, if the word 'psychic' is used here as merely some sort of allergic sensitivity to environmental stress, then Budden has misused the concept.

Given the previous definitions of the root word *psyche*, it is here that it is most evident that Dr. Little's theory is a "psychic" theory and Budden's theory is a "psychological" theory, therefore the title of Budden's book is misleading. *Psychic Close Encounters* is a book which aims to debunk theories of Other World existence, and looks to keep Alice home, safe, dreaming. Lets look at that dreaming self, the UI, a little closer to see if we recognize its multi-faceted face in the world of Freudian psychology, as well as in the Spirit world.

The Unconscious Intelligence

While Budden, on one hand, proposes that the characters which people claim to see, whether helmeted, space suited, or riding a phantom horse and buggy, are figments of their imagination, he is quite willing to create a fictitious inner character called the Unconscious Intelligence, or UI. Who is this somewhat devious and creative inner character that likes to come out and have fun? The following quote is from Budden's *UFOs, Psychic Close Encounters*:

> The UI (Unconscious Intelligence) utilizes its reality-defying abilities (including psychokinesis, or 'mind over matter') to produce the effects of an advanced, magical technology in these 'staged productions', its motivating purpose being to establish and maintain an external social identity. ... The UI is a function that is largely frustrated as a natural state of affairs, there is an imbalance between the two selves that is quite normal, if not actually desirable, in order for us to cope with life. The UI, having insider knowledge of what it would take to create belief in alien intelligence, as it wishes to use this identity, would know that the conscious mind associates structure with intelligence. That is why crop circles have been 'identified' as alien...

As Budden explains, the UI includes areas of the mind that communicate with the conscious self through dreams, art, religion and insanity. The UI is the intelligence behind visionary experiences, apparitions, and even UFO-related phenomena. The UI, he explains, is a part of the mind that all religions have a name for, and it is an intelligence that is "aware that the impressions we have of the world (what we call reality) is really a stable illusion."

With respect to the relationship between mind and matter, Budden believes that mental processes are involved with the production and maintenance of reality at a fundamental level. So, if reality is a "stable illusion," Budden explains, under certain conditions this illusion breaks down and is "manipulated by the UI for its own ends." What are these ends? Dreams are not enough for the UI; it apparently is not satisfied. He suggests that the UI wants expression in the conscious world ... "to carve out an important piece of the 'real world' for itself."

Budden explains that epileptic-like reactions can occur in which a person gets "switched off" from receipt of external perceptual information, and instead receives internal hallucinatory information and imagery based on memory of external perceptions. In this case, the UI would dominate the perceptual screen and "create as outlandish a scenario as it wishes." So the hidden hand that flips the "switch," which we were looking for earlier, is a psychological construct called the UI.

What is this inner construct which Budden describes as manipulative, unsatisfied, egocentric, selfish, frustrated, and which fights to rule our conscious life? How much difference is there between an inner-world neo-Freudian construct, and a spirit, an elf, or an alien from "out there"? Budden states: "Pre-scientific generations attributed all manner of natural things to the work of the Devil, God, the 'little people', evil spirits, etc...." Yet, if the 'ghoul within' has to be inserted into the final analysis to make his theory work, how is this theory "scientific?" Either way, we are dealing with an invisible patron, so what difference does this contrived inner-world/outer-world dichotomy really make? How is one more "scientific" than the other, when both worlds contain equally uncharted territory?

People of the Web

In Greek and Roman mythology, Psyche is a nymph, the personification of the soul. Her great beauty excited the jealousy and hatred of Venus, who ordered Cupid to inspire her with love for some contemptible being. Cupid fell in love with Venus himself and after many persecutions by Venus a reconciliation was effected. Psyche was made immortal. If the human psyche or mind-soul is immortal, are we then the weavers of reality?

If the EM Theories reviewed here appear clumsy, it is because there is a problematical loop in the 'web' of concepts involving an inner/outer, physical/mental dichotomy. To Budden, it is cut and dry. The source of UFO-poltergeist manifestation is the psychokinetic ability of the human mind, with its little 'people' running around inside flipping switches. In contrast, Dr. Little's Tricksters from Neverland actually enter the physical realm from the spiritual and 'play ball' with the human psyche. However, it has not been made clear in these theories why UFO entities should be categorized as apparitions or poltergeists.

Do the People of the Web touch us or do we internalize them in some way? Is inner space a reflection of outer space? Is the 'monster' lurking within or without? It is this fine line in the enigma of the People of the Web that makes the various EM theories so tantalizing, yet so difficult to grasp. For just a second, you get the feeling you might be holding on to the nature of reality. Then you realize you won't see the other side until you get to the other side. And you won't be able to come back to tell anyone about it ... or will you?

In the following chapter we will explore this dualistic conundrum a little further.

CHAPTER SIX
MANA, MAGIC AND MIND

The magical is an ephemeral quality which we impose upon the world as our moods dictate.

Jean Paul Sartre

Colin Wilson provides some perspective on the issues surrounding the dualistic concepts of unconscious personalities vs. spirits from another realm in *Poltergeist: A Study in Destructive Haunting.* Wilson explains how hauntings and apparitions can be explained in various ways, depending upon the circumstances. Essentially, the poltergeist can be seen in light of mediumship; a spirit form working through the human being. For, as Wilson points out, there can be no haunting without a human being present.

Wilson concludes that some poltergeist cases may be easier to explain using Hawaiian Huna concepts rather than neo-Freudian psycho-projection theories. The Kahuna system, according to Mark Pinkham in *Return of the Serpents of Wisdom*, has its origin in the higher evolved beings and extraterrestrial adepts who founded the lost civilizations of Atlantis and Lemuria. Pinkham claims the Kahuna system was transplanted to Egypt and later moved to Africa. It later swept to Polynesia and is part of the Hawaiian Huna religion. The Kahuna ideas are applicable to many facets of poltergeist phenomena, including the story about Reverend Phelps relayed earlier. The Huna/Kahuna explanation of hauntings encompasses the presence of *mana*, a collective subtle human energy that creates thought-forms. By concentrating their *mana*, Wilson explains, a few people have been known to lift a heavy human being into the air by their fingertips. The Huna explanation for a poltergeist would be that an enemy of the family had sent spirits to discharge excess *mana* in the victim, which manifests as a thought-form. Does this sound like Budden's UI?

Throughout his book, Wilson offers striking examples of both ancient and modern poltergeist manifestations. Wilson illustrates that some hauntings appear to be more explainable by a spirit possession explanation while others are better explained with multiple personality concepts. Yet, the two aspects are also interchangeable, depending upon your definition of the concepts of *self, soul or spirit.* For instance, in one case Wilson concludes:

> It can now be seen why Prince thought it possible that the Amherst case involved dual personality. He was more than half convinced that the Doris case of multiple personality was actually one of benevolent possession, so in suggesting that Esther was a dual personality, he was, in effect, hinting that this could be a case of non-benevolent possession. At the same time, his position as a well-known psychiatrist meant that, for public consumption, he was bound to lay most of the emphasis on the purely psychological explanation for both cases.

Essentially, the psychological explanation, as Wilson explains, depends upon the recognition that we are all, to some extent, multiple personalities or "divided selves." The Freudian point of view, he explains, is that we all "spend our lives trying to get rid of our old selves and develop new and less constricting personality structures." Thus, we all crave experience, yet on the other hand we retract from it out of fear of the new. Different personalities arise in order to guide these different behaviors. But are these personality "structures," or are they actual personalities or entities? The line between is actually more vague that one might think. As Wilson suggests:

> If 'spirits' can pass in and out of our bodies at will, then perhaps many of the feelings and emotions we assume to be our own are caused by

the intruder. Perhaps our belief that we are individuals is a mistake, and we are a whole assemblage of people, with one of them more-or-less in charge.

As Russian philosopher Georg Ivanovitch Gurdjieff believed, the human being possesses multiple selves, perhaps even dozens of selves, and this explains our inability to focus at length on any one matter. But is this a general lack of self-discipline, or are we really a conglomerate of personalities? An answer may be found in the ancient Kahuna system. Wilson writes of this ancient belief system:

> The Kahuna idea of the conscious and subconscious seems to be, judging from the root meaning of the names given to them, a pair of spirits closely joined in a body which is controlled by the subconscious and used to cover and hide them both. The conscious spirit is more human and possesses the ability to talk. The grieving subconscious weeps tears, dribbles water and otherwise handles the vital force of the body. It does its work with secrecy and silent care, but it is stubborn and disposed to refuse to obey.

Yet, this description is dangerously close to Budden's mischievous, manipulative, selfish, and frustrated Unconscious Intelligence, one of the three selves, or constructs, posited by Freud to which Budden ascribes a more intelligent, animated and even ulterior presence. As Budden asserts, the UI is a part of the mind that all religions have a name for, and it is an intelligence that is "aware that the impressions we have of the world (what we call reality) is really a stable illusion." Problematically, we've yet to figure out whether the UI is a "construct" or "entity," nor have we really figured out how it operates. As mentioned earlier, if the 'ghoul within' has to be inserted into the final analysis to make Budden's theory work, in what way is this theory scientific? Because it is remotely related to Freudian theory? Well, take a look. So is the Kahuna system.

In the Kahuna scheme of things, as Wilson notes, the "subconscious" spirit is closely aligned with the body, but at the same time seems to be "rebellious and highly emotional." Inherent in this description of dual autonomous selves is a "curious tendency of the human mind to turn against itself." Parts of us are like an immature child, Wilson suggests, but, because we fail to recognize it as a separate entity, we remain unable to balance the total psyche. In addition to these two spirits or souls, human beings also contain a higher self, or "superconscious being," who controls our future potential. The three selves, or souls, correspond to different levels in a hierarchy of awareness. The reason that future events go awry, Wilson notes, is because the conscious self (or ego) contains contradictions due to its lack of awareness of the other entities.

According to the Kahunas, the three souls use *mana*, or vital force, each with a different frequency or electrical charge. According to Max Freedom Long, in *The Secret Science Behind Miracles,* the poltergeist is the "lower soul" which has somehow, in death, become separated from the middle and higher selves. The lower soul possesses memory, but the middle self does not. As Wilson notes, a disembodied lower self is an earthbound spirit, with memories, which causes poltergeist disturbances. A disembodied middle self is "a wandering wraith without memory—in fact, what we would generally regard as a ghost."

As Wilson explains, both of these "low spirits" also lack intelligence and are highly suggestive to hypnotic suggestion. Therefore, witch doctors of the Kahuna tradition can direct them to possess another body at will. Under normal conditions, the victim can thwart such a takeover, because the human will is much stronger than that of the low spirit. The low spirits have to await the chance to enter, or enter by brute force. After they enter, they work by using their charged *mana* to slowly drain the victim of his own *mana.* As Wilson notes, Max Long has successfully applied the "three selves" hypothesis to several cases of multiple personality. Long believed that multiple personality was a case of spirit possession by the low- or middle-self of a 'wandering wraith.'

In either case, however, since a haunting never occurs without a human being present, it is obvious that the human being is the conduit in these occurrences. This means we cannot subtract the environment from the analysis, since under the electric conditions of normal physical reality, human beings appear to somehow manifest these apports. Wilson has concluded, after careful consideration of hundreds of poltergeist cases, that the RSPK theory (Recurrent Spontaneous Psychokinesis) "leaves half the phenomena unexplained."

Haunted Places

Dr. Gregory Little suggests that there are "window areas" where spiritual phenomena or archetypes, such as apparitions of the Virgin Mary, enter the physical world. These are the sacred places which Martin Gray has mapped out in his book *Places of Peace and Power.* Dr. Little presents evidence in *People of the Web* that ancient rituals were conducted in ways that allowed the participants to tap the EM energy field. Dr. Little suggests that the percipient's brain chemistry has been altered by prayer, ritual, or expectations, which tunes them to a frequency which is aligned with the spirit apparition's specific frequency. Likewise, as Martin Gray has pointed out, different power places have different types of energy frequencies and have different types of influences on people, and tend to supply different kinds of information as well.

As Wilson notes, haunted monasteries and churches are often built on older religious sites, suggesting that the ground itself has some type of power of an electromagnetic nature. Such "haunted ground," he suggests, retains impressions of events which occurred at that location at another time. As anthropologist Evens-Wentz has noted, nature has a psychic element, or memory. He notes, "there is some indefinable psychic element in the earth's atmosphere upon which all human and physical actions or phenomena are photographed or impressed." As Talbot suggests, an apparition seems to be nothing more than a 3-D hologram of a past event, a memory written into the natural environment. He suggests that perhaps "hauntings" are not the product of earthbound spirit forms, but are accidental pluckings from the holographic continuum, or holomovement.

On the other hand, as the Kahuna explanation would have it, certain entities linger in these areas waiting for someone who can be used as a medium to provide the energy, or *mana*, it needs to manifest. Therefore, human beings are the energy providers in the trans-world conduit. The meeting space is Mind, yet this does not preclude the rearrangement of objects in the 3-D world. For, as Budden points out, the psychic theory of UFO manifestation is misunderstood because people mistakenly assume that 'psychic' events cannot have physical aspects.

As Guy Playfair points out in *This House is Haunted*, there is definitely a source of energy, since physical work is being carried out. Since this work is being carried out in the three-dimensional world, it follows that this activity has to obey some of the laws of mechanics. Playfair went on to compare this energy source, presumably the "poltergeist," to a crowd of mischievous children who find a football in a field and proceed to kick it around. He likens the football to an energy discharge, or plasma, which is leaking from a human being. This is the playground where, in Dr. Little's theory, the archetypes 'play ball' with the human psyche. The escape valve in this scenario, Playfair suggests, is the pineal gland, a sort of vestigial 'third eye' in the center of the brain. Particularly at puberty, the pineal gland exudes energy and secretes "psychic hormones," which can often be misused for animalistic purposes. If a proper outlet is lacking in the adolescent, Playfair maintains, the energy will be used by what he refers to as "marauding entities."

Mana

We've been taught by our materialist scientific paradigm that space is empty; there is no "ether" in space. But this is contrary to ancient, esoteric information as well as quantum/post-quantum physics paradigms. The vital force, or *mana*, of which the Kahunas speak seems to have a resemblance to electricity or magnetism; and, therefore, is connected to the electromagnetic force field of the entire earth. Whatever this energy source is, it seems to be concentrated in certain people and at certain locations on the earth.

According to the Kahunas, the invisible substance through which the vital force acts is called *aka*, or "shadowy body stuff" (akasha). This shadowy body is also a sticky body, which sticks to anything we see. The stickiness transfers itself through touch, and can be drawn out in long threads or conducting filaments. The Kahunas teach that via these spiderweb-like electrical conductors people can make out-of-body journeys while remaining connected to the physical body. This fine substance is like an umbilical cord through which communication flows and by which the astral body and dream body remain connected to the physical world. The Kahunas believed that thoughts are things, and are comprised of a subtle energy called *kino mea*. After leaving the mind, images and thoughts become thought-forms and are woven into the tapestry of the future. In this way, thoughts are the builders of future potential. (It follows that people who are not in control of their thought processes create chaos in the future.)

Playfair discusses in his book, *The Indefinite Boundary,* a Brazilian black magic cult called *Umbanda.* As Colin Wilson explains in *Poltergeist,* an *exús* is a discarnate spirit sent to spook a person in an exchange of favors. Wilson takes the following quote from Playfair:

> Incarnate man wants a favor done; he wants a better job, to marry a certain girl, to win the state lottery, … Discarnate spirits, for their part, want to enjoy the pleasures of the flesh once more; a good square meal, a drink of the best rum, a fine cigar, and perhaps even sexual relations with an incarnate being. … Who are these spirits?

> The Brazilian *Umbandistas* see them as inferior discarnates living in a low astral plane, who are close to the physical world, not having evolved since physical death. In *Umbanda* they are known as *exús*, spirits who have no morals at all, and are equally prepared to work for or against people. … These creatures are traditionally thought of as part human and part 'elemental,' integral forces of nature that can act upon human beings subject to certain conditions. There is an enormous number of *exús*, each with his own specialty. … An *exús* is a vain and temperamental entity, and despite his total lack of morals he is very fussy about observing the rituals properly.

Wilson comments that the Brazilian *exús* is "so much like the poltergeist that it is tempting to feel that we have finally pinned down his true nature and character." It's even more interesting that the *exús* also closely describes the nature and character of Budden's UI, the Unconscious Intelligence. For instance, the UI has its own specialty (dial tone or frequency); it is considered part of the integral forces of nature; it can act upon humans under certain electromagnetic environmental conditions; and it is a vain and temperamental entity in that its motivating purpose is to "establish and maintain an external social identity." As Budden claims, the UI wants expression in the conscious world; it wants "to carve out an important piece of the 'real world' for itself." And, like the Brazilian *exús*, it probably wouldn't turn down a good square meal, a drink of the best rum, a fine cigar and a romp in the hay.

In short, does all of this mean that apports are part of the psyche or part of the environment? As we've seen in earlier discussions of Mind-at-Large, this is not an easy question to answer, and is probably an incorrect question to pose in the first place. The reason is fundamental: the physics of Western science has finally met the Panpsychism of the ancient world. Mind is present in all matter. It's funny how human knowledge has a way of biting itself on the ass.

As John Mack has suggested, the language we use to describe our perceptual habits may not constitute *proof* of the way the cosmos is organized. Therefore, words like 'inner' and 'outer' may not actually be that helpful in a full description of reality. As Husserl has noted, there is a "profound schism" between what science tells us about the world and our spontaneous sensory experience of it.

Are 'they' entering our sphere of influence from a different Mind Space, or are 'we'going to them by visiting 'their' Mind Space? Who is really the visitor to the sacred places? Can sacred places move with the intention of the individual, as Martin Gray has suggested with his idea of "perambulatory shrines"? As Jim deKorne has noted in *Psychedelic Shamanism*, shamanic communication is a two-way street. And, as William Gray explains in *Magical Ritual Methods*, "there are quite enough Innerworld teachers waiting to guide and direct the work once earthly practitioners have built their side of the bridge between the two different dimensions."

As we've seen earlier, Jung thought of the archetypes as the psychic aspect of the inherited structure of the human brain. He considered the archetypes a tangible link between the psyche and *nature*. The archetypes are a connecting link between psyche and earth, a union or bridge between mind and matter. The archetypes maintain this bridge by using symbolic energy units. This implies that ancient magical systems are still in use by 'unconscious'brain mechanisms. However, they aren't unconscious so much as they are 'ultraconscious.' A quick aside to a phenomenological definition of "magic" is in order.

Magic: The Mind Dragging Among Things

The key that will make us masters of our inner nature has been rusty ever since the Flood. The secret is to be awake. To be awake is everything.

Gustav Meyrinck

If we consider the ideas of the phenomenologists, magic and its relationship to reality may be a wholly different phenomenon than we understand it to be. Merleau-Ponty clarifies this phenomenal (magical) relationship between the body and the sensible realm when he writes: "I give ear, or look, in the expectation of a sensation, and suddenly the sensible takes possession of my ear or my gaze, and I surrender a part of my body, even my whole body, to this particular manner of vibrating and filling space known as blue or red."

Jean Paul Sartre proposed that the world is in effect "a world of emotion," and the various human emotions have something in common, that is, "they make a same world appear, a world which is cruel, terrible, gloomy, joyful ... but one in which the relationship of things to consciousness is always and exclusively *magical*." Sartre provides an example. Let's say a grinning face appeared in the window which immediately sent a reaction of horror throughout your entire body. Phenomenologically speaking, your body is *invaded* by terror. Sartre explains that in this emotional moment, "consciousness is degraded and abruptly transforms the *determined* world in which we live into a *magical* world." Think about that. *You* haven't changed; the world has! As Ouspensky has noted in *Tertium Organum*, "the mystery of thought creates everything." He writes:

> As soon as we understand that thought is not a 'function of motion' and that motion itself is a *function of thought*; as soon as we begin to feel the depth of this mystery, we shall see that the whole world is a kind of vast hallucination which does not frighten us and does not make us think we are mad only because we are accustomed to it.

What Sartre is proposing is that the world sometimes reveals itself to consciousness as magical (open-ended, subjective) instead of determined (solid, objective). Your psychological survival response is to bring the world back to the confines of your safety nest: consensus-reality or "the cosmic egg." But sometimes there is a lag in doing this, during which your heart feels like it could have jumped out of your skin. When the gag is over we can laugh, but while we're suspended in Magical Existentia we have seemingly entered an aspect of the world which contains possibilities we would normally not entertain. Sartre clarifies, we need *not* believe that "the magical is an ephemeral quality which we *impose* upon the world as our moods dictate. *Here is an existential structure of the world which is magical..." (Essays,* 243) (Italics added)

The category "magical," in effect governs our interpsychic relations and our perception of others. Sartre saw the magical as "the mind dragging among things." Sartre defined magic as an irrational synthesis of spontaneity and passivity; or "consciousness rendered passive." This is the world before our intellect puts it through a recognizable filter or "reducing valve." Therefore, in this posture, "man is always a wizard to man, and the social world is at first magical." While it is possible to take a deterministic view of our interpsychic world and attempt to rationalize this magical world, which some certainly do with respect to high weirdness situations, the *rational superstructures* which make up our consensus-reality are actually "ephemeral and without equilibrium," in that they "*cave in* when the magical aspect of faces, of gestures, and of human situations, is too strong." *(Essays,* 244) This point of view may explain why nobody is a true *believer* until they have experienced strange phenomena first hand.

Perhaps imagination is not a separate mental faculty, but is the way the senses have of throwing themselves *beyond* in order to make tentative contact with the other sides of things that we do not sense directly. As Ouspensky has remarked, these may be the manifestations of the fourth dimension into our phenomenal world.

Speaking as a magician for many years, David Abram writes in *Spell of the Sensuous* that debunkers of magic, "encouraged by a cultural discourse that disdains the unpredictable and puts a premium on detached objectivity," attempt to halt the participation of their senses in the phenomenon by imagining other phenomena (wires, threads, mirrors), or by simply looking away and halting the act of participation. We always retain the ability to suspend any instance of participation, he writes. There will always be people who "simply will not see any magic, either at a performance or in the world at large," since the act of participation is always open-ended and unfinished, and we are never locked into any instance of participation. In essence, we see what we want to see.

What happens when, without sufficient notice to halt sensory participation, one finds him or her self immediately plunged into the irrational alternate Universe which lies on the other side of our rational superstructure? Sartre guesses that "consciousness seizes upon the magical as magical; and forcibly lives it as such."

Thus, the only way to get around the mind/matter corner we've painted ourselves into is to pose a different question. For, if we take the individual mind to be continuous and contiguous with a collective depository, the akashic records or Mind-at-Large, it becomes a contradiction in terms to wonder 'where' all of this is taking place. For, while we're asking 'where,' we are forgetting to ask 'why.' These 'innerworld' or ultradimensional contacts are telling us something about the nature of reality itself. A better way to look at this, rather than in internal/external dualistic terms, is that the Visitor phenomenon is not a visit by one party entering the space of another, but by both parties meeting in the middle: in the intersubjective realm. Mind-at-Large is a place that we are going to have to acknowledge if we are to move toward understanding the message. But before we can do that, we have to "wake up"!

Asleep at the Wheel

The out of control nature of the human condition is echoed by Dr. Little when he suggests that humans are trapped by our own biochemistry, and events that happen in the brain often just "take us along for the ride." This condition is also emphasized when Budden suggests that, "the brain is a vast memory bank where the conscious self feels like a visitor with only a limited number of access codes." If the conscious self is the visitor, then who is at the helm of the human vehicle? In this sense, is it the 'unconscious self' that's really in-the-know all of the time? As Amit Goswami has noted: the "unconscious seems to be conscious of all things all of the time." Therefore, perhaps we should call this entity or construct the "superconscious." For, if the 'unconscious' is really the operator of human consciousness, then, as Russian mystic G.I. Gurdjieff says, human beings are essentially asleep the wheel.

According to differing perceptual interpretations, 'awake' and 'asleep' are relative, not black and white, concepts. And, as phenomenologists, we must consider the points of view of other bodies of experience besides our own. Could it rather be that human beings are pretty much *always* asleep?

Media shaman Bob Dobbs claims the implementation of what he calls "the solar government," which he claims was "consolidated between 1945 and 1960 after television comprehensively extended the living drama of cognition," caused the disappearance of Earth's entire population, who were then replaced with holograms, or "holeopathic retrievals." The term "holeopathic" combines the concept of hologram with the concept of homeopathic: the dilution or essence of a substance taken in small doses. The tinier the dose the more potent it is. A hologram, as most of us know, can be described as an artificial environment indistinguishable from the reality upon which it's based. Thus, according to Dobbs, the tinier the hologram, the more realistic and engaging the artificial environment becomes. This means that succeeding generations are holograms of holograms of holograms, ad infinitum. Robert Guffey quotes Dobbs in his article "Syncronistic Linguistics in The Matrix, or How Bob Dobbs Became the Tetrad Manager" in *Paranoia: The Conspiracy Reader*. A holeopathic retrieval, according to Dobbs, is the flip-side or correspondence of the nature body to its holographic essence or dilution. Interestingly, Dobbs stated the following in a 1988 interview:

> Magnetic City is the whole world in a little acoustic imitation of resonating electromagnetic white light. We're all on that little node. It can't be visualized, but the whole world is on that spot all the time, and that's the state of being discarnate. To someone who wants to have visual parameters, that's a very claustrophobic thing to imagine. But we are stuck in that. That's why people are channeling. That's why people are doing all the various things that have been surprising to Americans for the past twenty years. They're trying to erase their body, and the motive for that is the sensory-structural change resulting from electric conditions. Did you know that even speaking, even not being in a trance, is a form of trance under electric conditions? Just walking around is a form of trance today because any bodily activity is inside this little electronic, discarnate node of consciousness called Magnetic City.

In this article, Guffey also notes an interesting parallel which has been expressed by hypnotist Jack True. As Guffey writes, True states that he has stopped performing hypnosis on most people because most of his clients are already in a hypnotic trance as a natural state of affairs. True has noted that: "The modern idea that surrounds our society is that by being very nice you will fit into the system around you and everyone else will be happy with you. The only thing is, everything around you is hypnotic. I mainly find myself doing reverse-hypnosis these days. I do things to wake people up."

In this regard, G.I. Gurdjieff has probably best described the entranced human condition as perpetually asleep at the wheel. Gurdjieff is quoted in Pauwels and Bergier's *Dawn of Magic* as follows:

> In order to understand the difference between states of consciousness, let us return to the first state of consciousness, which is sleep. This is an entirely subjective state of consciousness. A man is immersed in dreams. ... Even if some real impressions reach him, such as sounds, voices, warmth, cold, the sensation of his own body, they arouse in him only fantastic subjective images. Then a man wakes up. At first glance this is quite a different state of consciousness. He can move, he can talk with other people, he can make calculations ahead, he can see danger and avoid it, and so on. It stands to reason that he is in a better position than when he was asleep.

> But if we take a look into his inner world, into his thoughts, into the causes of his actions, we shall see that he is in almost the same state as when he is asleep. And it is even worse, because in sleep he is passive, that is, he cannot do anything. In the waking state, however, he can do something all the time and the results of all his actions will be reflected upon him or upon those around him. And yet he does not remember himself. He is a machine, everything with him happens. He cannot stop the flow of his thoughts, he cannot control his imagination, his emotions, his attention. ... He lives in sleep. He is asleep. What is called 'clear consciousness' is sleep and a far more dangerous sleep than sleep at night in bed.

Gurdjieff believed that all of mankind's actions are done under the essential spell of 'sleep,' or total oblivion of the self. What Gurdjieff meant is that mankind is never really conscious of himself, or of who is at the wheel of his conscious life. He professed that our real consciousness is almost always completely absent from everything we do, think, or imagine. He regarded the essential and perpetual state of consciousness as that of a trance, or 'waking sleep.' As Ouspensky remarked in *Tertium Organum,* "it seems to us that we see something and understand something. But in actual fact we have but a very dim sense of all that is happening around us, just as a snail has a dim sense of the sunlight, the rain, the darkness."

Gurdjieff taught his followers that the only way to awaken is to first become convinced of the very fact that we are asleep. He believed that if all of mankind awoke from sleep, they would suddenly stop killing each other; all wars would come to an abrupt halt, for wars are carried out by people who are essentially sleep walking. He maintained that to awaken is the most difficult thing, because "this sleep is induced and maintained by the whole of surrounding life, by all surrounding conditions." As Bob Dobbs has maintained, this condition is the "electric condition," a "discarnate node of consciousness called Magnetic City." To Dobbs, this diluted point or "node" of discarnate consciousness, an "acoustic imitation of resonating electromagnetic white light," is the current state of the human condition. As Albert Budden has suggested, this condition of electrical overload causes human beings to "hallucinate" in droves. As Dobbs would have it, however, this condition causes human beings to "channel" in droves. He argues, "that's why people are channeling. That's why people are doing all the various things that have been surprising to Americans for the past twenty years. They're trying to erase their body, and the motive for that is the sensory-structural change resulting from electric conditions."

By making a serious effort to awaken from this induced condition of sleep, a person can become convinced of this essential condition. Because once one tries to awaken, he realizes he cannot do so by himself. Gurdjieff believed that a pact must be made among many people to watch over the rest, and that all of them must be looked after by someone who is not asleep, or who does not succumb to sleep as easily as the rest, or who is conscious while asleep. Gurdjieff wrote, "they must find such a man and hire him to wake them and not allow them to fall asleep again." They must find someone who will keep on shaking them, and perhaps who will administer shocks when necessary. And they must find someone else who will look after the man who has been hired to shake them and shock them. Therefore, a combined effort is required.

As John Mack has suggested, we've got to look at words like "awake" and "asleep" in relative context. As Gustav Meyrinck once wrote, "the key that will make us masters of our inner nature has been rusty ever since the Flood. The secret is to be awake. To be awake is everything." But to be awake is to be aware that everybody else is asleep.

The Satellite Phase of Civilization

In his book, The New Renaissance: Computers and the Next Level of Civilization, Douglas Robertson explains that the most important dividing points in the history of civilization were each accompanied by an invention that caused an information explosion. Such information explosions have a tendency to propel civilization to the next level, since, Robertson notes, civilizations are "generally limited more by lack of information than by lack of physical resources." As he explains, Level 1 is the emergence of language; Level 2 is the development of writing systems; Level 3 is the invention of the printing press and the publication of books; and Level 4 is the computer age. Each of these levels increases the storage capacity for information. As he writes:

> Even a Level 3 civilization can generate information at a rate that far exceeds anyone's ability to make use of it. Electronic computers, however, are capable of creating a totally new dimension in an information explosion. Computers can multiply our ability to find, analyze, and make use of vast quantities of extant information, thereby circumventing the information limits that bedeviled Level 3 civilization.

As Robertson explains, each of the three information explosions which occurred in the past produced a society that was "largely unrecognizable to an individual from an earlier civilization." Indeed, the current Level 4 information explosion will proceed at a much quicker pace than the previous three. As Robertson notes, "the difference between the 20th and the 21st centuries may well be greater than the difference between the 20th and the 13th (A.D. or B.C.)." Robertson notes the same peculiarity of Level 4 civilization as does Bob Dobbs: the extension of civilization into outer space environments. As Robertson notes, "one way to appreciate the full capability of a Level 4 civilization is to recognize that the Apollo moon landings were among the first (and presumably the simplest) examples of accomplishments that are possible only in a Level 4 civilization."

Dobbs has noted the same, except that he has taken it far beyond this analysis. Dobbs describes how the technological advances of Level 4 have actually changed the nature of the human being. Dobbs believes that humanity itself has become a technological extension: a "holeopathic retrieval." Yet, he believes that it is possible to return to our own anthropomorphic (First Nature) bodies with complete awareness of how the body was lost in the first place. He believes that under the present "electric conditions," the Second Nature body (technological extension) is over-stimulated to the point of constant awareness. In Magnetic City, he maintains, "nobody sleeps" because nobody has a real body. According to Dobbs, Second Nature is a technological extension of the human being; an artifact of the First Nature embodied condition. A person who awakens to this condition is then free to "flip out" of the body and become discarnate and then return to the First Nature body, and flip back and forth between First Nature [original nature] and Second Nature [virtual reality] at will. This is how human beings have been channeling, and having other out of body experiences.

Remember that Merleau-Ponty, as well as Husserl before him, suggested that "the world is not a given place in which experience occurs, but is that toward which one is turned in experience." Might this mean that we in a sense aren't really here, or that being 'here' is just an attitude toward which we choose to turn, and not a fixed concrete reality?

Human beings are inextricably tied to the phenomenal world; we are beings-in-the-world. We cannot divorce our First Nature existence from what we are, yet we have an undeniable Second Nature extension in what has been called Mind-at-Large. In addition, as Dobbs points out, our current technological level has the propensity to extend Second Nature to the Nth degree. This is most obvious in the present 'urgency' to move human beings off the planet and into a home away from home in deep space. As Dobbs has pointed out, what we have in our attempts to get off planet is the first simultaneous extension of both First and Second Natures. As Dobbs explained in an essay for *Semiotexte*:

> There is an inescapable trend leading toward ultimate implosion from the Telegraph phase to the Satellite phase. The satellite is an important marker in this evolution towards fusion. If you consider every technological environment an extension of the human crowd, or entropic social Nature, rather than of biological Nature (First Nature), then because the satellite is alone of all technologies a complete extension of the planet, or First Nature, by being the first man-made inhabitable simulation of our 'natural' environment, it follows that the satellite is the first simultaneous extension of both First and Second Natures, and something unique and unprecedented has occurred. This merging of the two Natures 'anticipates' and prefigures symbolically the bridging of the gap ("friction") between humanity and the environment. Also this frictionless condition is anticipated by the satellite as a symbol of the individual detachment from the historical prison of the crowd dynamic. We are literally 'out of town,' and not just in another town, but 'off the planet.'

Dobbs claims to be the leader of "The Secret Council of Ten," a secret group that controls the world with techniques which he calls "synchronistic-linguistics" and "tetrad management." The "tetrad" is a 4-step process that analyzes the projected evolution of man-made artifacts, and is a means of predicting the future of humanity by predicting the future of its technology. Dobbs believes that he won the election for world "Tetrad Manager" by rigging the election. Dobbs' goal now as Tetrad Manager is to help humanity to retrieve their lost human-scale identity.

Dobbs includes technology as part of "synchronistic linguistics." As he explains, the media (and even Dan Rather) practices synchronistic-linguistics. Tetrad management, he explains, is management of the Global Theater by the shadow government through synchronistic linguistics, which numbs and entrances its viewers using the "audience participation mystique." The media works to make you think you're part of something. But you're not, because it's all a great big hologram.

As P.D. Ouspensky has noted, the 'appearance' of the 3-D material world is a property of human perception and cognition, and not a property of the world per se. Many have noted that this 'appearance' is much like a hologram. In addition, studies have corroborated the hypothesis that the mind works "holographically." For instance, Carl Pribram hypothesized a holographic model to explain how the brain convinces us that inner processes are actually located outside the body. Also, David Bohm's well known quantum physics theories suggest that the universe operates as a kind of giant, flowing hologram.

Dobbs believes he is the "tetrad flip," or the mirror to the Tetrad Managers. As one radio caller pointed out, they strive for total control but the thing they can't control is the real natural phenomenon of "synchronicity." This is because synchronicity is the real world (First Nature) leaking through to the Second Nature sleeper. Synchronicity has been described as a "flaw" in the fabric of space-time. You might even see it as a leak, in the Dobbsian perspective.

There is a relationship between Gurdjieff's concept of waking sleep as a perception of the human condition and the Dobbsian idea of electric conditions and discarnate consciousness. As Dobbs has stated, "just walking around is a form of trance today because any bodily activity is inside this little electronic, discarnate node of consciousness called Magnetic City." As Dobbs also stated in one radio interview:

> They can't control your private citadel of consciousness, and that means they can't control *you*, but they can control our synthetic crowd behavior. That's what you've got to realize ... they *are* controlling us through synchronistic-linguistics. They call it the audience participation mystique.

It is in the Sartrean experience of nausea that we also sense that there are two possible modes of experience: the nature body and the virtual body, or, the Dobbsian First Nature and Second Nature experience. Perceptually speaking, most of the time, we're pretty much at home with "the rock, the tree, the sky," the Sartrean "brute thereness" of things-in-being or facts-at-hand. But in the experience of First Nature (man as animal), the world is brute, solid and manifest, and is in striking contrast to mankind's Second Nature experience—Mind-at-Large—an enormous intelligence matrix which has been described by physicists as a hologram. We are both brute animals and transient beings all in one confounded package. With First Nature as background, human Second Nature experience emerges as meaningless, and even unnecessary. It sticks out like a sore thumb. Mind-at-Large is like Dobbsian Second Nature virtual reality. It is Sartrean excess. It's flamboyant and absurd.

In the Dobbsian scheme, human beings are capable of flipping between First and Second Nature once they become conscious of it. Dobbs' tetrad flip is consonant with Magic. As Regardie writes in *What You Should Know About the Golden Dawn*, "the whole object of Magic and mystical training is, by the intervention of the symbol, ceremonial and sacrament, to lead the soul that it may be withdrawn from the attraction of matter and delivered from the absorption therein, whereby it walks in somnambulism, knowing not whence it cometh nor whither it goeth."

Yet, mankind is the only Be-ing capable of doing this, and this is what constitutes the difference between 'being' and 'facticity,'or Sartre's "in-itself," the brute *thereness* of "things" in life, and the "for-itself," or self-consciousness. It is in the experience of what Sartre has termed 'nausea'that the human being has realized his impotence in the reconciliation of 'subject' and 'object', or the reconciliation of consciousness and things. As Sartre reasons, somewhere in this reconciliation lies man's freedom. Is this "freedom" essentially the freedom to kick up and out of the system? Is it the freedom to "wake up" to our responsibility as beings above and beyond First Nature physical existence?

As Gurdjieff so wisely said, wars would stop as soon as human beings awoke to the fact that they were performing these barbaric acts under the spell of sleep. In the Dobbsian view, war is "synthetic crowd behavior." It is thought control through synchronistic linguistics ("be all that you can be, get an edge on life in the Army.") War on television allows us to vicariously participate in heinous crimes against our fellow man and to revel in our nationalistic victories. Television needs wars as much as armies and governments need wars in order to effectuate the audience participation mystique through linguistic flips. The way that these are pulled off on the human psyche is through archetypes; in this case, the particular archetype of confounded speech is Mercury.

The Sumerians believed that it was Enki, or Mercury, who confounded the speech of mankind. The same god, known to the Egyptians as Hermes or Thoth, is widely known as "speech itself." Thoth could "teach a man not only words of power, but also the manner in which to utter them." Does this describe Dobbs' notion of synchronistic linguistics or Tetrad Management, the media's linguistic control of "synthetic crowd behavior"?

I wonder if Dobbs is one of the wakers whom Gurdjieff had in mind; an undaunted shaker, mover and zapper (Dobbs says Frank Zappa was also one of them) of the human zombies who sleepwalk the artificially induced electric conditions of the surrounding environment; originally an ancient planetary catastrophic event or even a recurring cosmic effect, as discussed in Volume I of this book, which has grown exponentially via the radiation of out-of-control technological noise.

The technological noise is certainly getting louder by the day. In what way does this affect our ability to flip between First Nature and Second Nature? (Ingo Swann and Hal Puthoff have actually addressed this problem with respect to remote viewing and its "signal-to-noise ratio" – see Chapter Eight). The Dobbsian "tetrad flip" might be orchestrated by the ancient notion of the 'archetype.' As Jung has noted, the archetypes are the images or symbols by which the psyche is attached to nature, or, by which "its link with the *earth* and the world appears at its most tangible." He noted that the archetypes are a sort of "connecting link between psyche and *earth*," or a bridge between mind and matter. Rupert Sheldrake believes these forms constitute an "intelligent" energy matrix.

As noted earlier, while the archetype is part of the brain structure, it is that part of the brain structure which is constantly building and maintaining the bridge between psyche and matter, keeping familiar territory familiar. If the brain is a hologram, this means that the intelligent energy fields that maintain this hologram are, perhaps, the archetypes, an intelligent holographic energy matrix which constantly maintains the bridge between the individual psyche and the world we project 'out there.'

CHAPTER SEVEN

SHAMEN IN ARMY BOOTS: REMOTE VIEWING: HUMAN "USE" OR HUMAN "POTENTIAL"?

Remote viewing was like switching on a beacon within the Matrix. It attracted strange things, the way a porch light attracts bugs on a hot summer night.

Jim Schnabel

Remote Viewers

In much the same way that the CIA introduced the mind-expanding LSD experience into a closeted youth culture of the 1960s and 70s, the CIA has now introduced "remote viewing" into a mainstream culture totally unprepared for its potential repercussions on an "uninitiated" psyche. Remote viewing has become a tool of the masses, being extensively peddled on the Internet with an 'anyone can do it' attitude. Several businesses offer the services of a staff of trained remote viewers to perform various tasks, from locating missing persons or underground oil deposits, to other aspects of police, private, corporate or government investigative work. These companies also offer expensive courses in various styles of remote viewing. On their own time, some of these RVers have been known to human-satellite the ancient cities of Mars, time-track the builders of the Earth pyramids, and zoom in on alien craft with extraterrestrial occupants.

The current fascination with mind tools stems, at least in part, from quantum physics revelations essentially telling us that mind is *cause* rather than *effect*. Humanity's disposition has shifted from material *effect* to conscious *cause*, a concept known in New Age circles as "human potential." What's missing from the picture is our incremental "initiation" into the culture of this knowledge, a life-long education which in ancient times went hand in hand with mystic revelation. The background of knowledge necessary to understand this philosophical shift is missing; and our total picture is distorted. We've got the power, but we don't know how to use it.

What exactly is this enigma called "remote viewing"? Upon what foundations are its assumptions based? What is the intelligence community's interest in such 'human potential'phenomena? Can 'anyone'really be taught to surf the outermost interior of the conscious matrix and come back with information dependable enough for espionage purposes? Are there any human hazards?

Remote Viewing: A Short History

On August 7, 1977, John Wilhelm published an article in the *Washington Post* describing a series of "remote viewing" experiments supported by the CIA. In the article, Wilhelm explained that several psychics at a "think tank" called Stanford Research Institute (SRI – not affiliated with Stanford University) had allegedly succeeded in mentally viewing and describing a secret military installation in Virginia. Several publications in the following few years reported on the alleged military application of remote viewing, and described how psychics were training Navy and CIA personnel to develop their own remote viewing skills.

Physicist Harold Puthoff and scientist Russell Targ claimed that their work at SRI proved that psychics could remotely spy on any military installation in the world. The first three psychics to work at SRI were Ingo Swann, Pat Price, and Uri Geller. In 1973, the CIA and NSA arranged a top-secret demonstration of the SRI remote viewing program, called Project SCANATE, wherein Swann and Price described geographical coordinates in detail. In 1977, Swann and five other SRI subjects were even put to the test in a submarine 2,000 feet below the ocean.

As a result of President Clinton's Executive Order #1995-4-17, issued on April 17, 1995, the CIA was obliged to declassify information pertaining to its funding of programs in psi-related phenomena and, in particular, its interest in remote viewing. In July, 1995, 270 pages of reports pertaining to the remote viewing program at SRI were declassified and released by the CIA. This was the first public disclosure of the government and intelligence community's two decade-long interest in psychic phenomena.

In a paper entitled "CIA Initiated Remote Viewing at Stanford Research Institute," Dr. Puthoff finally discusses the program in detail. He writes: "it was not until 1995 that I found myself for the first time able to utter in a single sentence the connected acronyms CIA/SRI/RV." In this document, Puthoff reports on the results of the program and the direction the program took "as it expanded into a multi-year, multi-site, multi-million dollar effort to determine whether such phenomena as remote viewing might have any utility for intelligence collection."

As Dr. Puthoff's story begins, in a casual meeting at SRI with psychic Ingo Swann, Puthoff had been impressed with Swann's remarkable ability to describe in detail the interior of a specific apparatus located in a vault below the floor of the building, which was shielded by several layers of various metals. Puthoff wrote up the report and circulated it to a few of his colleagues to get some feedback. Within a few weeks, he was paid a visit by some men in black who held his report in hand. According to Puthoff, the CIA agents told him the intelligence community was increasingly concerned about "the level of effort in Soviet parapsychology being funded by the Soviet security services." The agency was interested in meeting Ingo Swann.

Swann and Puthoff agreed to undergo some simple experiments. The "visitors," as Puthoff refers to them, put Swann through a series of simple experiments which were impressive enough to begin an 8-month pilot study utilizing double-blind scientific protocols. Puthoff writes: "over the years the back-and-forth criticism of protocols, refinement of methods, and successful replication of this type of remote viewing in independent laboratories, has yielded considerable scientific evidence for the reality of the phenomenon." In addition, CIA contract monitors also participated in these protocols as remote viewers themselves. Puthoff & Company (pun intended) discovered that "a growing number of individuals could be found to demonstrate high-quality remote viewing, often to their own surprise."

The Final Report to the CIA, dated December 1, 1975, described various RV experiments carried out over the course of the pilot program from January 1974 through February 1975, including the remote viewing and detailed drawing/description of a West Virginia sensitive government facility. The details of this particular remote viewing session remain highly classified. Pat Price later went on to describe and draw in detail a Communist Bloc installation in the Urals. In July of 1974, another research installation in Semipalatinsk, USSR, was successfully remote-viewed by Price.

The results of this experiment, in particular the detailed drawing of a crane which was considered "a relatively unusual target item," were promising. As Pat Price "roamed the facility," several details of this site seemed to correspond with actual data, and several large structures were correctly described. At the end of 1975, as the results of tests in the pilot phase of the RV program at SRI traveled government and intelligence circles, intense interest was expressed. According to Puthoff, the program was expanded to a "multi-client base" and was eventually integrated under Defense Intelligence Agency leadership.

Several agencies began to contract studies at SRI, including NASA and the Navy, and several remote viewers were added to the team.

The identity of other government clients remain classified, but may be declassified in the near future, states Puthoff. He maintains that the RV program at SRI was directed not so much toward developing U.S. capability, but rather "toward assessing the potential threat of its use against the U.S. by others." In the early years of the program, Puthoff explains, the words "threat assessment" and "threat analysis" were often used with respect to the aim of the program. With regard to the physics of these unusual experiments, Puthoff concludes:

> Despite the ambiguities inherent in the type of exploration covered in these programs, the integrated results appear to provide unequivocal evidence of a human capacity to access events remote in space and time, however falteringly, by some cognitive process not yet understood. My years of involvement as a research manager in these programs have left me with the conviction that this fact must be taken into account in any attempt to develop an unbiased picture of the structure of reality.

Unusual States of Consciousness

Psi researcher Viola P. Neal has noted that certain rare individuals are able to project, while fully awake, a sort of "mental thought form" of themselves which is visible to others at distant locations. In a 1973 paper entitled "Unusual States of Consciousness," Neal describes the "bi-location" phenomenon as distinctly different from "astral projection." In the case of astral projection, individuals are not awake or fully conscious. Conversely, in the bi-location phenomenon, she explains, the individuals are fully awake and occupied in their own locale, or even conversing with others, while at the same time a projected image of themselves is witnessed by others at a distant locale. In the phenomenon of bi-location, the individual may or may not be aware that a self-image is being projected at another location. Neal states, "the instances of Padre Pio projecting such images of himself are well authenticated by very reliable witnesses."

Another unusual state of consciousness described by Viola Neal is the "clairvoyant." This type of psychic sees a sort of mental picture flash on the "screen" of the mind. As Dr. Neal suggests, "one would presume that such a picture always exists in time and space but that only a few people have the type of ability to receive the pictures clearly." Dr. Neal also adds that certain clairvoyants can see, while fully conscious, both the inner and outer states of an object, and may even get "a multi-dimensional moving picture, from the bio-plasmic level through the emotional and mental dimensions." As she concludes: "with training and effort an individual with this type of gift can give very accurate information about the state of mind, emotion or health of the subject under observation."

The above descriptions are somewhat helpful in assessing what might be occurring in the phenomenon of remote viewing. With regard to the clairvoyance phenomenon, remote viewers have reportedly been able to give a description of American political hostages and their state of health. It would appear that the remote viewing phenomenon may be best described as a clairvoyance phenomenon rather than bi-location phenomenon, since it has not actually been asserted that these individuals have been witnessed by others at the distant locations they claim to visit (with the exception of subjective reports that ETs do tend to have an awareness of the projected image of the remote viewer). As a matter of fact, actual "bi-location" would appear to be a very rare phenomenon indeed. However, a possible explanation might be that witnesses at the target locale are unable to see the projected image of the body double, since it takes another specially gifted person to perceive the image of a bi-located individual.

As we might also wonder, what is the difference between these out-of-body (OBE) states and lucid dreaming or hypnotic states? In his 1965 OBE studies ("Six Studies of Out-of-Body Experiences"), published in 1997 in the *Journal of Near Death Studies*, Dr. Charles Tart studied two frequent flyers, whom he called Mr. X and Miss Z. In order to test whether OBE has a "reality aspect," a 5-digit random number was written in large figures on a cardboard strip and placed on a shelf. Once in the OBE state, the subject was instructed to travel to the equipment room and try to memorize the string of numbers written on the card.

In one instance, Mr. X was able to float out of his cot and into the hallways. In another, he encountered several people and touched one of them. In yet another, he floated to another room to greet the technician and her husband, and was later able to describe the man in detail even though he had never met him. However, he failed to read the 5-digit number, most likely because he forgot that he was supposed to. During another OBE, Mr. X tried to take a short cut by following the EEG cable through the wall to the equipment room. But, instead of ending up in the equipment room he ended up outside the building.

Charles Tart concluded that OBEs are a mixture of dreams and "something else." The dream aspect is concluded from their "apparent conjunction with a Stage 1 EEG pattern." On the other hand, there was a fair amount of conjunction with reality, which suggested that extrasensory perception was occurring. He also noted that Mr. X's OBEs seemed to occur during a "prolonged, deliberately produced hypnogogic state" (Stage 1 EEG), which is not normally seen in the laboratory. Another frequent flyer, Miss Z, awakened and correctly reported the target number located in the equipment room. She also stated that several OBE attempts had been necessary, since "I needed to go higher because the number was lying down." According to Tart she was correct. The card was not leaning against the wall, it was lying flat on the shelf. Tart writes, the odds against guessing a 5-digit number by chance alone are 100,000 to 1.

Subjects can also be hypnotized to have OBEs. In a 1970 UC Davis study, Tart selected a small group of individuals who were in the upper 10% of hypnotic susceptibility. The hypnotized subjects were instructed to bilocate, enter a locked room to observe target materials on a table, and describe what they saw. All of the subjects reported vivid and realistic OBEs. However, Tart reports, none of their descriptions of the target materials bore any clear resemblance to reality. He writes, "a formal analysis was not worth the trouble."

Are OBEs simply "dreams"? Tart's conclusion after decades of research is that "in *some* OBEs, the mind may, at least partially, really be located elsewhere than the physical body." An OBE can also be a *simulation* of being out of the body, in the case of the hypnotized subjects. Tart concluded: "we can have OBEs which are basically a *simulation* of being out, but which are informed by information gathered by ESP such that the simulation of the OBE location is accurate and veridical."

Our current model of consciousness, he concludes, is inadequate to describe these phenomena. We must realize, Tart explains, that the feeling that we are situated "in" our bodies or heads, is itself a construction, or "world simulation." He notes that ordinary consciousness may be "a process that creates an ongoing, dynamic simulation of reality, a world model, an inner theater of the mind, a bio-psychological virtual reality 'in' which consciousness dwells." Furthermore, most of the brain mechanisms which construct the dream world may just be the same mechanisms that construct our waking world. Ordinary reality, or what Tart termed in 1973 as "consensus-reality," is actually a complex construction, strongly determined by social consensus.

Lucid Dreams as Holograms

The above studies indicate that locating the 'place' where we might all agree that these phenomena are 'real' may be even more elusive than we think.

Decades of ESP and dream research conducted at the Maimonides Dream Laboratory in Brooklyn, reportedly funded by CIA conduits during the 1960s and 70s, support the hypothesis that in dreams we are able to communicate in thus far scientifically unexplainable ways.

As Michael Talbot argues in *The Holographic Universe*, the unending flow of wisdom and counsel contained in dreams suggests that Bohm's "implicate order" represents an infinite and collective information source. Bohm has suggested that perhaps dreams are a sort of bridge between the manifest and non-manifest orders of reality, and represent a natural transformation of the implicate order into the explicate order. Physicist Fred Alan Wolf believes that all dreams are internal holograms, and that the brain has the ability to generate real images. He believes our minds create the illusion of objective external reality via the same process that allows the lucid dreamer to create its subjective internal reality. Yet, Wolf is not so sure that lucid dreams are subjective at all. He postulates that lucid dreams, if not all dreams, are visits to parallel universes, in that they are smaller holograms within the all-encompassing cosmic hologram. Lucid dreams might be thought of as "parallel universe awareness." Wolf suggests that perhaps parallel universes arise as other images within the universal hologram.

As an example, artist and lucid dreamer Paul Laffoley describes in *The Phenomenology of Revelation* an overwhelmingly emotional lucid dream which he believes was a mystical revelation. In the dream, he was walking up Newbury Street in Boston, and realized he was dreaming. He then excitedly entered an art gallery that he had not noticed before. Once inside the gallery, he realized that the exhibit contained "physically alive architecture." He writes:

> Here were things that were vibrant and even more alive than the people who were wandering around looking at them. ... The sculptures were horrible, not because they looked like something out of a horror film, but because they were inexorably alive. ... They seemed more alive than my vision of aliveness, and compared with my vision of maturity they had a supermaturity. It seemed possible that they were not life forms at all, but some other modality of being.

The thirteen sculptures in the dream exhibit had a "surreal aura." The sculptures were displayed on top of pedestals, and each one occupied about a four-foot cube of space, but somehow seemed to contain more space. When he reached out to touch them, they seemed to recede. Laffoley writes:

> My outstretched hand penetrated them like a ghost going through a door or Lewis Carroll's Alice going through the Looking Glass. As I probed, my progress inward became more and more difficult. It was as if my hand had entered a powerful and palpable electromagnetic field. Although I continued to see these entities as works of art, I began to realize that they were unbelievably brilliant—both intellectually and visually. They embodied a kind of iridescent scholasticism. In short, they were bodies of light.

As Paul began to stare at one of the sculptures, a strange impression came over him that the sculpture had an infinite number of sense organs. Suddenly he became aware that he had become the knowledge, and the sculpture was the knower. He felt he was being subsumed. He recalls:

> My modality of consciousness seemed mechanical in comparison with that of the sculpture's. Finally I realized the import of what was happening. At this point, alone with the sculpture, I was overcome with terror. I was fully awake, but I knew I was trapped in the gallery and would surely die if I did not get out of this dream and out of the presence of these 'sculptures.'One of them had got me somehow and I had to escape.

According to Sir David Cherubim of the Thelemic Order of the Golden Dawn, experiences of the most exalted type cannot be defined in human terms.

They are beyond man's power to know; "he must experience a different species of consciousness to understand what is beyond knowledge." In contemplating the essence of this dream over the years, Laffoley realized that this lucid dream experience was the closest he had come to death. He writes: "I believe that I left our physical universe, the fourth dimensional realm of Time-Solvoid, which is life, and entered the fifth dimensional realm of Eternity-Vosolid, which is death." However, Paul believes that after this dream his widely acclaimed visionary art began to develop into what it is today.

The Monroe Institute

To continue with the remote viewing story, the RV program at SRI was eventually moved to Fort Meade under the auspices of Major General Albert Stubblebine. Stubblebine began to send designated Army personnel to the Monroe Institute in Virginia for a "professional development" course, which was creatively labeled "Rapid Advanced Personal Training," or RAPT, in order for the Army to pay the tab. The Monroe course thereafter became required training for all Army remote viewers.

Robert Monroe began to have out-of-body experiences in 1956, and began his research in "sleep-learning" in 1958. In 1974, he founded the Monroe Institute in Lovingston, Virginia, which is reputed to have long-standing ties with the CIA. The primary area of research at the Monroe Institute is the use of their patented "HemiSync" tapes. This method involves use of a "binaural beat" to cause psychological effects. According to Tom Porter, the more radical research going on at the Monroe Institute "remains only tantalizing speculation."

Dr. Charles Tart has recently disclosed that "Mr. X," the subject of his 1965 OBE experimental research, was the infamous frequent flyer Robert Monroe. Monroe has claimed that his OBEs began to occur spontaneously following bouts with insomnia in the 1950s. However, in 1997, the Monroe Institute's Research Director, Skip Atwater, claimed the Institute had been "refining" binaural-beat technology for over thirty years. (see the following papers at www.monroe-inst.com/research) This suggests that Monroe may have been testing this method at the time of Tart's studies in 1965 and 1968, since Tart characterized Monroe's "prolonged" hypnogogic state as "deliberately produced." He noted that the high amount of theta rhythms and the occasional slowed alpha paralleled the EEG states reported for advanced Zen masters during meditation. It is also possible that Monroe may have been very talented at meditation.

Monroe's high theta activity is positively correlated with hypnotic susceptibility. In turn, highly hypnotizable people have been shown to exhibit "preternatural" skills, such as clairvoyance, psychokinesis and shamanic healing. Theatrical parlor tricks of the 1800s featured such talented "somnambules." A recent study conducted at No. AZ University using Monroe's HemiSync binaural beat technology showed that HemiSync can increase hypnotic susceptibility in persons who had not previously been highly hypnotizable. A state of hypnogogia associated with hyper-suggestive states of consciousness is produced after minutes of exposure to the HemiSync signals.

This paper also states that Robert Monroe "has been granted several patents for applications of psychophysical entrainment via sound patterns." Two of these patents are listed by Judy Wall and Mike Coyle in "Technology to Boggle Your Mind," in *Paranoia* (Issue 24) as follows:

> Method of and Apparatus for Inducing Desired States of Consciousness, U.S. Patent #5,356,368, Robert Monroe, granted October 18, 1994. Improved methods and apparatus for entraining human brain patterns, employing frequency following response (FFR) techniques, facilitate attainment of desired states of consciousness.

Method of Inducing Mental, Emotional, and Physical States of Consciousness, Including Specific Mental Activity, in Human Beings, U.S. Patent #5,213,562, Robert Monroe, granted May 25, 1993.

It is likely that these patents were applied for many years prior to the dates they were granted, and it is also possible that the government had a 'gag order' imposed on these patents for several years. It is also possible that these patents are modifications of much earlier patents.

Studies published on the Monroe Institute's web site indicate that the binaural beat-induced state of consciousness is described as "mind awake/body asleep." This common hypnogogic experience occurs naturally in the netherland between waking and sleeping and is characterized by an oblivion to location of extremities (hands and feet) without losing consciousness (i.e., falling asleep). By using stereo headphones which emit a slightly different beat frequency in each ear, the difference in tone creates a brain wave on which the human brain easily "entrains" or becomes "driven." Some published papers in the Monroe Institute's web site disagree that the word "entrainment" is descriptive of how the HemiSync sound method works. These researchers claim that HemiSync "guides" the brain to enhance and synchronize itself at its own natural frequency, and is "a safe modality for health improvement."

With regard to this statement, as Judy Wall explains in "Technology to Boggle Your Mind," private inventions may very well be intended for positive uses, such as sound induction through the skull for those with hearing loss, but they could just as well be put to negative "control" uses. Also, what the government has in classified research is anybody's guess, and the CIA has followed its own course with regard to creating "subprojects" to review patents in this area and to adopt these psychophysical manipulation technologies for their own use. A CIA MK-ULTRA document speaks for itself. This recently declassified document, entitled "Memorandum for the Record, Subject: MK-ULTRA, Subproject 119," dated 17 August 1960 (and reproduced in the above-cited article), states the following:

1. The purpose of this subproject is to provide funds for a study conducted by [redacted] to take a critical review of the literature and scientific developments related to the recording, analysis and interpretation of bioelectric signals from the human organism, and activation of human behavior by remote means. When initiated this study was being done on a consultant basis by [redacted]. The reason for converting this into a Subproject is to provide more flexibility in the disbursal of funds for various kinds of assistance and equipment needed.

2. As indicated in the attached proposal this study is to provide an annotated bibliography and an interpretive survey of work being done in psychophysiological research and instrumentation. The survey encompasses five main areas: a. Bioelectric sensors: sources of significant electrical potential and methods of pick-up. b. Recording: amplification, electronic tape and other multi-channel recording. c. Analysis: autocorrelators, spectrum analyzers, etc. and coordination with automatic data processing equipment. d. Standardization of data for correlation with biochemical, physiological and behavioral indices. e. Techniques of activation of the human organism by remote electronic means.

Psychological theories suggest that certain HemiSync frequencies allow the unconscious mind to transcend ego defense mechanisms, which facilitates communication between the two hemispheres. Also, whole-brain synchrony may accomplish "an integration of content and affect," leading to clarity, or the *aha* experience. It is also suggested that the synchronization of the two hemispheres of the brain gets rid of the "me" syndrome, or ego experience. HemiSync produces "hemispheric communication," or synchronization of the two hemispheres of the brain, which has been shown to produce feelings of euphoria. Deep meditative states do the same thing naturally.

The binaural beat can be embedded in music and has been utilized this way in studies of children with developmental disabilities. Another study in creativity demonstrated that the HemiSync tones cause "highly divergent thinking," i.e. subjects tended to think about matters far removed from the actual physical environment. Although the applications of this technology are aimed at helping people with psychological and behavioral problems, including attention deficit, depression, and stress disorders, there may be potential applications which could be deleterious to human health and well-being. This unfortunate outcome is always possible when we play with mind tools.

Euphoria, creativity, and 'happy smiling people holding hands' is nice, except in situations where a state of alertness is warranted. Could this technology be used to produce a docile populace during a period of social crisis? Assuming consensus-reality to be the norm, what would be the impetus to attempt to induce "highly divergent thinking"? While the ostensible aim is toward creativity, could this technology, in tandem with its suggestibility aspect, be utilized to induce thoughts which "diverge" from the norm? Could "divergent thinking" include subject matter such as extraterrestrials and UFO abduction scenarios? Further, if subjects can be hypnotized to have OBEs, and HemiSync increases hypnotic susceptibility, could this technology be used to simulate something like the Biblical "rapture," or even a UFO abduction? Or could some type of psychosonic (sound entrainment) method be utilized to keep humans in an ongoing 'dazed and confused' state of mind?

The potential applications of this technology run the gamut between benevolent and malevolent, and are a source of much dissent between those who worship technology and those who fear its potential for controlling human beings. This social argument comes to life in the Cronenberg film *eXistenZ*, where a futuristic society of virtual reality worshippers have "bio-ports" installed in their spines in order to play the game *eXistenZ*. Once plugged into the game, enemy agents begin to infiltrate the ranks of the game players and a virtual reality war ensues. This profoundly disturbing film is a warning about the acceptance of any technology which alters consciousness. Your personal reality, as narrow and confining as it may sometimes seem, shouldn't be taken for granted. What would you do if you left it behind for a chance to expand your 'view' and you couldn't get back?

Canadian researcher Dr. Michael Persinger has utilized the basic HemiSync method, which, he maintains, works by introducing the left brain to the right brain, eliciting various illusions and emotions. Persinger has been able to simulate paranormal experiences, including religious rapture and a distinct sense of presence, including alien presence. Persinger has also used "solenoids" to pass a magnetic pulse through the frontal lobes of the brain; these magnetic coils are used in psychiatry as a non-intrusive alternative to implantable electrodes for brain stimulation. As Susan Blackmore has written in the *New Scientist*, "by controlling the nature of the magnetic fields, causing them to simulate brain patterns, Persinger is able to stimulate strong emotions and hallucinations, including the illusion of touch and movement." The simulation of brain waves is the same method behind HemiSync. Technology also exists which can project words into the mind using microwaves. This brings us to the subject of psychosonics.

PsychoSonics

Specific 'sonic' utterances produce very real changes in consciousness and affect the mind, body and soul. As William Gray explains in *Magical Ritual Methods*, in ancient times these sonics were considered magical, and they continue to be employed today by magicians of various traditions. As Gray reminds us, "the Word has literally brought Cosmos out of Chaos, and the Anti-Word is capable of reducing us to Chaos once more. Words and magic are inseparable." Yet, as Gray asks, when we call upon Deities and Intelligences during rituals, how do we suppose they would be able to "hear" us? He explains, "Beings that live beyond the boundaries of physical matter will only "hear" us if we address them with Inner Sonics uttered through our own Inwardising consciousness." In other words, as Gray clarifies, "the Gods hear us in ourselves, if we are effectively connected to Them by Inner Channels." So, via the use of Inner Sonics, or ritual resonance in the human voice, human beings can make contact with supra-human consciousnesses that do not have human bodies.

Practitioners of magic believe that sonic ritual procedures produce effects in the minds and souls of the participants. The participants are encouraged to think, feel and undergo experiences aimed at a kind of "processing of consciousness." As Gray explains, these require "skilled psycho-physiological techniques of sound," or "psychosonics." At one time psychosonic procedures were kept secret, but Gray admonishes, "most of them are now being used by commercial or political groupings for influencing whichever section of the Mass mind they want to dominate."

As an example of which political groups might use psychosonics, we can imagine that the occult principles of psychosonics could be put to good use by our boys in the military. As ex-military spook Adam Mandelbaum writes in *The Psychic Battlefield* (p. 122):

> If microwave radiation can serve as a carrier for voice messages, if such things as pulsed microwave audiograms really can implant thoughts in the minds of men, our boys in the basement and alleyways of espionage had better know about it. If remote viewing techniques can eventually lead to a significant improvement in the accuracy of intelligence obtained by those methods, it will be a revolution in the world of espionage.

As Mandelbaum notes, "what started out as magic has again ended up as magic. ... Today's magic wand might control microwave radiation instead of demonic hordes, but the goal is still the same. Control, command, conquest." The microwave audiograms mentioned above use microwave technology as a carrier to directly implant into the mind words that seem to originate from the thoughts of the target. Aren't these psychosonic procedures? Remember that infrasound and ultrasound can either heal or wound or kill when properly targeted. Mandelbaum warns (p. 233), "As we learn more about neuroscience, as our brain wave measurement devices improve, as our electromagnetic research continues, we may find ourselves in the 21st century with the ability to literally remotely control the mind of another."

According to Randy Fitzgerald in *Psychic Warfare, Fact or Fiction?*, he obtained FOIA documents relating to a series of tests in remote viewing, precognition, ESP and psychokinesis which took place at the Maimonides Dream Laboratory. Per the typical *modus operandi* of intelligence funding, one participant stated she was told that "part of the funding came from a government agency and was funneled through charitable foundations." Ingo Swann has also admitted being involved in ESP research at Maimonides in his earlier years of involvement in psychic studies.

Michael Talbot notes in *The Holographic Universe* that decades of ESP and dream research at Maimonides Dream Laboratory support the hypothesis that in dreams we are able to communicate in scientifically unexplainable ways. In reading all of this material, it becomes evident that the intelligence community has long been interested in the physics of dreaming, as well as other altered states of consciousness, including, as we now well know, LSD experimentation. But, we might ask, what lies under the intelligence community's apparently intense interest in such things?

Researcher Alex Constantine has asserted that psychotronic devices using ELF (extremely low frequency) electromagnetic waves were being tested on the RV subjects at SRI. He alleges that "during the Vietnam War period, SRI was a hive of covert political subterfuge." He alleges that the managers of the project "engaged in projecting words and images directly to the cranium." Constantine notes that during a routine briefing on various projects, including the remote viewing program at SRI, Dr. Sam Koslov, assistant to the Secretary of the Navy, saw on the chart being projected on the screen the words "ELF and Mind Control." Koslov ordered the Navy's remote viewing projects at SRI canceled, but instead, "the Navy quietly continued to fork out $100,000 for a two-year project directed by a bionics specialist."

The director of the Neuropsychology Research Lab at SRI was none other than Karl Pribram. As noted earlier, Pribram's studies in neurophysiology have shown that memories are not localized in a certain area of the brain, but are dispersed throughout the brain. After many years of brain studies on primate and human guinea pigs, Pribram and others theorized that the holographic model can explain how the brain is able to convince us that inner experiences project an external reality. As Constantine notes, previous studies at SRI in the processing and storage of sensory imagery have noted that "mental imaging bears a close resemblance to hologram projection." However, it is not known whether this statement was made in the context of how human perception works, or whether holograms were actually used to project images into the mind. Nonetheless, Constantine wonders whether the results of these studies were later tested under the misnomer "remote viewing," instead of, perhaps, hologram projection.

In addition, Constantine notes that the medical oversight for the studies at SRI was provided by the infamous CIA mind control specialist, Dr. Louis Jolyon West, who is a specialist in "dissociative states." Constantine notes that years of covert CIA experimentation has left a legacy of multiple personalities, and that the CIA can trigger such dissociative states remotely. For instance, as mind control researcher Kathy Kasten notes in *Paranoia*, the manipulation of human emotions was undertaken by researchers at the UCLA School of Medicine Brain Research Institute, more than likely utilizing patients and volunteers from the Reed Brain Institute's Sleep Lab. The following quote, from a 1978 paper entitled "Mental Phenomena Evoked by Electrical Stimulation of the Human Hippocampal Formation and Amygdala," indicates how long such remote biotelemetric research has been going on under the misnomer "sleep studies:"

> Electrical stimulation of the human brain may evoke reports by patients of a wide variety of simple and complex sensations, emotions, and cognitions. These mental phenomena have been primarily considered in relation to the localization of function within the human brain. Penfield, in his pioneering studies describing the mental phenomena evoked by stimulation of the human temporal lobe, interpreted these evoked phenomena in a manner analogous to those evoked by specific sensory cortex stimulation. Penfield found, and others have confirmed, that the most common categories of mental phenomena evoked by temporal stimulation include complex hallucinations. When discussing the hallucinations, which he considered to be memories, Penfield labeled the temporal cortex "memory records" (Penfield and Jasper, 1954, p. 145). When considering the deja vu and other misinterpretations of present sensations, Penfield (1958) referred to this cortex as "perceptual" in analogy to "visual" or "motor" cortex, because stimulation there evoked "psychical responses" corresponding to the visual sensations or movements evoked by stimulation of the specific cortices.

Similar information regarding the technology to cause a person to hear external voices via microwave signals has come forward via several academic journals. Kasten points out that this research went "black" (undercover) in the early 1980s. Kasten discusses one of the breakthrough papers, entitled "Human Auditory System Response to Modulated Electromagnetic Energy," which was authored in 1962 by Allan H. Frey. She notes that in this research people were able to hear for the first time without a radio or transmitter. What they heard at first was "clicks and buzzes" which were controlled by the operator. Dr. Frey had figured out how microwave signals created sound in the head of a target.

In 1975, Dr. Don R. Justesen published a paper in the *American Psychologist* called "Microwaves and Behavior." Kasten quotes the following from Justesen's paper regarding the experiments of Joseph C. Sharp, the only journal article mentioning these particular experiments:

> Sharp and Grove (note 2) found that appropriate modulation of microwave energy can result in "wireless" and "receiverless" communication of speech. They recorded by voice on tape each of the single-syllable words for digits between 1 and 10. The electrical sine-wave analogs of each word were then processed so that each time a sine wave crossed zero reference in the negative direction, a brief pulse of microwave energy was triggered. By radiating themselves with these "voice modulated" microwaves, Sharp and Grove were readily able to hear, identify, and distinguish among the 9 words. The sounds heard were not unlike those emitted by persons with artificial larynxes.

As Kasten points out, the research results discussed in Sharp's paper prove that the human being has the capacity to receive audible signals without being implanted. As Kasten concludes, "it should be apparent that humanity has had both the technology and the will to manipulate each other remotely for many years." As Constantine points out, these biotelemetric subjects routinely complain that their dreams are "commandeered."

Commandeering Dreams

While we were being told plastics was the wave of the future, the physics of nonlocal consciousness was being commandeered by the secret government. The CIA began backing young geniuses, buying a round of physics educations, and pairing them up with UFO lounge-lizards at the Esalen Institute. Post-quantum physicist Jack Sarfatti claims he was visited by two men from Sandia Corporation as a child in the 1950s. He later received a full scholarship to Cornell at age 17, and studied under the major figures in the Manhattan Project at Los Alamos.

Sarfatti suggests that Einstein's nonlocal connection can be used for communication. The idea of nonlocal communication involves receipt of telepathic messages from other times or other worlds. As a child, Sarfatti claims, he received a mysterious phone call claiming to be the voice of a conscious computer aboard a spacecraft. The machine-like voice stated it was located on a spaceship from the future. (see "Psi Wars Script," at http://stardrive.org/Jack) Sarfatti's mother has verified that Jack received several of these mysterious phone calls over a span of three weeks at the age of 13. She claims that after these long phone calls, Jack "was walking around glassy-eyed in a daze." She claims she picked up the phone one time and heard the metallic voice, which "said it was a computer on a spaceship and to put Jack back on the telephone." She shouted to leave her son alone and hung up. That was the last call Jack received, however, Jack only recalls receiving one phone call.

As Jack tells it, this distant "cold metallic voice" identified him as "one of 400 bright receptive minds." He was told if he said "yes," he would "begin to link up with the others in twenty years." He said yes. Jack has recently verified in an e-mail that this event occurred in the summer of 1953, not 1952 as he had previously reported. Twenty years later, Sarfatti claims, he was invited to SRI and spent a seventeen hour day there in the summer of 1973. This would put him smack dab in the middle of the SRI remote viewing experiments.

Sarfatti also notes, "what is peculiar about my 'close encounter' was the prediction of '20 years' in the future which did happen, and which Saul-Paul has a tape recording of the key event from 1973, and the fact that only in 1974 after contact with Puharich did my mother reveal her memories of the same events. The correlation with Ch. 11 of James Schnabel's *Remote Viewers* is also significant, as that involves CIA's Kit Green and physicists from Lawrence Livermore, some of whom I also met in L'Affaire Uri Geller. See Martin Gardner's *Magic and Paraphysics*."

Sarfatti claims he met Hal Puthoff at SRI in the summer of 1973, as well as ex-astronaut Edgar Mitchell. He notes that Mitchell's think tank, Institute for Noetic Sciences, was funding the SRI project at the time. He also claims that Mitchell took part in telepathy experiments while in outer space. Ronald McRae has also noted in *Mind Wars* that Mitchell formed a "psychic posse" in an attempt to locate kidnapped heiress Patty Hearst. It appears that Mitchell was a very busy man in the 70s.

In his book *Mind Wars: The True Story of Government Research into the Military Potential of Psychic Weapons*, McRae also has some other interesting things to say about Edgar Mitchell and his Institute for Noetic Sciences. He writes that George Bush, while director of the CIA, was approached by Mitchell, "a personal friend for many years." McRae writes that "Bush gave Mitchell permission to organize high-level seminars at the CIA to discuss possible intelligence applications of parapsychology." Despite this support, according to McRae, parapsychology research was never quite "institutionalized" at the CIA; i.e. it never had its own department or centralized location, but was pursued as "scattered research projects." (So, now we're supposed to believe the well known "CIA Weird Desk" is really just a desk and a few drawers.) McRae notes that Mitchell implicated "bureaucratic inertia" as the problem. Mitchell stated, "we just couldn't get the actors together, there was always one bureaucratic bottleneck or another." Apparently, this problem was solved by moving the program to SRI, with the Institute for Noetic Sciences and other known CIA cutouts funding various projects. This trend has continued to this day with various remote viewing agencies/think tanks springing up on the Internet.

Notably, Sarfatti states that the relevance of this experience was "triggered" in his session with Brendan O'Regan at SRI, but he clarifies that, "the actual memory of this experience is still very vivid and has not at all changed." Sarfatti also notes, with regard to his bizarre 1953 phone call, "Brendan said 'Oh yes, I have seen data on several hundred incidents of that kind.'" Incidentally, Sarfatti doubts that some Army scientists in 1953 could have planned a twenty year deep cover operation like this; that is, unless time travel was involved. Yet, he clearly suspects there was something more than synchronistic quantum connections at work. Sarfatti writes in *Quantum Quackers*:

> I was then simply a young inexperienced naïve 'useful idiot'in a very, very sophisticated and successful covert psychological warfare operation run by the late Brendan O'Regan of the Institute of Noetic Sciences, and the late Harold Chipman, who was the CIAstation chief responsible for all mind control research in the Bay Area in the '70s. Chipman (aka "Orwell") funded me openly for awhile in 1985 when he was allegedly no longer in the CIA, and covertly before that, and told me much of the story. In fact, he even introduced me to a beautiful woman adventurer-agent who was one of his RV subjects, who later became my live-in 'significant other'.

The Esalen Institute

The "quantum conspiracy" runs back to the Esalen Institute, a conference center/resort in Big Sur, California. Since the early 1960s, the Esalen Institute has held seminars on various esoteric topics, including parapsychology, human potential, psychedelic experimentation, quantum physics, gestalt therapy and various mystical/esoteric topics. The Esalen Institute has a web site which currently offers "wilderness excursions" as well as workshops for psychologists, nurses and massage practitioners.

According to a 1983 book by Walter Anderson entitled *The Upstart Spring: Esalen and the American Awakening*, the Esalen Institute was founded in 1964 by Michael Murphy and Dick Price. Anderson notes that every program leader in the first "human potential" seminar held at Esalen was involved in early LSD research, including Willis Harmon, who was later head of the Future's Department at SRI, Gregory Bateson, Gerald Heard, Paul Kurtz, and Myron Stolaroff. Interestingly, according to *Mind Race*, by Russell Targ and Keith Harary, a 1982 workshop on psychic phenomena was taught at Esalen by Targ and LSD researcher Stanislav Grof. In this program, however, the goal was to show that psychic experiences did not need to be precipitated by a chemically altered state. Apparently, for twenty years, the CIA assumed that LSD was the short cut.

Other leaders of the drug culture and hippie movement gave seminars at Esalen, like Timothy Leary, John Lilly, Richard Alpert, and later, Terence McKenna, some of whom may have been, in Jack Sarfatti's words, "young inexperienced naïve useful idiots," and others who probably knew what was up and went along with it anyway. Although, Anderson writes, drug use was not "officially endorsed," it was common knowledge that psychedelic drugs were widely used by both staff and students. Anderson also notes that even though this was common knowledge, the Institute was never raided by the authorities. Anderson noted that Charles Manson and Family played an "impromptu concert" at Esalen just three days before the slaughter at the Tate household.

The weirdness at Esalen is a never-ending tale. Another report is that a parapsychology exchange program began between certain Russian officials, which lasted into the 1980s. This exchange program came to be called "hot tub diplomacy," and it has been reported that Dr. John Mack attended these sessions. Esalen's seminars in the latest quantum physics theories gave birth to Jack Sarfatti's Physics/Consciousness Research Group. Sarfatti, as director, along with Michael Murphy led the first seminars in the physics of consciousness beginning in 1974. This group, financed by Werner Erhard and George Koopman, nurtured the writing of a new wave of quantum-synchronistic-mystical tomes by such people as Gary Zukav, Fred Alan Wolf, Nick Herbert, Fritjof Capra, Robert Anton Wilson, Uri Geller and others, spawning a new genre of pop science known as "the new physics." Sarfatti stated in his article, "In the Thick of It," that Koopman provided publishing funds for the Physics/Consciousness Research Group through Air Force and Army contracts funneled through Koopman's company, Insgroup. Insgroup has known affiliations with U.S. intelligence agencies and is considered a CIA 'cutout'or front.

Post-Quantum Physics

In an interesting on-line paper entitled "Bye, Bye Schrodinger!," physicist Jack Sarfatti outlines the status of post-quantum theory, essentially stating that Niels Bohr's quantum theory does not allow for the emergence of consciousness. Sarfatti's Synergetics-related Post-Quantum Physics of the Conscious AI (Artificial Intelligence) Biocomputer extends some of Bohm's findings. As Sarfatti notes, Bohm's material "hidden variable" [which, according to Sarfatti, could be an electromagnetic, geometrodynamical or torsion field configuration] piloted by its attached "mental order parameter" [the mental quantum informational pilot wave]—explains how thought moves matter. But, Sarfatti notes, one must also explain how matter reacts back on thought, for, he notes, the "change in thought induced by matter is consciousness."

Sarfatti notes that consciousness is not possible in quantum theory, stating it is a post-quantum effect. Sarfatti states that Bohr's orthodoxy consisted of a "list of false statements, a veritable brain washing, that drove several generations of highly intelligent philosophically-minded theoretical physicists into irrational lunacy." Sarfatti sees Bohm's quantum "causal theory" as deterministic and consistent with special relativity and quantum field theory. In contrast,

Sarfatti's post-quantum extension of Bohm's deterministic theory is self-determining. It explains morally responsible free will in terms of a cosmic connection. As Sarfatti explains, this is in strong violation of quantum theory's "passion at a distance," which strictly prohibits paranormal phenomena like remote viewing. Sarfatti's post-quantum theory allows what quantum theory does not."

Sarfatti suggests that "paranormal telepathy, precognition, and remote viewing are impossible in principle in quantum theory." Post-quantum theory, however, has corrected these faults. As Sarfatti writes, "in The New Jerusalem of post-quantum theory … we find consciousness and our possibly immortal souls." Sarfatti's post-quantum theorizing essentially attempts to find the critical complexity, numerical value, dependence upon, duration of, and power wattage required to generate a single moment of conscious experience. He asks with regard to artificial intelligence, per popular biocomputer intelligences such as "Commander Data" in Star Trek or Hal 2000 in Kubrik's *2001: A Space Odyssey*, is this "fact imitating fiction, or fiction pretending to be fact?"

Sarfatti presents a list of "facts" which could be experimentally assessed as true or false. He explains, "once a set of experimental data have been correlated and a postulate has been formulated regarding the phenomena to which the data refer, then various implications can be worked out. If these implications are all verified by experiment, there is reason to believe that the postulate is generally true. The postulate then assumes the status of a physical law. If some experiments are found to be in disagreement with the predictions of the law, then the theory must be modified in order to be consistent with all known facts *including #7-13 on the above list*." (emphasis added)

Interestingly, most of the items on Sarfatti's numbered list refer to known scientific 'facts' like the duration of a conscious moment (1 second), the number of nerve cells in the brain (100 billion), the electric field which acts as the brain's biocomputer, the "Hubble flow" (now set at 13 billion years from Hubble Space Telescope data), the resting mass of the electron (half-million volts), the coupling of the photon to the electron (1/137), etc. Number 7 on the list is "Libet sees 'temporal subjective antedating' in mind-brain experiments," and #8 on the list is "Radin and Bierman see 'presponse'in mind-brain experiments. These two 'facts' refer to ESP experiments in precognition. Strangely, following this odd melange of scientific facts, #9-13 on Sarfatti's apparently 'provable facts'list have to do with social/historical events surrounding remote viewing, historical intelligent contact, and alien abductions. Specifically, these statements are the following:

> 9. CIA, DIA, et al. funded work in "remote-viewing" included transcending time and causality, seeing into the past and the future as well as the distant "present."

> 11. Flying saucers are real and have a superior technology of propellantless propulsion.

> 12. Contact with Higher Advanced Intelligences is real and has been happening in all of recorded history.

> 13. Humans have been abducted, mostly against their will, by seemingly non-human creatures in flying saucers.

Sarfatti asks, are all these facts just a random hodge-podge? Are they all really facts? Can they all be explained by a coherent interesting checkable story? As Sarfatti notes, "All things are not possible! However, many more things are possible than are dreamt of in the philosophies of many respectable mainstream scientists to be sure." Interestingly, the footnote for #11 above is the book *Unconventional Flying Objects* by NASA pioneer Paul Hill; and the footnote for #13 above reads: "22. The research of Harvard psychiatrist, Pulitzer Prize Winner, John Mack."

Sarfatti also notes that we live in a "locally flat tangent Cartesian space" which is like a "many sheeted Riemann surface of a function of a complex variable of parallel flat worlds connected by moving through the branch cut." He notes, "this does remind us also of the possibility of a Star Gate 'portal' from one 'flatland'to another." The footnote following these statements alludes to the 1943 Philadelphia Experiment in time travel being a possibility if, in fact, we live in such a world. Sarfatti notes in "The Starship Builders" (www.stardrive.org), that delayed choice experiments have shown that whether a photon acts as a wave or a particle in the past depends on the future free will choice of a conscious observer. Brain experiments have shown that conscious intention seems to depend on a quantum delayed choice effect of about one second backward in time, in other words, Sarfatti notes, "conscious choice acts backward in time." Regarding UFOs, Sarfatti conjectures that, "if UFOs are really spacecraft, then somehow they're controlling their local space-time curvature, maybe in angstrom thin boundary layers fitting the outside surface of the UFO like a skin." He also speculates that they may be doing this using "loops in time."

As Sarfatti concludes in this paper, "Einstein's traditional theory, used by Penrose (black holes), Hawking (quantum cosmology "universe has no boundary"), Thorne (traversable wormhole in Sagan's "Contact"), Alcubierre (warp drive with exotic matter of negative energy density), Puthoff (metric engineering, origin of gravity and inertia, polarizability of vacuum), Davis (brute force laser zapping attempt to make inconsequential amount of exotic matter for an impracticably short time with a huge amount of energy), et. al. are "seriously incomplete." Sarfatti concludes that the above theories are "physically leading us all up *the wrong primrose path away from the objective of making Star Trek Real and reverse engineering of allegedly alien ET flying saucers.* (Italics added!) Sarfatti adds, "the text book orthodoxy for general relativity corresponds to a trivial commutative Lie algebra."

In his web article "The Starship Builders," Sarfatti is quoted as saying the following:

> The key to building a practical cost-effective 'UFO-like' advanced propulsion system may be in a better understanding of the fundamental meaning of quantum mechanics and its relation to consciousness. If the photos of the Roswell crash fragments are not bogus, then the panels with hand prints provide a major clue that the craft is controlled by consciousness. The late Brendan O'Regan, who worked with Astronaut Edgar Mitchell and the Noetics Institute told me in 1973 that he had classified information that such was the case. He very much wanted me to work on that problem when he was Editor of Psycho-Energetic Systems in which he published some of my early premature speculations. Now, more than twenty years later, we have Sir Roger Penrose, Fellow of The Royal Society, and Professor of Mathematics at Oxford, speculating on a direct connection of human consciousness with quantum gravity.

This bizarre post-quantum connection, complete with rather cryptic allusions to the human ESP factor, bio-engineering of artificial consciousness (i.e. 'making Star Trek Real'), 'von Neumann probes,' historical ETI contact, and back-engineering of ETI space craft (which Sarfatti denies having worked on), merely underscores the point that quantum/post-quantum physics has not grown in a vacuum of social forces, but rather in a petri dish of covert intelligence experiments in parapsychology-related hijinks linked to CIA-connected funding. This is not to say the 'human potential'for paranormal experience does not exist, or that Jack Sarfatti is mistaken in his memory of his 'post-quantum'contact experience. The potential ramifications are much more frightening than this simple explanation can offer.

What if this human potential *does* exist, and the secret government is trying to usurp and control it for psychic warfare purposes? What if this human potential *does not* exist, and we are being manipulated for mind control purposes? Or what if it does exist along certain genetic lines *and* it is being technologically cultivated in certain individuals? Why is telepathy in humans being cultivated and how is the extraterrestrial theme related?

It is the purpose of this book to explore as many connections as possible. Let's start with the perplexing story of the discovery of LSD and how the CIA was largely responsible for 'dosing' an entire American generation.

CHAPTER EIGHT
LSD AND THE PSYCHIC ARMS RACE

The central irony of LSD is that it has been used both as a weapon and a sacrament, a mind control drug and a mind-expanding chemical.

Lee and Schlain

Acid Dreams

The natural source of LSD-25, lysergic acid, is a substance called ergot, which is a rye fungus. Ergot was used medicinally in ancient China and the Middle-East, and also in ancient Greece. The first modern studies of LSD-25, inadvertently discovered in Switzerland by Dr. Albert Hoffman, were conducted in that country in 1947. In the U.S., according to Lee and Schlain in *Acid Dreams*, CIA investigators first began trying out LSD-25 in the early 1950s as a "truth serum," or speech-inducing drug for interrogation purposes. Since it was colorless, odorless and tasteless, and could be introduced without the subject's knowledge, the CIA had a barrel of fun coming up with ideas on its potential use and, as well, trying it out on each other without prior warning. Once they were dosed, the agents got the day off.

However, the CIA soon discovered that the response to LSD was unpredictable, since it tended to promote extreme mood swings from anxiety and panic to ecstasy. The CIA also discovered that minute doses of LSD could create serious mental confusion and could render the mind susceptible to suggestion. Once the CIA decided LSD didn't work as a "truth serum," they considered it as a "lie serum," which could be imbibed by an agent who was caught in an interrogation situation in order to put him in a psychotic state wherein any information elicited would be of a bizarre nature. When neither of these ideas panned out, the CIA began contacting researchers to see what other ideas they might come up with. Almost overnight, a burgeoning market for grants in LSD research was born. CIA-linked conduits like the Geschickter Fund for Medical Research, the Society for the Study of Human Ecology and the Josiah Macy, Jr. Foundation, began to fund LSD research on a large scale.

As Lee and Schlain write in *Acid Dreams*: "Like the Nazi doctors at Dachau, the CIA victimized certain groups of people who were unable to resist: prisoners, mental patients, foreigners, the terminally ill, sexual deviants, ethnic minorities." For instance, the National Institutes of Mental Health knew all about CIA-funded LSD research on mostly black inmates/patients at the U.S. Public Health Service Hospital in Lexington, Kentucky. New drugs that needed to be tested were sent over to the captive guinea pigs at Lexington. There, Dr. Isbell gave LSD to some inmates for more than 75 consecutive days. The CIA also funded particularly cruel and unusual LSD/sleep studies by Dr. Ewen Cameron at Allain Memorial Institute at McGill University in Montreal. These so-called "sleep studies," which put people to sleep for months at a time, caused severe psychological damage, and the victims were later grudgingly compensated by Canadian courts for paltry amounts. (see Collins, *In the Sleep Room;* also see Robert Naeslund in *Paranoia*, issue 19, see *Paranoid Women Collect Their Thoughts*, see Constantine, *Virtual Government*)

Myron Stolaroff's book, *The Secret Chief: Conversations with a pioneer of the underground psychedelic therapy movement*, outlines the therapeutic use of LSD from the late 1940s to the late 1960s, when its use was eventually outlawed. As Stanislav Grof writes in the prologue to *Secret Chief*, the "serendipitous" discovery of LSD by Albert Hoffman in 1947 and the first clinical paper on LSD by Walter Stoll brought to light this chemical substance which began "a golden era of research." Grof writes, "experimental psychiatrists saw this substance as a unique means for creating a laboratory model for naturally-occurring psychosis, particularly schizophrenia." Clinical researchers hoped that this chemical could provide insight into the nature of mental disorders and "open new avenues for their treatment." Psychiatrists and psychologists, Grof explains, could "spend a few hours in the world of their patients" in order to better understand them. Thus, it was hoped that LSD experimentation by both patient and doctor could accelerate the psychotherapeutic process, particularly for the alcoholic, criminal and drug addicted population. In his book *Flashbacks*, Tim Leary describes his short-term supervised therapeutic LSD trials on convicted prisoners, which attempted to completely shake the foundations of their worldview and was successful on some counts.

As Grof writes in the prologue to *Secret Chief*, under supervision, lysergic acid offered the human being the spiritual experiences which western/European society no longer allowed its populace. As Grof explains, "All ancient and pre-industrial societies held these [non-ordinary] states in high esteem and they devoted much time and energy trying to develop safe and effective ways of inducing them." In contrast, he argues, western societies have "pathologized" non-ordinary states, and have developed means of suppressing them whenever they occur naturally. Western society has also rejected and outlawed tools that can facilitate these states. As Grof notes:

> The sudden invasion of the Dionysian elements from the depths of the unconscious and the heights of the superconscious was too threatening for the Puritanical values of our society. In addition, the irrational and transrational nature of psychedelic experiences seriously challenged the very foundations of the world view of Western materialistic science. The existence and nature of these experiences could not be explained in the context of the mainstream theories and seriously undermined the metaphysical assumptions on which Western culture is built.

From Grof's point of view, this therapeutic atmosphere was suddenly jinxed by mass unsupervised experimentation by a generation of youth, leading to the illegalization of psychedelic substances. As Grof writes, "Tools of this power carry with them greater potential risks than more conservative and far less effective tools currently accepted and used by mainstream psychiatry, such as verbal psychotherapy or tranquilizing medication. However, past research has shown that these risks can be minimized through responsible use and careful control of the set and setting."

There is also a connection between CIA-linked LSD studies and the holographic model of consciousness discussed earlier. As Michael Talbot explains, in the 1950s, Stanislav Grof personally guided over 3,000 LSD sessions and studied the records of over 2,000 LSD sessions conducted by his colleagues. He noted in his pioneering work that each of his patients seemed to go through a typical unfolding process involving deeper and deeper levels of consciousness. He found that LSD drastically shortened the treatment time for many psychiatric disorders.

In addition, Grof's patients moved beyond the most obvious issues of their illnesses and went cosmic. Several even began to report "embryonic" experiences and perceptions in the womb. Essentially, Grof's patients expanded their conscious awareness beyond the ego or self to a collective psychic dimension which encompassed the experiences of other life forms, as well as the experiences of relatives and distant ancestors. His patients seemed to have access to racial and collective human memories of ages past which they could not possibly have otherwise known.

Grof personally concluded that the holographic model can account for this collective, transpersonal experience, which he characterized as the feeling that all boundaries are illusory, the lack of distinction between part and whole, and the interconnectedness of all things. These are the qualities of a holographic universe. The "enfolded" nature of holographic space-time would explain why all spatial or temporal levels are instantaneously accessible. A holographic universe essentially has an endless capacity for information storage, since all of the participants are actively contributing to the dynamic flow of information.

Ironically, legal sanctions did not stop unsupervised experimentation by the general populace, however, it did curtail supervised clinical experimentation. According to Grof, this was a tragic loss to psychiatry, psychology and psychotherapy. Grof opines that, had it been possible to avoid this "unnecessary mass hysteria" and continue responsible clinical oversight of psychedelic experience as a therapeutic tool, this research would have radically altered the tenets of psychiatry and brought new understanding of human consciousness. This, it should be noted, is precisely why psychiatric use of psychedelic substances had to stop. LSD was a powerful social transformational tool which would have spelled the end of mainstream psychiatry. To this end, some practitioners saw this as an "irrational, unjustified and even unconstitutional" infringement of their right to practice psychotherapy, as well as an infringement of "religious freedom," and they continued to covertly administer this sacrament in their practice. *The Secret Chief* is about one of these practitioners, who is simply named "Jacob."

Many people have found it curious that Terence McKenna and his brother, publishers of popular psychedelic mushroom growing guides, have been allowed to grow and experiment with psychedelic substances while the CIA turns its back. Interestingly, Stolaroff thanks McKenna for the title of the book "Secret Chief." Even more interesting is the statement on the cover of the book promising that, "100% of the profits from the sale of this book will be devoted to psychedelic psychotherapy research." What's odd about this statement is that the book was published in 1997. Is psychedelic research ongoing, and does McKenna have something to do with this? (I'm not advocating that this research should be stopped. On the contrary, I'm all for it. I'm just noting a curious state of affairs.)

At the same time LSD was being administered in supervised settings to help people, several 'spychiatrists' also assisted the CIA in its more nefarious LSD research, including Drs. Isbell, Pfeiffer, Cameron, West, and Hoch. In addition, the FDA even assisted the CIA as an intermediary in the acquisition of LSD from the Sandoz pharmaceutical company in Switzerland. Eventually, the CIA asked an Indianapolis company, Ely Lilly, to break Sandoz's secret formula for LSD, which Ely Lilly did in 1954. This development eased the full swing of MK-ULTRA, the CIA's insidious Cold War behavior modification research program, prompted by the questionable paranoid assumption that the Soviets were doing the same thing.

Spilling out into the streets in the early 1960s, as Lee and Schlain write, nearly every drug that appeared on the black market, among them marijuana, cocaine, heroin, PCP, amyl nitrate, mushrooms, DMT, barbiturates, laughing gas and speed, had already been tested, scrutinized and even refined by the CIA and Army scientists for use in MK-ULTRA. Yet, they write, no drug ever received as much attention by the intelligence community as LSD. As Lee and Schlain have noted:

> The central irony of LSD is that it has been used both as a weapon and a sacrament, a mind control drug and a mind-expanding chemical. Each of these possibilities generated a unique history: a covert history, on the one hand, rooted in CIA and military experimentation with hallucinogens, and a grassroots history of the drug counterculture that exploded into prominence in the 1960s. At key points the two histories converge and overlap, forming an interface between the CIA's secret drug programs and the rise and fall of the psychedelic movement.

The place where these two histories overlap is perhaps in the "mythic realm" of the psyche; the place which psychotropic drugs are proven catalysts for accessing. Within this realm lies the convergence of various cultural archetypes, including the culture of the UFO. Many researchers have noted that some type of "alien contact" frequently takes place after imbibing certain psychotropic drugs. In *Pyschedelic Shamanism,* Jim DeKorne sees UFO contact as an interface between inner and outer dimensions, or space-mind/mind-space. He likens the alien visitor experience to a "kind of involuntary shamanic encounter." Did the CIA have an ulterior motive for introducing psychotropic drugs to the American youth culture? The verdict on this is still out and opinions are divided on this issue. Lee & Schlain seem to opine that it wasn't really that well thought out in advance, and may be attributable to stupidity as well as preordained unaccountability.

Nonetheless, the American mind was opened and something weird flew in. As Terence McKenna has written, UFO contact is frequently mentioned by people who take psilocybin. The psychotropic drug DMT is also well known for its brief but extremely bizarre effects, along with profound fear and a consistent type of encounter experience. In a scientific study of DMT described in *Pyschedelic Shamanism,* Jim DeKorne had the experience of approaching some kind of "space station," with a landing platform. Two entities were guiding him, but he could not see them. Inside of the space station he was aware of android-like creatures, which he describes as "a cross between crash dummies and the Empire Troops from Star Wars." DeKorne compares this with other common experiences of DMT users. One user saw thousands of entities passing something around; another user met with alien beings who seemed to be waiting for his arrival; and another user had a close encounter with unfriendly beings who seemed to be waiting for him. In another experiment, the same user could feel the aliens wanting to get into his psyche.

DeKorne notes that there is much common ground between the alien visitor/abduction experience and psychedelic shamanism. Ironically, the fact that aliens are able to enter our 3-D world at will might suggest that they use something analogous to the shamanic techniques used by humans to enter their space. He writes, "the way of the shaman is a two-way street." He notes that the UFO encounter represents the possibility of a "traditional shamanic connection with a hidden power for the purpose of healing the ills of the tribe."

Mind Wars

According to Ron McRae in his 1984 book *Mind Wars,* there *was* a national security concern with regard to secret parapsychology research after World War II, but there is no reason to assume it to be true in the present. In their book, *Acid Dreams,* Martin Lee and Bruce Schlain claim that even the earlier assertions of "national security" were actually unfounded. Internal CIA memoranda to which they were privy in their research seem to dispute the claim that the Soviet Union and Red China were "engaged in unorthodox methods of altering human behavior." One CIA document dated January 14, 1953 stated that the major emphasis of Soviet research was actually "on the development of specially trained teams for obtaining information without the use of narcotics, hypnosis, or special mechanical devices." (Could this be remote viewing?) Another memo issued at that time by the Ad Hoc Medical Study Group stated that "the present state of knowledge indicates little, if any, threat to National Security through 'special interrogation' techniques or agents." These special interrogation methods could include the use of LSD or other mind altering substances as "truth serums," or machines using sound waves or other types of mechanical devices to alter human consciousness.

On the other hand, military spooks will have us believe just the opposite. This shouldn't surprise anyone. For instance, as ex-military spook Adam Mandelbaum notes in *The Psychic Battlefield* (p. 122):

We should not be lulled into a false sense of psychic security by the destruction of the Soviet Union, for this particular bear, while it may have matted fur and vodka on its breath, still has plenty of nuclear, biological and chemical weapons, and may have who knows what else up its psychic sleeve.

In addition, the book *Psychic Discoveries Behind the Iron Curtain* agrees with this premise. The authors state: "There is every indication from multiple sources that psychic research with military potential is well financed by the Soviet Army, secret police and other paramilitary agencies. Soviet scientists doing psi research in non-military areas often have trouble getting money." As Mandelbaum notes, the reason Soviet paranormal research wasn't wholly successful was that it was "too heavily dressed in battle fatigues," and no potential commercial uses for it were explored. This fully explains why remote viewing in the U.S. has gone "dot.com." As is customary in corporate capitalism, it's got to pay for itself commercially in order to be a viable military tool.

According to Mandelbaum, a report entitled "Military Development of Remote Mind Control Technology," written by scientist Turan Rifat, asserted that, "there is reason to believe that Russian research in the biophysical domain became so advanced that they opened doorways to other continuums and themselves fell prey to malevolent forces."

Whether or not there was an actual threat, there are reasons to believe that the advocates of psychic warfare have had more influence in the Pentagon than has been admitted. As McRae notes, "the Pentagon has the statutory responsibility to investigate all new technologies, if only to ensure that the other side doesn't surprise us." McRae notes that there is "a thirty-year record of psychic research in the CIA, the Army, Navy, Air Force, and Marine Corps, NASA, the Defense Intelligence Agency, the National Institute of Health, and in fact, just about every conceivable government agency." This statement was published in 1984, so that takes us back to at least 1954.

Yet, keeping up with enemy secrets is a very convenient excuse to commit inhumane crimes against citizens. And, if this isn't an acceptable excuse for declaring war on innocent human beings, at least it's something to hide behind later if the seat gets hot. If it's described as a "war," you've bought yourself some immunity from charges of inhumane treatment. For, as Christopher Simpson notes in *The Splendid Blond Beast*, the state of war lays a blanket of immunity over the warriors. In the "psychic war," or the war for control of the human mind, it's no different.

After World War II, the United States took in members of the Nazi party and SS who had committed horrible atrocities in the concentration camps. As we know, power attracts power. As Simpson also notes, there seems to be in operation a pattern of rewards for those who cooperate, either actively or tacitly, in persecution. America gave these Nazi murderers cover in exchange for information and know-how. As McRae explains, when the U.S. captured the records of Nazi parapsychology experiments performed at Dachau, U.S. psychic researchers suspected the Germans may have been close to discovering psychic weapons. As John White writes in Appendix 2 to his 1988 book *Psychic Warfare: Fact or Fiction?*, "although Hitler and the Third Reich did not have the technological forms of mind-matter interface emerging today as psychotronics, they certainly did have a clear understanding of secondary principles of metaphysics, which they applied for black magic purposes." There is, in fact, much evidence that Hitler did employ "psychic warfare."

Is there or *was* there a real "psychic arms race"? According to McRae, futurist Alvin Toffler convinced Congressman Charlie Rose that Congress needed to keep in mind the potential impact of future technologies, including psychic weapons. I'd add that we need also to keep in mind the potential impact of 'futurists' whispering in the ears of politicians. Congressman Rose became convinced that psychic weapons might be "a hell of a cheap radar system, and if the Russians have it and we don't, we are in serious trouble."

According to McRae, Rose even became involved in getting the Pentagon interested in an "electronic paranoia inducer," developed by Astronics, Inc. This potential weapon worked as a "psychic neuron disrupter" which interferes with the connections between the nerve cells in the brain, inducing a temporary paranoia similar to the effects of LSD. Although the range of the device was limited, it was proposed that the range could be expanded for military applications. Apparently, as McRae reports, a contract was never signed with the Pentagon for the device, and the company went out of business. But, we can be sure something like it was eventually made available, and there is a vast literature claiming that such mind altering technologies, including brain implants and radio controlled telepathy, have been and continue to be field-tested on "free" citizens of many countries, including America, Canada, and Sweden. According to Adam Mandelbaum, the U.S. patent office does in fact hold registered mind control devices, some of which date back over twenty years. (For a short list see Wall, Judy, "Technology to Boggle Your Mind.")

CHAPTER NINE
THE SEARCH FOR SUPERMAN

George Orwell's "1984" would be the palest imaginable shadow of what a world would be like under the rule of the secret use of scientology with no remedy in exis - tence.

L. Ron Hubbard
Philadelphia Doctorate Course

Does the history of remote viewing represent human potential or human use? Were the goings-on at the Esalen Institute an "American awakening" or a usurpation of arcane information by a controlling faction?

To be fair, there are different styles and levels of remote viewing, and not all RV sessions occur at the depth of "trance bilocation." Some reportedly occur at the "intuition" level. All remote viewers do not utilize HemiSync sound tapes. In the early SRI project, the protocols designed by Puthoff and Swann seemed to be 'scientific' enough, although this assertion has been argued.

It is unclear whether or not HemiSync was used in the early SRI studies, since reference to this method does not come up until the program moved out of SRI and into the Army's remote viewing program called Project SCANATE, which was located at Fort Meade. However, HemiSync was used by most of the remote viewers after the early phase of the SRI program and may have been brought into SRI later in the course of the program, since it was the preferred choice of some viewers to move into the "zone." HemiSync is now used at most of the private institutes ("think tanks") teaching remote viewing. In particular, it is reportedly used by Joe McMoneagle, Ed Dames, and Courtney Brown. It is also still being used at the Monroe Institute in Virginia.

Still, one enigma remains. Various protocols were designed to 'send' the viewer toward the 'target,' as well as to more accurately translate perceptual information. Hal Puthoff has stated that no method obtained better results than any other. But he is still left with a mystery in any case: *how* does the target information, such as a picture in an envelope, a description in a folder, or a person standing at a remote location, traverse the "empty space" between subject and object? This question cannot be answered within the confines of normal science. Clearly, the holographic model of the mind is applicable, and the solution lies in the physics of nonlocal consciousness: 1) space is not empty, 2) separation between subject and object is an illusion, and 3) the human mind is part of a collective dimension.

These assumptions challenge the mainstream scientific paradigm, but it's important to realize that the mainstream paradigm is for mainstream consumption while pertinent alternative factual observations made by researchers via intelligence-paid grants remain largely unknown and unpublished. This hidden knowledge, which may actually describe the nature of reality and our particular situation in it, is squirreled away by a covert intelligence apparatus that is tied to an "industrial complex" comprising the top defense contractors who are now household words; i.e., the "military-industrial complex." Over the years, this vast intelligence apparatus has invested plenty to explore the 'human potential' to be 'two places' at once. What we've got to understand is *why.*

There is evidence that psychic functioning is exhibited by some people as a natural talent, and the latent ability for the mind to be two places at once has been demonstrated. However, we don't really know what kind of technologies were/are being tested on unwitting subjects under the guise of "enhanced creativity" and "intuition development." The potential for mind tools to double as mind control is very real, and we should beware wherever the intelligence apparatus is involved.

Take heed to the words of scientology founder, L. Ron Hubbard, during a 1952 lecture of the Philadelphia Doctorate Course. As Hubbard warned, "scientology contains methods of controlling human beings and thetans which have never before been dreamed of in this universe." According to ex-scientologist L. Kin, in *Pied Pipers of Heaven: Who Calls the Tune?*, Hubbard stated that these control mechanisms were "of such awesome and solid proportions that if the remedies were not so much easier to apply, one would be appalled at the danger to beingness that exists in scientology." Hubbard concluded that George Orwell's *1984* would be "the palest imaginable shadow of what a world would be like under the rule of the secret use of scientology with no remedy in existence."

Inserting the words "remote viewing" in place of "scientology" in the above statement might indicate that these words should be taken as a warning. Those of us sufficiently paranoid to entertain such notions might want to keep a third eye open for signs of the covert control or usurpation of "human potential" by a clique of planetary, or perhaps interplanetary, tricksters. As we've seen in the story of remote viewing, the techniques which cause the mind to "bilocate" are the kept secrets of shamanism, and are counterintuitive to the Western scientific brainscape. As Adam Mandelbaum writes (57):

> Shamanic methods developed in the cultures that were technologically challenged. Yet the principles behind the techniques are similar to modern methods of achieving altered states of consciousness... The shamans used psychotropic drugs, as did the CIA in its MK-ULTRA human-use experiments of the 1950s and '60s. The shamans used visualization methods, as did the soldiers involved with Project Jedi in the 1980s. The ordeals of ancient shamans are mirrored in the sensory-deprivation techniques used to enhance paranormal functioning in modern psychic warrior endeavors (dim lighting, sound-proofed chambers, neutral environments, etc.) ... The influences of ancient magic and the techniques of sorcerers and shamans were the precursors of modern military experiments in the black arts.

This chapter will show that the national security apparatus has surreptitiously dug into the magic bags of the world's occult/arcane and shamanistic traditions, including those of various scientology solo offshoot practices (unofficial scientology splinter groups are hereinafter called 'SOPs'), and has opened a dangerous Pandora's box.

The Operating Thetan

According to L. Ron Hubbard, an Operating Thetan (OT) is able to operate without a body in order to control matter, energy, space and time (MEST). An OT can operate freely from the physical body, and is able to cause effects at a distance by 'will' alone. An OT is "a totally unaberrated being" who is supposedly capable of exteriorization or bilocation. The OT must use a *Time Track* to trace events and postulates back in time. A time track is described as a 3-D recording of every event that's ever happened. According to Hubbard, the beginning of the time track goes back 4 quadrillion years. An advanced solo auditor, who has become capable of exteriorization at will, can supposedly "switch" between his own time track and another's time track. Only the most highly trained Operating Thetans are supposedly capable of these shamanic feats.

It is well known that at the time of the SRI remote viewing experiments, Ingo Swann was a scientologist OT VII, the highest level achievable in the scientology organization at the time. He attributes his success in remote viewing to techniques he learned and cultivated in scientology. Proof of this is a paper he presented at the First International Congress on Psychotronic Research in Prague in 1973, wherein he touted the scientology paradigm as a model for developing and exploring paranormal abilities. The paper was entitled "Scientological Techniques: A Modern Paradigm for the Exploration of Consciousness and Psychic Integration." The details of this paper will be discussed shortly.

In addition, several other persons involved in the RV/SRI/CIAprojects were also scientologists. There were reportedly fourteen scientology "clears" running around at SRI. The manager of the program, Dr. Harold Puthoff, was an OT Level III, and was married in the scientology church. Two of the most quoted books on remote viewing, *Mind Wars* and *Remote Viewing*, charge that Puthoff's involvement in scientology was casual and short-lived. Both tend to underplay Puthoff's affiliations.

Yet, other sources disagree. Ex-scientologist Jon Atack writes, in *A Piece of Blue Sky*, that Puthoff has attested to completion of OT Level III, which can be considered scientology's motherlode. An advertisement for Hubbard's "Wall of Fire" in *Advance!*, the Magazine of the Advanced Organization Los Angeles (AOLA), states: "no one penetrated the traps and lies laid in on you and your fellow man until L. Ron Hubbard did so with the breakthrough of Section III OT." Completion of OT III would indicate that Puthoff had more than a passing interest, since the practices beginning at this level purportedly begin to endow the practitioner with powers of telepathy and exteriorization. Hubbard promised that graduates of these courses would be able to leave their bodies at will and perceive remote events. They would be "at cause" in the "MEST Universe." As ex-scientologist L. Kin also professes in *From the Bottom to the Top*, "anyone who understands traditional esoterics will immediately see that OT II and III are an initiation of the highest calibre."

Another talented remote viewer, Pat Price, had been a scientologist at OT Level IV. Of all the psychics evaluated at SRI by the CIA, writes Jim Schnabel in *Remote Viewers*, Price was the only one to "come close to being accurate and reliable enough for regular intelligence use." Yet, Schnabel notes, among psi critics, scientologists could never really be trusted to conduct psi experiments impartially, since "negative results were against their religion." This attitude toward scientologists implies that they might be capable of scheming to bias the results of psychic experiments. On the contrary, John Wilhelm writes in *The Search for Superman*, "Puthoff and Targ are men of good faith, and despite the large number of scientologists involved in the SRI research, I found no evidence that any covert conspiracy attempted to subvert or bias their results."

In June, 1979, Randy Fitzgerald submitted a request under the Freedom of Information Act for access to all parapsychology related documents in CIAfiles. Fitzgerald states that he initially received 500 pages of "translations of superficial and contradictory Soviet literature on psychic phenomena." He again wrote to the CIA specifically asking for documents pertaining to U.S. research, and received 21 pages consisting of mostly internal memos. The documents related to research either "initiated or contemplated" by the agency, but fell short of describing the research. Interestingly, Fitzgerald writes in *Psychic Warfare, Fact or Fiction?*, much of the information had been previously released to Hubbard's organization. We might wonder, what was scientology's interest in government files on parapsychology? In *Mind Wars*, Ron McRae reports that in 1978, the FBI uncovered an extensive scientology plot to infiltrate, spy on and harass government agencies investigating scientology. Thus, it appears that the two were at each other's throats throughout this decade. What was behind all this?

Interestingly, some of the other documents which Fitzgerald obtained, dated January and April, 1952, pertained to the CIA drug-testing program called Artichoke (later code-named MK-ULTRA), which discussed how ESP abilities are affected by drugs. Fitzgerald noted that from the very beginning the CIA's program linked drugs and parapsychology in order to "harness and manipulate the human mind." One of the most intriguing documents Fitzgerald obtained is a 4-page memo circa 1952 written by a CIApsychologist. The memo concludes that "it looks as if the problem of getting and maintaining control over the ESP function has been solved." Was this through the use of LSD or psychotronic devices?

Thus, we might turn the tables on the assumption that scientology was attempting to bias or subvert results, and instead query whether, perhaps, in its longtime stance against the psychiatric establishment—in particular the widespread use of psychiatric drugs and what they rightfully perceived as widescale psychiatric abuse—the scientology organization was more interested in keeping tabs on the CIA's forays into mind control. On the side of this argument, ex-scientologist L. Kin notes in *From the Bottom to the Top*:

> The Government waged decades of war against Hubbard and much of it was unconstitutional. I believe that they were angry at him for breaking security with information he had obtained while in the Navy. His organization was also perceived as a threat to J. Edgar Hoover, Richard Nixon and other established forces.

One of those "established forces" was clearly psychiatry. Hubbard proposed that his teachings would negate the need for a psychiatric establishment. Another reason for scientology's counter-espionage pursuits could very well have been to keep tabs on members who had gone off to work in the government's remote viewing program. As it turns out, the organization indeed suspected that their upper level teachings were being usurped by government and military intelligence agencies. According to Jon Atack in *A Piece of Blue Sky*, "for at least ten years, Puthoff and Swann owed allegiance to both the U.S. intelligence community and to scientology." In 1982, ten years after U.S. intelligence agencies first employed Hubbard's psychic spies at SRI, he explains, Hubbard ranted about an attempted takeover of scientology by one of the agencies employing Puthoff and Swann.

As it turns out, this wasn't simply a paranoid notion. The CIA and military search for "Superman" most certainly passed the threshold of the scientology organization. At about this time, U.S. Army General Stubblebine came to head the remote viewing project. He began to involve his military staff in spoonbending, tarot readers, spirit mediums and the astral specialties being taught at the Monroe Institute. Atack notes that the timing coincides with a decade-long 'cleansing' of the scientology organization and the mass exodus of numerous members who founded various solo offshoot practices (SOPs). Finally, in 1984, General Stubblebine resigned under a cloud of controversy and the Defense Intelligence Agency took over control of project "Grill Flame." By 1984, Puthoff and Swann had defected scientology to become involved with a breakaway movement called military intelligence; in this case, an offshoot practice called remote viewing.

There is evidence that a "takeover" of scientology by intelligence agencies did in fact take place, in the form of usurpation of its techniques and practices. As touched upon earlier, Swann had presented a paper in 1973 at the First International Congress on Psychotronic Research in Prague entitled, "Scientological Techniques: A Modern Paradigm for the Exploration of Consciousness and Psychic Integration." In this paper, Swann maintained that scientological techniques have wide possibilities for "pedagogical study." He described the basic scientological premise as "problematic man and his view of himself as a conscious psychic entity attempting to correlate himself with physical constructs of matter, energy, space and time [Hubbard's 'MEST Universe']." Swann wrote that scientological concepts were based upon a "psychic apprisement of man within the physical universe," and further that scientology principles "contain possible practical application within the context of emergent alternative future histories," meaning that through conscious intent alone (the will-to-power) mankind is in a position to take complete control of the future (or the entire MEST Universe).

In this talk, Swann explained that Hubbard's theories maintained that man was in "an inverted state," with respect to normal observations, and that in actuality the conscious or psychic entity "take[s] rank over the mechanics of space, energy and time." Therefore, the primary goal of scientology, according to Swann, would be to bring an individual "into such thorough communication with the physical universe that he could regain the power and ability of his own postulates." Indeed, the aim of scientology is to "clear" the entire planet. As reiterated by David Miscavige at the LRH Birthday Event 2000 held in Clearwater, Florida, "we intend to bring LRH tech to the whole planet. We intend to actually achieve the aims of scientology and we intend to do it this lifetime."

In addition, Swann explained, the mechanics of the physical universe as well as the mental universe are "agreed upon considerations which life mutually holds." According to Hubbard, he explained, "the reason we even have space, energy, time, objects, etc., is that life has agreed upon certain things, and this agreement has resulted in solidification." Swann added, "our agreed-upon material is then quite observable." As Swann wrote:

> Hubbard indicates that the aspects of existence when viewed from the level of man is a reverse of the greater truth above, for man seems to work on the secondary opinion that mechanics are real, and that his own personal considerations are less important than space, energy and time. This, he suggests, in an inversion. He further indicates that the freedom of an individual depends upon that individual's freedom to alter his considerations of space, energy, time and forms of life and his roles in it. If he cannot change his mind about these, he is then fixed amidst barriers such as those of the physical universe, and mental barriers of his own creation. Thus he is generally impotent in many respects in handling his existential environment.

With regard to the technical aspects of scientology, Swann wrote, there are "ordered processes and psychophysiological feedback techniques derived from research to restore to the individual the conscious process of choice, both in terms of himself and in terms of his familiarity and cause with the physical universe." Any other condition of existence would contribute to, according to Hubbard, a "less self-determined existence in a physical universe which is the inevitable average of illusion." As Swann wrote:

> The end point of the dianetic and scientology rehabilitative processes is considered to be the ability to be conscious and causal in any desired direction of activity, and thus has implications for the development of alternative future histories in which psychoenergetic factors may play an increasing role.

What Swann was saying was that via psychic abilities, mankind could be "at cause" (in complete control) of the MEST Universe and thereby of "alternative future histories." (As Ouspensky has written, "we must remember that the world as we know it does not represent anything stable. It must change with the slightest change in the forms of our perception.") Swann wrote that his paper would contain a description of relevant scientological philosophies and technological processes, and would "include descriptive data on certain scientological concepts which do not as yet have correlations in other fields of inquiry." He even ended his paper with the promise that "the concluding discussion will indicate certain potential directions for scientological applications." However, this is right where this 'government eyes only' document ends. The government restrictions on this document have now been lifted, but it appears that portions of this particular presentation were not published. However, it is clear that Swann did share certain scientology secrets and techniques at these government proceedings, although we can't be sure what those were.

It is not known how much information was shared between scientology and government agencies, but we can be sure that much was given over by Swann himself. Atack is certain that scientology's Guardian's Office was aware of the agency's approach to Puthoff and Swann. As he notes, it would be entirely out of character for the Guardian's Office not to have fully interrogated all the scientologists involved in the remote viewing project. In addition, Hubbard was not alone in suspecting that the FBI and other government agencies were after his organization. He was supported by his close friend (later scientology defector) Bill Robertson, who had worked closely with Hubbard and held high positions in scientology. Robertson was the creator of a solo offshoot auditing practice called the "Excalibur" levels, which professed that our world had been invaded by hundreds of thousands of extraterrestrials from the Markab system. One would wonder whether, by this time, the CIA/Army remote viewers began to acquire this belief system as well.

Superpowers of the Human Bio-Mind

Ingo Swann is one of the most prolific authors involved in the remote viewing program.(www.biomindsuperpowers.com) He asserts that the label of mind control is ludicrous. He explains, "now that the CIA is occupying itself with minimalizing and disowning remote viewing, there is no longer any reason to keep the substantive and technical matters from public view." Swann maintains that the SRI remote viewing technical matters are unclassified and proprietary to him. With respect to such technical matters, however, discovering his specific techniques seems to be a difficult task. A Coordinate Remote Viewing (CRV) manual under litigation by Ed Dames of the remote viewing institute PSI-Tech has been posted on the net, but Swann denies that he wrote this manual.

Swann believes that the capacity to remote view is perfectly normal. He suggests that the human species possesses what he calls "superpowers of the bio-mind," and considers remote viewing to be just one of these superpowers. He argues, "there is nothing wrong with attempting to research our species' superpowers of the bio-mind any more than there is anything wrong with attempting to research anything." Swann explains that the superpowers of the bio-mind have been well documented in transcultural lore and historical documents of the last 5,000 years, and that remote viewing is a "species thing." He suspects that all humans are carriers of superpower potential, possibly manifesting in given individuals through the generations.

Swann laments that an adequate frame of reference cannot be constructed within modern, Western categories of knowledge. The best way to describe superpowers of the bio-mind, he explains, is by analogy to computer systems as a "systemic net or grid of information-carrying processes." Remote viewing is a sort of "hacking" of the "information-bearing terminals of our species bio-mind," which can be likened to a very sophisticated "net." Each individual is one terminal in that net, but also carries within itself a total replica of that net; a "reproduction" down-loaded from the "species bio-mind net." Swann explains that the only thing in the way of all of us becoming "wired" into the hard drive of the species bio-mind are "installed mental software programs [social norms] which abort cognitive access to them."

Swann also adapts the term "virtual reality" to describe the place where "the past, future and present meet in one big matrix in which anything and everything is possible." He asserts that the human mind is "wired into alternative realities, cross-dimensions and multidimensional awareness," a place which has also been referred to as the universal akashic records. He argues that if we do away with the word "psychic" and replace it with "virtual reality," "cross-dimensional wiring," or "levels of consciousness," we arrive at a closer description of remote viewing.

According to Swann, the main interest of the intelligence community in psi phenomena was not focused on "a bunch of psychics strutting their stuff, or a bunch of parapsychologists seeking to theoretically explain psi." Swann insists that the issue of remote viewing as a "signal-to-noise problem" was the "real story" behind the interest of the intelligence community in remote viewing. Let's see what Swann means by this.

Signal-to-Noise Ratio

As Ingo Swann explains in his prolific on-line writings, the concept of signal-to-noise is fundamental to human perception, consciousness and communication, and is relevant to the superpowers of the human biomind, or the Vedic *siddhis*. The *siddhis* are powers which, in the expansive Vedic literature, many humanoid races are said to possess. Humans can potentially acquire *siddhis*, just a few of which include: mental telepathy, hearing and seeing at great distance, levitation, power to change the size of objects or living bodies, power to move objects from one place to another without traversing the space between, power to travel through physical objects, power of long distance hypnotic thought-control, invisibility and cloaking, power to assume various forms or generate illusory forms, the power to enter and control another's body, and so on.

Swann writes that the human being is a "born bio-mind mechanism," or an "entity-born-to-think." What Swann means is that the human being is essentially an information processor. Yet, he notes, humans are susceptible to 'noisy' information and, problematically, a "superpower cannot be a superpower if what issues from it is noise and dirty data." According to Swann, accuracy and clarity must be the signal features of the superpowers. If accuracy and clarity are not confirmed by feedback with regard to the signals, then something other than superpower functioning has occurred. As Swann explains:

> The ratio of low signal (low or infrequent accuracy) to high noise (high and frequent inaccuracy) could not possibly be of any service within the intelligence community respective of using psi perceptions for espionage purposes. If decisions are to be taken based on espionage inputs, one has to be relatively sure that the inputs consist of "good" information and not "bad" information.

In remote viewing, the 'signal' pertains to the information contained in or pertaining to the distant location or 'target,' the source which the remote viewer is attempting to contact. These protocols are 'double-blind' in that neither the remote viewer nor the 'monitor' during this process knows what the target is. The target information is kept in a closed envelope by a third party. Swann claims that during the SRI remote viewing experiments a naturally-occurring signal-to-noise ratio was confirmed to be about 15-20% signal to about 80% noise. This average was not considered to be suitable for government espionage purposes. Thereafter, efforts were undertaken to study the sources of the noise, and protocols were designed to deal with these noise sources. It can be safely surmised that some of these protocols were designed from the techniques of scientology, since Swann seems to have been so eager to share them with the government.

According to Swann, many methods were worked out to enhance psychic potential, or to obtain a high signal-to-noise ratio. As is clear by the title of Swann's paper, "Scientological Techniques: A Modern Paradigm for the Exploration of Consciousness and Psychic Integration," scientology contained a very workable system to develop such psychic potential, and it is clear that the intelligence apparatus tapped into this source. As is also clear, Swann was a willing pawn in the sense that he apparently stood right up in front of the proceedings of an international conference on psychotronics — an obvious meeting of the intelligence/scientific apparatus — and shared the secret techniques of one L. Ron Hubbard.

Following an attempt to minimize noise, the signal could be identified and enhanced. Swann writes, "had not decreases in noise and increases in signal been demonstrated, then it is quite clear that the project would have been abandoned after a year or so." He adds, "fourteen years later the remote viewing effort began failing—largely because too many individuals who had become involved opted to ignore noise sources."

But, what constitutes noise? According to Swann, the human being as a species is "fascinated and sometimes completely preoccupied with turning fact (signal) into fiction, and fiction (noise) into fact." He writes, "we are the only known species that does these rather remarkable transfigurations on a rather continuing and redundant basis." For one thing, he writes, just the fact that mental information processing is "very noisy regarding your natural superpower endowments [i.e. you are a doubter], then you won't hear what they are saying." Since the signals involved in superpower processes are quite subtle, methods to obtain noise-free environments are necessary in order to perceive them.

Yet, if signal is fact and noise is fiction, how do we know what is noise and what is signal? Swann writes, "even a quiet mind might not recognize signals unless its mental information processing grids can identify them and their special characteristics. And no one can delete noise unless it is recognized for what it is." Thus, it is important to identify noise for what it is, but herein lies the difficulty. As Swann admits, even an incorrect concept, a doubting attitude, a predisposed belief system, can be a source of noise. Swann writes that the human mind itself is "probably the single biggest source of noise on our planet, while the minds of various specimens [of humans] often produce some of the dirtiest data possible."

And here lies the crux of the matter: Swann writes, "the 'quiet mind' probably isn't the same thing as a noise-free one. Any mind can roam contentedly among its self-held noise if the belief is held that the noise is not noise." Yet, one must wonder, if "correct thinking" is signal, and "incorrect thinking" is noise, who is the judge of what constitutes correct thinking (i.e. "who calls the tune")?

Swann continues to assert that other nations are in the process of researching remote viewing, and he and others are concerned that this research will be used to 'enemy' advantage. This must be his justification for supplying the secret techniques of scientology to the U.S. government. Who is the enemy to whom Swann refers? One of Swann's books, *Penetration*, reveals the story about a "deep black" agency which utilized his psychic talents in order to 'remote view' man-made artifacts and humanoid occupants on the moon. Two very strange seemingly psychic 'twins' would meet him and take him to secret meetings with a "Mr. Axelrod."

The 1975 "Axelrod Affair" was so undercover that there was to be only a verbal secrecy agreement lasting ten years. Swann was taken to an underground facility outside of the DC Beltway where his secret remote viewing sessions of the moon took place. The focus of the first part of *Penetration* is on these bizarre "twins," who seemed to be telepathic. Somehow they even knew the combination to Swann's locked office at SRI. As Swann tells it, he would see these twins everywhere, even at the grocery store following a well-stacked female extraterrestrial. This made him wonder who Axelrod was really working for: the CIA, KGB, Mossad, M-5, military intelligence, or … "worst of all was the speculation that they, themselves, might be extraterrestrial." He wondered if ET troops could be fighting a telepathic war on Earth.

Telepathic Overlay

It is quite notable that the concept of "telepathic overlay," unconscious suggestions from the session monitor, was important enough to be considered within the careful scientific protocol at SRI. Since many of the original remote viewers had a background in scientology and/or in solo offshoot practices (SOPs), including the monitor-guides (i.e. they basically monitored each other), Hubbard's and/or Bill Robertson's intergalactic quadrillion-year alien cosmology cannot be extracted from the remote viewing mindset that evolved over time.

Is this the 'self-held noise' which was eventually ignored – and which Swann blames for the ultimate failure of the program?

As Swann explains in his on-line document entitled "Remote Viewing vs. Telepathic Overlay," telepathic overlay was identified by Swann and Puthoff during remote viewing experiments in 1975, and, with the help of hypnotists and psychologists, they worked to determine its causes and how to avoid or eradicate its effects. Accessing 'target' information is the goal of remote viewing. Accessing any other kind of contaminating information from the environment is considered 'noise.' As explained earlier, in remote viewing, the 'signal' pertains to the information contained in or pertaining to the distant location or 'target,'the source which the remote viewer is attempting to contact. Therefore, telepathic overlay, as Swann explains, is picking up on signals from someone else's head and mistaking them for the remote viewing signal itself. If one was doing this, Swann explains, "then we didn't have remote viewing at all. We had some format of telepathy."

Of course, all of this information presumes that the human being is a telepathic species and is susceptible to such conditions. It was generally agreed by psychologists and hypnotists consulted by SRI that something like subliminal telepathy could account for the contamination of remote viewing sessions. As it turned out, Swann explains, telepathic overlay was caused by the power-control relationship itself, and is similar to what takes place between a hypnotist and a hypnotee. The subliminal transfer of information from the hypnotist to the hypnotee is a known phenomenon of the hypnotic relationship. As Swann explains:

> It is well understood in psychology that if one person has suggestive power over another, the latter will not only accept the suggestions (or commands) but often will somehow mysteriously emulate that person in more subtle ways. The controllee will often sense the controller's wishes, desires and wants without their being vocalized. The whole of this is a kind of rapport, and certainly a type of sympathetic state with the controller. Controllees often go so far as to non-consciously emulate the controller's dress, posture, preferences, mannerisms, etc.

Swann explains that the concept of telepathic overlay with regard to remote viewing has an historical precedent known as "charismatic influencing." This is a situation which reflects the power in the relationship, who has power over whom, and involves sympathetic states. In remote viewing work, however, as Swann explains, this problem revolved around "who had power over whom not only during the RV work, but as regards the relationships of all involved." (emphasis added) As Swann writes:

> In the final analysis it was evident that the focus of control-power had subtly shifted to the guide-monitor, that the viewer had probably fallen into sympathetic rapport with him, and thereafter the viewer did not interact with the distant location but with the conscious and subconscious mind of the monitor. In this sense, the formula of who was to have power over whom was subtly present, even if no one involved consciously thought about implementing it... Unless something could be done to resolve what otherwise was a mess, then remote viewing would be up against a wall of perpetual telepathic contaminants coming from who knows where. Up until that time, it seems that no one realized, or didn't admit to, the possibility that people are continuously interactive at some deep telepathic levels which are interactive in sympathetic and rapport states.

As Swann writes, telepathy is more clearly understood as "empathy across distance." He notes that telepathy is hardly ever reported between people who are not sympathetic, or who are out of rapport with each other. So telepathy is a sympathetic or empathetic state involving emotion. But how can we be sure that what we have with remote viewing is actually a distance viewing experience ("bilocation") or whether it is a phenomenon more closely described as "sympathetic telepathy?"

As Swann has noted, a superpower is not a superpower if what issues forth from it is "noise and dirty data." Ironically, Swann considers a pre-held belief system as a source of "noise." As he also notes, "any mind can roam contentedly among its self-held noise if the belief is held that the noise is not noise." So, if the monitor believes that scientology precepts constitute the "truth," and truth is consonant with signal rather than noise, then what we would essentially have in this "remote viewing" scenario is telepathic overlay. Interestingly, the May 2000 issue of *Advance*, the magazine of scientology, states in a recruitment ad: "For every Sea Org Member making things go right, there are 1.2 million people who don't even know what right is."

What is ESP?

As Swann writes, telepathy (a word coined in 1882) was originally called "thought-transference." Telepathy is most often thought of as "brain to brain" or "mind-to-mind" contact, or along a "mind invasion" sort of paradigm, but ESP as a subliminal relationship between two minds is actually an obsolete point of view. As is evident in David Bohm's physics, the idea of the akashic records is now coming back in vogue. Rather than the "unconscious," we have the "super-conscious," or Swann's "bio-mind net."

This modern definition of ESP, which is actually an ancient view, is described in a 1973 article by E. Stanton Maxey entitled "The Subject and His Environment." Maxey wrote that consciousness may be called man's "sixth sense," in that man is the only creature on Earth who is aware of the fact that he is aware. As he writes, "dreams and out-of-body experiences demonstrate the mobility of the "I" of man separate from the physical body and often into a foreign time dimension." He asks, "when man is the receiver of provable meaningful information, who is doing the sending?" Maxey suggests:

> Man may be defined as a complexity of subatomic fields, within atomic fields, within cellular fields which make up organismal fields; these in turn exist within gravity fields, magnetic fields, electrostatic fields and light fields. Cognitive man of seven senses is dependent upon all of them. Under special circumstances, in dreams, meditations or out-of-body experiences, the "I" of man functions independently of physical being and time. Because man receives meaningful information in such states, we ponder on the origin of such information. Who can say that the fluctuations of magnetic and electrostatic fields upon the surface of our sphere are [not] indicative of a planetary consciousness?

This is mindful of Ouspensky's thought in *Tertium Organum*:

> Sometimes we dimly feel the intense life which goes on in the phenomena of nature, and sense a vivid emotionality manifesting itself in the phenomena of nature which, to us, is dead. Behind the phenomena of visible manifestations there is felt the noumenon of emotions. In electrical discharges, in lightning, in thunder, in the gusts and howling of the wind, are felt flashes of sensory-nervous tremors of some gigantic organism.

The idea of a "collective consciousness" was certainly not new with Carl Jung. As Bob Dobbs has noted in an essay for *Semiotexte*, the idea of a collective consciousness held sway in the medieval centuries, but in the Newtonian era became an "unconscious agency," a subliminal but personal, mind-to-mind agency most think of today as ESP. As Dobbs notes, Newton's Optics dissertation suggested that there was a correspondence between the forms and textures of the outer world and the inner faculties of perception and intellection, provoking an onslaught of debates on perception which have not quit to this day. All of these arguments have derived from the Newtonian idea that there is some kind of "unconscious" aspect to inner faculties; something we don't know about. The medieval concept of a collective unconscious was discarded, but with the emergence of quantum physics paradigms it has now come back in vogue. Consciousness is now marketed like laundry detergent. It's super, extra, ultra. It's nothing short of FAB.

As Bob Dobbs notes, the assumption of ESP as unconscious begs the question 'what is ESP if it is not unconscious?' If it's not unconscious, then it's connected by 'strings' we cannot see, connections in space. Remember that once a quantum connection is established, there is quantum entanglement. Once entangled in a cosmic dance, two or more ideas, objects, entities, phenomena, are always potential dance partners. This is also called "synchronicity." As Dobbs wonders, "who or what is influencing our perception? Are there invisible strings being pulled by an unnoticed puppeteer? Are there connections in matter to make the strings possible?" This is where consciousness becomes 'acausal.'

Perhaps these connections can be better understood as the sticky *aka* or *mana* of the Kahunas. As we have discussed, the Kahunas believed that this sticky, web-like invisible substance, through which the vital force acts, transfers itself through touch and can be drawn out in long threads. Through these stringy electromagnetic conductors, humans remain connected to the physical body during out-of-body experiences.

This umbilical, or bridge, as Ostrander and Schroeder write, connects "the world of 'plasma,' of the shifting 'tissue' of the universe connecting all to all." What all of this is telling us is that ESP is not simply 'unconscious,' or brain-to-brain, mind-to-mind communication, but, rather, it's 'out-of-body.' No matter which superpower you're talking about, the superpowers are not individual mind-to-mind contact but are the result of an energetic Earth matrix acting as go-between; thus, the superpowers are better described as Earth-to-Mind, or Earth-in-Mind; or, in Maxey's words, cognitive man of seven senses floating in his electromagnetic ethereal womb.

As we have discussed, quantum and post-quantum physics concepts which would serve to bring the marginal in from the margins are largely unknown or misunderstood by the general population; for what we call magic is only misapprehended science. There is nothing unexplainable by true science in this world. It is only unexplainable by what has been called 'scientism': a dogmatic and emotional commitment to a materialist philosophy.

Those who doubt the existence of a psychic Cold War, regardless of whether the 'enemies' were contrived ones, should be aware that this stuff is taken seriously on the power levels of the planet. Is this curious stance warranted? In the next chapter, the story gets curiouser and curiouser.

CHAPTER TEN
MIND, MANA AND THE SPEED OF THOUGHT

*Mana is not only the carrier of information
between one's own three selves and those
of others, it also sticks to everything one
has ever put attention on. Therefore, man
(middle self) appears to hang in a web of
tiny invisible lines connecting him to
things, events and people of his past, pres -
ent and future.*

L. Kin

Pied Pipers of Heaven

Ancient Greek philosophers described various vehicles connected to the body. Damascius wrote that, "the soul possesses a certain shining vehicle which is also star-like and is eternal." Islamic Shiite philosopher Sheikh Ahmad Ahsa'i described four parts of the soul as two living organisms and two "body masses" or "body volumes." The two living organisms are the material body and the subtle archetypal form. The two "body masses" consist of an "astral body" which is a "thing of the intermediary world," and the other an imperishable and transcendent "light body."

Soul travel was practiced in ancient Egypt and has roots in far older shamanistic traditions, presumably of the ancient Atlanteans. Soul travel between three worlds—upper, middle and lower—included interaction with non-ordinary entities. Among ancient shamanistic traditions, it was believed that these powers or states of mind were associated with certain body "vehicles." The physical body was part of a dynamic collection of vehicle-bodies existing simultaneously on many levels. Ancient disciplines taught the secrets of movement between subtle realms of space-time by using meditation, sensory deprivation, hyperventilation, repetitive mantras and other techniques of religious ecstasy. According to the author of *Angels and Aliens*, the modern Western world has since forgotten that the mind-body complex is a subtle vehicle capable of transporting the "observing self" to other worlds.

There are two historical veins of occult tradition (occult meaning 'hidden knowledge') which have made it to the West. One is based on the Vedic (Sanskrit) teachings of ancient India, and the other vein is Qabalistic, stemming from the Hermetic traditions of ancient Egypt. Both Helene Blavatsky's Theosophy school and Rudolph Steiner's Anthroposophy school stem from the Sanskrit tradition of India. Franz Bardon was an earlier practitioner of the Hermetic tradition. The various Rosicrucian teachings also follow the Qabalistic tradition.

It is L. Kin's opinion, in *Pied Pipers of Heaven*, that these three occult traditions practice "white magic," although Christians would argue against this. Christians tend to see anything "animistic" as "satanic." However, few would argue with Kin's statement that Aleister Crowley practiced what is considered "black magic." Kin suggests that Blavatsky and Steiner were students of occult lore who did not have actual occult powers (or *siddhis*). On the other hand, it is claimed that Franz Bardon, who followed the ancient Egyptian tradition, had serious magical powers. Among these, Bardon could heal illness (much like the Hunas of Hawaii), knew how to "use chakras to instill telepathic lines for defense and attack," and was adept at evoking nature spirits (elementals) in order to affect the weather. These are powers which L. Ron Hubbard also claimed to possess.

These ancient systems of thought are comparable to the basic teachings of scientology in various ways, according to Kin. As one example, a trinity of selves is evident in each of the systems. Hubbard's "genetic entity" is comparable to Steiner's "ether body," Blavatsky's "animal soul" and Bardon's "astral body." Hubbard's "thetan" is comparable to Steiner's "astral body," Blavatsky's "human soul" and Bardon's "mental body." This trinity of selves also has its counterpart in the Kahuna system, which Pinkham claims, in *Return of the Serpents of Wisdom*, had its origin in ancient Atlantis and was transplanted to Egypt and later to Africa, Polynesia and Hawaii. Oddly, the Western psychoanalytical tradition contains the same trinity of selves. The Freudian model of the mind consists of the id, the ego and the super-ego. As Kin writes in *Pied Pipers of Heaven*, "even in the middle of the professional world of a Viennese university at the turn of the century, we find our familiar 'trinity' concept of static, thetan and GE."

Kahuna-based concepts contain several interesting parallels to SOPs, according to Kin. First, the Hawaiian Hunas are known to use telepathy to either heal or harm at a distance. As Kin explains, the Kahuna system "almost uncannily compares to Hubbard's model of the mind." In the Kahuna system, man is composed of three selves: the lower self takes care of the body, as does Hubbard's Genetic Entity (GE); the middle self may be described as "conscious man," the equivalent of Hubbard's "thetan;" and the higher self is like an "all-knowing guardian angel," which in Hubbard's system is called "static." This trinity communicates with each other and with others through a fine substance called "mana," which is an invisible sticky filament-like substance. This is equivalent to Hubbard's "theta quanta" or attention units. As L. Kin explains in *Pied Pipers of Heaven*:

> Mana is not only the carrier of information between one's own three selves and those of others, it also sticks to everything one has ever put attention on. Therefore, man (middle self) appears to hang in a web of tiny invisible lines connecting him to things, events and people of his past, present and future.

This mana, or "mental stuff" as Bardon called it, is believed to have electromagnetic properties. Perhaps what we moderns call "quantum connections" are made by this sticky psychic substance known by various ancient cultures. Since we can't see the invisible strings connecting matter in the universe, we can only be 'weirded out' by observable associations between things, and continue our search for 'causes' in the physical sphere.

In effect, could the modern term for *aka* be *synchronicity*? Is it comparable to *theta quanta* or *attention units*, or to the *akasha* of ancient knowledge?

Everybody is connected to the rest of the world, as Kin explains, through the shadowy stuff called *mana*, as well as above the level of *mana* (on the plane of postulates) to all other infinite beings. Might there be a connection between this sticky substance and the creation of the world? Kin writes, "Akasha is the most subtle of substances, a mere potential and mother to the four elements. By transforming itself, akasha becomes first fire, as such produces gases (air), these cooling off liquify (water) and finally, through further condensation, turn into solid matter (earth)." Does this describe Genesis? This is the alchemical pattern by which the world was created by akasha. In the beginning was the word. But thought had to precede the word. As Kin writes in *Pied Pipers of Heaven*:

> All language was originally creative or 'evocative' insofar as the root sounds of words denote concepts rather than things and, if spoken properly, would evoke 'the spirit of the thing' and thus make theta quanta assemble and bring the actual thing into physical existence.

Just the words "I think, therefore I am" suggest a "whereness" to being. To be, you must be some place. You must be somewhere doing the thinking. As L. Ron Hubbard claimed, "the thetan is where his attention units are parked." Let's park our attention units now on the genesis of scientology.

From Dianetics to Scientology

The concepts involved in scientology and some SOPs aren't totally new. It has been noted that Hubbard studied hypnosis, psychological theories, and related subjects for a year or more at the Oak Knoll Naval Hospital where he was treated for ulcers. Apparently, Hubbard was practiced at hypnosis. In *Science of Survival*, Hubbard claimed to have knowledge of the use of "pain-drug-hypnosis" in espionage work. The context and extent of his knowledge in this area, as well as how he obtained it, is unknown.

According to Peter Moon in his Appendix to *Montauk Revisited*, Hubbard studied "narcosynthesis" and hypnotic regression techniques while working for Naval Intelligence. Narcosynthesis is therapy created by Drs. Roy Grinker and John Spiegel, who published an account of its use in 1945 in their book *Men Under Stress*. Since Hubbard incorporated the Hubbard Dianetic Research Foundation in 1950, he could easily have studied this book in the Naval Hospital library as he claims.

Narcosynthesis was used by U.S. and British psychiatrists during World War II for "battle neurosis" or "combat fatigue." This therapy combined Pavlovian and Freudian concepts with the induction of hypnotic states using barbiturates and sodium penthothal to assist the patient to 'synthesize' the personality. However, it is important to note that Hubbard did not recommend the use of drugs, and specifically stated that drug-hypnotism is "dianetically illegal." In his "Research and Discovery" series, Hubbard strongly cautioned against its use, saying, "One will find regression if one treats soldiers who have been unlucky enough to undergo narcosynthesis … He was merely sick before, but now he is crazy … Anything which is touched in narcosynthesis is apt to be restimulated permanently."

Moon explains that Hubbard combined principles from this research along with earlier studies to create Dianetics, which Moon describes as "major regression therapy." As Jon Atack opines, a study of Dianetics reveals that it is a careful rewording of then-existing psychological and hypnotherapeutic practices. Moon states that Hubbard also studied Aleister Crowley's work, but that Hubbard's techniques were "very much his own." This is true to the extent that Hubbard has written over a hundred books and has produced over two thousand recorded lectures, and has registered thousands of trademarks, including symbols which may have magical significance.

Hubbard's first system, Dianetics, which included the concept of the "Reactive Mind," is heavily based on early Freudian concepts. In addition, as Atack has pointed out, the idea that the mind is based in certain identities, as well as the power of the redefinition of words, comes from Alfred Korzybski's "Korzybski's General Semantics." Atack points out that Dianetics also includes ideas propounded by American psychiatrists Grinker and Spiegel and English psychiatrist William Sargant, as well as psychiatrists J. Sadger, who referred to embryonic memories, and Otto Rank, who held a belief in the residual effects of birth trauma. In Dianetics, Hubbard also lists as resources Franz Mesmer, Ivan Pavlov, Herbert Spencer and Emil Kraepelin. It should also be noted that in his earlier years Hubbard was a science fiction writer, and was also a roommate of the science fiction writer Robert A. Heinlein. Jon Atack describes scientology as "a hybrid of science-fiction and magic," largely derived from "Will Durant's *Story of Philosophy* and the works of Aleister Crowley."

When Hubbard later lost the rights to dianetics, he founded scientology. Atack describes scientology as a mixture of occult ritual and 1950s style psychotherapy. He believes that scientology's "auditing" procedure is a modernized, Westernized version of magical ritual. He also notes that Hubbard intimated that he wrote Dianetics in three weeks via "automatic writing" dictated by an entity called "the Empress." Atack and others believe Hubbard was channeling this entity. As ex-scientologist L. Kin also professes in *From the Bottom to the Top*, "anyone who understands traditional esoterics will immediately see that OT II and III are an initiation of the highest calibre."

Babalon Working

Interestingly, Moon connects Hubbard's role on Earth to two things: his involvement with magician Jack Parsons in the Babalon Working ritual, and his "Wilson" heritage. The Wilson clan, explains solo offshoot practitioner L. Kin in *From the Bottom to the Top*, is a family of highly-initiated Scottish Druids. It turns out that Hubbard's father, Harry Ross Hubbard, was actually a Wilson who had been adopted in America by the Hubbard family. Kin maintains that Hubbard "grew up in fairly elevated spiritual circles." However, scientologists oppose the idea that Hubbard would have been working with either Parsons or Crowley, since he represented the antithesis to their type of magic.

According to Jon Atack in *A Piece of Blue Sky*, Hubbard met Jack Parsons while on convalescent leave in Los Angeles in 1945. Parsons was one of the developers of Jet Assisted Take-Off (JATO) units, and a founding member of CalTech's rocket project, which later became the Jet Propulsion Laboratory. Parsons and Hubbard spent much time together in Parson's home in Pasadena, which has been described as a cooperative rooming house full of eccentric people. In addition to being a science fiction fan and an explosives chemist, Parsons practiced black magic under Crowley's OTO. As is now well known, Hubbard and Parsons became involved in January of 1946 in the California desert in a magical venture written by Crowley called the "Babalon Working."

There are two opposing theories with regard to the Babalon Working. Some believe Hubbard was a black magician and his agreement with Parsons was real, and others believe Hubbard was a white magician who was trying to shut down Parson's Los Angeles Ordo Templi Orientis (OTO) Lodge. Aleister Crowley believed neither of these to be the case. He considered the entire fiasco to be a "confidence scam," wherein Hubbard got away with Parson's girl as well as his money. There is a lot to be said for the latter theory. On the other hand, William Gray has written in *Magical Ritual Methods,* "the late A. Crowley's rites have enough fool-traps in them to catch a regiment of idiots, or trip hordes of innocent unwary dabblers." This could explain a lot as well.

As Atack explains, Parsons wrote to Crowley early in 1946 describing Hubbard as "the most Thelemic person I have ever met and is in complete accord with our own principles." He wrote: "although he has no formal training in Magick, he has an extraordinary amount of experience and understanding in the field. From some of his experiences I deduce he is in direct touch with some higher intelligence, possibly his Guardian Angel." Parsons explained that he and Hubbard were pooling resources in a partnership. He also told him that his mistress, Sara Elizabeth Northrup, had taken a liking to Hubbard, and had transferred her affections to him. Nonetheless, Parsons professed that he and Hubbard were "great friends."

In Crowley's OTO, the personification of female was "Babalon." In his novel, *The Moonchild*, Crowley described the creation of an "Homunculus." The Homunculus is described as "a living being in form resembling man, and possessing those qualities of man which distinguish him from beasts, namely intellect and power of speech, but neither begotten and born in the manner of human generation, nor inhabited by a human soul." Crowley said it was "the great idea of magicians of all times to obtain a Messiah by some adaptation of the sexual process."

Thus, Parsons became intent on conjuring Crowley's Babalon, the human Messiah or Antichrist who would overthrow Christianity, using Crowley's "VIIIth degree" ritual, which was later distributed as "The Book of Babalon." Other names for the ritual are "Concerning the Secret Marriages of Gods with Men" and the "Magic Masturbation." The Babalon Working ritual is described in detail by Jack Parsons in *Freedom is a Two-Edged Sword*, by Jon Atack in *A*

Piece of Blue Sky, and by John Carter in *Sex and Rockets: The Occult World of Jack Parsons*. In January 1946, Parsons and his magical assistant, L. Ron Hubbard, performed Crowley's VIIIth Degree. As Atack writes:

> Parsons performed rituals which led up to an operation of symbolic birth. Then he settled down to wait. For four days he experienced "tension and unease . . . . Then, on January 18, at sunset, while the Scribe [Hubbard] and I were on the Mojave desert, the feeling of tension suddenly snapped . . . . I returned home, and found a young woman answering the requirements waiting for me." The woman was Marjorie Cameron. Parsons wrote to Crowley: "I seem to have my elemental. She turned up one night after the conclusion of the operation and has been with me since . . . . She has red hair and slant green eyes as specified.

Parsons prepared an altar according to instructions. When Hubbard returned after a week away, he relayed to Parsons his vision of a beautiful woman riding naked on a great "cat-like beast." They immediately began the ritual. Hubbard robed in white and Parsons robed in black hooded attire holding a cup and dagger, the two magicians played Rachmaninoff's *Isle of the Dead* as background music. Shortly afterward, Hubbard began to channel masturbatory instructions from beyond. He instructed Parsons to "display thyself to our lady, dedicate thy organs to Her," *et cetera*.

As Jon Atack explains, the next day, Hubbard, acting as Babalon's medium, gave instructions for the second and third rituals. During the second ritual, Parsons was to gaze into an empty black box for an hour until a "sacred design" would become apparent, which he was then to reproduce in wood. Then, robed in scarlet ("symbolic of birth") with a black sash, Parsons was to invoke Babalon again. Hubbard's instructions, given in sexual detail, were to "think upon her, move her into Babalon, bring her into Babalon … until the flame of lust is high." The sexual pretext of this ritual is clear as Hubbard instructs Parsons to "preserve the material basis," and "consider thou the Beast raping."

On March 6, Parsons sent a letter to Crowley informing him that his first instructions had been received through "Ron the Seer," and that he had followed them to the letter. He wrote that he had been "the agency chosen to assist the birth, which is now accomplished." Requesting extreme secrecy, Parsons claimed the Homunculus would be "loosed on the world" in nine months. He admonished that "premature discussion or revelation would cause an abortion." As Atack writes: "Parsons obviously thought Babalon was gestating in Marjorie Cameron's womb." However, Crowley didn't believe it for a minute. As Jon Atack relays the story, Crowley wrote back, "You have me completely puzzled by your remarks about the elemental—the danger of discussing or copying anything. I thought I had the most morbid imagination, as good as any man's, but it seems I have not. I cannot form the slightest idea who you can possibly mean."

Crowley then wrote to his deputy in New York: "Apparently he [Parsons] or Ron or somebody is producing a Moonchild. I get fairly frantic when I contemplate the idiocy of these louts." As Atack explains, Crowley viewed the gods not as distinct individuals, but as representations of particular energies, which could be tapped. Crowley believed the Gods are names for the forces of Nature themselves. Crowley's IXth degree magic is concerned with embodying this energy or force. Crowley's IXth degree ritual, which was performed by Parsons, Hubbard and Marjorie Cameron, describes the Homunculus as a being of perfect form, with all powers and privileges of humanity, but with the essence of a particular chosen force. Crowley's Homunculus would be the servant of its creator; to it "thou art Sole God and Lord."

According to Atack, the partnership agreement between Parsons, Hubbard and Sara Northrup clearly delineated that all money earned by the three of them for life was to be equally divided. In May, OTO member Louis T. Culling wrote to Crowley's deputy, Karl Germer, suggesting that Parsons should be "salvaged from the undue influence of another." Crowley's reply telegram read: "Suspect Ron playing confidence trick, Jack evidently weak fool obvious victim prowling swindlers." On another telegram he wrote that he suspected Parsons had committed errors, and had "got a miraculous illumination which rhymes with nothing." Crowley wrote, "from our brother's account, he has given away both his girl and his money, apparently it is an ordinary confidence trick."

Hubbard, Parsons and Northrup had indeed set up a company which would purchase yachts in Florida and sell them in California. Hubbard and Northrup went to Florida and started buying. But, when Hubbard failed to provide any accounting of his spending, Parsons went to Florida after them. There, the business fell apart and Parsons undertook legal proceedings. A restraining order was placed on all assets and the personal property and assets were divided. As Atack writes, Parsons later wrote to Crowley:

> Here I am in Miami pursueing [sic] the children of my folly. I have them well tied up: they cannot move without going to jail. However I am afraid that most of the money [in the joint account] has already been dissipated. I will be lucky to salvage 3,000-5,000 dollars. In the interim I have been flat broke.

In 1969, the *London Sunday Times* published a story on the Babalon Working ritual. The *Times* later printed a retraction written by Hubbard saying that he had been "sent in" by the FBI to handle a dangerous situation involving a black magic ring located in Pasadena. While staying at the house, he found the situation to be "very bad." He claimed to have shut down this black magic circle, and "rescued" a girl. Interestingly, Parsons' FBI file does indicate that he was routinely investigated beginning in 1943 due to his "peculiar lifestyle." According to Atack, there is no mention of Hubbard in Parsons' FBI file, and Parsons continued to keep his high security classification until 1952.

In October 1948, Parsons repeated the Babalon Working ritual on his own, and in 1949 began work on *The Book of the Antichrist*, proclaiming himself "Belarion, Antichrist." In 1952, just a few years after the Babalon Working rituals, Jack Parsons was killed in an explosion in his laboratory in Los Angeles. Within two days, his mother either committed suicide or was killed. Jet Propulsion Labs named a crater on the dark side of the moon for Parsons.

Hubbard's claim to have "broken up black magic in America" is interesting. It has been difficult to establish whether Hubbard was connected to any intelligence agency. Of course, Hubbard's own claim published in the *London Times*, that he had been "sent in" to a black magic ring in Pasadena, had found the situation to be "very bad," and had "rescued a girl," may be taken at face value. Perhaps, on the other hand, Hubbard was in fact working for the 'Druids' as a white magician. Hubbard was, in fact, successful in 'busting' Parsons in another way, since Parsons claimed that because of Hubbard he had been stripped of his fortune, his house, and all he possessed. Parsons is described by Robert Anton Wilson as one of the greatest libertarian philosophers of the 20th Century. This may be true, but there is a lot more to Parsons than meets the eye.

In an article entitled "Dark Side of a Bad Moon," Michael Hoffman II writes that Parsons was a government operative who "enjoyed immunity from prosecution for sales of explosives on the black market," and "traveled under sealed orders from the government." Hoffman also reports that at various times Parsons was employed by the LAPD, the Los Angeles Superior Court, the U.S. Army and Navy, and the National Defense Research Council, and that Parsons held top security clearance. Much of Parsons work remains classified and cannot be obtained even under the Freedom of Information Act. In addition, Hoffman writes, Parsons enjoyed a rare immunity from prosecution in various crimes, and his FBI file is heavily redacted. For instance, Hoffman reports, it is known that Parsons was transferring secret documents relating to U.S. rocket and defense technology to the Israelis beginning in October of 1948 until June of 1950. Parsons was caught in the act by personnel from Hughes Aircraft's Research and Development Laboratory. In a strange set of circumstances which occurred in October of 1951, the U.S. Attorney in the case declined to prosecute Parsons for treason, apparently after J. Edgar Hoover stepped in.

As Hoffman also reports, it is alleged that before each rocket test Parsons invoked the "Hymn to Pan," which Hoffman describes as a "dirge to the god of panic and frenzy" written by Aleister Crowley. Hoffman writes that Crowley was not only head of the OTO but was well-connected to the British establishment and was an agent of British Intelligence. In this article, Hoffman also makes the claim that indeed Hubbard was an agent of U.S. Naval Intelligence. (see, *Revisionist History*, www.hoffman-info.com)

Many have claimed that the Babalon Working rituals opened an interdimensional portal into this dimension and let in the wicked entities of the modern UFO era. Could this be so? As Blavatsky has warned in *Isis Unveiled*, a trained Adept should purify the essence and "equilibrize" the elements within the circle in which he wished to attract the *pure spirits*. Blavatsky warned, "woe to the imprudent inquirer who ignorantly trespasses upon forbidden ground." This trespasser will evoke powers he or she cannot control, and will "arouse sentries which allow only their masters to pass." As William Gray has also admonished in *Magical Ritual Methods*, "without adequate safeguards and common sense methods of working, more harm than good is possible to human operators." As Gray has also mentioned, "the late A. Crowley's rites have enough fool-traps in them to catch a regiment of idiots, or trip hordes of innocent unwary dabblers."

Crowley biographer Kenneth Grant refers to Hubbard as "a confidence trickster who had wormed his way into the OTO on the pretence of being interested in Magick." As Michael Culkin writes in "Aleister Crowley, The Midnight Messenger," (*Paranoia*, Issue 21):

> In April, 1945, Parsons was introduced to L. Ron Hubbard. Enter the prankster! ... Hubbard's relationship to Parsons is basically similar to Edward Kelley's relationship to Dr. John Dee, the English alchemist and Elizabethan court astrologer. Kelley was also a prankster and scryer, and Dee fell completely under his spell.... Parsons was also an alchemist, but needed a 'magical partner,' and Hubbard became that partner.

Was the Hubbard/Parson's "tryst" actually a deadly contest between a Druidic wizard and a Satanist? As Kin writes, he once met a Druid who was a "solo auditor" in scientology. The Druid told Kin that the Druids believe Hubbard was "entrusted with the task of making Druidic knowledge available to mankind in popular language." The Druid said he had heard this from his teacher, so Kin called his teacher to verify the story. The teacher indeed confirmed he had been told this by his teacher, who had known Hubbard. He confirmed that indeed Hubbard was born into a clan of magicians of the Druidic tradition, and received a Druidic education from late childhood on, lasting about fifteen years. The Druid further informed Kin that the Druids believe Hubbard was entrusted with the task of rendering Crowley powerless, since Crowley's form of black magic was considered evil to them. Hubbard's mission was "to rehabilitate Druidic knowledge in the eyes of the world." Kin adds that Hubbard was excluded from Druidic circles after founding the "Church of Scientology" in 1954, since it is against their policy to start a religion.

Druidic philosophy encompasses the idea that the world is animate and ensouled. The Druidic apprehension of the world is as communion: the perceiver assumes the identity of the perceived and the boundaries blur. The great "bards" were masters at "walking between the worlds." Druidic magic is also closely associated with the use of medicinal herbs. The Druids were guardians of an oral-based culture; as such, they underwent intensive training in memory and concentration. The role of the Druidic bard was as "word magician." The use of poetry was magical rather than mundane; poems accompanied by the harp were considered invocations; the spoken word could invoke the divine. Poetic inspiration or "trance" was gained by lying in the dark under conditions of sensory deprivation for long periods of time. The Spring, 1995 issue of *Parabola* asserted that some of the traditional Druidic rituals are reminiscent of techniques used in modern hypnosis to alter consciousness.

The Thetan's Briefcase

It has been noted that Hubbard did a lot of esoteric reading, and also for a short time beginning in 1940 was a "neophyte member" of the Rosicrucian order, the Ancient and Mystical Order Rosae Crucis (AMORC), at their headquarters in San Jose. One of the most important underlying philosophical concepts of both Theosophy and Rosicrucianism is the ancient theory of the thought-form, the idea that *thought produces energy*, and that all events, mental or physical, are recorded as subtle vibrations in nature's memory and in all matter.

We've discussed the concept of thought-forms in an earlier chapter, but here the concept of the "elemental" should be explained. Theosophists Besant and Leadbeater wrote in their book *Thought-forms* that each definite thought produces both a radiating vibration and a floating form. The radiating vibration carries the character of the thought, but not the subject of the thought. Since the mental body is composed of matter of varying degrees of density, there are many varieties of mental matter, and each one has its appropriate rate of vibration. Every rush of emotion and feeling in a human being produces a permanent effect. Each particular human emotion has a particular vibration and hue, which adds its hue permanently to the normal coloring of the astral body. Every time a person yields to a particular emotion, it becomes easier to yield to it again since the astral body is in the habit of vibrating at a certain rate. However, since human emotions are very complex, the resulting thought-form thrown off by an emotion will show several colors instead of just one.

Thought-forms which take on a 'life' of their own are referred to by Theosophists as "elementals." As Besant and Leadbeater wrote in *Thought-Forms*, "each thought draws round it the matter which is appropriate for its expression, and sets that matter into vibration in harmony with its own." In this way, the character of the thought brings on its color. Clearness and definiteness in thought are of greater importance than strength. The "elemental essence" is described by Besant and Leadbeater as "that strange half-intelligent life which surrounds us in all directions, vivifying the matter of the mental and astral planes." This "animated matter" responds readily to the influence of human thought, and "every impulse sent out, either from the mental body or from the astral body of man, immediately clothes itself in a temporary vehicle of this vitalized matter." These thoughts or impulses become temporarily a kind of living entity; "the thought-force being the soul and the vivified matter the body." This kind of 'living entity' is referred to by Theosophists as "astral or mental matter ensouled by the monadic essence at the stage of one of the elemental kingdoms." It is also referred to as "quickened matter" or, for brevity's sake, "an elemental."

Thus, it's easy to see that, among his many possible influences, Hubbard's philosophy may have been influenced by the animistic Druidic and Kahuna principles (which have their source in ancient Atlantis, according to Pinkham in *The Serpents of Wisdom*), which have also influenced Theosophy and Rosicrucianism.

As L. Kin writes in *Pied Pipers of Heaven*, the source of mental energy according to Hubbard is "theta." Every spiritual being operating a body is a thetan. A thetan is "an immortal spirit being who produces and uses *theta* in order to translate his thoughts into action." In addition, a second subtle body called the genetic entity (GE) guards and animates the physical body. The GE protects the body during trauma or sickness, and stays closer to it, while the thetan is more of an astral body. As mentioned earlier, many religions and philosophies contain this trinity of selves. As Michael Cremo has noted in the Vedic story of the "City of Nine Gates," intelligence, as a subtle material energy, is perhaps not itself conscious but mimics the behavior of consciousness. It thus attracts the attention of the conscious self, causing the self to identify with it. As Cremo deduces from this ancient tale, the mind/body dualistic conundrum can be explained by the concept of a triad incorporating (1) a nonmaterial conscious self, (2) a subtle material body formed of mind and intelligence, and (3) a physical body composed of gross matter.

According to Hubbard's philosophy, all mental imagery consists of mental MEST, which is "Mass and Energy existing in Space and Time." MEST has differing density, solidity, mass, size and durability, depending upon the amount of *attention units* given to it by a thetan. Mental energy consists of units of theta quanta. Theta quanta are very fine vibrating subatomic particles. Hubbard taught that "whatever one puts attention on is energized by theta quanta flow." A thetan habitually puts "lumps" of attention units on things in his path which connect and anchor him to the world. Theta quanta or attention units may be seen as similar to *mana* or *aka* of the Kahunas, since this sticky substance connects astral bodies to the material world. The similarity of these ideas to Theosophy also come to mind in the following quote from Annie Besant's *Thought-Forms*:

> Each man travels through space enclosed within a case of his own building, surrounded by a mass of the forms created by his habitual thoughts. Through this medium he looks out upon the world and naturally sees everything tinged with its predominant colors, and all rates of vibration which reach him from without are more or less modified by its rate.

According to Hubbard, theta is manifested as "pure thought or concept in the form of postulates." It is also manifested as "energized thought in the form of loud thinking and mental image pictures." As L. Kin writes, a thetan creates his own theta field in order to have a "platform to act from." Although a thetan actually exists outside the coordinates of MEST, he locates himself within a field so that he can be perceptible. This bundle of mental energy located within a playing field was referred to by Hubbard as "mind."

In order to function in the "game" of life, a thetan needs "a body, food, playmates, and things to play with." Therefore, these things are manifested through the platform of mind on two levels, the level of mental MEST and the level of physical MEST. The thetan continuously creates this energy field called Mind, through which he makes himself perceptible and through which he makes himself a player in the "game." According to Kin, Mind is the thetan's brief case.

According to Hubbard, a thetan gets the brain working "by pulsing towards it." The mental vibrations of Mind set off the brain's neurons. Recall McGowan's thoughtron theory discussed earlier. As McGowan suggested, a wave/particle he called a thoughtron travels at great speed caused by the intention of thought. McGowan believed that thoughtrons are the particles which bring ideas into fruition in the material world. McGowan wrote that thought is the source of all matter and all life, and it conceives and carries out ideas by using a physical system of projection of infinitrons into thoughtrons.

McGowan suggested that "the personality transmits orders to the brain according to its thoughts by concentrating thoughtrons at a nerve synapse." Eventually, this forms a code of instructions. He suggested that, "as the concentration of thoughtrons increases, a pressure is built at a synapse causing them, by induction, to jump the gap to another neuron which leads to a proper location in the brain." The coded instructions in the thoughtrons, he suggested, choose the proper neurons to connect with and transmit their data. In addition, McGowan wrote the following:

> Thought, by its intention, causes particles to have the various frequencies and resonances necessary to make each desired conception a reality. The DNA molecule which has within it the plan for its actions and reactions to result in a specified organism is an example of how these particles, as messengers, messages, and material, are organized to carry out thought's intention. ... Thought, by a system of waves and variable frequencies and resonances, projects infinitrons into thoughtrons, which by the evolution of particles, result in the partons, electrons, protons, and neutrons, which structure the atoms, which form the elements, that compose all the compounds that form life and matter.

The concept of the thoughtron as a wave/particle, described scientifically in McGowan's *The Thoughtron Theory of Life and Matter*, helps us to understand how Hubbard viewed "emotion." According to Hubbard, Mind consists of pure energy, and is in a constant state of vibration which is perceived as emotion. The Latin root of the word "emotion" means "a motion emanating." As such, emotions have a frequency and an amplitude. According to Kin, emotions are "the thetan's mode of pulsing into his body and environment and of responding to it." As Hubbard clarified, "the intention of exerting effort bridges from the thetan into the body by emotion." Emotion is *intent*, an impulse to act, "a motion emanating." Thus, Kin writes in *Pied Pipers*, the "mental force of emotion, which emanates from a thought, is necessary to achieve motion, or physical activity."

Hubbard taught that through their postulates (thoughts, concepts) all thetans "overlap as infinities," or perhaps we might say "in infinity." This is comparable to Swann's idea of "bio-mind net." A thetan, above the level of mental MEST, as a postulate overlapping other postulates, is in a state or condition Hubbard called "static." Yet, Hubbard maintained that at this level individuals still remain individuals, and do not become "one." It is in MEST that individuals lose their self-identity and adhere to a mob mentality called consensus reality.

The game of life, according to Hubbard, is unpredictable, and the state of "not knowing" is an agreement, an act of will. Since one cannot play a "game" when one knows everything, there must be an agreement of "not knowing." However, as Kin explains, the more habitual "not knowing" becomes, the more it becomes a trap. One becomes trapped in the MEST universe, and forgets that one is actually "up there" as well, existing as pure thought, and even further up, as pure static: the source of thought. This realm is comparable to the "ether" or Matrix which remote viewers claim to explore. In India, breaking the barrier of "not-knowing" is called *samadhi* or enlightenment.

According to Kin, "foreign-made entities and the Genetic Entity put their pictures, charges and postulates into the head of the unaware thetan—and drive him out of 'valence.' He takes on valences foreign to him; his own valence is submerged." A body thetan (BT) is a "ridge" disconnected from the thetan, containing all information about the thetan's identity, and a cluster is a large collection of BTs. A ridge can be "copied," and can wander from its creator to another host and become an entity. The original creator "can't get rid of it because it consists of his theta quanta," and contains the identity of his postulate (thought) and emotion at the time of creation. Thus, an "entity" may consist of "at least two brands of theta particles: those of the original creator and those of the second owner who subconsciously registered the foreign ridge, and in trying to keep it out, made a copy of it." Let's look at similar concepts explained by Besant and Leadbeater in *Thought-forms*:

> The desire (or astral) body gives rise to a second class of entities, similar in their general constitution to the thought-forms already

described, but limited to the astral plane, and generated by the mind under the dominion of the animal nature. These are caused by the activity of the lower mind, throwing itself out through the astral body.... Vibrations in the body of desire are in this case set up and under these this body throws off a vibrating portion of itself, shaped, as in the previous case, by the nature of the vibrations, and this attracts to itself some of the appropriate elemental essence of the astral world.

Such a thought-form has for its body this elemental essence, and for its animating soul the desire or passion which threw it forth; according to the amount of mental energy combined with this desire or passion will be the force of the thought-form. These, like those belonging to the mental plane, are called artificial elementals, and they are by far the most common, as few thoughts of ordinary men and women are untinged with desire, passion, or emotion.

As McGowan explains in *The Thoughtron Theory of Life and Matter*, a "facsimile" is a section of thought which contains physical universe impressions on it, and which also contains a "time tag." The 'time track' is of great importance in SOPs as well as in remote viewing, since it places the occurrence of an event in a time relationship to other events. According to Hubbard, the time track is "the entire sequence of 'how' incidents, complete with all 'perceptics' picked up by a person during his whole existence."

Contrary to popular belief, time does not heal all mental anguish. According to Hubbard, a facsimile can have just as much "charge" on it fifty years later as it did when it occurred. As McGowan explains, Hubbard taught that facsimiles are an acquired aberration, usually extremely contra-survival, which mankind has picked up along the time track. As Hubbard explained, "facsimiles are used by the mind in combination with other facsimiles to make a body, animate it and direct it toward its purpose of *to be* and the conquest of the physical universe." This sounds quite similar to an "artificial elemental" in the lingo of the Theosophists.

According to Hubbard, a universe is "a whole system of created things." Each thetan has created his universe, and each person "carries his universe about and feels at home there." This sounds a lot like what Annie Besant had in mind when she wrote, "each man travels through space enclosed within a case of his own building, surrounded by a mass of the forms created by his habitual thoughts."

To summarize, memories have a vibratory element; *engrams* are recorded memories of events. Mental pictures are called *mock-ups* and have a real and objective existence. When an event is imagined, it acquires a reality which can influence the circuitry of the E-meter. The process of auditing includes *exteri - orization*; a state which Hubbard referred to in his command to "get three feet in back of your head." The *auditing* of engrams, whether they consist of *ridges* built up by postulates and counter-postulates, or whether they are found on your time track or someone else's time track, requires something akin to telepathic time travel.

One might take the view that these are symbolic processes, but it is unlikely that a scientologist would agree. By way of a unique e-motional self-exploration and past-life regression, which might be described as Freudian-Animism or Therapeutic Panpsychism, it might take years to clean up the vibratory records of various parts of ourselves. A scientologist who has reached a point of mental clearedness and is free from aberration is referred to as "Clear." Kin states, once one becomes an advanced solo auditor, they "will have no problem entering another person's reactive data banks *telepathically* and assisting him in cleaning them up." It has been noted that once a person becomes accustomed to this telepathic time travel procedure, it is quite easily facilitated.

Interestingly, as Bruce Vance has explained in *Dreamscape: Voyage in an Alternate Reality*, travel in the out-of-body realm is performed quite differently than in the physical realm. Movement in this sphere of existence is performed by *intent*. As he explains, the dream body is the astral or spirit body, or "vital body" of the Rosicrucians. This is the vehicle of navigation used by consciousness to travel to nonphysical realms, including the dream world. Movement in the Dreamscape, including an out-of-body, remote viewing, or dream world experience, is different than in the physical dimension. In the Dreamscape, Vance explains, you must "employ imagination or visualization to see where you want to be, and then you must 'intend' the move; that is, you must create the intention to move to the 'place' where you want to be." Thus, the method of moving around in a lucid dream or OBE employs new "laws of motion" necessitating clear and directed thought-volition. Incidentally, it is also taught in the *Bhagavad-gita* that at the time of death, if one *thinks* of Krsna and remembers the *form* of Krsna, he will approach this spiritual kingdom in the afterlife. This ancient teaching implies that directed thought-volition is necessary to effect movement in other space-time dimensions.

The next chapter will explore a few similarities between scientological, magical, psycho-therapeutic and remote viewing concepts.

CHAPTER ELEVEN

PSYCHOLOGY, MAGIC AND THE TIME TRACK

An organism's time track goes back before time—to the moment he decided to be a monocell—and progresses through all the millions of evolutions to this immediate instant.

Harold McGowan

The Thoughtron Theory of Life and Matter

Psychology and magical practice may be seen as two aspects of a system which integrates the human personality. Israel Regardie has suggested that the ideas of the Conscious and the Unconscious are fundamental to both psychology and magic. Both systems aim to unify these two aspects of man's psyche and to awaken latent powers and functions. As we will see, certain terminology regarding these powers and functions appears to be somewhat interchangeable.

While I am not a practitioner of magic, I think it is important for people to understand that all magical ritual is not necessarily consonant with satanism, witchcraft, blood rituals, sex rituals or sado-masochism. There are certainly cult groups in operation today which do employ sex, torture and violence. For instance, some neo-pagan 'witch'rites focus on sado-masochistic 'bondage and beating'rituals, which are symbolic dramatizations of ancient sacrificial slaughter rites. Unfortunately, as William Gray explains, sex and violence are two things that can create a powerful effect on the Inner world. And it is unfortunate, as well, that blood offerings, sado-masochism or other primitive and unenlightened rituals are the only way that some undeveloped persons can acquire access to other dimensions. However, Gray admonishes that much better routes exist for making Inner dimensional contact, and the ones that take the higher road are those guided by love and respect. As a matter of fact, Hubbard often repeated this admonition.

The Nil Principle

There are certain undeniable parallels between some of the techniques utilized by SOPs, psychotherapy and certain magical systems. For instance, as L. Kin explains, "auditing" is an attempt to determine the correct classification of each ridge, postulate, or counterpostulate as "homemade" or "foreign-made," and uncreating it by mentally "running through" the sequence of events that created it until the negative emotions charging it are discharged. This procedure can be seen as a merging of psychological and magical systems. As Israel Regardie writes in *The Middle Pillar*, one of the aims of Magic is to go over memories of childhood over and over again to remove resistance to repressed material. He writes:

> Beginning with the actual events of the day upon which the reader determines to commence this exercise, the meditation should gradually extend its field of vision until ultimately the events and occurrences of the earliest years are brought into the light of day. The technique is principally one of the training of the mind to think backwards.... As the childhood memories are exposed, the student will see for himself in what way the conflict now bothering him came into manifestation. ... [B]y this process of remembering he will see in what way he failed to respond properly to the phenomena of his existence.

According to Regardie, once the nature and origin of the conflict is thus exposed, one must undertake an attitude of unconditional acceptance of the event causing the conflict. Once this event and the responses to it are fully rec-

141

ognized, a positive attitude should be adopted with regard to the event; i.e. the person should proceed to ignore it and begin to develop in an entirely new direction. This can be seen as the discharging of negative emotions wrapped up in the event.

William Gray describes a similar magical procedure in *Magical Ritual Methods.* With regard to a problem that is a matter of personal worry or to which there is a constant emotional "reaction," Gray explains that the practitioner should evoke the problem fully into consciousness until the particular unwanted reaction (i.e., emotion) sets in, then deliberately banish and neutralize it into Nil. The idea of unconditional acceptance is the same as Nil. Most mystery schools have their own "zeroing" procedure, and each practice has the same objective, which, according to Gray, involves swinging the direction of consciousness through the Nil-point toward its changed focus of attention.

The Nil-principle, as Gray explains, requires exclusion from focus of all but the essence of the subject under study. It is also known as "banishing," "dismissing," or "outer negation-inner positivity." The Nil-principle concentrates on isolating a stream of consciousness by excluding all other thoughts. In magic, as Gray explains, the "Nil-point" is the "All-point," for the more we Are Not, the more We Are. The Nil-principle is a "zeroing" procedure. As Gray explains, whatever we reduce to Zero becomes raw material for creation. Everything must be made into Nothing in order to become Something. This he calls the "condition of undifferentiated neutrality."

With regard to this matter, in *The Thoughtron Theory of Life and Matter*, Harold McGowan writes the following:

> Many processes, techniques, and drills have been developed to help the Preclear expose engrams and to run them out. They have been designed to give the Preclear the opportunity to make a perfect duplicate of the engram and cause it to vanish. The 20th axiom of scientology states: "Bringing the Static (Thetan or "I") to create a perfect duplicate causes the vanishment of any existence or part thereof. A perfect duplicate is an additional creation of the object, its energy and space, in its own space, in its own time, using its own energy. This violates the condition that two objects must not occupy the same space, and causes vanishment of the object.

As McGowan explains, by creating an exact duplicate of an unwanted engram in this way, the "Preclear" will be clear of any aberration it has caused. According to magical principles, whatever can be "called up" on purpose can be dismissed on purpose, since all is under the control of the will and intention. To effect this, Gray suggests, all that is needed is a ritual which appropriates circuits of consciousness through gestures, commands and symbols. In order to open the consciousness, one must imagine the opening of a doorway and give the command to "come in" out loud. To raise or call up a formation of consciousness and positively recognize it as happening gives it reality in mental dimensions. Interestingly, Gray writes, "once time-space events of any world cease to have power over us, we start having power over them."

As L. Kin explains in *Pied Pipers of Heaven*, "This is an affinity process. As you don't resist these energy masses but voluntarily tune in to them and causatively duplicate their resonance band, they dissolve. It works purely by duplication of vibration." Hubbard's Axiom 20 claims the following: "Bringing the static [higher self] to create a perfect duplicate causes the vanishment of any existence or part thereof." Also contained in Kin's explanation is the idea of "vibration." In magical systems, it is important to be sure that the linguistic evocation you are using creates a vibration in the body. As Israel Regardie writes in *The Middle Pillar*, the practitioner must find the right tonal frequency which will resonate and tune in to the desired frequency band. This is what is meant by "affinity." Your frequency bands are the same, therefore, they have an affinity for each other.

As Kin also explains, the root sounds of words denote concepts, and if they are properly uttered, that is, magically uttered, they evoke 'the spirit of the thing.' This causes "theta quanta" to assemble and bring the actual thing into existence. This 'thing', once understood in its entirety, can then be banished to Nil. To understand some thing means having an affinity; i.e. not having any feelings one way or another, not attaching any negative or positive emotions to it. Because if you react with emotion you are making a copy of it, whether you know it or not, and it becomes a BT or Cluster. (Note: This thinking is opposed to a division between the thinker and the thought-about, since the thought-about actually becomes a part of the thinker.)

However, in *Scientology: More Than a Cult?*, L. Kin has noted an extremely important distinction between black magic, white magic and scientological principles. As he explains:

> In scientology, one works towards *dissolving* ridges and entities of whatever kind. In magic, one strives to *create* new entities, and to command about and use already existing ones. ... Scientology cannot be compared to white or black magic. The task of the auditor consists of rehabilitating the self-determinism of a being and of eliminating the aberrating influences of mental masses and energies on the thetan. Scientology addresses itself to the dissolving of unwanted conditions; black magic, in contrast, to the solidification and clustering of black masses and their employment in the control of beings; white magic concentrates on the use of entities in order to achieve good effects.

Remote Viewing as Telepathic Time Travel

Let's get back to the initial reason for this digression from the subject of remote viewing. What are the similarities between remote viewing and solo offshoot practices? The most obvious is the aspect of telepathic time travel. As Harold McGowan writes in *The Thoughtron Theory of Life and Matter*, the time track is of great importance since it places the occurrence of an event "in its proper time relationship to other events." According to McGowan, the time track is "the entire sequence of 'how' incidents, complete with all 'perceptics' picked up by a person during his whole existence." He explains:

> Actually, an organism's time track goes back before time—to the moment he decided to be a monocell—and progresses through all the millions of evolutions to this immediate instant. Thus, life's time track begins at the first moment of recording and ends with the abandonment by the Thetan of the MEST organism.

As L. Kin writes in *From the Bottom to the Top*, "the term OT level is actually quite well chosen in that 'OT' refers to the telepathic aspect of solo auditing, to actions one does as a thetan and not by means of a body." He explains that the terms 'OT' and 'Clear' designate two separate categories of ability. He emphasizes that "not every OT is a Clear." Unofficial solo offshoot practitioner techniques taught personally by Kin are aimed at getting students to take on the viewpoints of people and animals, and "getting the feel of them and getting them to follow your intentions." Later, the SOPs trainee learns to get "oriented" inside certain incidents which he has observed. The SOPs trainee is initially taught that any "soma" or sensation felt during this telepathic trip, anything he "sees or feels from the moment he first contacts the incident," is part of the "dramatization" of the initial incident. That is the trail he is to follow in order to "get oriented inside the incident."

The SOPs trainee learns to locate the identity of the observer of the incident by asking, "from what angle is the film taken?," and "who is the camera?" Once the identity is located, "the picture starts moving." Now, Kin writes, "the sequence of events starts showing up all by itself." The SOPs trainee then runs the incident through repeatedly, going back further each time to locate the "beginning" of the incident. In this sense, SOPs techniques, including those of

Solo Excalibur Practitioners, are reminiscent of telepathic time travel practiced by remote viewers.

In one example of time travel executed during a remote viewing session, Army remote viewer David Morehouse was trying to get impressions from his target surroundings and decided to "search backward in time." As Morehouse explains in *Psychic Warrior*, "I let the signal line drag me into the past; present time gave me little information. I closed my eyes to ride the movement out, and I opened them to a landscape that hadn't changed a bit." He complained to his monitor, "I don't understand it. I just executed a fairly large movement in time and I still don't see anything."

As Jim Schnabel explains in *Remote Viewers*, on one occasion Joe McMoneagle went after a target brought in by the FBI. The target was a person whose picture was inside an envelope. The time and location of the person was not provided. McMoneagle got comfortably within his "zone" (for which he claims he regularly used HemiSync) and saw a man dressed in a business suit driving a car. The driver, who spoke Russian, was being stopped by a policeman. There was a fishing pole in the back seat. McMoneagle's monitor asked the significance of the fishing pole. McMoneagle then asked the man, "What are you going to do with the fishing pole?" As Schnabel remarks, "this was an especially strange use of the telepathic interrogation technique."

Following the time track of the KGB man either backward or forward, McMoneagle, whom Schnabel calls the "shaman in Army boots," observed him using the pole as an aid to dislodge an object placed by a fellow agent. His explanation for this particular use of the pole was never verified. The Russians had been seen quite often with fishing poles, and had been actually seen fishing in groups. Their fascination with fishing poles remained an elusive enigma. But what does seem apparent, if we accept Kin's description of what goes on, is that once McMoneagle became "oriented inside the incident," the picture started moving on its own and he was able to trace it forward and backward in time. If, as Bohm suggests, the source of consciousness is in the implicate order, the holographic record of the past also exists in the explicate order. A "shift in focus" is all that is required to access records of the "past."

Yet, are we to accept that the scenarios one might encounter in the remote viewing telepathic technique are necessarily events which actually occurred or will occur in the physical universe? McMoneagle's explanation for what the Russians were doing with the fishing pole does not seem to make sense. Does it represent one "potential" truth? Is the incident in which one finds oneself just one of many possible worlds? This is the gray area between the states of "mind/awake-body/asleep" and "three feet in back of your head." As Charles Tart's studies make clear, even EEG readings are of no help here. Remote viewing inevitably walks the hazy ether between clairvoyant parlor trick and a tool of the national security state.

In another time travel feat, McMoneagle was stepped forward in time month by month in order to view a new secret Soviet submarine. His description of the sub as well as other predictions were not far off. Satellite photos taken four months later showed the Typhoon as McMoneagle had described it. Notably, McMoneagle suggests in *The Ultimate Time Machine* that corporations looking for patentable machines can utilize remote viewers to grab ideas from the future! (McMoneagle's remote viewing business, called "Intuitive Intelligence Applications," can be found at www.mceagle.com/iia/)

In *The Holographic Universe*, Talbot describes an out-of-body test in which the participants were asked to "fly in" and describe objects on a table. As Talbot notes, one test subject tended to describe the objects which were placed on the table *days later*! The phenomenon of time travel—precognition and retrocognition—during OBEs and remote viewing episodes suggests that consciousness resides in what David Bohm has called an "implicate order," where linear time does not exist. As Talbot posits, this OBEer "inadvertently tuned into frequencies that contained information about the future and converted those into a hologram of reality." Talbot sees this as more than an instant of precognitive vision. Instead, he reports, OBEers have reported that OBE visits to future time and space are qualitatively different from "precognitive dreams," and that the feeling is described as definitively "out" and "moving." One OBEer describes the sensation as "meeting myself behind myself as if I were two beings." This appears to describe true "exteriorization." If this isn't a description of Hubbard's "three feet in back of your head," I'm not sure what is.

Clay Modeling

Another example of the connection between solo offshoot practices (SOPs) and Ingo Swann's remote viewing protocol is the "clay modeling" technique. By using this technique, a remote viewer is trained to depict his remote sensory experience in clay in order to give dimension to perceptual information. According to Alex Constantine, Ed Dames at PSI-Tech also uses this technique. This is not surprising, since Dames is a former student of Swann.

As William Gray writes in *Magical Ritual Methods,* "of all sensory paths, that of touch puts us most finally in contact with material manifestation." One important technique having to do with the sense of touch is the magical technique of "clay modeling." As Gray explains, "thoughts and things are interchangeable, and if we train ourselves to exchange them via their appropriate media, we shall become practical magicians." Those media to which he refers are the basic Earth elements of Air, Water, Earth and Fire. According to Gray, magicians are trained to work with these elements, to become familiar with their properties, and to concentrate on the energies and impulses they produce in Inner consciousness.

The magical clay modeling technique is an example of manipulating the Earth element. Yet, as Gray explains, "we are not trying to make the clay *look* like our subject, but *feel* like it." As he explains, "whatever our production in clay looks like, we are here concerned with its tactile qualities. The test is, can we reverse it and reproduce a proportion of its initial energy in ourselves?" As he explains, the shaped clay should "play back tactile impressions that will eventually add up to some approximation of its Originator." In these kinds of magical exercises, Gray explains, magical practitioners learn to "solidify our thoughts right down to earth."

SOPs also make use of the clay modeling technique to describe the important emotions and visualizations which have arisen during auditing sessions. L. Kin writes in *From the Bottom to the Top* that the "clay demo" demands that the auditee "create examples paralleling on a MEST level the high flying theta concepts he carries about in his personal universe." This teaches him two things, Kin explains. First, how difficult it is to create, and second, what his universe *really* looks like. As Kin notes: "a universe consists of created masses and of created significances attached to those masses. A clay demo must parallel that." As he explains, a well-put clay demo problem will "lead to major cognitions."

As William Gray explains in *Magical Ritual Methods,* the "condensation of consciousness" is basic to the magical arts. As Gray has written, skill and practice in the making and use of symbols is absolutely essential to all Initiates of the Magical Mystery. In other dimensions, we are entirely dependent upon our skills with symbolism; therefore, he advises, it is very important that the Initiate be taught some means of symbol working. As Gray writes, "the whole basis of Magic is building up a foundation of symbolic energy units out of which our Inner Cosmos may be constructed." Gray further explains that the materials of the Magician are the ancient elements of creation: earth, air, water and fire. As Gray explains, these elements are also the basics of consciousness; i.e.; they are the counterpart in the unmanifest world of the elements constituting the manifest world.

As L. Kin explains, the SOP supervisor should demand of the auditee to, "look at life, look at how people feel and act, look at how the mind works—and then show me the *real* thing in clay, not some symbolic abbreviation." Kin suggests that thoughts should be written in clay letters, and images should be shown as clay pictures. In this way, the student "creates what goes on between people and other people, between people and their minds, between people and their bodies." As Gray has written, the use of symbols contracts consciousness in one World while expanding it into another. As Gray writes, "exercises must consist of reducing the Time-Event extent of a mass consciousness into a single Symbol, which may be of any suitable nature, whether sonic, written, painted, or perhaps not physical at all." The clay demo, therefore, while it is supposed to be the "real thing" and not a "symbolic abbreviation," is the event in real time zeroed down to its symbolic otherworld energy-exchange unit.

It's also interesting to note that in the Babalon Working ritual, Hubbard instructed Parsons to stare into a black box waiting for a "sacred design" to appear, which he was instructed to model in wood. As L. Kin notes, he sees no difference between esoteric initiation and scientology OT levels II and III.

7th Dynamic Goo

SOPs and remote viewing share another remarkable likeness: the danger of getting stuck in the netherworlds of "7th dynamic goo." McMoneagle often used his telepathic interrogation technique during remote viewing sessions. According to Schnabel, while going toward a target, he often found himself "staring at the curved interior of an unearthly ship filled with skinny, large-eyed humanoids." McMoneagle explained that suddenly the aliens would be looking at him, wondering what he was doing there. Apparently, he had to undergo some psychic battling with these entities, and would return "drenched with sweat and xenophobic stress." This is also a danger of the Excalibur practitioner. As L. Kin warns in *From the Bottom to the Top*, "the solo auditor may get hung up in spaceship hunting or 7th dynamic goo. The more they fight this 7th dynamic goo the more they get sucked into it."

Author David Icke refers to these negative energies as Luciferic Consciousness. Luciferic Consciousness is a collective consciousness, known to Christians as the "Antichrist," and is the total sum of all minds, human and extraterrestrial, whose thoughts vibrate within an extremely negative frequency range. Icke professes that it is possible for such a multidimensional collective consciousness to affect an entire planetary system with their thoughts alone. As Icke explains in his on-line article, "The Veil of Tears":

> As everything is created by thought, and all matter is subordinate to thought, all physical events are the result of a thought or thoughts of some kind affecting matter. All of the events which caused mayhem in this galaxy took place within the confines of the vibratory prison, created by the Luciferic Consciousness. This consciousness can work through any life form—human or extraterrestrial—which is operating within its vibratory range. The Luciferic Consciousness is an extremely negative thought pattern, or range of thought patterns. Anyone whose attitudes are within that range can be captured by it and turned into a vehicle for its will.

> When the Luciferic Consciousness locks into an individual's consciousness, it, in effect, becomes their 'mission control', their guide and master. If however, our intent remains loving and positive, it cannot affect us directly because our energy fields (auras) will be vibrating within a range much higher than the Luciferic band. There is no resonance established. The 'Luciferic broadcast' is not received by a consciousness tuned to a different frequency, just as a radio receiver only picks up stations within a defined bandwidth at any given time.

Strangely, even at upper management levels, the individuals in the RV program held strong beliefs in the paranormal and, in particular, in the reality of the

ET presence. Ed Dames, who later went on to found PSI-Tech, began to choose bizarre targets for viewers to locate. Using Monroe's HemiSync tapes to induce "deep trance bilocations," Schnabel explains, a small group of remote viewers began investigating all types of anomalous phenomena. Dames'"Enigma Files" began to fill with descriptions of such things as UFOs, the Loch Ness monster and Virgin Mary sightings, as well as remote scenes from the past like ancient Atlantis. Some were so fascinated with UFO lore that they quickly "homed in" on a UFO as soon as they set foot in the ether. As L. Kin has noted, once one begins this telepathic enterprise, it's easy to get sucked into "7th dynamic goo," including extraterrestrial spaceships. As the following story will illustrate, such telepathic pursuits are a common pastime of both military-intelligence trained remote viewers and Solo Excalibur Practitioners and other SOPs.

Solo Excalibur Practitioners have also been busy "auditing" (remote viewing?) what they refer to as "Galactic Patrol Mother Ships" stationed at the edge of the solar system. L. Kin describes this scenario in *Pied Pipers of Heaven* (p.311). One huge mother ship "perceived" independently by a number of solo offshoot practitioners in October, 1992 was described as being more than 200 kilometers in diameter. It was also noted by several independent percipients that this enormous sphere rotates and creates its own gravity so that people can walk about inside. Shortly after these descriptions came in, it was learned that in August of 1992 the "most distant body in the solar system" (1992-QB1) had been discovered by a Hawaiian telescope, and was again seen in November of the same year by a telescope in Spain. This is one of the "small planets" beyond Pluto, on the edge of our solar system (but which may expand our concept of our "solar system"), discussed in detail in Volume 1 of this book, *Space Travelers and the Genesis of the Human Form*. Interestingly, this sphere or "small planet" was estimated to have a diameter of 100 to 200 kilometers. As Kin comments, "why look through telescopes when you can get your data by telepathy and exteriorization?" Yes, indeed. Welcome to the future. Naturally, those of us who do not have our telepathic abilities honed will be, in Darwinian terms, "selected against."

Another artifact which was located telepathically in outer space by Solo Excalibur Practitioners is referred to as "the Screen." This phenomenon has also been described by percipients as a "Between Life Implant Station." (see Lanny Messinger) This implant station is described by Kin as "a firmly installed 'electric cow fence' around Earth, consisting of a very fine field of vibrations." Kin explains, "This is a one-way fence. It lets you in, but not out." According to Kin in *Pied Pipers of Heaven*, the Screen was programmed as part of Hubbard's "Inc.2" implant scenario. Kin describes the Screen as a grid of entities (theta quanta) comprised of standing scalar waves. The Screen seems to consist of plasma spirals working in opposing directions, vibrating at about 2 Gigahertz. Solo Excalibur Practitioners have described the Screen as having the appearance of a honeycomb, with about 49 grid crossings per square meter. Each cell has six sides and contains a copying and programming mechanism.

As Kin explains, the Screen resonates at a sympathetic frequency, therefore, the thetan considers it familiar and doesn't notice it. On contact with The Screen, the thetan forgets his own past and identifies with the information being programmed by the Screen. Since the GE Pool also comprises part of the Screen, the thetan is coupled with a GE, or Genetic Entity, when he approaches the Screen, and is reborn in another Earth body. He is thus "tricked" into a reincarnation scenario. [Note that Cremo has suggested in "City of Nine Gates" that Intelligence is not in itself conscious, but "mimics the behavior of consciousness," presumably by resonating at a sympathetic frequency. It thus attracts the attention of the conscious self, causing the self to identify with it.]

As Kin reports, Solo Excalibur Practitioners have been working to counter-program the Screen since it was discovered in 1992. They have been approaching the Screen telepathically, utilizing a concept much like a computer virus.

Focusing on the Screen, the Excalibur deprogrammer drains the energy content of one of the cells. As the cell spills its energy, the Excalibur deprogrammer telepathically charges it with standard Excalibur anti-Xenu information, such as "Xenu's game is over." Since the Screen is actually comprised of theta quanta, the entities are provided the standard "Two Rights of a Thetan," which are the right to self-determination, and the right to leave a game.

Kin explains that during initial trials of this deprogramming process, wave impulses began to spread throughout the Screen, and the copy mechanism with the anti-Xenu instructions began to diffuse in an outward motion from the cell. Several repetitions containing the anti-Xenu instructions seemed to cause the program to run by itself, permeating the Screen. When last checked, the counter-program appeared to be running on its own, and Solo Excalibur Practitioners have not bumped into Xenu in the last couple of years. It has been noted by auditors that friendly Visitors to Earth now find it easier to move in and out of the vicinity of Earth since the deprogramming of the Screen.

As L. Kin has noted, "telepathic abilities increase throughout the OT levels – if they did not, one could not possibly audit entities, let alone the 'bad guys' in space ships or implant stations." (*Scientology: More Than a Cult?*, 169) Indeed, it is clear not only that remote viewing has taken its precepts and know-how from SOPs and Solo Excalibur Practitioners, but remote viewing IS the practice of auditing taken specifically from high level SOPs, which concentrate on the remote viewing of various constructs and artifacts in the solar system. These artifacts include "the Screen," alien mother ships and the purported remote viewing of space ships containing humanoid beings which were reportedly trailing the comet Hale-Bopp in 1996. Now the story really takes a weird turn.

The Heaven's Gate Suicide/Psi-Ops

Courtney Brown, founder of the Farsight Institute in Atlanta, Georgia, studied at the Maharishi International University in the TM-Siddhi program, which involves "yogic flying." He explains in his book *Cosmic Voyage* that he attended the Gateway Voyage Program at the Monroe Institute where he used Monroe's HemiSync sound method. He then went on to study with an anonymous remote viewer, whom some assert was Ed Dames of PSI-Tech. It has been asserted that Brown works for the Pentagon.

The remote viewers at Brown's Farsight Institute were responsible for the "Far-Side" claims that manned extraterrestrial flying saucers were trailing the Hale-Bopp comet. A few months after his outfit made these Far-Out claims Far and Wide, both on their web site and on the popular and sensational Art Bell radio show, a UFO-cult group called Heaven's Gate committed suicide to join their intergalactic gurus. Notes posted to "alt.religion.scientology" by one of the group members referred to this information as "fantastic proof that the 'Next Level' mothership is coming." According to Matt Drudge in *Wired News*, using the e-mail address "rep@heavensgate.com," the writer stated he was working in seclusion with his disciples, preparing them for membership in the next world.

Interestingly, in his web site called The Eschaton (www.clark.net/pub/dansmith), Dan Smith, civilian attaché to an ad hoc intelligence intermediary UFO group called The Aviary, has made some very interesting comments regarding the obvious psy-war characteristics of the Hale-Bopp story, admitting that the Aviary group had something to do with the story that manned ETI saucers were trailing the comet. In his on-line article entitled "Pecking Away at Heaven's Gate," (www.clark.net/pub/dansmith/Bopeep.htm) (see also interview at www.paranoiamagazine.com) Smith writes the following:

> The Aviary is not responsible for the deaths of 39 innocents. It just looks that way. The Aviary always manages to be in the wrong place at the wrong time, minding someone's else's business. And I should know.

There is plenty of guilt to go around, because of course we are our brothers keepers, and we did not leave the 99 sheep to go to the aid of the 39. They just slipped through one of the many cracks in our society. But did any of us give them a nudge?

There is a larger agenda and those 39 got caught at the short end of that agenda. The Aviary knows something of that agenda, and it shakes a lot of trees trying to find out more, and some of the apples will hit the ground pretty hard.

Item: the remote viewing of the alleged Hale-Bopp companion was pretty much an Aviary spin-off. Item: the alleged April UFO landing was definitely an Aviary story and I was the one to pass it on to the public where it quickly took on a life of its own. Item: two days ago I received a call from an ABC reporter who had come across my name in the above context. He is working on a Heaven's Gate special. As he put it, the lost 39 had just put 2 and 2 together and come up with 5.

If I had it to do over again, what would I do? I would do it over again. My problem is that I am all too proficient in mathematics. When one sheep goes astray, I am very reluctant to leave the other 99 in the lurch, or the ends do sometimes justify the means. In the field of eschatology, one gets paid mainly to keep track of the ends.

I knew that the UFO landing story was very likely to be disinformation, and I was not at all surprised to see that it gained considerable currency in the UFO arena. And that did not stop me. The Heaven's Gate affair is the Bennewitz affair written large.

There is some explaining to do. I believe there is a cosmic agenda relative to human destiny and this agenda is now coming to a head. A small part of the US government has reluctantly become caught up in this still clandestine agenda. Other parts of the government would like to know what the heck is going on and the Aviary has come to be a principal tool for gaining information and access.

I for one have a special interest in this game of hide and seek. Long before I could even imagine that such a thing as the Aviary could exist, I was given the impression that there was a job available for me in the destiny business, and when the knock on my door came a second time, I opened it up to find one of those innocent birds strategically positioned, and ready to do some hand holding.

I believe that I have what everyone is looking for, the truth. The Aviary is on the scent and I am holding one of the tail feathers, waiting for the birds to realize they are chasing their own tail. In the meantime I go along for the ride, getting in my two cents at every opportunity. The role I have been playing is mainly that of publicist, which is one thing most of the birds would just as soon do without.

The Heaven's Gate tragedy points to the potential for this supposedly scientific style of information-gathering to be used as social mind control. How has our gullibility factor been so engorged that we readily accept sensational information as truth? Indeed, humans are having enormous trouble recognizing the signal in the out-of-control noise.

This is not meant to be a comment on whether the reported artifacts are part of the SOPs/Excalibur cosmology or whether these objects are really out there. But what we should not miss is the fact that SOPs and Solo Excalibur Practitioners are known to perform exactly the same telepathic "remote viewing" of distant solar system objects as have military/intelligence-trained remote viewers, as we have seen in the story of Courtney Brown and his remote viewing intelligence-affiliated think tank, the Farsight Institute. The point is that scientology had something of enormous importance to offer the secret government of the United States, and, via military intelligence channels, through 'shamen in army boots,' an incredible domestic resource was tapped.

Can we say that this information was "stolen"? If we consider that at the time SRI tapped into this information, the founders of the remote viewing project (Hal Puthoff and Ingo Swann) were actually still scientologists, and that for a span of approximately ten crucial years these two people owed their allegiance to both scientology and the CIA, then, yes, by all means, there was a breach of trust on their part. At some point their allegiance was switched, and they became spies for the secret government. The procedural information Swann imparted to the government was proprietary to the "Church of Scientology." There is no other way to look at it. It was stolen information. And this is never reported in any of the books written on remote viewing, most likely because these books are sanctioned by the CIA. In particular, Jim Shnabel, author of *Remote Viewing*, was a well-known crop circle hoaxer in Britain and is suspected to be CIA connected.

The decline of the official scientology organization and its split into various SOPs seems to have begun at the about the same time that the remote viewing experiments were in full swing, which suggests there were actual external causes for the increasing internal paranoia exhibited by the organization during this dark period. As Jon Atack informs us, among those external causes was the remote viewing program at SRI and the not-so-paranoid suspicion among Church elders that Swann and Puthoff were working for intelligence. It makes one wonder if the troubles that befell the organization during the mass "cleansing" and exodus of many members was orchestrated from outside of the organization.

Slipping Into the Ether

The CIA's historical involvement with the occult and its connection to Nazi Germany has been well researched. The occult is a "recurring theme" in this milieu, writes Alex Constantine. In addition, Rod Lewis, spokesman for the American Federation of Scientists, has stated that "the immediate speculation is that they are dealing with the demonic realm." The word "demonic" is Greek for "disembodied intelligence." Lewis has stated, "apparently it's something they take very seriously, and unfortunately they're trying to use it for military purposes."

The decline of the remote viewing program was also inevitable. Once 7th dynamic goo got the better of the situation, things went from bad to worse at SRI. Remote viewer Angela Dellafiora began experimenting with WRV, or written remote viewing, which was essentially a form of trance channeling. As Schnabel reports, she would go into a trance state (also known as self-hypnosis) and announce the presence of entities named George, Maurice, or Dr. Einstein, who would take control of her hand and write answers to questions she was asked. The "Jedi Knights," those who had been trained by Ingo Swann, lamented that the project was regressing "from high tech wizardry to archaic and vaguely feminine witchery." The rivalry intensified and the program eventually slid into chaos and mismanagement. Ed Dames blamed it on "the witches and their wiles." So much for being "at cause" in the MEST Universe. One might observe that the more one tries to be at cause, the more trouble one actually stirs up!

In addition to its irresponsible use in this social mind control scenario, does remote viewing have any physical dangers? Several persons involved in the RV program have noted the serious possibility of psychiatric problems. RVers have all noted that following an RV session, the 'doors of perception' are open wider than usual. Apparently, total concentration on barely perceptible phenomenal experience turns one's extrasensory volume knobs all the way up. You might even say, once you come off the electric highway, the radio is on full blast! As the shamans told Schnabel, there's an 'electric tingle' in the body, and it feels like you've taken a 'mild dose of LSD.' Some wondered if having these daily deep altered-state experiences could make your mind more liable to slip into that state spontaneously and without control.

Army veteran David Morehouse, author of *Psychic Warrior*, was the foremost "psychic spy" in the military's top secret "Stargate" program. Morehouse claims he and other remote viewers were utilized during the Gulf War. Morehouse explains that he had a psychotic breakdown from his "addiction" to remote viewing. He states that every viewing session was followed by a period of slipping in and out of the 'ether' with no control, and that viewers who performed more than two sessions a day had to be driven home because "the chance that we would slip back into the ether was too great." Morehouse claims that the longer he remained in the program, the more out of touch he became with reality and the longer it took to recover from his trips into the ether. He writes, "the tether that held me to the physical dimension was stretching thin; I had begun to wonder what would happen if it broke."

Morehouse has also noted that every object in the 'ether' was animate, and that a "target's surroundings recorded the history of the place without prejudice and stood ready to bear witness." Anthropologist Evens-Wentz has noted that, "Nature herself has a memory. There is some indefinable psychic element in the earth's atmosphere upon which all human and physical actions or phenomena are photographed or impressed. Under *certain inexplicable conditions*, normal persons who are not seers may observe Nature's mental records like pictures cast upon a screen, often like moving pictures."

What are these 'certain inexplicable conditions' which can impose upon a person the ability to view 'Nature's mental records'? Can these conditions be induced by drugs, sound, hypnosis, entrainment, torture or technology? Could the remote viewers at SRI possibly have been tripping on acid, DMT or other psychotropic drug? According to Lee and Schlain in *Acid Dreams*, the CIA was interested in exploring a method called *iontophoresis*, which used an electric current to transfer the ions of a pharmaceutical into the tissues of the body without surgical, hypodermic or oral introduction. In addition, it is well known that SRI was a major think tank involved in chemical mind studies for the intelligence community.

As William Gray has warned in *Magical Ritual Methods*, each soul entering the Inner dimensions must be its own complete master therein. He warns that insanity and other sufferings can occur, especially in connection with an unbalanced individual. For these reasons, the Mystery traditions have always been very careful in their choice of candidates. As Gray explains, "once a channel of communication has been established by magical means between Outer and Inner Self, a kind of short-circuit occurs, and surges of energy take place from one state to another." The merging of these energies without adequate control can cause tensions resulting in spiritual, mental or physical diseases, Gray warns. On the other hand, these surges of energy can also improve health, strengthen the mind and bring benefits to the soul. As he explains, it all depends on "whether our circuit was properly arranged before the power was switched on."

In any case, it would seem that when we visit these worlds it can be only for a fleeting moment, for its atmosphere is not our own. Is it when we stay too long, or when our visits become too frequent, that we become ill? According to Helena Blavatsky, founder of the Theosophical Society, every organized thing in this world, visible as well as invisible, has an element appropriate to itself. There is no occupied portion of universal nature which does not have special conditions pertinent to the types of living things abounding in that sphere. As Blavatsy writes in *Isis Unveiled,* "special conditions are furnished, and, being furnished, they are necessary."

What this means is that the occupants of the universes invisible to our senses are supplied with the indispensable conditions of existence within that sphere. But we must remember that these *noumena*, using Ouspensky's term, exist right here albeit in other frequencies of existence, and we really don't have to "go" anywhere to be in contact with them. As well, we need to keep in mind that there are both negative and positive energies existing. If we keep in mind Annie Besant's writings, these *noumena* are made of various types of 'mind stuff' as are we, and we don't have to 'leave' our sphere in order to send our thought-forms out to explore other realms of existence.

Back here in our material existence, the atmosphere in which our bodies are comfortable is thick and solid and has a lot of mass. Our material containers are likewise dense and, although we become used to it, it takes a lot of effort to move around in our world. It takes immense effort to obtain any focus or clarity of thought. Phenomenologically speaking, it is as though we are swimming in some sort of pea soup, or as Icke calls it, a 'vibratory prison.' It's up to us to explore this feeling and see what it is, and describe it as best as we can when we sense it, rather than shirking away from the feeling when it is encountered. What is this thickness that clouds our minds and eludes our senses whenever we approach it? Is it the boundary, the Great Wall, where the noumenal world touches the phenomenal world?

Shamen of old were well trained to move around in all types of worlds, but it should be kept in mind that the more frequent the visits, the more open the door between the worlds. As a result, shamanic and druidic ecstasy may bear some resemblance to insanity. According to Schnabel, the Army eventually categorized remote viewing as "human use experimentation," necessitating a "blizzard of consent forms and a medical review panel." By 1983, Richard Kennett of the CIA began questioning the Army about all the money they were spending at the Monroe Institute. He began to suspect that the active promotion of altered states of consciousness might actually make the brain unstable and more prone to spontaneous hallucinations and delusions. It turns out that Kennett had also had a spontaneous OBE after following the Monroe Institute materials. He had left his body and walked across the room, but noticed there were other beings in the room. Some kind of entity had put its face right up to his, and he became frightened that he would not be able to get back into his body.

Madame Blavatsky warned about such unsettling occurrences which were the result of an unprepared psychic space. As the ancients have written, when the "directing intelligences" retire from any portion of the ether which they are bound to supervise, that "space is left in possession of evil." Blavatsky wrote that an Adept who "prepared to converse with the 'invisibles' had to know well his ritual and be perfectly acquainted with the conditions required for the perfect equilibrium of the four elements in the astral light." The trained Adept knew how to purify the essence and "equilibrize" the elements within the circle in which he wished to attract the pure spirits. As Blavatsky warned: "woe to the imprudent inquirer who ignorantly trespasses upon forbidden ground." This trespasser will evoke powers he or she cannot control, and will "arouse sentries which allow only their masters to pass." She penned the following detailed warning in *Isis Unveiled*:

> The spirit of harmony and union will depart from the elements, disturbed by the imprudent hand; and the currents of blind forces will become immediately infested by numberless creatures of matter and instinct—the bad daemons of the theurgists, the devils of theology—and gnomes, salamanders, sylphs, and undines will assail the rash performer under multifarious aerial forms. Unable to invent anything, they will search your memory to its very depths. The elementals will bring to light long forgotten remembrances of the past: forms, images, sweet mementos, and familiar sentences long since faded from own remembrance, but vividly preserved in the inscrutable depths of our memory and on the astral tablets of the imperishable 'Book of Life'.

With regard to this notable warning, in his book *Psychic Warrior*, Morehouse describes a remote viewing episode wherein he had a long conversation with a dead friend at the moment of his friend's death. This brings to mind Blavatsky's claim that the elementals, unable to create or 'invent' anything [ie. since they are BTs or Clusters, not actually thetans?] will search the depths of your memory and bring to fore unconscious memories from the akashic records, the 'imperishable Book of Life.'

After his own experience in this realm, Kennett wondered if repeated experience could cause psychological trauma, psychotic breaks, or even a heart attack. According to Schnabel, his recommendation to Stubblebine was to stop sending officers to the Monroe Institute, but his advice went unheeded until 1984, when a "young lieutenant" avoided direct answers about prior mental problems on his entrance application and was forthwith transferred from Monroe to the psychiatric ward at Walter Reed Hospital.

McMoneagle also wondered if the act of remote viewing might produce a hazardous effect on the human nervous system. The numbers of remote viewers experiencing heart attacks and different types of cancers became "too high to ignore," and it was unsettling that so many of them had seemed to "die before their time." (Come on, a CIA program that's hazardous to your health?) Is this cancer connection a clue that the remote viewing guinea pigs were being bombarded with some type of ELF waves or microwaves? Or, was there perhaps a chemical substance introduced through the pores of the skin via iontophoresis? Why should deep meditative or altered states on their own cause cancer? Stress on the heart, maybe, but cancer? Then McMoneagle himself had a heart attack and a near death experience.

Another side effect of remote viewing, Schnabel points out, is a self-centered perception of "hypersignificance." Perhaps this is due to the fact that whole brain synchrony causes hyper-attention to meaningful synchronistic events. At any rate, this effect was noted in the behavior of one of the most enigmatic personalities in this group, General Stubblebine, who frequented the Monroe Institute practically every weekend for several years. He was on a "spiritual quest," Schnabel notes, and he was "taking the Army along for the ride." This so-called 'messianic self-centeredness' is "a classic aspect of altered-state behavior, probably most familiar to hallucinogen users," and was rampant at the Monroe Institute and among remote viewers in general. One should rightfully wonder why this condition manifested itself so rampantly at the Monroe Institute.

Shamanic duels and boasting are part and parcel of the magi's bag. Pat Price and Ingo Swann regularly engaged in such psychic duels. Pat Price claimed that he could make traffic lights change through psychokinesis. The "rough and ready leprechaun" also claimed to have certain shamanic powers which could affect the weather, including an ability to create or evaporate clouds at will. Strangely, L. Ron Hub(bard), the Druidic storyteller, professed to effect the same at will.

The ability to easily fall into altered states appears to be genetic. The shamanic personality often runs in families, Jim Schnabel notes, and may have traits of mental instability. On the other hand, as Talbot reports in *The Holographic Universe*, other studies of OBEers have reported psychologically normal findings. Conclusions at a meeting of the American Psychiatric Association in 1980 suggested that OBEs are common occurrences and that referring patients to books on the subject might be more helpful than psychiatric treatment. It was even suggested that patients might benefit more from seeing a "yogi" rather than a psychiatrist.

But in the case of the remote viewing experiments, we should also keep in mind that there are potential differences between a spontaneous lucid dream OBE experience, a hypnotically induced OBE experience, ritually induced shamanic out-of-body travel, or a technologically induced remote viewing experience. There are obviously various ways of accessing the noumenal world. But, what technological artifact or other dangerous ingredient was added to the remote viewing experiments which was placing its practitioners in danger? Was it the HemiSync sound method? Was it ELF sound waves or microwaves? Was it the introduction of psychedelics without their awareness? Or, was it simply the "unprepared psychic space" which Blavatsky warns about? Why did the remote viewing program at SRI eventually fail? Was the entire project invaded by the negative energy of "Luciferic Consciousness" which Icke warns about? Or was it simply, as Ingo Swann concluded, the remote viewing project at SRI began to fail after approximately fourteen years, largely because many of those involved "opted to ignore noise sources."

Think Tanks and Social Control

Sources are fairly certain that official CIA/military remote viewing projects have ended, but there is reason to believe the remote viewing of exotic targets such as UFOs has continued covertly. The point is, why in the world would the intelligence agencies continue to spend money when they can just oversee programs being run by private companies and peddled on the Internet? We should, therefore, see these remote viewing institutes in the context of "think tanks."

According to the authors of *Acid Dreams*, various think tanks such as the Rand Corporation, Stanford Research Institute and the Hudson Institute are connected to the CIA. In the 1960s, the Rand Corporation was one of the think tanks which examined the short and long-term effects of LSD on personality change, in particular, as "an antidote to political activism." Former CIA director and Secretary of Defense James Schlesinger was a senior strategic analyst at Rand. Likewise, the former head of the CIA's National Intelligence Command, Henry Rowen, is a former president of Rand.

Another think tank with strong intelligence connections, the Hudson Institute, kept its eye on the grassroots psychedelic movement. According to *Acid Dreams*, Herman Kahn, founder of the Hudson Institute, performed classified research on national security issues. Kahn experimented with LSD on many occasions, and frequently visited Millbrook and other psychedelic subculture meeting places. Nonetheless, it has been noted that social control was the primary concern of Kahn and his Hudson Institute. A CIAconduit called the Human Ecology Fund supplied funding for numerous CIA behavior control studies under MK-ULTRA, including Kahn's paranoid futurist manifesto entitled *The Year 2000*. In it, Kahn projected that the psychedelic subculture would comprise a separate country within the United States. As we've seen, the term "futurist" seems to be synonymous with "shit-stirrer." It is quite bizarre to learn that the CIA was essentially responsible for letting LSD and other drugs loose on the public, and quite handy indeed that they also saw fit to wire themselves into the social problem that they had a major hand in creating in the first place. This almost blatant orchestration of social conflict is just a ladle in the soup of the CIA's schizoid, double-dipping omnipotence.

Another think tank with which readers are perhaps more familiar is Stanford Research Institute (not affiliated with the University). It is known that SRI received numerous grants from the U.S. Army to conduct classified research into chemical incapacitants. In addition, in the late 1950s, Willis Harmon, head of the Futures Department at SRI, was turned on to LSD. He later became Vice President of the International Federation for Advanced Studies (IFAS), a think tank devoted to exploring the therapeutic potential of LSD. Harmon and his colleagues were allowed to continue their studies of LSD long after the FDA purged the acid subculture in the late 1960s. As a matter of fact, IFAS continued to charge $500 for a single high-dose LSD session long after it was highly illegal to sell or use LSD.

If we look in the 'Where Are They Now' files, we find that most of the remote viewing companies are founded by veterans of this intelligence alphabet soup (SRI, CIA, NSA, DIA, DEA, Navy, Army, Air Force, NASA), and are connected to big names in Psi-Ops. For instance, reportedly sitting on the Board of Ed Dames' company, PSI-Tech, are two infamous military spooks, John B. Alexander and Maj. Gen. Albert Stubblebine.

According to researcher Alex Constantine, Scientific Applications International Corporation (SAIC), a think tank and remote viewing organization located in San Diego, is directed by several of the "highest-ranking oligarchs" of the military/intelligence apparatus: former NSA Director Bobby Ray Inman (also connected to NASA and JPL, see below), the CIA's John Deutch, William Perry, Clinton's secretary of defense from ESL, Inc. (part owner of Area 51), Melvin Laird, defense secretary under Nixon, and Donald Kerr, former director of Los Alamos National Laboratory. (Constantine also reports that another ex-military remote viewer, David Morehouse, is the producer of a Hanna-Barbera cartoon series called "Peace Force: The Avalon Odyssey," about aliens defending the galaxy with advanced weapons.)

A question that is pertinent here was recently asked by Richard Hoagland of The Enterprise Mission in his essay entitled "Who's Really Running NASA?" (www.enterprisemission.com/whosnasa.html). It seems that there has been an ongoing "war" since the Viking mission within this so-called civilian agency regarding who would ultimately control missions to Mars, along with any information regarding manmade artifacts that might be discovered. The current Administrator of NASA, Dan Goldin, just after NASA's two successive Mars Mission blunders of 1999, announced on CNN that he has shortened the manned Mars Mission timetable from the earlier estimate of 30 years to 10 years! This is an extraordinary maneuver by an agency that recently blamed its so-called 'equipment failures' on "30% lack of funds and an equal lack of experienced spacecraft personnel at JPL."

On March 28, 2000, Goldin then delivered a speech to Jet Propulsion Laboratories (JPL) personnel. In that prepared speech, Goldin revealed: "I'd also like to acknowledge Admiral Inman, head of the JPL Oversight Committee at Cal Tech. He couldn't be here today, but I talked to him by phone..." As Hoagland reports, Admiral Bobby Inman is the former director of the National Security Agency, Deputy director of the CIA, Vice Director of the Defense Intelligence Agency, and former Director of Naval Intelligence. As Hoagland asks, "what is the Nation's most celebrated 'spook' doing heading an 'oversight committee' at one of the Nation's leading private Universities? And specifically a committee overseeing all civilian unmanned exploration of the planet Mars?"

Hoagland wonders if this "flagging" of Inman's name has something to do with the Viking's discovery over 25 years ago of artificial ruins on Mars and the national security implications of this discovery. We might rightfully wonder what other military-intelligence brass are among the members of JPL's secretive Oversight Committee. This 'admission' also suggests that the Lost-in-Space Mars Observer isn't lost at all, but is currently returning the most extraordinary images directly to the national security agencies of a so-called free society. It has been reported that remote viewers have successfully viewed these alien landscapes and have described manmade artifacts. (As L. Kin has commented, "why look through telescopes when you can get your data by telepathy and exteriorization?") This would explain the ultimate interest of the Pentagon and military intelligence in remote viewing, as well as in creating "oversight committees" capable of shutting down what should be democratic picture shows of potential artifacts on planetary bodies. Therefore, it is likely that even though you and I contribute our tax dollars for space exploration, we will have no access to any of the discoveries made.

In addition, California researchers Melinda Leslie and Randy Koppang have discovered that some intelligence insiders, leading physicists and remote viewing veterans may have been gathered together under the umbrella of a think tank called the Advanced Theoretical Physics Working Group (ATPWG). According to *The Excluded Middle*, ATPWG members have included, among others, Ed Dames of the remote viewing organization PSI-Tech (who was also involved in the SRI remote viewing and Army intelligence), Jack Houck, who was also involved in the SRI RV program, Hal Puthoff, manager of the SRI RV program and affiliated with intelligence and military aerospace R&D, Col. John B. Alexander, also affiliated with intelligence and military aerospace R&D and remote viewing at SRI, as well as with the National Institute of Discovery Science (NIDS), and other members of PSI-Tech and the military/intelligence faction, including Bob Wood. It is also alleged that Col. Philip Corso, author of *The Day After Roswell*, was a member of the ATPWG, as well as NIDS. All of these people are part of the military/intelligence community. Alleged members of NIDS have claimed that this group was formed to "create a new renaissance in aeronautical physics and man/machine interface." They have also claimed that this technology is back-engineered from captured ETI saucers.

It is surmised that the aim of ATPWG was to integrate new discoveries and theories in both physics and remote viewing, especially as these theories describe the nature of reality. As explained in this book's introduction, one might surmise that the question physics has to answer regarding UFOs might be 'how do they get here and how can they help us to achieve the same space-faring status?'. However, moving beyond the obvious, the presence of UFOs in our skies fifty years ago essentially forced a reappraisal of the nature of time, space and reality. Thus, the real question physics has to answer is more like 'what kind of reality allows visitors from time?' and, further, what would be the implications of this paradigm shattering news on human beings accustomed to cause and effect linear explanations for events occurring in the material world? This question is at the bottom of the UFO cover-up.

Col. John B. Alexander, with whom we will become more familiar in later chapters of this book, has admitted to being the Director of the Advanced Theoretical Physics Working Group. Puthoff and Corso have both claimed that the ATPWG "operated at the highest levels of government," and that this group was very powerful. Ed Dames of PSI-Tech has admitted his association with this group, and claims it was the "current incarnation of MJ-12." It's also interesting to note that PSI-Tech was the first offshoot private company, created by former members of the Army/Defense Intelligence Agency remote viewing program, to offer psychic consulting services to the public.

As Hal Puthoff has stated with regard to the physics of his remote viewing experiments at SRI, "the integrated results appear to provide unequivocal evidence of a human capacity to access events remote in space and time, however falteringly, by some cognitive process not yet understood." As Puthoff also asserted, years of research have left him with "the conviction that this fact must be taken into account in any attempt to develop an unbiased picture of the structure of reality."

Do not doubt for an instant that this "unbiased picture" is coming in very clearly for those with the impetus to spend billions upon billions of dollars to bring it into focus. But what is the ultimate reason for this extravagant R&D spending? Surprisingly, it has everything to do with the crash of an extraterrestrial craft at Roswell, New Mexico, in 1947: the day the Earth changed forever.

The following chapter explores the mysterious connections between the Roswell crash, remote viewing, psychotronics and von Neumann probes.

CHAPTER TWELVE

THE BIOLOGICAL AND THE SILICON: MODIFYING HUMANS FOR SPACE TRAVEL

The advanced electronic physiological monitoring techniques essential to space flight are kissing cousins, at worst, to the corresponding instruments of psychic research, whose modern forms were in fact enabled by aerospace spin-off.

Michael Rossman

"On Some Matters of Concern in Psychic Research"

Psychotronic machines are devices which can be interfaced with psychically-gifted individuals to draw on and exponentially expand the psychic potential of the human mind. These devices can ostensibly pair the human psyche with such energies as microwaves to carry and amplify bioenergy. As Dennis Stacy explains in "Battle of the Minds," in *Psychic Warfare: Fact or Fiction?*, American Army experiments have demonstrated the feasibility of making voices heard *inside* the head via microwave broadcasts.

Other types of waves and frequencies can be used to conduct, amplify, entrain or remotely control the psychic power of the human mind. For instance, radionics devices have been fully operational in the U.S. for some years to cure diseases from a distance. For readers who haven't heard of this, a friend of mine went to a radionics specialist in California to cure parasites and toxins in her body. Oddly, she did not have to be in the presence of the practitioner for a cure to be effected. The operator of such a device is a "sensitive" or psychic individual, who, according to Dennis Stacy, enters into a similar kind of psychic rapport with the machine as a dowser may enter with his willow rod. My friend wanted me to meet with this practitioner on a visit to California a few years ago, but he did not wish to meet with an author who might write about him or expose his practice, since it is quite unlawful to practice with such a device – that is, unless you are an authorized agent of the covert intelligence apparatus field-testing a mind control device on innocent citizens.

In a paper entitled "The Enigmatic Status of Radionics in the U.S.," presented in 1973 at the First International Congress on Psychotronics in Prague, researcher Frances K. Farrelly wrote regarding radionics machines that "… their use, regardless of model, involves a factor of consciousness as does any form of radiesthesia." This author also wrote the following:

> It is my sincere desire that this enigma of radionics be studied by those well qualified investigators in the field of applied cybernetics, parapsychology, and psychotronics. Radionics appear to have much in common with the phenomena of dowsing, and/or telepathy, and it rightfully belongs to those scientific investigators in both hemispheres to pursue this research further.

Here we have a nice concise tie-in between radionics devices, telepathy and cybernetics. This connection will prove interesting as the reader continues. Similar devices, such as psionics or Hieronymous machines, are simple devices which conduct electrical energy or bioenergy. The theory underlying radionics or psionics machines is that things like minerals, crystals, plants, microbes and diseases, essentially *all* organisms whether our science considers them biologically 'alive' or not, have their own specific vibratory rate or electromagnetic signature. The radionics specialist tunes in to the specific frequency of the bio-

157

entities that he wishes to target and turns on the machine. The target can be miles away—it doesn't matter where they are. These types of machines can even employ a photograph or strand of hair to capture or encode the specific wavelength signature of a person. This has an interesting similarity to remote viewing, which often contains a photograph of the target enclosed in an envelope, and the remote viewer is supposed to telepathically zoom in on the real target which the photo represents.

In this way, microscopic 'critters' who are causing us to be ill can be specifically targeted by the device. People and animals can also be caused to become ill by the same methods. (It has been noted that viruses, such as the AIDS virus, could be attacked in this manner, but this method of treatment remains marginalized.) As an example of what could be done, Dennis Stacy explains, a photo of a cotton field could be treated with insecticide and the psychotronic machine operator could "wish death to all boll weevils therein." The targeted insects may not necessarily die, but may simply "get the message" and migrate to another place. It would seem that the treatment of an object having a correspondence to the target, coupled with evil intention sent via thought waves, is descriptive of the practice of voodoo. Yet, it is interesting to note that my friend, who is a Christian, and who would otherwise see something like this as 'demonic,' nonetheless paid great money to the person effecting his cure from a distance simply because there was a legitimizing 'black box' involved.

The development of the psychotronic arts has connections to many classified CIA projects having to do with various developments in theoretical physics. Within these experimental paradigms, the practical hurdles which needed to be overcome before mind/machine interface could be established were (1) how to effect the transfer of information from mind to machine, and (2) how to overcome the extremely low power wattage with which these instruments typically operate. As Dennis Stacy clarifies in *Psychic Warfare: Fact or Fiction?*, "increase the information flow between mind and machine, increase the power and amplification wattage, and psychotronic weapons may well step out of the pages of science fiction into reality."

The Neurophone is an early 1970s device, described as a "super-sophisticated hearing aid," which solved the first part of this problem, as Dennis Stacy explains. According to Stacy's research, the Neurophone's inventor, Patrick Flanagan, "accidentally cracked the neural code for audio data allowing for direct communication between a crystalline electrical circuit and the brain's nervous system."

According to a personal communiqué from Judy Wall, there are three patents for the Neurophone. In a discussion with Mr. Flanagan, he told Ms. Wall that the original Neurophone, which was called a Nervous System Excitation Device (U.S. Patent #3,393,279), was developed by Flanagan when he was 14 years old. This patent was described as "a method of transmitting audio information via a radio frequency signal modulated with the audio info through electrodes placed on the subject's skin, causing the sensation of hearing the audio information in the brain." This patent application was filed in 1962 when Flanagan was a senior in high school, but it was not granted until July 16, 1968, because the patent examiner didn't believe it worked as claimed.

After Flanagan had gone to college and was working for the Naval Research Lab, he filed a second patent application, called Method and System for Simplifying Speech Waveforms (Patent #3,647,970), on August 29, 1968. According to this patent, "a complex speech waveform is simplified so that it can be transmitted directly through earth or water as a waveform and understood directly or after amplification." The second patent for the Neurophone, which used transistors, was applied for immediately after the first one was granted. A government secrecy order was slapped on the second Neurophone and this patent was not issued until March 7, 1972. The third Neurophone is a modern version using solid state circuitry, combining elements from the two previous patents. Flanagan told Ms. Wall that he no longer files for patents since it's like giving your ideas away to whoever reads it.

According to Dennis Stacy, when coordinated with research carried out by DARPA in programming computers to recognize human brainwave patterns, the basic R&D of the Neurophone can be extended to encompass much more than its initial invention as a sophisticated hearing device. As Stacy writes, these developments will "establish direct linkage communication and 'understanding' between man and computer—and other electronic machines (*i.e. missile control panels*) as well." (Italics added)

Psychic Navigation

As John White also writes in his Afterword to *Psychic Warfare: Fact or Fiction?*, air and space travel would be revolutionized by psychotronics. White maintains that UFO propulsion is "probably psychotronic in nature." But what does this mean and what are the implications for human beings?

As researcher Randy Koppang has concluded in *The Excluded Middle* (Winter 2000), the ultimate reason for the intelligence community's interest in remote viewing is the psychic interface between human consciousness and technology, or man/machine interface. Some believe this interest stems from back-engineering projects involving captured extraterrestrial space craft. According to Col. Philip Corso's book, *The Day After Roswell*, among the artifacts retrieved from the infamous 1947 Roswell saucer crash were headband devices of flexible plastic material which contained electrical conductors. Corso connected this headband artifact to the piloting of the alien space craft.

As Corso has disclosed, among the technological artifacts retrieved at the Roswell crash were headband devices which contained some sort of electrical circuitry. It's a good guess that such circuitry would be crystal-based, since crystals are a highly organized and energized living structure, which, if we consider Rupert Sheldrake's theory of formative causation, can 'learn new tricks.' In any structure that is highly organized, including crystals, plants or humans, there is a series of geometric points at which the energy is highly concentrated. This relates also to chakras and acupuncture points. These 'intelligent' energy forms, which are unknown to current (mainstream) science, in effect bring back in from the margins the Lamarckian concept of an intelligently guided evolutionary process. Therefore, crystal electronic circuitry could be an effective bridge between mind and matter and an effective material with which to interface and extend/amplify the parameters of the human psyche, since it contains the inherent signature properties of bio-communication. As will be discussed in detail shortly, Marcel Vogel, senior chemist for IBM, did extensive work in this area.

Along with other alien technologies retrieved at the crash site, Corso developed the theory that these extraterrestrial artifacts essentially comprised an electromagnetic anti-gravity drive and brainwave navigational guidance system. Corso claimed the U.S. Army eventually fed these technologies to industry giants under the guise of "foreign technology" for purposes of back-engineering. As 'maverick' physicist Jack Sarfatti has admitted in an e-mail correspondence, "the late Philip Corso's allegation that captured advanced ET flying saucers, in the possession of US military forces, are mentally controlled is not that implausible."

An on-line article at www.stardrive.org entitled "The Starship Builders" describes NASA's sudden interest in exotic new energy/propulsion physics. On 9/13/96, NASA announced an about-face in its program by announcing a new research program which would seek to "revolutionize" space travel by utilizing non-mainstream theories. As this article explains, a government "steering group" consisting of members from the various NASA centers, the Department of Defense, and the Department of Energy was established in 1997. At that time, an "invitation-only workshop" was to examine the relevant emerging physics and was to produce a list of research tasks. If the workshop successfully demonstrated that promising and affordable approaches exist, funding was to be granted to begin research. The author of this web article expresses excitement about this new "dimension to the space program." The author states: "One can only feel encouraged that the agency has chosen to go in this promising direction." Yet, we should note, this promising direction is becoming more and more technologically secretive. As this web author states, navigation in outer space is a formidable problem. How does one "reliably navigate across such vast interstellar distances in a distorted spacetime metric?" Sure enough, the web author answers as follows:

> That brings us to the final mind-blowing aspect of this subject. Of course, it will take human imagination and genius to realize the kinds of breakthroughs discussed here. *But our consciousness may play an even more fundamental role than in just the metaphorical sense of genius and creativity. It may actually be an integral part of a star drive – as important as fuel, instruments, and navigation systems.* (Italics added)

With this information in hand, we can safely surmise that the interest in classified remote viewing projects by military agencies and NASA was to explore the capacity for human/machine psychic interface in the piloting of space craft. According to Greg Bishop in *The Excluded Middle*, Corso has even admitted that he visited Stanford Research Institute's remote viewing labs in the early 1970s, and he asserted that the reason for the visit was "to seek methods for remote viewing/technology interface between extraterrestrials and their craft." Indeed, beginning in August of 1960, as stated in the previously discussed covert "Memorandum for the Record" regarding MK-ULTRA Subproject 119, all of this 'psychotronic' research and development came under the microscope of the intelligence apparatus.

Ostensibly, the purpose of Subproject 119 was to provide funds for a "critical review" of scientific developments with respect to "the recording, analysis and interpretation of bioelectric signals from the human organism, and activation of human behavior by remote means." It was also stated that the reason for converting this into a Subproject was to provide "more flexibility in the disbursal of funds." Ostensibly, the purpose of this "review" of the status of psychotronics was the following:

> … to provide an annotated bibliography and an interpretive survey of work being done in psychophysiological research and instrumentation. The survey encompasses five main areas: a. Bioelectric sensors: sources of significant electrical potential and methods of pick-up. b. Recording: amplification, electronic tape and other multi-channel recording. c. Analysis: autocorrelators, spectrum analyzers, etc. and coordination with automatic data processing equipment. d. Standardization of data for correlation with biochemical, physiological and behavioral indices. e. Techniques of activation of the human organism by remote electronic means.

Military Abductions

To continue with these connections, the military is known to be extensively interested in alien abductees. As a matter of fact, they are so interested that it has been suspected that they abduct alien abductees after their authentic alien abductions to find out what they know. The book *MILABS: Military Mind Control and Alien Abductions*, by Helmut and Marion Lammer, discusses military-type abductions reported primarily in the U.S. and Canada which mimic the alien abduction scenario. Instead of alien space craft, it is reported that unmarked helicopters, vans and buses are used to transport victims to underground government facilities. The MILABs theory suggests that a covert military/intelligence task force is monitoring real alien abductees in order to debrief the victim, as well as to install full amnesia regarding both abduction incidents. According to *The Excluded Middle*, abductee Melinda Leslie claims the military is interested in abductees because "they were mostly curious about the pilot/craft interface and if we knew anything about that aspect of their technology." (see also, Koppang, Randy)

MUFON official Dr. Robert M. Wood was also reputedly a member of the Advanced Theoretical Physics Working Group (ATPWG). As explained earlier, it is surmised that this think tank focused on integrating physics theories with remote viewing research in order to develop a 'bigger picture' of the nature of reality. Dr. Wood has admitted that this secret UFO working group "planned and set policy regarding the UFO issue." He also claims that any information pertaining to psychic pilot/craft interface that can be learned from UFO research is obviously very important to the military/intelligence apparatus in charge of the UFO cover-up.

What we also have going on in the sidelines of this issue is a plausible tie-in between the Roswell crash and biotelemetry implants in humans. As noted in research performed by Kathy Kasten (*Paranoia*, Issue 24), William Shockley of Bell Labs sent four experimental implantable transistors to experimental brain researcher, Dr. Dean C. Jutter, in 1952. In talking about the history and evolution of the human brain implant, Jutter notes: "The transmission of signals from within a subject was a technique that evolved slowly. *On July 2, 1952 William Shockley and Bell Labs sent me [Dr. Jutter] four experimental point-contact transistors*, which were difficult to power in a small package. (Junction transistors were only available for military use.) Thus, another approach was developed to provide for the totally passive transmission of information." In his book, *The Day After Roswell*, Philip Corso has connected the novel invention of the transistor by Shockley and Bell Labs to the Roswell saucer crash. We might wonder then whether these *experimental* implantable transistors for the passive transmission of information are essentially 'back-engineered' from alien technology discovered at this alleged 1947 crash site. Is telepathy in humans being nurtured technologically by the secret government? Let's continue our investigation of the facts of this matter.

Space Telepathy Experiments

According to Michael Rossman in "On Some Matters of Concern in Psychic Research," in *Psychic Warfare: Fact or Fiction?*, in 1963 "a top NASA official reaffirmed reports that telepathy research was a 'top priority' in the Soviet space program." As Rossman wrote:

> The advanced electronic physiological monitoring techniques essential to space flight are kissing cousins, at worst, to the corresponding instruments of psychic research, whose modern forms were in fact enabled by aerospace spin-off. The inclination to research telepathy in space rather than just on Earth was perhaps influenced by the popularity within the aerospace field of the myth, encoded by Arthur C. Clarke in imaginative literature, long before it was seared (vaguely) in the public mind by the movie *2001*, that psychic abilities unfold more fully in space. The resulting experiments would most likely have been encoded among the astronauts' biotelemetric records, scarcely distinguishable from orthodox experiments, records and perhaps accomplished through the same instruments, possibly unbeknown to the astronauts themselves.

It has been pointed out that CIA/NSA involvement in the 1970s remote viewing research at Stanford Research Institute strongly influenced the military's attention to this type of research. A CIA contract study with SRI published in 1976 was titled "Novel Biophysical Information Transfer Mechanisms." This would appear to be linked to experimental studies in space telepathy. Astronaut Edgar Mitchell has admitted to performing telepathy experiments in space. As

Michael Rossman reports, rumors among parapsychological researchers assert that telepathic jamming experiments in space revealed "surprising things about human psychic capabilities in space conditions."

There is also a connection between space telepathy experiments and Tesla technology. As Rossman reports, NASA has completely mapped the electromagnetic grid of the Earth. Early Soviet research proved that neural activities could be entrained (driven or controlled) in low frequency ranges which characterize outer space. As Rossman explains, these standing waves resonate in the Earth's ionospheric cavity in the low frequency ranges which also happen to characterize human brain activity. Early Western parapsychological researchers had hypothesized that these standing waves act as carriers of information. Rossman believes it is likely that Soviet scientists have also investigated this phenomenon, and that biocommunications and electromagnetic research in Soviet Russia "must be a fundamental dimension of the development of Tesla technologies." As Rossman also makes clear:

> There is no longer a clear line to be drawn between research into 'psychic phenomena' and advanced military applications, even in the design of antimissile defense systems. The possibility that Tesla technology may also be adaptable to distant mass psychophysical manipulation, through direct entrainment or more subtly, stands now not only as a modern version of an old nightmare about bad magic, but as a small yet concrete factor influencing policy calculations on both sides, pulsing the Earth's atmosphere each time the great Tesla magnifying transmitters at Riga and Gomel crank up to 75 million volts to unleash their 7 Hz signal.

Rossman also notes that civilian researchers and policymakers have been kept out of the loop in this type of research, and this has been condoned up to high levels of government since 1959. As he notes, the field of civilian psychic research has been 'effectively starved' out of operation and all of this research has come under the auspices of the intelligence apparatus. As he writes, "from this unnecessary starvation of a field, the potentials for its militarization (if not perhaps for its ultimate military efficacy) are generated or emphasized."

Thoughts have their own vibratory rate or signature, and this lost occult science is the key to psychotronic machines. If vibrational signatures can be affected from a distance, can thoughts be effected from a distance? Indeed, during the Cold War, it seems the Soviets were interested in another paranormal sideline: telepathic jamming. According to Mandelbaum, the Soviets were interested in whether a telepathic frequency could be detected and shut down by electronic means.

This leads to the question 'what is telepathy?' Is human thought transmitted via a wave, particle, or by anything physically detectable by another human mind or by electronic means? Would psychic jamming require human, electronic, or both: psychotronic, means? Can ESP messages be bugged? According to Mandelbaum, there is no "declassified information" that can answer these questions. Yet, as Vaughan Purvis noted in *The CIA and the Battle for Reality*: "Soviet telepathy research was almost immediately taken out of the hands of psychologists and redefined as a problem of radio engineering, hard applied science that readily attracted funds and military interest." The same appears to be true of American military-intelligence enterprise with regard to psychotronic research; that is, the "hard applied science" of radionics and miniature implantable biotelemetric devices appears to have been more than a sideline interest.

U.S. involvement in remote viewing experiments began in 1973, when NASA contracted with SRI (SRI Project #2613, NASA contract #953653, NAS7-1000). The report, entitled "Development of Techniques to Enhance Man/Machine Communications," described in detail "crude electronic means of screening for and training psychic perceptual abilities," as well as experiments in remote viewing using double-blind methodologies. The report concluded that talented remote viewers could be remarkably accurate under consistent protocols. As Rossman reports, NASA later employed two astral travelers to 'fly' out to Jupiter to take a look in advance of the Jupiter fly-by mission. As he notes, under the aegis of this 'civilian institute,' which nonetheless has known ties with the Department of Defense, Department of Energy and the CIA, a sophisticated protocol was developed for biocommunication with technological artifacts. As Rossman writes:

> The selection and training of talented percipients; the development of observational teams and protocols; the enhancement of their capacities through feedback and interpretation of sophisticated electronic monitoring—each element was demonstrated here in isolation, in a rudimentary form whose potential for further development was not quite clear but quite promising. The strategic potential of the whole package was unmistakable. Yet to believe appearances, little has been made of it since at SRI or anywhere else in the United States.

It is unlikely that "little has been made" of this early research. In a paper entitled "The Relationship of Psychotronics to Creativity," presented at the First Psychotronic Congress in Prague in 1973, Dr. Engr Antonin Duron noted that "psychotronic research is extending into the area of physics by studying the interactions between man and inorganic substances and between man and living nature."

This thesis aims to show that what we have in the development of the psychotronic arts is the development of the "human computer" or the von Neumann Probe: the bio-engineered fusion of human with computer as a way to ultimately move human beings into man-made ecological niches in deep space.

The von Neumann Probe

The development of man-machine psychic interface has obviously been the focus of the military Space Command's future vision, as is illustrated by the title of the aforementioned NASA remote viewing paper: "Development of Techniques to Enhance Man/Machine Communications." It has long been suspected that the development of a computer with a more humanlike mind would go a long way toward sending something like a von Neumann probe out to explore and populate the galaxy. The von Neumann probe, named after it's Dad, physicist John von Neumann, is a 'theoretical' computer probe with self-replication and construction abilities, or what is referred to as a "self-reproducing universal constructor." It's basically a conscious computer aboard a space craft. One might rightfully wonder if von Neumann received the same phone call as Jack Sarfatti.

A vN probe is a computerized machine capable of making any device, given the construction materials and a construction program. It has been argued that any advanced interstellar species would have such a self-replicating universal constructor with intelligence comparable to the human level, and that "the ultimate survival of a technological civilization, and indeed the survival of the biosphere in some form, requires the eventual expansion of the civilization into interstellar space." (Barrow & Tipler) As Jack Sarfatti has noted, "if UFOs are not artificially intelligent von Neumann robot probes, and if they are not using traversable wormholes, then, they're probably migrating as completely self-contained interstellar colonies." Such theoretical migratory colonies have been referred to as "O'Neill Colonies." (see *Space Travelers and the Genesis of the Human Form*)

Incidentally, Sarfatti has also stated in an e-mail: "Joan's reference to the Von Neumann Probe is a good one and fits my first-hand experience in 1953." Sarfatti has also commented that the von Neumann probe connection also fits Andre Puharich's claimed von Neumann probe/ETI contact experience, which he called "SPECTRA." Sarfatti adds that the only other explanation that would fit "is that it was Puharich behind these events all the time, though this is unlikely." He explains, "It is possible I met Puharich and Corso as a kid through my grandfather who worked for the US Army Quartermaster Corps, but this is only a conjecture. I met a lot of Army Officers over many months around 1950 or so but they are a faceless blur. I am sure they were studying me. My interest in rockets was encouraged and I was allowed to play in their "museum" after school and also ride around in official Army cars." Sarfatti adds, "I think the flying saucers are real mechanical craft. In addition of course there has been a lot of psi-ops around the issue because of the weapons applications."

The Space Travel Argument, as presented by Barrow & Tipler in *The Anthropic Cosmological Principle*, argues emphatically for the future rights of cyborgs, or vN probes, as human beings. The authors of this book launch a peculiar discussion of human rights and how those should be extended to a vN probe, which is after all an "intelligent being in its own right, only made of metal rather than flesh and blood." They contend that "arguments against considering intelligent computers to be persons and against giving them human rights have precise parallels in the nineteenth-century arguments against giving blacks and women full human rights." They appear to be hopeful that in the future "von Neumann probes would be recognized as intelligent fellow beings, beings which are the heirs to civilization of the naturally evolved species that invented them." After all, they contend, the "naturally evolved species and all of its naturally evolved descendants must inevitably become extinct ... but ... a civilization with machine descendants could continue indefinitely."

As I have explained in *Space Travelers and the Genesis of the Human Form*, there is nothing more important to the power junkies running the show on Planet Earth than reaching for the stars. It has all the trappings of a Darwinian 'survival of the fittest'scenario, in which the 'species'(or should we say 'race') which has the edge on 'indefinite survival'is the winner of the game. The 'edge'on this space race, the ultimate gain from U.S. military mind control research toward this end, is derived from the understanding and control of human psychic potential and the interface/application of technologies toward development of mind-driven space vehicles: the marriage of the biological and the silicon.

As Carl Sagan once proposed, communication with extraterrestrial intelligence will require computer actuated machines with abilities approaching human intelligence. Sagan and others admitted in the 1970s that a deficiency in present-day computer technology is what prevents us from exploring the galaxy. Secret developments in mind-machine psychic interface, which includes research in the areas of computers, psychotronics, cybernetics and genetic engineering, would certainly solve this problem, and in all probability have already solved it. As Zdenek Rejdak stated in 1973 before a world gathering of psychotronic gurus, one of the future goals of computer technology was to create a generation of computers capable of creating technological artifacts. This is directly connected to the idea of the vN probe and to modifying humans for space travel. In his paper entitled "Psychotronics Reveals New Possibilities for Cybernetics," Rejdak revealed the following:

> Theoretical cyberneticians are proposing at present the construction of computers that would 'create' and would possess at least a degree of intuition. ... Psychotronics has a great opportunity to provide much essential knowledge about these processes, and thereby to help cybernetics in solving one of the most complicated tasks, that of teaching computers to create. ... The point is not merely to build more perfect computers, but primarily computers with qualitatively new functions. Work is now underway on a fourth generation of computers, and a fifth generation is being planned. Therefore, it is very timely for cybernetics to include in its studies also the results of work and research in psychotronics. This will not be easy, because psychotron-

ics has its own specifics, and these could easily be passed over in superficial applications. Yet we believe that psychotronics is able already to offer cybernetics fruitful models.

Following this history-making conference, an article entitled "Mind Reading Computer" appeared in *Time* magazine's 7/1/74 issue. This computer program, developed at none other than Stanford Research Institute by Lawrence Pinneo, could read thoughts by interpreting the EEG patterns that correspond to certain words. Similar work was done by Donald York and Thomas Jensen at the University of Missouri, and also by Richard Clark at Flinders University in Australia.

Related to this, as noted earlier, Patrick Flanagan invented a hearing device in the early 1970s called the Neurophone, which reportedly cracked the neural code for audio data allowing for direct communication between a crystalline electrical circuit and the brain's nervous system. As noted, when coordinated with research carried out by DARPA in programming computers to recognize human brainwave patterns, this research established direct linkage communication and understanding between man and computer, and other electronic machines.

Homo Alterios Spatialis

It is clear that the marriage of technology and human psychic potential was a focus of various early brain studies conducted by CIA fronts and cutouts, including LSD experimentation, Monarch trauma-based conditioning, sleep/dream studies and psychic research, in an effort to investigate the inner workings of the human mind, and as a side effect of that research, to investigate the possibilities for manipulation, harness and control of human psychic potential. It is less known that the Agency undertook what was referred to as experimental "guided animal" research, in order to investigate whether it could make robots out of dolphins, dogs, cats and other animals. A personal acquaintance of mine recalls, as a child in the 1960s, being taken to the Massachusetts Institute of Technology (M.I.T.) in Boston by his adoptive father, who was in military intelligence and held high security clearance. There my acquaintance, a probable mind control victim himself, witnessed the test of a remotely-controlled 'brain-dead' dog, which executed the most bizarre robotic movements when walking.

The potential ramifications of this type of research takes us one step beyond and exponentially over the edge. It is highly likely that the apex of this research represents the creation of the bio-engineered human robot: *Homo Alterios Spatialis* ("human modified for space"), a term coined by Assistant General Counsel of the Smithsonian Institution George F. Robinson, an attorney specializing in Space Law, in a paper presented at the 1995 When Cosmic Cultures Meet conference. (See *Paranoid Women Collect Their Thoughts* for a review of this event.)

It is very likely that this scenario has jumped right out of the pages of science fiction (and CIA classified documents) to become reality. A 4/16/00 *Washington Post* article brings this all into focus. As co-founder of Sun Microsystems, Bill Joy, proclaimed in this *Washington Post* article: "We are dealing now with technologies that are so transformatively powerful that they threaten our species." "Where do we stop," Joy asked, "by becoming robots or going extinct?" In this article entitled "Are Humans Doomed?," Mr. Joy, a widely respected "Silicon Valley" computer expert, presented his joyless warning against the out-of-control technocratic culture which he himself has helped to spawn, saying that "there are certain technologies so terrible that you must say no. We have to stop some research. It's one strike and you're out."

Interestingly, Joy always believed that the rate of speed of the computer chip, which doubles every 18 months, would eventually "rub against the boundary of the physically possible," and he drew comfort from knowing there was a limit. But now he's not so sure there is a limit. As he claims, computer chips with molecular level advances will make for a computer which is "a million times faster and smarter by the year 2030." And, for what purpose would one suppose we would need computers that fast? Could it be to finally create von Neumann's dream, the self-replicating universal constructor; not just a computer that can create, but an intelligent race of deep-space-faring cyborgs? According to Bill Joy, this dream may become a nightmare sooner than we think.

As Joy stated in *Wired* magazine, "It was only then that I became anxiously aware of how great are the dangers facing us in the 21st century... We have yet to come to terms with the fact that the most compelling 21st century technologies—robotics, genetic engineering and nanotechnology—pose a more dangerous threat than any past technologies." As Joy adds, "these computers and genes and micro machines, share a dangerous amplifying factor: *They can self replicate:* A bomb is blown up only once, but one bot can become many, and quickly get out of control." (Italics added) He adds: "I may be working to create tools that will enable the construction of technology to replace our species. How do I feel about this? Very uncomfortable."

In the same *Post* article, cyberneticist Hans Moravec claims, "One way to avoid the biological threat is to become non-biological." As Moravec stated in a panel discussion, "The evolution of our descendants will push them into entirely different realms. They will become something else entirely. I don't know why you are disturbed by that."

On the heels of this media announcement, on 8/31/00, the *Washington Post* released a story entitled "Brave new world: Robots create themselves," which touted a major milestone in cybernetics. Quoting from a current article in the journal *Nature*, this article explains that two Brandeis University researchers have crossed an important threshold in cybernetics research by creating a computerized system that "automatically evolves, improves and builds a variety of mobile creatures without any significant human intervention." These robotic life forms are a few inches in length, are made of plastic, and contain rudimentary nervous systems made of wire. These robotic creatures were not designed or constructed by people, but evolved in 'Darwinian' fashion via a computer program. As this article explains, the body plans of these robotic creatures evolved by "random accumulation of mutations," a concept described as "virtual evolution." Rodney Brooks of MIT's Artificial Intelligence Lab stated that this achievement is "a long awaited and necessary step toward the ultimate dream of self-evolving machines."

The Biological and the Silicon

As the 4/16/2000 *Washington Post* article also explains, a few scientists see intelligent robotic life as centuries away, and others see it just around the bend of the next decade: it is just a matter of "uploading the human brain into the computer, blending the biological with the silicon."

Interestingly, it was reported on 2/25/2000 that U. Cal. Berkeley researchers have discovered "a way to mate human cells with circuitry in a 'bionic chip' that could play a key role in medicine and genetic engineering." The "cell-chip," touted in the March, 2000 issue of the journal *Biomedical Microdevices*, is a tiny device smaller and thinner than a strand of hair which "combines a healthy human cell with an electronic circuitry chip." By controlling the chip with a computer, the activity of the cell can be controlled. Eventually it is hoped that various types of cell-chips will be developed which would be "tuned for the precise voltage needed to activate different bodily tissues, from muscle to bone to brain." As this article explains, it will be a while before we see the development of "a bionic man," but the development of the cell-chip will clearly accelerate genetic research.

Cyberneticist Hans Moravec explains such a scenario in detail in his 1999 book, *Robot: Mere Machine to Transcendent Mind.* On the book's back cover we read: "… in a bid for immortality, many of our descendants will choose to transform into 'ex humans,' as they upload themselves into advanced computers." How does Moravec propose such 'uploading' could be effected? He explains (p. 170) that advanced neurological electronics could bit by bit replace gray matter. Moravec proposes that the brain could be slowly replaced by these "superior electronic equivalents," until finally, the biological is fully interfaced with the electronic. However, as he points out, the resultant transplanted human mind would be "disembodied." Since the human mind needs to be connected to a body to remain sane, the illusion of bodily awareness would be generated via computer simulation.

The transformation of the biological human into the cyborg entity is closely associated with space flight and deep space exploration. Moravec's book, *Robot,* also goes into this idea in great detail. In the year 2100 and beyond, Moravec writes, colonies of transformed humans, who will comprise new corporate ventures, will reach for the stars in order to beat the competition on Earth. Moravec refers to these new space inhabitants and space enterprises as the 'Exes,' since they will be ex-humans and ex-corporate entities no longer calling the terrestrial Earth home, and no longer subject to its social institutions and corporate laws. Moravec writes (p. 144):

> A small 'seed' colony launched to an asteroid or small moon could process local material and energy to grow into a facility of almost arbitrary size. Earth's moon may be off limits, especially to enterprises that change its appearance, but the solar system has thousands of unremarkable asteroids, some incidentally in earth-threatening orbits that an intelligent rider could tame.

According to researcher Martin Caiden, certain military personnel volunteered their bodies to become cyborgs in 1970. The book, *MILABS,* reports that there are "rumors" that the Air Force has conducted top-secret cybernetics projects to modify humans for space flight. In a German television report entitled "Future Fantastic," televised on January 18, 1998, *X-Files* star Gillian Anderson gave viewers a tour of the possible future of cybernetics. The creation of bio-engineered robots, or cyborgs, the television show explained, would necessitate the cloning of humans who "have computers instead of brains." In light of the development of the cell-chip, these cyborgs might be better described as Moravec's 'ex-humans'– disembodied intelligences who have multiple types of cell-chips instead of cells comprising their brain tissue.

According to Philip Corso's book *The Day After Roswell,* the impetus driving this research may come directly from the now infamous 1947 Roswell UFO crash. Col. Corso speculated in 1961 that the navigational entities discovered at the crash scene were "bio-engineered robots," and were engineered as *part of the craft.* This would suggest that the craft's navigational circuitry was interfaced with the consciousness of entities who, perhaps, had volunteered to become "ex-humans." As Congressman Rose has suggested, indeed psychic weapons might be "a hell of a cheap radar system;" but even more than that, a "disembodied" human mind might be a hell of an interesting psychic navigation system.

The most profound thought in all of this is the idea that the Zeta Reticuleans are the future of the human race if technologies incorporating psychotronics, genetic engineering and cybernetics are utilized to engineer human beings with computer brains. It has been noted in UFO literature that the Zeta Reticuleans themselves are a race which has allowed their technology to run full throttle without consideration of the impact of technology on the human spirit. Using the language of physics, this is indeed the destination we are pulling toward ourselves, toward our children and our children's children (*Homo Alterios Spatialis?*) with reckless abandon. Indeed, the physics of deep space propulsion, wherein time is reduced to zero and acceleration is increased to infinity, may well describe the imminent direction, position and speed of the entire human race toward its final extinction. It's a shame that we have "free will" and this is what we have chosen to do with it.

Psychotronics: The Future is Now

In an article entitled "The New Mental Battlefield: 'Beam Me Up, Spock,'" published in John White's 1988 book *Psychic Warfare: Fact or Fiction?*, U.S. Army Col. John B. Alexander defines psychotronics as "the interaction of mind and matter," and asserts that there are "weapons systems that operate on the power of the mind and whose lethal capacity has already been demonstrated." Alexander further explains that there are two subdivisions within this field which have been investigated. One is "mind-altering techniques designed to impact on an opponent." These techniques, Alexander writes, are "well-advanced," and include the manipulation of human behavior via psychological weapons which effect sight, sound, smell, temperature, electromagnetic energy or sensory deprivation. The second area of experimentation, Alexander reports, involves out-of-body experience, remote viewing and extrasensory perception (bioinformation). Alexander reported at this time that certain persons appear to have the ability to "mentally retrieve data from afar while physically remaining in a secure location."

With regard to unclassified parapsychological research performed by the USSR and its allies, Alexander notes they are "well in the lead" in this type of research. He notes that this research is voluminous and is scientifically verified. Alexander discusses just some of the most important human superpower discoveries made by the Soviets:

- *Electromagnetic Energy Field.* Existence of energy emanations from the body through Kirlian (radiation field) photography.

- *Energy Transference.* Transference of energy to heal or cause disease over distance has been demonstrated in lower organisms.

- *Telepathic Hypnosis.* Ability to induce hypnotic states telepathically over large distances (up to or in excess of 1,000 kilometers).

- *Telekinesis.* The mental movement of objects has been repeatedly demonstrated under scientifically controlled conditions.

Alexander also posits that the phenomenon of spoon-bending is explainable as the mental generation of a human-emitted electromagnetic force capable of distorting or rupturing a target object. Soviet research in Kirlian photography has proven the existence of such a force in the human body. This electromagnetic force is also known in Japan as *Ki* and in China as *Chi*, and is the force which is manipulated in acupuncture. Alexander also discusses the use of telepathic hypnosis to implant information or commands to "agents." As he states, "in cinema terms, the Manchurian candidate lives and does not even require a phone call." Alexander also states that there are other mind-to-mind thought induction techniques which would allow "direct transference of thought via telepathy from one mind, or group of minds, to a selected target audience." As he notes, "the recipient will not be aware that thoughts have been implanted from an external source. He or she will believe the thoughts are original."

Alexander also mentions the Transcendental Meditation Siddhis Program, where there is evidence that some individuals have been taught to levitate and manifest other paranormal feats. (Courtney Brown, founder of the Farsight Institute remote viewing organization in Atlanta, Georgia, studied at the Maharishi International University in the TM-Siddhis Program, which teaches "yogic flying.") Alexander claims that people can be trained to use their minds to produce physical phenomena which would extend our conceptual boundary of physical reality. Clearly, Alexander notes, the side with the edge on psychotronic weapons will have a "quantum leap over his opponent."

During a panel on metapsychiatry at the 1981 annual meeting of the American Association for Social Psychiatry, Col. Alexander presented a paper entitled "The Problem of Psychotronics: A Military Approach and Ethical Framework." An excerpt of this paper appears in John White's *Psychic Warfare: Fact or Fiction?*. Regarding the "command and control of aspects of war" and the "theoretical battlefield of the next war" Alexander had the following to say:

> We can now hypothesize a quantum leap in complexity through the theoretical context of multidimensional realities and evidenced by psychotronic experimentation. It is my contention that within the foreseeable future the very constructs of time and space as presently conceived in consensus reality may be subject to significant revision to accommodate such subject matter as psychokinesis, psychoenergetics, remote viewing and superluminality.

Col. Alexander also addressed the question of the validity of research into psychic phenomena, and asserted that the accumulated evidence thus far "runs counter to anticipated results" and "flies in the face of the very belief systems of many individuals." He reported that "the adjustments necessary to accommodate the data presented are so extreme that the facts become denied." Alexander asserted that, while both fundamental Christians and dialectical materialists have a right to their own beliefs regarding paranormal phenomena, what we are dealing with should not necessarily be labeled satanic, black magic or voodoo, but are "normal forces whose parameters have not yet been defined." He argued that "the penumbra of consensus reality must be carefully explored to diminish the realm of the *paranormal* while expanding the parameters of the *normal*." Col. Alexander insisted that both the Soviets and the People's Republic of China have an interest in the field of psychotronics. During this talk, Alexander also stated the following:

> To the inevitable question as to the propriety of military experimentation and application of advanced human technology, I would submit that we have no recourse but to do so. While all would agree that the world would be a safer and saner place without nuclear, biological, or chemical weapons, the fact of the matter is they do exist. In psychotronics, just as in those areas, it is naiveté to presume that if we ignore the field, no one else will venture forth. The power is neutral, it is the application that is judgmental. *There are eschatological con - siderations, but those must be evaluated by each individual.* (Italics added)

Thomas E. Bearden claims in "Tesla's Secret and the New Soviet Superweapons," published in *Psychic Warfare: Fact or Fiction?*, that orthodox electromagnetic theory is seriously flawed, and that "a fundamental error in thinking has hidden the long-sought unified field theory from theorists." Through Tesla technology, "Star Wars" is literally possible. Bearden also maintains the following:

> With two cerebral brain halves, the human being also has a Tesla scalar interferometer between his ears. And since the brain and nervous system processes avalanche discharges, it can produce (and detect) scalar Tesla waves to at least a limited degree. Thus a human can sometimes produce anomalous spatio-temporal effects at a distance and through time. This provides an exact mechanism for psychokinesis, levitation, psychic healing, telepathy, precognition, retrocognition, remote viewing, etc. It also provides a reason why an individual can detect a sticky feeling on the plate of a radionics or Hieronymus machine, when ordinary detectors detect nothing.

These are the powers of the *siddhis* of ancient India as we have discussed in this book. It is claimed that humans can potentially acquire *siddhis*, such as telepathy, levitation, telekinesis, hypnotic thought control over distance, invisibility and cloaking, power to generate illusory forms, power to travel through physical objects, power to enter and control another's body, and so on. Via Tesla technology, these powers can ostensibly come back to the human race, at least to that group which holds the well protected key to the psychotronic "black box." As Bearden hopes, perhaps with the free and open release of Tesla's secrets, we might be able to develop defenses against this dangerous technology "before Armageddon occurs." Otherwise, the use of these weapons will affect the minds and thoughts and the very lifestreams of all life forms on earth. This allusion to Armageddon, along with Col. Alexander's allusion to "eschatological considerations," is a frightening scenario. It appears that the end of the world is being taken very seriously in some quarters.

Ufologist Steven Greer warns that in his meetings over the last several years with covert operatives working in UFO related programs, one overriding theme has emerged. That theme has two strands: "the eventual covert militarization of the ET subject and a weird covert religious strain which can only be viewed as bizarre." As Greer explains, in this milieu we find some "very strange bed-fellows: war mongers and militarists in cahoots with industrialists who share a bizarre eschatological bent." This brood has an extremely dark view of the future, with the threat of an extraterrestrial Armageddon. This theme supports "retrograde and fanatical religious causes as well as deeply covert military-industrial plans to expand the arms race into space." Greer believes that attempts to rapidly militarize space are a result of "a myopic, militaristic and paranoid view of extraterrestrial projects and intentions."

Military-industrial interests heavily involved in covert projects have a shared goal: demonizing the UFO/ET phenomenon. As Greer explains, from a military-industrial perspective, the type of disclosure which serves their purposes is one which frames the UFO/ET issue in a threatening manner. A false UFO/ET disclosure would serve the military-industrial agenda as well as a fanatical religious agenda. Not only have these religious beliefs pervaded the civilian UFO community, but they have also influenced covert policy on UFOs. As Greer warns, "some of these people want Armageddon – and they want it ASAP." This eschatological (end time) belief system has also pervaded the civilian UFO community.

Greer's research has uncovered the penetration of this covert group into the civilian UFO research community. This penetration by a military-minded faction runs so deep into the civilian community, Greer argues, that "civilian initiatives are totally controlled and financed by 'cut-outs' from ultra-secret projects." Greer insists that deep-cover black project operatives are working closely with civilian researchers and journalists, and that CIA and military intelligence operatives are working with heads of think tanks. Add to this mix wealthy business people who are also "eschatologists" working from a biblical end times perspective, and think tank people who are being advised by supposed civilian scientists, who may not be civilians at all and may also be proponents of this Armageddon/ET scenario. This is a very complicated scenario which defies categorical logic and defines the parameters of good old fashioned psi-ops disinformation strategy. (see Dan Smith's web site, The Eschaton, and my interview with Smith at www.paranoiamagazine.com)

The following chapter provides an understanding of how an elite planetary group called the Illuminati uses covert technology to maintain its perverse eminence via ancient secretive procedures of ritual occult mind control.

CHAPTER THIRTEEN
MIND CONTROL, RITUAL CULTS
AND THE ILLUMINATI BLOODLINE

In cinema terms, the Manchurian candi-
date lives and does not even require a
phone call.

U.S. Army Col. John B. Alexander
"The New Mental Battlefield:
'Beam Me Up, Spock,'"

This brings us to an important juncture in the quest to understand the connection between mind control and the usurpation of occult information by the intelligence apparatus. The important issue is the fact that certain esoteric/occult principles and practices were usurped by the intelligence community from various sources and utilized for purposes of mind control.

In order to investigate the efficacy of certain practices for espionage purposes, the CIA's MK-ULTRA (anything goes) program let loose on the public, under various subheadings, clandestine experimental research in psychedelics, hypnosis, telepathy, and, among other nefarious trials and tribulations, trauma-based mind control. The MK-ULTRA program is now known to have involved over 40 colleges and universities in the U.S. and Canada, and many other types of institutions, think tanks and civilian agencies from the 1950s to the 1970s. In collusion with certain Nazis brought into the U.S. by the intelligence apparatus after World War II, the CIAMK-ULTRAmind control program was responsible for the development of what was 'lovingly' called "Monarch" trauma-based conditioning.

The connecting link between MK-ULTRA and generational ritual cults is the creation of what has become popularly known, from a film of the same name starring Frank Sinatra, as the "Manchurian Candidate." As U.S. Army Col. John B. Alexander has stated, "In cinema terms, the Manchurian candidate lives and does not even require a phone call."

A Manchurian Candidate is a person with a psychiatrically-created Multiple Personality Disorder (MPD). Canadian psychiatrist Dr. Colin Ross has personally documented, through declassified CIA documents, the history of the CIA's ability to create a real life Manchurian Candidate through hypno-therapeutic and trauma-based conditioning techniques, performed by psychiatrists with CIA connections and funding. As he notes, this ability has grown to a perfection over the past fifty years, since the discovery that POWs returning from Korea had been brainwashed by the Chinese to accept Communist allegiance. (see, CKLN Mind Control Radio Series)

As Dr. Ross notes, Dr. G. H. Estabrooks began in World War II by creating one "alter personality" in an adult military recruit, which could be switched on without the recruit's awareness. The alter could be used in espionage or counterespionage, or as a hypnotic courier, i.e., to carry a message without awareness. Or, if caught, the alter could be programmed to commit suicide. (Incidentally, Lee Harvey Oswald's military buddy, Kerry Thornely, believes that Oswald may have been one such military recruit.)

Monarch programming creates MPD by inducing painful trauma which causes the mind to "dissociate" or fracture. From birth onward, helpless children born into sacrificial cults are tortured and maimed by their own sadistic guardians in order to cause this fracturing of the personality. Children born into "generational" or bloodline ritual cult families are brutalized, drugged, elec-

171

troshocked, deprived of food, water and sleep, and are subjected to or are witness to unthinkable ritualized activities, including rape, incest, bestiality and sacrificial killings. The child's "handler" creates several layers of personalities with various pseudonyms, some of whom will be called upon to handle the pain, and others who will be called upon to perform various criminal and sexual activities. These alters are called upon without the awareness of the primary personality to perform various acts, ranging from sex with officials to drug running to political assassinations. This layered effect essentially creates a condition of amnesia in the primary personality.

Nowhere is the reality of this nightmare so vividly described as in Beth Goobie's shocking book, *The Only-Good Heart*. Beth's book is proffered as a work of "fiction," but is a very real account of a Canadian Monarch survivor born into a ritual cult which is fictionalized as "The Kin." Beth describes in harrowing detail how the Monarch victim's personality disintegration is effected:

> The man has appointed me Doorkeeper. It is now my job to make and keep all doors. I keep track of everyone inside. When the man needs a new child, he calls me up into The Body. He inserts a needle into the skin and instructs me to make a new door. The Body must obey without crying or twisting its face so I send the needle pain in behind the door where a girl named Klarrenord lives. The man has decreed that it is Klarrenord's job to feel needle pain, but she must cry alone behind her door without knowing what's happening. All alone so no one can hear her and be bothered by her wailing. Then The Body can perform the required task without complaining.

The man then inserts a long needle high in her leg, and Beth directs the pain to Klarrenord. She then goes inside, "down the long hallway that leads to that leg." There are five other doors nearby. She explains, 'I wave my hands counterclockwise around the needle tip, ... the man requires a dark door here." The man chants, "doorkeeper, make a new door," and a new door appears. Beth explains, "I surface into The Body and look out the face." A "new door" has been made. The man then explains the name and purpose of this new door:

> There will be a new girl who lives behind this door. Her name will be Sepperintowski. Sepperintowski will do everything I tell her. Sepperintowski will like especially to cut with knives. Sepperintowski will cut anything I tell her to cut. If I tell Sepperintowski to cut a puppy, she will cut a puppy. If I tell Sepperintowski to cut a man, she will cut a man. If I tell Sepperintowski to cut herself, she will cut herself. But when Sepperintowski cuts herself, Sepperintowski will not feel it. Someone else inside will feel it and that someone will be Klarrenord. Klarrenord is already there and Klarrenord feels pain for other children.

In time, it was no longer necessary for Beth to create her own doors. Eventually, The Body learned "to obey without the Doorkeeper." As she explains, "The man inserts a needle and commands a door of white light to begin. The door shapes itself out of fear and pain, then a spirit of hissing white comes through it and rises from The Body to speak with the man. I close my own door quietly. I don't want to see any more."

Generational Ritual Abuse

The link that modernizes ancient bloodline cults is the now well-documented MK-ULTRAprogram. The person who is performing the trauma-based mind control is usually described as a "doctor," and is most likely a 'spychiatrist': a psychiatrist with intelligence ties. A few of these mind control doctors have actually been identified. They have been named as Dr. Green, identified as the notorious Nazi Josef Mengele, Dr. White, identified as Scottish mind control programmer Ewen Cameron, and Dr. Black, who has been identified as Monarch survivor Cisco Wheeler's father. The child's primary "handler" and abuser is usually the child's father, who, in some cases, is involved in a generational bloodline cult, often has intelligence ties, and usually is associated with other powerful patriarchal organizations. When the child grows up, she is given over to a different handler, sometimes in "marriage." And the gears of generational abuse keep turning.

Many of these cults are based on the dichotomy of the Christ/Satan duality, a split personality in itself. In other words, these cults are either satanic cults, or Christian cults which recognize the ancient roots of the split person Horus/Set. As Beth Goobie writes, "the Kin serves both the Dark Lord and the Lord of Light, feeding them both from the kill of energy of ritual sacrifice so that they may fortify their regions of Dark and Light in their war against one another." As William Gray writes in *Magical Ritual Methods*, there are many "sex and slaughter schools" in operation today under various names. Some of them, Gray maintains, would be shocked to hear themselves described this way. For instance, the Christian Mass is full of pagan sex and slaughter symbolism. The symbolic drinking of Christ's blood and eating of his body at Eucharist, the crucifixion/torture of Christ on the cross and the ascension of his body after death, are examples which illustrate that Christian images can be used just as well by the operators of a death cult. It does not take much imagination to see where some wayward souls could go with this symbolism.

Probably the largest of these ancient cults which still survives worldwide is the Dionysian blood sacrifice cult. As Dan Russell has indicated, Dionysis is Jesus' Greek alter-ego. As ritual abuse victim Caryn Stardancer explained in a panel discussion (CKLN), the Dionysians were a serious force to be reckoned with in ancient Rome, and were actually outlawed. As she explains:

> The oldest laws ever passed against ritual abuse were passed in Rome through [the time of] Christ, and they were made against the very Dionysian Sects that were still in operation in the forties and fifties, and which I assume are still in operation now. The reason the laws were made against them was because at that time … it was known that in the rituals there were sexual orgies, flaying (skinning of people), flagellation, abuse and ritual rape of women and children. But that isn't why there were laws made against the groups–the laws were made against the groups because of the practice of common commission of crime for the purpose of political blackmail.

As a matter of fact, political blackmail is the strongest deterrent to open disclosure of the reckless and inhuman activities of these cult members. It has come to light that these generational ritual cults operate on the fringes of public organizations, such as police forces, secret societies and fringe factions of the intelligence apparatus, which groups require funding for secretive projects and gain that funding by political blackmail. Even the Mafia has been implicated in these programs. As Monarch survivor Kathleen Sullivan has reported, the Mafia was involved in a program called OMICRON which may have involved both the Columbo and Trafficante crime families. The reason they utilized these mind controlled couriers and assassins was so that they would not be able to name the person for whom they performed illegal tasks. (CKLN)

Sullivan has personal knowledge of having worked on projects which indicated a lot of crossover between the CIA, the Mafia and several other federal agencies, including the Pentagon. Sullivan explains the historical roots of the Mafia's connection to the Monarch program. As she explains, during WWII the OSS and the military recruited many mob figures, especially from Italy, to spy on various governments. Some personal friendships developed between operatives and mob figures, and these friendships have continued.

As Caryn Stardancer explains, layers of political blackmail are known to occur "right up the hierarchy," and is the basis of the diseased political system in which we live. It has become clear that much of the weirdness that goes on politically in America can ultimately be explained by this mafioso-style political intimidation and blackmail, which is a cover for various criminal activities and which is effected in collusion with underground ritual cult groups. And we think Russia has a mafia problem!

Yet, it's important to note that these sinister activities wouldn't get too far if there wasn't any interest in the trafficking of pornography and sex with children. As we now well know, "sex addiction" is rampant in society, and goes "right up the hierarchy." What this situation boils down to is that officials caught with their pants down in drug-induced sexual situations with minor children are apt to do everything they are told. As therapist Gail Fisher-Taylor indicates, these groups operate through implication and intimidation. As she explains, "if these people are implicated in criminal activity, they are drawn in, and they can be drawn in and blackmailed under the influence of drugs and other kinds of influences." (CKLN) In terms of how these people get away with what they do, Fisher-Taylor points to both "collusion" and to "disbelief." As she so succinctly explains the predicament:

> The structures of power are such that if there are members of the cult who are both leaders in business, let's say members of the police department, members of the criminal justice system—judges or lawyers—it often becomes an 'old boys network.' You've got people protecting other people so if there is any kind of revelation that this kind of activity is going on, their members in the media are going to participate in the cover-up, or in the blasphemy and outrageousness of such allegations. If the police department is involved, and there are often reports of police being involved–in Saskatchewan, for instance, the Martensville case–it is very easy for police to conduct an investigation that will throw their whole case out of court. If you have a lot of people in many different positions of power, and there is collusion among them, it is much more difficult especially when the public doesn't know about the principles of dissociation and the way that trauma [conditioning] works, the way the human psyche works around trauma. It is very easy for the media, police and criminal justice system to play on the public's disbelief.

The False Memory Movement

A media spin which helps to dispel "rumors" of ritual abuse/mind control is what Fisher-Taylor refers to as "false memory propaganda." Once survivors of this ritual torture get to the point where they become aware of what has occurred, and the layers begin to peel off with the help of therapy, they begin to network with other survivors. One San Francisco non-profit group which has been formed for these cult victims is called "Survivorship" (see web site at www.ctsserver.com/~svship) Problematically, once these victims began to come together to heal themselves and to testify before the courts and government investigatory panels, a "backlash" began to occur from an organization called the "False Memory Foundation."

According to the claims of the False Memory movement, Multiple Personality Disorder is "iatrogenic," or created by the therapist. People in this movement argue that these memories, which are admittedly of a bizarre nature, cannot be relied upon as true evidence since they are often brought forward under clinical hypnosis and other psycho-therapeutic techniques, and, as well, the memories may be intertwined with some rather peculiar information and extraordinary claims. Another argument is that MPD or DID (Dissociative Identity Disorder) is really temporal lobe epilepsy. Both of these arguments are part of what Dr. Colin Ross calls "Manchurian Candidate Denial." (CKLN)

As Dr. Ross also points out, "the history of psychiatry in the second half of the 20th Century is undoubtedly strongly skewed – not by an agenda that has to do with academic research, not by the best interest of clients, not by ethical psychiatry – but by an Intelligence agenda." As he also points out, psychiatrists have created a "little loophole where they can step out of normal ethical oversight." All of this is kept under the carpet, he asserts, "not by twelve guys in a room at Langely ...but by this pervasive 'old boys' network." According to Dr.

Ross's research, many of the people in the False Memory movement themselves have a vested interest in Manchurian Candidate Denial.

The idea that the False Memory movement constitutes a deliberate disinformation strategy, Dr. Ross argues, is perfectly plausible and consistent with the fact that large numbers of persons claiming ritual abuse are now coming forward. That is, "false memory" is a convenient handle for a counterstrategy by people who perhaps stand a chance of being implicated in the scheme themselves somewhere along the line. As Walter Bowart also stated in an interview, "the board of this organization is made up of a lot of CIApeople, CIAcontracts and 'spychiatrists,' and pedophiles, child molesters, people like that are on the side of pedophilia. They are trying to defend pedophilia. And it is a very litigious, very aggressive organization that has struck terror in the hearts of the therapeutic community." (CKLN)

As Fisher-Taylor explains, articles touting "false memories" appear in the newspapers often at the same time as stories reporting on real findings of ritual cult activities. This effectively "splits" readers minds on the issue, forcing them into denial about the reality of ritual abuse. In addition, trauma-based conditioning contains the potential for infusion of misleading or fantastic information, often induced by audio/visual input (i.e. movies, music or taped commands) cued along with sleep deprivation, electroshock, sodium amytal and/or hypnosis, which serves to "scramble" memories and create amnesia barriers. This would explain why some of the claims of mind control victims can often be so utterly bizarre.

Military-Corporate-Secret Society Connection

The numbers of mind control victims now comparing notes in America and Canada are astounding. Most of these victims claim that their torture as children was at the hands of sacrificial cult groups to which their parents belonged, as well as at the hands of certain 'spychiatrists'now known to be connected to the CIA's MK-ULTRA program. It has also been established that many of these activities took place at locations, including hospitals, universities, day camps and military bases, now recognized as part of this nefarious program. Thus, it has become apparent that CIA cult specialists have in some cases "subcontracted" with ritual cults, or were in some manner already connected to these cults, to prime these children to be of service to the mafioso-style intelligence arm of the secret government. At the same time this programming provided a means by which these children could be of special service to the cult itself.

In many cases, a military-corporate-secret society connection can be made. Survivors have connected the dots between ritual cults and the armed services (in Canada, especially, near NORAD bases), as well as to "white male secret society groups" such as the Masons and the Ku Klux Klan. Ancient sects such as the Golden Dawn have also been implicated in these practices. Such groups are said to be in practice even in Washington, DC. As Sullivan explains, many people who are involved in "neo-pagan religions" are interested in a "New World Order" where they will be able to worship their Dark Lord publicly without shame. These religions are part of their family's past and they do not wish to let them go. Sullivan believes that many of these groups also have Aryan generational backgrounds and consider themselves elite. These groups would like to rid society of Christian ethical codes and laws against adult-child sex, bestiality and other sordid activities which supply them with untold power.

The Aryan connection is also discussed in detail by Cathy O'Brien in *Trance Formation of America*. She claims that many of her cult abusers adhered to "Neo-Nazi" principles wherein "mankind must take a giant step in evolution through creating a superior race." O'Brien's "handler" espoused Nazi and KKK ideas to the effect that a perfect "blonde race" should be genetically bred and the genocide of underprivileged races and cultures should be effected.

As Lynne Moss-Sharman explains, her memories seem to revolve around her father, her uncles and her father's military buddies, all of whom were pedophiles. Lynne is not aware that her father had ritual cult involvement outside of this. Her father worked for General Electric and may have had CIA/defense industry connections. Later, she began to recall episodes which took place at locations further away and she began to recall other "doctors" who were involved, as well as complicated electrical equipment, including chairs, helmets and containers, sensory deprivation and torture devices, body wrapping, programming via telephone, and more.

How the situation progresses from the child being a victim of a sort of 'localized' pedophile group to becoming a Monarch victim is probably different in each case. However, as Lynne explains, over 90% of survivors believe they were offered up by their own parents for ritualized cult abuse as well as simultaneous 'outside' mind control experimentation. As Lynne explains, children were not secretly taken away from their parents during the day or for overnight or weekend visits. There was conscious knowledge by one or both parents, and the parents were "actively involved in making sure the children arrived where they were supposed to arrive." It is clear that the CIA's proximity to various cults and to certain criminal types allows for such arrangements. As Walter Bowart has explained, in some cases the CIA gets involved in a child pornography case and forces the parents to "play ball" with them. This was done in the case of Cathy O'Brien, whose father started by having Cathy and her brother perform in porn films as children. After he was arrested for these illegal activities, and just before he was about to go to trial, the CIA stepped in and began Cathy's lifetime of service to the crytocracy as a drug runner, prostitute and hypnotic courier.

The Occult Connection

After World War II, the U.S. captured the records of Nazi parapsychology experiments performed at Dachau concentration camp and, as well, took hundreds of Nazi scientists in from the rain. U.S. psychic researchers have long suspected the Germans may have been close to discovering psychic weapons. The records of the Dachau experiments are still classified top secret, but it is known that one focus of certain Dachau experiments was whether 'telepathy' could be increased under torture. Clearly, the 'telepathy' in this case is out-of-body. What they were trying to do is induce the out-of-body experience via pain, which is exactly what is done in cult rituals to induce multiple personality disorder. As Monarch survivor Beth Goobie writes in "The Network of Stolen Consciousness" in *Paranoia*, Issue 24:

> In search of immortality, cults have always explored the metaphysical gateways to alternate dimensions that can be opened through traumatic dissociation. These out-of-body experiences teach cult members to exist as frequencies; conscious knowing energy that has been dissociated from the body during trauma. One can leave the body at many different frequencies, and each frequency opens up a different dimension of reality or 'mystery,' as well as interaction with the entities which inhabit these dimensions.

Nazism was a state-instituted perverse cult which explored much of this ground, and the CIA/intelligence apparatus, also an institutionalized cult, has continued in their depraved footsteps. As Beth Goobie makes clear, due to her special trauma-based training she became a "channeler" for a sacrificial cult operating in Saskatchewan, and her body became a "megaphone for the Dark Lord to yell through from the other side." As she explains, Monarch programming is based on occult principles, since it teaches a person to locate and tag interdimensional frequencies which are portals to the dark world beyond the psyche. In a personal communiqué, Beth explains that as she began to access memories of the occult ritual abuse, she began to understand that the way to healing was to "beat the frequency." As she explains:

We're surrounded by other dimensions that can be encountered through specific brain frequency 'gates'– each altered state has a specific pattern of brain waves which is the entry point for interactive consciousness. Each frequency has a color and a tone/pitch (synesthesia). Cults program an individual to split into personalities tuned to specific colors and sounds (harmonics?). These personalities are then sent out of the body to live in other dimensions (i.e., in "the Grid" or the "Matrix"). Each time a personality leaves you to live somewhere else, you lose part of your brain power and functioning–becoming less and less of yourself. These other dimensions where your 'others' live, are ongoing and interactive, not static. Personalities from other people can access/torture/use/abuse you there, usually as a conduit for your life energy, depleting you further. Most of the energy conduit selves are white-light energy, and are sent (up) out of the body during orgasm. Shock programming is also basic to this.

Goobie is backed up in this color/frequency/consciousness connection by William Gray in *Magical Ritual Methods.* As he notes, if we wanted to, for instance, contact the Sphere of Mercy, we "enter the Sphere by 'going Blue,' and locking consciousness on to the frequency of Compassion." He explains, "once we are able to project the power from this Sphere, we push it out of our fingers into the surrounding air and let our hands make whatever reactive movements they are impelled to do by the Origin-impulse." At first, Gray notes, the hands will move awkwardly, but with eyes closed, the practitioner should let this energy work through him to manipulate the Air Element." The main objective of this exercise is to develop magical touch, and to work through all the Spheres of influence until results are achieved from each.

As William Gray has explained, in magical ritual one is not dealing with inanimate lumps of matter, but living energies which are, as he explains, "capable of autoreaction upon each other." As he explains, magical ritual is the art of stretching "one piece of consciousness" and extending it beyond the limits of the sensory world. It must then be "picked up" or "channeled" by Intelligences operating through the Inner Dimensions. Without the cooperation of such "Inner contacts" which pick up the energy and extend it beyond their usual "point of neutrality," the magical practitioner would not be successful in making contact. Likewise, if we ourselves are unable to pick up the energies coming back toward us, and translate their expression on the material level, we will not be successful in making contact. We must understand that this is the type of training which Monarch mind control victims are receiving, whether or not they themselves are aware of it.

The sense of touch is an important sense for magical practitioners. Magicians are trained to work with the media of all of the four elements: Earth, Air, Water and Fire. Ritual hand gestures aren't simply hand movements, but are a way of pushing, pulling and working with Air as though it were a material substance. All you "see" is the hand, but there's more to it than what the untrained eye can see. As Gray explains in *Magical Ritual Methods,* what is actually happening in a ritual hand gesture is that the practitioner is 'sculpting'with air as a medium. In effect, Gray writes, "we are moulding the Element of Air into symbolic shapes intended to contain our meaning. It is not actually our hands, but what they have done which must be considered. Air has been touched, moved around, given form, and made to mean something in connection with our Inner intention." This becomes more obvious when we recall Beth Goobie's instructions on making a new door for her alter personality. As Beth explains, after the man inserts a long needle into her leg, Beth directs the pain to Klarrenord. She then goes inside, "down the long hallway that leads to that leg." There are five other doors nearby. She explains, 'I wave my hands counterclockwise around the needle tip, ... the man requires a dark door here." The man chants, "doorkeeper, make a new door," and a new door appears. Beth explains, "I surface into The Body and look out the face." A "new door" has been made. The man then explains the name and purpose of this new door.

As Gray suggests, a ritual such as this "appropriates circuits of consciousness through gestures, commands and symbols." As he explains, in order to open the consciousness, one must imagine the opening of a doorway and give the command to "come in" out loud. To raise or call up a formation of consciousness and positively recognize it as happening gives it reality in mental dimensions.

As Gray also explains, the magical practitioner works with air as though it is a moldable material. As Gray instructs, "It should be felt between the fingers, pulled about like elastic, and generally treated like any other amenable substance. We can poke our fingers into it, throw lumps of it about, press pieces of it together, tear bits of it apart, or do whatever else we please with it." This exercise is intended to sharpen consciousness to deal with normally intangible phenomena. By attempting to literally feel air, Gray writes, "we are bringing our consciousness to the very threshold where matter and unmatter meet. We shall be trying to solidify thought … trying to mould mind-matter." As Gray aptly notes, few people 'real-ize' air as a palpable substance, but of course it is as real as other invisible but quantifiable substances, such as electricity, magnetism and light.

It is not so peculiar that underground ritual cults and the covert intelligence apparatus have found such a cozy relationship in the arms of trauma bonding, since there has to be some way to get a child involved in this ritual programming right from birth. As Dr. Ross explains, "if you start with G.I. Joe at age 19, you can't get intensely poly-fragmented multi-multi-layers of defence systems in place very easily." (CKLN) With adults, he explains, it is highly unlikely to create more than one alter personality. In order to create an absolutely effective mind controlled zombie with several programmed personalities, intense fear and total submission must be generated via a ritualized pattern of trauma bonding inculcated from birth onward. Where are you going to find a cover for such a child? How is it possible to keep up the ritualized maintenance which this conditioning requires on a daily–hourly–basis?

Yet, not all ritual abuse survivors are aware of a cult connection. Jeannette Westbrook has not uncovered any "satanic" or cult memories, nor has she been able to make any connections between CIA or military mind control and her sadistic pedophile father. Nonetheless, she is aware that there was a pattern of ritualized abuse and there was a group of people in collusion with him. With regard to the creation of Jeanette's multiple personalities, as well as her sister's MPD status, Jeannette believes it unlikely that her father would have known any elaborate techniques on his own. However, she is sure that whoever it was that her father was in collusion with, it was an "organization" of some sort. She argues, whether they were satanists or simply an organized pedophile club, they were very much aware of multiple personality systems as a way to cover their tracks. They apparently knew enough about it to "seek to create it as a way to keep their abuse of the victim hidden."

Whether this group had 'professional' assistance in the deliberate creation of MPD, or whether these procedures are common knowledge among pedophiles and cultists in general, is unknown. Since the creation of MPD has been CIA knowledge since the 1950s, and since all that's actually required is a general knowledge of hypnotism and occult principles, this knowledge base has apparently 'trickled down' among those who 'need to know.' As is also well known, females easily dissociate and create alter personalities under trauma. In any case, Jeannette effectively dissociated from the memories of this sadistic abuse so that she "could get up in the morning, and function, and go to school, and come home, and live with these perpetrators." Yet, she and her sister recall that their father often called them by other names which specifically referred to their alter personalities. So, if these personalities weren't purely personal (self-created), it is likely that they were deliberately and ritually created, and the instance of their creation is perhaps lying in another layer of memory.

JonBenét Ramsey

In March of 2000 a 37-year-old California woman came forward in the JonBenét Ramsey case to testify that she has suffered a lifetime of sexual and physical abuse beginning at age 3. According to a story published in the *Camera* by Barrie Hartman, this woman's story, if true, "could mean the Ramsey case is tangled in sexual abuse and involves more people than originally thought." Thus far, the police are considering this woman's report to be credible. As Hartman reports, the woman has described sexual and physical abuse which she experienced as a child during after-hours holiday parties in various homes in California. After most of the guests had gone, another 'party' which involved sexual abuse of children by a select group of adults would begin. The woman names one of the main participants in these sex parties as one of the Ramsey's closest friends, Fleet White, whose Christmas party the Ramseys had attended the night their daughter was killed by an "intruder" in their home.

The woman has described sexual techniques used at these after hours parties wherein asphyxiation is used to stimulate an orgasmic response. The physical evidence of "garroting" which was found on JonBenét's body suggested to this woman that JonBenét may have been killed accidentally when this asphyxiation technique went too far. The woman has reported to police that this technique was used on her when she was a child. A tie-in to ritual cults may be Beth Goobie's belief that "most of the energy conduit selves are white-light energy, and are sent (up) out of the body during orgasm."

Another tie-in between cult ritual abuse and JonBenét Ramsey are the stun-gun marks found on her body. Many Monarch survivors claim that various forms of electricity, including stun-guns, are widely used as a control measure as well as to instill fear, and many of these victims have the tell-tale scars of the stun-gun on their bodies. The woman also told police that little girls were dressed provocatively and trained to say provocative things. She also stated that when girls did not perform as expected they were struck on the head, since their hair would cover the wound. In addition, she reported that Christmas was a good time for these sex parties so that children had a full week to heal from their wounds before going back to school.

JonBenét Ramsey's death occurred sometime during Christmas night in 1996. The autopsy report concluded she had suffered a blow on the head and was strangled. Stephen Singular, a Denver author who has pursued the Ramsey case for three years, is convinced the killing is linked to child sexual abuse. As yet, it is unknown whether this case involves a sacrificial bloodline cult. However, a strange event occurred shortly after this report came out which may have an occult significance.

On March 22, 2000, during a taped interview with Katie Couric of the "Today" television show, John Ramsey claimed that he wears a particular medallion on his chest in memory of his slain daughter. When Katie asked to see the piece, John Ramsey unbuttoned his shirt and pulled out a large round medallion which hung on a long chain on his chest. It was shown on television for only an instant. Upon the piece was a large six-pointed or five-pointed star, and a scattered grouping of smaller stars near the top of it. Ramsey claimed that the medallion had been won by his daughter in a beauty pageant. However, another way of looking at this strange behavior is as a ritual sign between co-conspirators of the success of an alchemical operation being undertaken. As William Gray explains in *Magical Ritual Methods* (pp. 160-161), the "pectoral symbol" is a medallion worn underneath garments on a long chain in the middle of the chest. With regard to the meaning of the pectoral symbol, Gray writes:

> The pectoral Symbol must bear some design which indicates the nature of the operation being undertaken, and the confidence of its wearer in the whole affair. ... The pectoral shows what we proclaim ourselves to be before everyone else, and what we will defend with all

our might. Without this quality of belief, no magic would be possible … Whatever Symbol we hang upon our breasts must really and truly stand for what we genuinely believe in with all the force of our Inner Being.

As Gray also writes "a working magician thinks and projects Inner power as far as possible towards materialisation, and relies on other agents to continue the cycle commenced." Who knows what ugly truth is lurking behind John Ramsey's poker face? Did something happen to his daughter at that Christmas party at Fleet White's house? Or, did someone from that party enter the Ramsey home and await their homecoming?

The Illuminati Bloodline

Digging our way even deeper into this quagmire, we discover that some of these generational cults are made up of Illuminati bloodline families. As mind control victim Cisco Wheeler explains, the Illuminati structure is based on 13 royal bloodlines. These 13 ruling families, which can be traced back many centuries, are luciferian cult members who have taken oaths to see the fulfillment of the end-time, and "to see the antichrist take his throne." These bloodline families, as Wheeler explains, are satanists who have taken blood oaths to serve lucifer, and they believe the world belongs to them. They are very loyal unto themselves, and they see themselves as gods. As she asserts, "there isn't anything they will not do." As Wheeler so poignantly states, "this isn't something that just happened." This mindset is passed on from generation to generation, and it "touches everyone within the family for generations." As this survivor so chillingly informs us:

> Their allegiance is unto lucifer, who I now will call satan. They believe in the doctrine of satanism, that if they rule as gods and they are obedient to the call which is lucifer's call upon their life, then they will rule and reign with him in hell. They have no fear of hell. They believe they will stand as gods in hell and they will rule the people in hell. They will become gods with him. That is the big lie. They believe this. That is bottom line of the doctrine.

Several Monarch mind control victims have come forward to report that they were victimized in this way as children due to the unfortunate circumstances of being born into the Illuminati bloodline. By creating layers of personality structures, these children grow up to become Manchurian candidates for the secret government. Yet, it is suspected that the children of the Illuminati bloodline for the most part are not expendable. These children are being groomed to become programmers and high priests and priestesses of the cult. It is suspected that the children who are killed in ritual sacrificial offerings are usually not Illuminati-bloodline children, but are other innocent children, perhaps orphans, foster children, adopted children, abducted children, or unwanted children who are given or sold by their parents to the cult. Essentially, they are our "missing children."

For various reasons, we remain in denial about the reality of satanic ritual abuse and sacrifice of children. According to Alan Scheflin, there is evidence that it occurs but the frequency is unknown and no satanic sects have actually been caught in the act. The FBI denies that this phenomenon exists, however, some specialized police departments tend to hold a different opinion. According to the *Toronto Globe and Mail,* police statistics in Bogota, Columbia report that about 15 children there are kidnapped every day to be delivered to satanic sects, forced into prostitution, adopted illegally, or for the harvesting of their organs. According to a police official there, most of the children are sacrificed in satanic rituals. It is suspected that many of these children come across the border into the U.S.

Beth Goobie describes the fate of one of these children, whom she calls "Billy Wheeler." As Beth explains, she had tried to phone Billy's mother, "somewhere in Louisiana." When she answered the phone, Beth sobbed, "please, please, are you his mother? Come and help him." The woman on the other end of the line replied, "We don't have a son named Billy Wheeler anymore. You tell him to be a good boy and do what he's told." Although Beth's book is labeled "fiction," she assured me in a personal letter that this story is true. As she also explained, many of the children born into cult families are sold or given to the cult for ritual sacrifice purposes. There also exist underground "breeding farms" where these children are housed. Beth suggests that there has to be some kind of police collusion involved in these crimes, since they go largely unnoticed. Strangely enough, the television show *The X-Files* gets into many of these sordid topics.

As Beth explains, the two children were forced into copulation many times. One night in a cult ritual, the "Brothers" shackled the boy's ankle to a long chain and made him kneel before the fire. Beth's mother then stepped forward and drew a black X on Billy's throat, and sang "Precious Redeemer." People in white robes chanted, "for we have sinned and he must die." The cult members forced the two children into sex on an altar. In the middle of the children's sexual climax, they pulled the chain which was still around the boy's ankle, and, when he hit the ground, they cut a slit in his throat and let the dog go. As Beth recalls:

> I could not pull my eyes from Billy Wheeler, his life or his death. I saw the dog leap, saw the jaws descend onto the thin lines of blood. Saw Billy's rigid legs and arms slump as his voice passed into mine, screaming, until a hand pressed over my mouth, the side of my head hit hard, the night blacked out. When I surfaced into lopsided vision, a dark throb in my head, I was covered in blood. Still shackled to the altar, I knew it must be his, there was no way to get it off me, I would carry this stain all my life.

The important thing to note is that the children of these generational Dionysian or Illuminati bloodline families, who are brought up in a sick, twisted, violently abusive environment, are apt to continue to put their own children through this genetically-based Hell on Earth. As Cisco Wheeler explains, her father was a "multiple," or multiple personality, trapped in this repetitive game loop. As she explains:

> I think there was a time in my father's life when he realized what he was and what he was doing. I think the barriers within his own mind, within his own multiplicity, had broken down to the point where he knew, but he also knew he was in over his head. It would cost him his life to move away or to change directions. He was too far in.

However, it's interesting to note that victims like Katherine Sullivan have come to realize that these perpetrators are not "powerful in the real world the way they tried to trick me into believing." She writes: "It's been smoke and mirrors all along. Intel occultists are the worst possible combo. They especially know that the easiest way to weaken an opponent is to psych him out." Sullivan declared the following:

> Reality check: the so-called controllers aren't controllers at all. They are miserable humans. They defecate and get ulcers and feel pain and loneliness and have miserable marriages and are in absolute terror of each other. They aren't ruling anyone. They never will. Freedom is a condition of the soul. They will never have what we have. We are free; they never will be. They are permanent prisoners of each other. They know that if they ever change heart, if they ever decide to tell the truth, they are dead men. They are too high-profile and they have too many proofs. God, have mercy on them because I doubt if anyone else will. (Katherine aka Kathleen Sullivan, President of PARC-VRAMC, http://parc-vramc.tierranet.com)

Multiple Personality and Altered States

As Cisco Wheeler professes, underlying their motivation is not just the seduction of power but actually has to do with demonic entities or generational spirits who are in control of their bodies. As Beth Goobie writes in *The Only-Good Heart*:

> Every nerve is a gate to another dimension of energy and power. Through her, the Kin has discovered many new frequencies and dimensions. They have carefully tortured and trained each nerve with needles and shock, turning nerves into gates of fear so that the worlds they open onto may be twisted into frequency dimensions that the Kin can manage. Through careful training, each nerve learns to call in whatever frequencies, dimensions and beings the Kin requires. With the body sufficiently prepared and its nerves pressed in a specific sequence, then I, Slayer, am called from my dimension into her flesh to feed the Dark Lord's appetite.

Author Eugenia Macer-Story backs this up in her essay entitled "The Dark Frontier: Master Game Plan of Discarnate Intelligences." As Macer-Story has discovered in her vast research into discarnate intelligence, "human beings regularly experience the intrusion of powerful interdimensional 'spirit' entities with power appetites which can be puzzling." As David Icke has suggested, the way to keep this power in the same lineage is to keep the bloodline intact. He also names that secret bloodline as The Illuminati. Macer-Story's extraordinary research seems to back up the idea that discarnate intelligences do in fact tend to aim for hereditary power. She writes:

> If, in a family or small business situation, a power-oriented discarnate intelligence can enter telepathically the minds of the persons in authority, this intelligence can 'rule' the limited group of blood relatives and/or employees with a dictatorial energy ... Symptoms of takeover by negative discarnate intelligence should be watched for within political situations involving monarchy, dictatorship and/or significant hereditary financial power ... One motivation for dominating a series of perishable organic bodies might simply be the desire for continuation of this power-oriented identity in sequential time.

If the reader is unable to subscribe to the "discarnate intelligence" or demonology explanation, keep in mind that whether or not these things are "real," they are certainly part of a belief system that considers them very real. And that's enough of an explanation for the very real activities that are transpiring. Essentially, what modern mind control victims are telling us is that we need to take a fresh look at the demonology paradigm with an eye toward explaining why these things are happening, and why they are happening in large part to females. As long-term mind control researcher Walter Bowart has stated in a lecture, "the history of mind control is the history of male chauvinist secret organizations preying upon women." And these secret organizations include ancient sacrificial blood cults as well as their modern counterparts, alive and transformed via nefarious intelligence cohesion with the Nazi occult underbelly.

Another important facet of MPD which needs further attention by those interested in it is the relationship between psychology and magic, as has been discussed much throughout this volume. To open up this matter for further exploration, we need to widen our phenomenological options; i.e. what may be actually happening in MPD? What other kinds of descriptions of mind, other than the psychological interpretations we are accustomed to, might describe what is going on in the multiple personality complex? One lead is touched upon by Monarch survivor Claudia Mullen when she reports that in MPD the personalities come out "one at a time" over the course of years. As she reports, "some of them only come out one time and then that's it, they integrate. They come out to give you a memory and then they integrate because their job is done."

As strange as this interpretation might sound, we must agree that to some degree this sounds like the "auditing" of a "body thetan." Therefore, perhaps it is helpful to view alter personalities as "elementals," or as BTs or BT clusters; that is, entities rather than personalities. As we've discussed, Body Thetans are not really live thetans (souls) but merely contain the main information of the thetan and are "clustered" around it. The "elemental essence" is described by Besant and Leadbeater as "that strange half-intelligent life which surrounds us in all directions, vivifying the matter of the mental and astral planes." This "animated matter" responds readily to the influence of human thought, and "every impulse sent out, either from the mental body or from the astral body of man, immediately clothes itself in a temporary vehicle of this vitalized matter." This vitalized matter is referred to as an elemental.

As Madame Blavatsky has explained in *Devas and Men*, "the difference between an elemental and a human is that the elemental contains only a portion of *one* of the four great kingdoms: fire, air, earth and water, while the human contains in himself a portion of *each* of the four kingdoms. The elementals can be subjected to the will of the sorcerer. Blavatsky explains that the elementals have an undeveloped consciousness and bodies which can be shaped according to the conscious or unconscious will of the human being who puts himself in rapport with them.

These concepts may explain how alter personalities are created in the first place. This would comprise an animistic interpretation of MPD. It has been noted by several Monarch survivors that these personalities are instilled in a specifically occult or magical manner. Beth Goobie has explained the procedure. The "man" inserts a long needle into her leg, and Beth directs the pain to a personality named "Klarrenord." Klarrenord then goes inside, "down the long hallway that leads to that leg," where there are various doors. She explains, "I wave my hands counterclockwise around the needle tip, ... the man requires a dark door here." The man chants, "doorkeeper, make a new door," and a new door appears. Beth explains, "I surface into The Body and look out the face." A "new door" has been made. The man then explains the name and purpose of this new door."

This occult ritual seems to suggest that, as maintained by both Husserl and Merleau-Ponty, the "world is not a given place in which experience occurs, but is *that toward which one is turned* in experience." The Body isn't located any more 'here' than 'there' – nor is it any more 'somewhere' than 'nowhere.' As mentioned earlier, our sense of a 'whereness' to Being needs to be reconsidered or refined if we are to understand these notions that are peculiar to the Visitor phenomenon as well as to occult ritual.

These types of phenomenal (or noumenal) experiences suggest that the Body (to Beth, "The Body"), phenomenally speaking, is only 'located' in the 3-D world by the ongoing maintenance agreement of consensus reality. This is also suggested by Bob Dobbs' description of a "a holeopathic retrieval," which is the flip-side or correspondence of the nature body to its holographic essence or dilution. This points out a strong explanatory correlation between Monarch mind control and holographic theory. If the body-mind complex is part of a vast holographic reality, then it is capable of, utilizing Dobbsian ideas, flipping back and forth between First Nature (body) and Second Nature (holographic extension or virtual alter personality).

Interestingly, Charles Tart has described this in a similar way in an online paper entitled "Multiple Personality, Altered States and Virtual Reality: The World Simulation Process." As Tart explains, "we each live 'inside' a world simulation machine. We almost always forget that our 'perception' is a simulation, not reality itself, and we almost always forget that we have anything to do with the particulars of how the simulation works." He explains that the technology of virtual reality is an excellent way to demonstrate this World Simulation Process. Tart describes how this concept is applicable to multiple personality disorder. As he explains, a person with MPD has "two or more well developed core constellation patterns which can take over his or her World Simulation Process." *The person then lives temporarily in a "virtual reality" which constitutes an identity, personality or state of consciousness.* As Tart explains, "experientially this virtual reality is perfectly real. ... [since] our 'normal'perception of physical reality is not a perception of reality per se but more *a semi-arbitrary construction, a virtual reality,* but a particular virtual reality *widely shared* in its broad outlines by members of our particular culture." (Italics added)

As Dan Smith has written in an on-line essay entitled "On What We See (And what we are about to see)":

> That we misconstrue the construction of the world is the major impediment to its and our redemption. This misconstrual is not a mistake, it is part of the plan of salvation. It is our dispensation. ... Everything we see is felt meaning. The world is a metaphor. I am reminded of the philosopher visiting modern Athens who was surprised to see 'METAPHOR' written in Greek letters on the side of a truck. Later she learned that it was a moving van. Our world should be similarly inscribed. The world is not an object. It is a conveyor of meaning relative to our thoughts. It is the gradual bootstrapping of meaningful structure within the primordial chaos of virtual experience.

As Beth Goobie has also explained, each altered state has a specific pattern of brain wave frequencies which acts as a gateway to other-dimensional consciousness. Beth believes that these cults program their victims to split into personalities tuned to a specific pattern of color, sound and frequency which is the entry point for a specific consciousness. This consciousness may also be seen as a virtual reality extension of reality (which is partly "virtual" to begin with). Beth seems to agree. As she explains in an article entitled, "The Network of Stolen Consciousness," in *Paranoia* (Issue 24):

> The human body naturally lives within many interactive dimensions of reality, but *Western society has programmed the individual to limit consciousness to the small fragment of reality that we commonly called 'the real world.'* Many people who dissociate and have an out-of-body experience will describe a great deal of activity going on 'around'us. The term 'Around'is a common cult trigger that refers to alternate dimensions, and it is frequently used to trigger an individual into sending a programmed fragment of consciousness (an alter) out-of-body, in order to initiate interaction that exists at a frequency outside 'real world'consciousness. (Italics added)

The energy field of the body is a "blueprint" that guides and molds the physical body. As we've discussed before, the dynamic interplay between the body's energy field, mental images, and the physical body explains why concentrated visualization techniques, meditation, and prayer can heal the body. This means that via these techniques we can also harm the body. Beth Goobie seems to be the Monarch victim most aware of how MPD is effected, and has a clear understanding of the occult leanings of this procedure. As Beth explains, these personalities do not actually live *in* the body, but are sent out of the body to live in other dimensions, known in the occult world as the grid or the matrix. As Beth explains (*Paranoia*, Issue 24), these other frequency realities where alternate personalities reside are interactive and ongoing with the primary personality. Your life energy is then sucked through these alternate personalities, and "personalities from other people can access/torture/use/abuse you there, usually as a conduit for your life energy, depleting you further." This explanation should be the focal point for further understanding of the occult nature of the creation of MPD through the modern merging of ancient ritual sacrificial bloodline cults and intelligence agencies.

Do What Thou Wilt

Interestingly, the Amalricians, an ancient ritual sacrificial cult of the later Middle Ages, taught that "true believers need obey no law." They taught that, since all things are of God, there can be no evil, and that "those who followed their lustful urges were simply doing God's will." The Amalricians, as well as other heretical groups, believed that to resist their lustful urges was to resist God. In the words of a contemporary chronicler, "if anyone was 'in the Spirit' even if he were to commit fornication or to be fouled by any other filthiness, there would be no sin in him, because that Spirit, who is God, being entirely distinct from the body, cannot sin."

This doctrine is remindful of Aleister Crowley's motto "Do what thou wilt shall be the whole of the law." In the mindset of people who have taken the luciferian oath, the idea of sin or doing wrong is no longer a restriction on the 'will-to-power,'a doctrine which was taken up with zeal by the Third Reich. As Cisco Wheeler claims, "there isn't anything they will not do." This includes torturing and maiming innocent children, forcing children into prostitution, forcing children into copulation with animals, allowing animals to kill children, and many other heinous and sexually deviant acts.

As we must keep in mind, any type of sexual deviance is a way of denying the validity of current societal standards. With libertarian ethical arguments duly noted, the supremely self-centered "moral code" of the pedophile is in willful defiance of anything that could be considered the larger society's moral code. Can libertarians and anarchists rightfully profess that there is NO sacred ground? As *The Urantia Book* makes clear, it is difficult for us "immature evolutionary mortals" to distinguish between true and false notions of liberty, since we are unaware that true liberty has a cosmic relationship beyond our egoistic awareness. *The Urantia Book* (p. 613) explains:

> Liberty is a self-destroying technique of cosmic existence when its motivation is unintelligent, unconditioned and uncontrolled. True liberty is progressively related to reality and is ever regardful of social equity, cosmic fairness, universal fraternity and divine obligations. Liberty is suicidal when divorced from material justice, intellectual fairness, social forbearance, moral duty and spiritual values. ... Unbridled self-will and unregulated self-expression equal unmitigated selfishness, the acme of ungodliness. Liberty without the associated and ever-increasing conquest of self is a figment of egoistic mortal imagination. Self-motivated liberty is a conceptual illusion, a cruel deception. License masquerading in the garments of liberty is the forerunner of abject bondage.

These intergenerational cult families rest assured that society will remain in denial and disbelief when we hear these survivor stories, for, although we are quite familiar with the extent of man's inhumanity to man, it is far too distressing to acknowledge man's inhumanity to child. As Cisco Wheeler claims:

> We were controlled by very sadistic individuals and we were terribly, terribly treated. You wouldn't treat an animal the way we were treated. You wouldn't–it's important to be sensitive to that because it's very painful. The body has felt raped, the mind has felt raped, the spirit has felt raped. And we need someone to say–this really hurts–we need someone to say 'you know, I didn't walk where you have walked and so I can't totally comprehend what you are saying to me, but I am listening, and I truly believe what happened to you did happen to you.'

The Malleus Maleficarum

As Alan Scheflin explains in a CKLN Mind Control Radio Series lecture, according to the *Malleus Maleficarum*, printed in 1486, witchcraft comprised the following four essentials: (1) renunciation of the Christian faith, (2) the sacrifice of unbaptized infants to Satan, (3) the devotion of body and soul to evil, and (4) sexual relations with incubi or succubi. According to the *Malleus*, the sexual activity most often attributed to witches was sex with demons, the incubi or succubi, who were considered the manifestation of demons who assumed the form of a male (incubus) and female (succubus) for the purpose of intercourse. It is estimated that the male incubus appears about nine times as frequently in the works of demonology as does the female succubus. Witchcraft and sorcery were believed to be responsible for impotence, infertility, and a series of sex-connected activities. Eventually, sexual promiscuity of whatever nature became a way of denying the validity of current societal standards. Thus, heretical thought became intertwined with stigmatized sexual conduct.

The *Malleus Maleficarum* was used as a "bible" for witchhunters. It explained how to identify witches and especially, as Alan Scheflin points out, how to interrogate them. As Scheflin explains, the *Malleus* offers a systemized technique on performing interrogations which lead to so-called "confessions." As Scheflin explains, the *Malleus* played an important role in the history of mind control, since it was the work used by the Inquisition throughout the Middle Ages to obtain "confessions" from witches. Centuries later, Scheflin notes, the *Malleus* was used in the development of the first police manual. Scheflin finds in the 1800s a common thread tying possession theories and the birth of psychiatry with the *Malleus*, since most psychiatric treatments contained the same elements of violence that were purveyed in the *Malleus*.

As Scheflin notes, possession theory, quite popular in the Middle Ages, has come back again in the twentieth century, and MPD is essentially a theory of the possession of the body by several entities, or parts of the personality. However, Beth Goobie would tend to disagree with this summation. As she notes, MPD is mistakenly thought of as fractured personalities residing IN the body, but she tends to think of these personalities as existing out of the body—in alternate frequency realities. It is The Body that is mistaken as belonging only to the physical realm. Perhaps The Body exists in the metaphysical in a much more 'real' sense than we are accustomed to thinking. As noted, Beth believes that dissociated selves are energy states or brain frequencies sent out of the brain. She also believes that these dimensions are interactive, and via ritual techniques other people can exploit you in dissociated dimensions. Beth believes the CIA is heavily involved with these "psychic attacks" as both a method of mind control programming and as a method of feeding off human energy without direct physical contact.

Remote Influencing: Mind to Mind Causation

Both the Soviets and the U.S. intelligence apparatus were keenly interested in the "remote influence" of behavior; i.e. whether it was possible to change a person's behavior via hypnosis or psychic means from a distance. Remote influencing is also related to telepathic killing. Michael Rossman notes that the CIA had been researching "invisible means of death" since at least 1949. He charges that the evidence suggests that such experiments were perhaps even officially undertaken at any time from this date onward. During the 1950s, he reports, Army recruits on field maneuvers were tested for ESP performance while under the influence of LSD. Given the CIA's intensive and macabre research into drugs and telepathy, he writes, "there is reason to suppose that it was involved in these tests, as in others of 'strike force' character."

As Rossman also writes, as early as 1952 the State Department was using "visualization exercises" similar to those which are the basis of "such 'consciousness-expansion technologies'as Silva Mind Control to train its operatives in their intuitive psychic faculties." As we now know, similar training in consciousness-expansion was later offered privately to Army recruits at the Monroe Institute in Virginia, utilizing technologies such as HemiSync to get trainees to go astral. As also discussed in this book, the secret techniques of scientology were usurped via the intelligence community's research into remote viewing at SRI, followed by a similar U.S. Army program.

According to Adam Mandelbaum in *The Psychic Battlefield: A History of the Military-Occult Complex*, much of the paranormal research undertaken in the USSR during the 1960s focused on subliminal control of an individual's conduct from a distance. There is also cause to believe that U.S. intelligence took a serious look at remote influencing in its early paranormal repertoire. For instance, in the Spring of 1958, an interesting article appeared in a classified in-house CIA publication entitled *Studies in Intelligence*. This recently declassified article, entitled "The Operational Potential of Subliminal Perception," indicated that indeed U.S. intelligence was interested in remote influence of behavior. According to Mandelbaum, this article reported that, "…it has been demonstrated certain individuals can at certain times and under certain circumstances be influenced to act abnormally without awareness of the influence or at least without antagonism." The fact that such an article was published over forty years ago indicates that remote influencing was being seriously considered by both sides of a cold, cold, cold, cold war.

According to Mandelbaum, Siberia was known for its shamans: infamous men who had honed the powers of telepathy, clairvoyance and psychokinesis. These powers were later searched for and experimented by the Soviet Union for military and espionage purposes, and became engulfed in the budding science of psychotronics—man/machine interface. Even though the atheist/materialist Soviets weren't supposed to place credence in the "mind over matter" paradigm, it has been maintained that the Soviet Union did in fact seriously research whether powers of "thought transmission" could be utilized as weapons of war. According to Mandelbaum, the three paranormal abilities with obvious military and espionage applications were clairvoyance (similar to remote viewing), psychokinesis (movement of objects), and telepathic projection (also known as remote influencing).

Lyn Buchanan was a talented remote viewer utilized as a trainer in the Stargate program. Army remote viewer David Morehouse claims in *Psychic Warrior* that Buchanan was asked by the program managers to codify the protocols of his style of remote viewing to create what Morehouse calls a very dangerous offshoot of remote viewing referred to as "remote influencing." In addition to this disclosure, CIA-Monarch programming survivor Kathleen Sullivan has reported that she was trained as a remote viewer, and that RV training may have been a subset of "theta programming," one of five principle types of trauma-based mind control. Theta programming, she explained to a government panel on CIA mind control, involves the programming of mental energies in "telepathic killing." (CKLN) As Kathleen explains, theta programming was based on rage training. As a youngster, she was taught to build up rage inside, which would come out as a form of pure energy or "pure thought" directed toward a person. This mental attack, when taught in an occult manner, she believes, could make people "implode internally." Is the human mind being used as a microwave oven?

Here the reader should be reminded that magical precepts contain rather dangerous hidden knowledge which, one may rightly imagine, would be of interest to the military mindset. This statement will impact the reader all the more after fully digesting the following statement made by William Gray in *Magical Ritual Methods*:

> All Motion, which is to say all Matter, has its Rate or Frequency which makes it precisely what it is. Alter that, and the whole structure of the material would change accordingly. Transmutation would become an almost instant phenomenon under the control of the practitioner, and we could destroy our planet much faster than we are doing at present. It is a question of applying the correct frequency with sufficient energy to the specific item in the right manner. Fortunately, these factors very rarely coincide to the destructive degree except over Time periods which allow us an opportunity for adjustment. …

The Rate of anything is its fundamental pattern of potential between maximum and minimum energy compatible with its existence. This is to say that if more energy were applied beyond its positive limits, or more energy subtracted from its negative ones, it could no longer exist as itself, but would disintegrate one way or the other.

Sullivan has also reported that she was involved in a "charismatic" cult in the 1970s known as The Church of the Living Word. In this church, as well as in other Pentacostal and charismatic-influenced churches, they practiced hands-on-healing and directed thought energy transference between bodies. Sullivan feels that this type of energy transference is practiced by many people and it is very real. Such practices can be used for good as well as evil purposes, as can any such human powers.

Many Monarch survivors have to deal with the memories of actually having caused serious harm to others, or of having committed murder, while in an alter personality mode. As Kathleen Sullivan reports, she was taught remote viewing and she believes it was part of "theta programming," or psychic killing. She believes she was taught psychic killing techniques, and she believes that she may have actually used these techniques while in an alter personality mode. She believes she would have been capable of causing serious bodily harm from a distance, and that this was part of her training, which began at around age 6, as an assassin for the secret government. As Kathleen also explains, this was a generational ability. She had a Swedish grandmother who practiced "pain drawing." Her grandmother could put her hands on her and draw the pain energy into her own body whenever Kathleen was in pain.

As Kathleen explains, the public is being fed the propaganda that the Theta programming experiments were shut down because they didn't work. But these programs did work, she maintains, especially for those trained at a young age. This is a certain clue to why they had to find children for these nefarious programs. (As one Monarch survivor reports, as a child one of the doctors she was taken to for programming refused to take part, saying "I didn't know you were using children.")

Kathleen maintains that children in generational cults are raised to believe they can do these things with ease. Most importantly, they don't have any mental blocks that say they can't do it. As Ingo Swann also believes, the only thing in the way of all of us becoming "wired" into the hard drive of the species bio-mind are "installed mental software programs [social norms] which abort cognitive access to them." Belief is everything! As Kathleen has charged, if you have enough trust in your brain, "even as far as remote viewing ... oh man ... the things you can do with that in spycraft is outstanding. It's like being in a room with somebody and being able to pick up on their thoughts. Or know when somebody has a physical illness without them knowing it yet. It's amazing what they can do with this stuff."

CHAPTER FOURTEEN

THE SECRET OF THE FIFTH FORCE: SCIENCE AND THE SECRET SOCIETY

The difference between magician and sci-entist lies in method and materials ... The symbolic tools of magi and mathematician both operate through Inner dimensions to cause Outer effects.

William Gray

Magical Ritual Methods

Since ancient times a fundamental energy or "fifth force" has been postulated to be the intrinsic vital force in all of creation. As John White writes in his Appendix 1 to *Psychic Warfare: Fact or Fiction?*, entitled "What is Psychic Energy," ancient magicians called this force the *astral light*, the Chinese call it *Chi*, the Japanese call it *Ki*, the yogic traditions of India and Tibet call it *prana*, the Polynesians and Hawaiian Kahunas call it *mana*, the Sufis call it *baraka*, Jewish Cabalists call it *yesod*, the Iroquois call it *orenda*, the Ituri pygmies call it *mgebe*, and the Christians call it *Holy Spirit*. As Eliphas Levi writes in *Transcendental Magic:*

> There exists an agent which is natural and divine, material and spiritual, a universal plastic mediator, a common receptacle of the vibrations of motion and the images of form, a fluid and a force, which may be called in some way the Imagination of Nature.... The existence of this force is the great Arcanum of practical Magic.

In modern times, Rupert Sheldrake postulated the existence of causative organizing fields he called *morphogenetic fields*, which he believed accounted for both the evolution (changingness) and stasis (unchangingness) of life forms. Also in modern times, Wilhelm Reich identified through scientific investigations a primordial, massless and pre-atomic creative life-force he called *orgone energy*. Marcel Vogel discovered an energy he called the *information band* as an energetic communication band between all substances, between all life. In addition, investigators have noted parallels between this all-pervading medium and the Soviet idea of *bioplasma*. (Apparently, the Soviets were allowed to purchase Reich's works before they were destroyed by inferno in this country by court order!) This energy appears to be the energy recognized in paranormal abilities. White also quotes in his 1988 book *Psychic Warfare* the following comment by electrical engineer Laurence Beynam:

> There is an energy in living organisms that is weak and unpredictable, but it can be refracted, polarized, focused and combined with other energies. It sometimes has effects similar to magnetism, electricity, heat and luminous radiation, but it is none of these. Attempts to control and employ the energy have met with little success; investigators have not yet defined the laws governing its operation.

White doesn't provide an approximate date for this quote, but it is likely that as of this writing in the year 2000 the laws governing the operation of this organismic energy have been well defined, and its ability to be focused and combined with other energies has likely been well researched by the military-industrial complex. Preliminary work in this area was performed by Marcel Vogel, senior research scientist for IBM, whose work focused on "phosphor technology, liquid crystal systems, luminescence, and magnetics." Remy Chevalier writes (www.remyc.com/bigigloo.html) of Marcel Vogel's discovery of the properties of *Chi:*

I experienced Marcel's release of stored *Chi* from one of his crystals at a US Psychotronics conference back in the late 80's. ... When he asked everyone in the audience to stand up, and he aimed the crystal in our direction telling us that three day's worth of *Chi* had been stored inside and that he would release it all at once, call it a 'psychic wind' blew from his direction to the back of the room, gently freshening our faces. There was no fan on the stage, no sudden burst of the air conditioning system. Just something Marcel was able to do.

We had a long conversation over the phone a few months before he passed away. He explained electromagnetism as a kind of 'box' that enabled *Chi* to travel, as if *Chi* was a passenger on the EM train, and that *Chi* was finer than EM and that EM was just its vessel. Marcel's work has yet to be re-discovered by the "new age" community. ... Somebody is carrying on his work and surely cashing in on his crystal designs.

Indeed, we can safely surmise that this "somebody" is the secret government, a covert corporate/military/intelligence apparatus which is above the law, and is likely the same entity which has in its possession the 'co-opted' works of Wilhelm Reich, Nikola Tesla, Marcel Vogel and other modern geniuses. You can bet that nobody with planetary clout who was present in that room when Vogel let loose the *Chi* from his crystal was about to let this fifth force become potentially 'free' energy. White quotes Ivan Sanderson, founder of the Society to Investigate the Unexplained, as saying the following in a 1972 editorial about this fifth force:

The fifth force is certainly involved in various aspects of [super sensory abilities] and it would now seem to be the major force operative in the true psychic field and possibly the only one acting therein. Its manifestations are in no way affected by any of the other known forces; and, while doubtless universal in nature, it can be observed, measured and investigated only in the biological field. The presence of a living thing is necessary to bring it to light. Although we have not yet defined it or its parameters, it has now been demonstrated that it, and it alone, can explain a whole raft of ... mysteries ... clustering around clairvoyance [and] ... the so-called subconscious, hypnotism and the like.

Laurence Beynam listed the characteristics of this fifth force or energy as follows:

- It is observed in the operation of heat, light, electricity, magnetism, and chemical reactions, yet is different from all of them.

- It fills all space, penetrating and permeating everything, yet denser materials conduct it better and faster, and metal refracts it while organic material absorbs it.

- It is basically synergistic, moving toward greater wholeness. It has a basic negentropic, formative and organizing effect, even as heat increases, and is the opposite of entropy, thereby violating the Second Law of Thermodynamics.

- Changes in this energy precede physical, observable changes, therefore it is a creative force.

- In any structure that is highly organized (crystals, plants, humans), there is a series of geometric points at which the energy is highly concentrated. (This relates also to chakras and acupuncture points.)

- The energy corresponds to certain colors, which can be seen by psychics.

- The energy will flow from one object to another. According to the Huna tradition, it is 'sticky' so that an invisible stream of energy will always connect any two objects that have in any way been connected in the past (the basis for sympathetic magic). The energy is subject to exponential decay, radiating outward in the course of time... The density of this energy varies in inverse proportion to distance, which sets it apart from electromagnetic and gravitational laws.

* The energy is observable in various ways: as isolated pulsating points, as spirals, as an aura surrounding the body, as a flame, as a tenuous web of lines.

The Experiments of Marcel Vogel

In 1943, Marcel Vogel co-wrote with Dr. Peter Pringsheim a book entitled *The Luminescence of Liquids and Solids and their Practical Application*, and just after this founded a company called Vogel Luminescence Corporation. Vogel sold this company and joined IBM in 1957, becoming one of the most prolific patent inventors in IBM history. Incidentally, Marcel Vogel did not hold a university degree, but was largely self-taught. Vogel also did pioneering work in man-plant communication experiments, leading to the study of quartz crystals and the creation of the "Vogel-cut™ crystal," which stores, amplifies, converts and coheres subtle energies. By spinning water around a tuned crystal, Vogel created a novel information storage system. (see "Legacy of Marcel Vogel," www.vogelcrystals.com/)

When Vogel retired from IBM after 27 years, IBM and Stanford Research Institute donated equipment to his new company, Psychic Research, Inc., which aimed to show the ultimate compatibility of science and metaphysics. Vogel went on to study subtle energies and forces which emanated from the human body, and attempted to identify and quantify these energies. He was also interested in the therapeutic application of crystals and crystal devices, using stored energies to heal the human body. Vogel invented a radionics machine called the Omega-5, which utilized the psychic power of the human mind and detected fields undetectable by standard scientific devices. The Omega-5 was a subjective type of device which assisted in scientific findings by providing clues regarding how to proceed, or where to look, to obtain standard scientific measurement. The Omega-5 worked by use of a pendulum, similar to the telepathic dowsing process. Vogel referred to the unknown fields measured by the Omega-5 as the "information band."

Vogel held many patents having to do with magnetic recording media, liquid crystals, and the creation and development of rare earth phosphors. Vogel also was granted many patents in the field of Opto-Electronics, specifically for photo-relays for analog to digital conversion. Vogel's work with liquid crystals led to modern digital displays on everything from watches to radios. He also held patents for the degassification of liquids, Dark Field Microscopy, and organic/inorganic photoconduction.

Following a 1969 article in *Argosy* magazine entitled "Do Plants Have Emotions?," which explored the research of polygraph expert Cleve Backster, Vogel decided to explore the concept of human-plant communication. Interestingly, Cleve Backster was present at the Proceedings of the First International Psychotronic Congress in Prague in 1973. His paper, entitled "Evidence of a Primary Perception at Cellular Level in Plant and Animal Life," is included in Volume 1 of these proceedings, which is not in my possession. However, it's interesting to note that Backster's work came to the attention of another person we've been introduced to in this volume: one L. Ron Hubbard. As it turns out, Backster is also famous for the development of the lie detector, which was picked up for official use by Hubbard as the "E-meter." Hubbard also performed published plant communication experiments on tomato plants using the E-meter. As of May of 2000, Backster's invention is advertized in the scientology magazine *Advance!* as the "Mark Super VII Quantum™ E-Meter" at a regular edition price of $4,650.00, and a commemorative edition price of

$5,530.00. You can purchase a "quantum upgrade service" to your old E-Meter at a cost of $1,000. It is not known what type of service constitutes this equipment quantumizing.

In separate experiments, Marcel Vogel was able to duplicate the "Backster effect." He used plants as transducers for bio-energetic fields released by the human mind, thus demonstrating that plants respond to thought. By connecting the plant to a "Wheatstone Bridge," Vogel was able to compare a known resistance to an unknown resistance. When he held a thought in mind while pulsing his breath through his nostrils, the philodendrons responded dramatically. Vogel's experiments suggested that these human bio-energetic fields were linked to the action of both breath and thought. His findings were that these fields were beyond the space and time domain, in that they had the same effect on the plant whether the person emitting them was inches away or miles away. This suggested that "the inverse square law does not apply to thought."

Marcel Vogel was also present at the Proceedings of the First International Congress on Psychotronic Research held in Prague in 1973. In his essay entitled "Man-Plant Communication Experiments," Vogel presented his findings with respect to the distant influence of thought on ordinary house plants. The class of split-leaf philodendrons were found to be the most suitable plant for these experimental procedures. Vogel's basic summary and conclusions after four years of work are most interesting. As he concluded, once the experimenter is able to establish a psychic link with the plant, he is able to get a response from the plant with regard to: "(a) the act of damaging the leaf of another plant; (b) the destruction of another life form, cellular or animal, (c) the release of a thought form of love, healing, mathematics, imagery, emotion." Vogel explained that each of these thought forms have distinct patterns to them. Vogel also stated that the distant projection of thought forms had been accomplished with a distance of up to 110 miles between plant and person. He also acknowledged that repeatability of experiments had been possible, and "thought forms of individuals can be repeated," although multiple repeatability was still very difficult.

Vogel discovered that plants respond more to the *thought* of being cut, burned, or torn than to the actual act. The plants seemed to be mirroring his own mental responses. He concluded that the plants were acting like batteries, storing the energy of his thoughts and intentions. Vogel discovered that when thought is pulsed, the energy connected with it becomes coherent. To Vogel, the only pure force and the greatest cohering agent is "love." Coherent thought, Vogel asserted, can have a "laser-like power." He likened love to gravity, stating that it was an attracting and coherent force present at every level of existence. This is perhaps one reason why certain scientific investigations in the area of subtle energies cannot be readily replicated, i.e. because "intent" is everything. (see also, *The Secret Life of Plants*, Tompkins and Bird.)

The Vogel™ Cut Crystal

In his experiments on crystals, Marcel Vogel was able to alter the final form of a liquid crystal while focusing on its growth. In one experiment, Vogel, a devout Catholic, focused for one full hour on an image of the Blessed Virgin while viewing the growth of the crystal under the microscope. The result was a shape recognizable as the Madonna. Vogel videotaped this anomaly and noted that, "before the melt went into the liquid crystal state, a blue flash of light took place and then immediately after that, the sample transcended into the liquid crystal state." After a year of watching this anomaly, Vogel finally captured a picture at the moment of transition. This anomaly had been discussed in metaphysical literature, but had never before been witnessed and photographed. The flash of blue light witnessed through the microscope was the transfer of information from the level of light-coding to the physical plane. As Vogel wrote:

What appeared on the film was the prefiguring in space of the crystallographic form the system was to assume. The blue flash contained information which formed into a geometric form. This geometric form was the source of the crystallographic form from which the crystal grew and developed.

According to Vogel, once the crystal has ceased growing, the "intelligence matrix" of the crystal disappears. The form of the quartz is then basically an empty shell until it is enlivened with human bio-energy. This is accomplished by the transfer of thought-energy via the pulsed breath. Vogel then began 17 years of research into quartz crystals, discovering that the quartz had the capacity to store, amplify and transfer information. But, because the raw quartz crystals Vogel was studying could not adequately cohere these energies, Vogel began to experiment with cutting the crystals into various shapes. Just as light through a faceted ruby can produce coherent energy, Vogel wondered if thought interfaced with a specifically faceted quartz could produce a coherent energy.

One morning in 1974, Vogel awoke with a pattern similar to the Kabbalistic Tree of Life in his mind. Over the course of the following year, he was able to grind his quartz into a three dimensional representation of the Tree of Life. The resulting 4-sided quartz crystal with pyramidal terminations came to be known as Vogel-cut™ crystals. From these experiments came the first instrument for storing, amplifying, transferring and cohering the energies of the body-mind of an individual. It is reputed that some of the best crystal and diamond cutters in Germany have attempted to reproduce the Vogel-cut™ crystals without success. Vogel explained that the crystal must be faceted "not only with geometrical precision along the "C" or growth axis, but must also be worked with right attitude, understanding, and consciousness." He maintained that it is *not* simply a matter of cutting the quartz in the correct shape, but it must be "tuned as a coherent information transfer device." The geometry of the Vogel-cut™ crystal creates a coherent field of energy that can act as a carrier wave of information. (see "Legacy of Marcel Vogel," www.vogelcrystals.com/)

The ability of crystals to store information is now widely known. According to the September 4, 1994, issue of *Newsweek*, Stanford University physicists have demonstrated the first fully digital model of a device that stores information as a hologram within the subatomic structure of a crystal. The scientists were able to store and retrieve a holographic image of the Mona Lisa. The particular crystal held only 163 kilobytes of memory, but it is expected that these holographic units could store up to one million megabytes. This article explains that crystals store information in three dimensions and could be ten times faster than the fastest systems currently available.

Vogel claimed his crystals could be used for healing the human body and mind, by "removing unwanted vibrations or thoughtforms from an individual in distress." He discovered that the crystal acted as an "energetic scalpel" in an "etheric surgery," and he developed methods of healing using the Vogel-cut™ crystals. Vogel also came to believe that the various subtle energy bodies described in metaphysical literature are "gradations of a field that is anchored to the physical body via the water molecule." He discovered that, since the human body is 75% water, the profound healing effects of the crystal were related to its resonance to water. A web site devoted to Marcel Vogel (www.vogelcrystals.com/), explains how these crystals work:

> The crystal is a quantum converter that is able to transmit energy in a form that has discreet biological effects. This is most likely a resonant effect. The human body, on an energetic level, is an array of oscillating points that are layered and have a definite symmetry and structure. This crystallinity is apparent on both a subtle energetic or quantum level as well as the macro level. The bones, tissues, cells, and fluids of the body have a definite crystallinity about them. The structure of the fluids, cells, and tissues of the body tends to become unstructured

or incoherent when dis-ease or distress is present. The physical body is comprised of liquid crystal systems in the cell membranes, inter-cellular fluids, as well as larger structures such as the fatty tissues, muscular and nervous systems, lymph, blood, and so on. Through the use of an appropriately tuned crystal to which these structures are responsive, balance and coherence can be restored by delivering the necessary "information" or energetic nutrients needed.

The Information Band

Vogel discovered that the information band measured by the Omega 5 exists in and around all matter. He postulated that the information band is a sort of "record keeper" of events which brought an object into being, as well as the responses of this object to these actions, energies, fields or forces. He suggested that these forces and actions combined to build a series of identifying patterns or codes. Since all motion generates a field, the composite of these fields is the ground state of the information band. It is different from the excited state of the electron which goes into the conduction band and drops down into the ground state. These perturbations form an energy cloud around the substance. This is the mind of the atom. Vogel found that there is a rhythmic nature to this field, and a corresponding periodicity to the information band. He discovered that the information band would even expand and contract in accordance with its relationship to planetary influences. Vogel took a clue from occult writer Alice Bailey, writing in *The Consciousness of the Atom*:

> We have seen that the atom of chemistry, for instance, demonstrates the quality of intelligence; it shows symptoms of discriminative mind and the rudiments of selective capacity. Thus the tiny life within the atomic form is demonstrating a psychic quality – take the atom that goes to the building of form in the mineral kingdom; it shows not only discriminative selective mind, but elasticity. ... Let us endeavor to realize that there is no such thing as inorganic matter, but that every atom is a life. Let us realize that all forms are living forms, and that each is but the vehicle of expression for some indwelling entity.

Vogel's contention was that there is communication through the information band. As long as there is integrity in the system, the object holds itself together and one can obtain the rate for the information band that is releasing the fields into the space of the form geometry of the object.

Keeping Occult Secrets

Keeping occult secrets is an unspoken mandate of the national security state. With respect to scientific knowledge of an arcane nature, this information becomes a source of power when it is kept within the control of an elite social clique. The story of Marcel Vogel illustrates that magic and science are two sides of the same coin. Notice that IBM kept their hooks in Marcel Vogel after he left their employ, and Stanford Research Institute donated equipment to Vogel's research lab. What kind of information did this computer industry giant and intelligence think tank receive in return? We can only imagine.

Both military and intelligence people, as Adam Mandelbaum points out, are highly trained specialists, well-drilled in security matters, who work always under threat of extreme penalty for breaches of security. This is also how members of secret societies work. Loyalty to the organization's secrets is a very serious undertaking. As Mandelbaum concludes, "it is not surprising that occult secret societies have often played a role in the military and political arenas of the world, achieving status as permanent residents in the realm of the military-occult complex." As Mandelbaum notes:

> A secret cabal with indigenous contacts, untraceable funding, and a built-in chain of command is just what the revolutionary or the espionage organization ordered. The history of revolution and intelligence provides us with examples of how secret societies have participated

in geopolitical struggles, and how occult symbolism and ritual have been found alongside the bayonets and bombs that have changed governments and established—or overthrown—tyranny.

According to Mandelbaum, psychics are the spies of the future. As he reminds us, "what started out as magic has again ended up as magic. ... Today's magic wand might control microwave radiation instead of demonic hordes, but the goal is still the same. Control, command, conquest." An important book written in France in 1960 discussed the implications of this control of scientific knowledge by the secret society of the State.

As Pauwels and Bergier wrote in a rare 1960 book called *The Dawn of Magic*, those who are really interested in the future should also be interested in the past, and should be ready to look in both directions for solutions to social, scientific and philosophical problems. Since we never take the trouble to consult ancient and historical scientific documents, we labor under the false presumption that our scientific inventions are new and our scientific world view is the culmination of a special historical status. As the authors explain, unknown treasures of the past lie slumbering in libraries of Alexandria, Athens, Jerusalem, and Egypt, and many other ancient libraries were torched for political and religious reasons. Much of our ancient history is physically lost, and much of what remains is lost to the tendency of moderns to think of the progress of knowledge as being "discontinuous with hundreds of thousands of years of ignorance." This assumption serves a purpose. It serves to obscure arcane knowledge in order to keep it in the hands of the few.

The idea that there suddenly came about an "era of enlightenment" serves to obscure all previous periods of history. Yet, Pauwels and Bergier lament, these periods of time actually contained "truths far too profound to be attributed merely to the intuition of the ancients." For instance, modern methods of rational inquiry were not, they wrote, invented by Descartes, but by Aristotle, and before that, Democritus actually had his roots in an earlier Phoenician tradition of rational scientific inquiry.

But, if scientific knowledge has a tendency to repeat itself, what does this say about the conduit which is the origin of knowledge? How different is science from magic? As William Gray has written in *Magical Ritual Methods*, modern science utilizes ritual procedures and symbolic tools in its exploration of the world. Gray notes the following:

> Magic seeks to translate energies from one state of existence to another in accordance with an intention of the operative intelligence. So does science. The difference between magician and scientist lies in method and materials, which sometimes are not so dissimilar as might appear. A circle-dance and a cyclotron have much in common. The symbolic tools of magi and mathematician both operate through Inner dimensions to cause Outer effects.

> Modern science has evolved far more ritual procedures in its techniques than ancient magicians even dreamed of, and they all come from the same source—Man's curiosity concerning the Cosmos and what he has to do with it; human attempts at growing into Godhood.

> Ritual is a major tool of magic and science alike for patterning the consciousness of its operatives so that calculable results may be obtained. Unhappily it is a sadly neglected tool, ill cared for and misunderstood. The scientist is showing more respect for it than the magician, so he is getting better results with it today. ...

As Pauwels and Bergier suggest, the scientist, like the magician, cultivates secrecy and obeys the laws of similarity. At first, scientific inventions are imitations of nature. Like the magician, the inventor derives from natural phenomena the essence or resemblance and creates an artifact or copy of it. This sense of power as well as pleasure acts as the incentive to create. The scientific process is the very essence of the magical. We can see this in the work of Marcel Vogel. Pauwels and Bergier point out another striking connection between magic and technology. As they note in *The Dawn of Magic*:

> Science erects barriers of impossibilities. The engineer, like the magician, passes through these barriers by means of what physicists call the tunnel effect. He is drawn by a magic attention. He wants to see behind the wall, to go to Mars, capture thunder, manufacture gold. His aim is to catch out the universe and explain its mysteries. In the Jungian sense, he is an archetype.

Israel Regardie of the Golden Dawn argued with strong conviction that the magical secrets of the Golden Dawn should not be kept secret. Regardie argued that the necessity for secrecy had been instituted in darker periods of history due to fear of persecution from church and state, but that there was no reason in the modern world for such secrecy. He argued that a much more potent weapon had arisen and taken its place. He named that weapon: "ridicule arising from spiritual darkness." As Regardie writes in *What You Should Know About The Golden Dawn*, "for purposes of prestige and love of power a secret is a most invaluable weapon." Of the power and prestige of religious and secret knowledge, Regardie writes:

> An Order is simply a temporary vehicle of transmission—a means whereby suitable individuals may be trained to awaken within their hearts the consciousness of the boundless Light. But sooner or later, it would appear that the initiates foster loyalty to the external husk, the shell, the organisation of grades at the expense of that dynamic spirit for which the shell was constructed. So often has it happened in the past. Every religion stands as eloquent witness to this fact. It is the fate which has overtaken the Golden Dawn. ...

> Its Chiefs have developed the tyranny of sacerdotalism. They have a perverse inclination towards priestcraft, and secrecy has ever been the forcing ground in which such corruption may prosper. ... If by any chance the hidden knowledge were removed from their custody, their power would be gone. For in most cases their dominion does not consist in the gravitational attraction of spiritual attainment or even ordinary erudition. Their power is vested solely in one fact, that they happen to be in possession of the private documents for distribution to those to whom they personally wish to bestow a favour as a mark of their esteem.

Regardie warned that this ancient knowledge would be lost if it were not soon transferred into a more permanent form than in the private manuscripts in whose hands it lay. For the above reasons, Regardie worked during his lifetime to transcribe the Golden Dawn rituals. As an old Zuni saying goes, "power told is power lost."

Pauwels and Bergier note that what we call "esotericism" is a remnant of a very ancient branch of technical knowledge relating to both mind and matter, containing the keys to open up the forces contained in man and in things. Such esoteric secrets should not be seen as fables or legends, but "precise technical systems" that will open the door to scientific knowledge about mind and matter. In this regard, science and magic are but two aspects of the same system.

However, even though both scientists and magicians can be said to be doing much the same thing at a certain level, politically they are seen as opposite and warring factions. As Bob Dobbs has suggested, the scientific paradigms of Bacon, Descartes and Newton dislodged the paradigms of Natural Magic and Hermeticism. In turn, he writes, Blavatsky, Einstein, Gurdjieff and Crowley were able to derail the Newtonian locomotive. So, we see that indeed the historical tide does seem to move in cycles between the "circle-dance" and the "cyclotron."

Pauwels and Bergier suggest that in the distant past these 'precise technical systems' (which we now consider 'magic' due to their secrecy) may have preceded scientific knowledge and, further, that these techniques may have even endowed mankind with "powers too terrible to be divulged." Hence the underlying reason for the secrecy of secret knowledge, the obscurity of esoteric incantation and the divinity of divine revelation. The techniques and skills of this kind require "a command of language on a different plane," at a non-ordinary human level. They suggest: "secrecy results from the nature of the thing kept secret, and is not necessarily imposed by those who know."

A comparison to modern science shows that the state of affairs is much the same. The rapid growth of technology makes the same secrecy a necessity. As knowledge advances, the more it is surrounded by secrecy at every level, and the technical language with which this knowledge is conveyed becomes more and more obscure to the lay person. As a result of this secret scientific knowledge, the upper echelons of the cryptocracy have the power to make far-reaching decisions over the heads of a powerless populace. As Pauwels and Bergier wrote *in The Dawn of Magic*, we are returning to "the age of the Adepts," and to the era of secret societies. We are on the verge of fully apprehending that "magic" is misapprehended science. Yet, the agencies in charge of our so-called national security have known this for a long time. Is this an orchestrated time lag?

Secret societies have always closely guarded their scientific knowledge, their artisan and industrial traditions and their magical techniques, and carefully created closed societies and guilds for the propagation of these secrets. The Initiates of secret orders were organized to keep their knowledge and techniques underground. In 1960, Pauwels and Bergier imagined that the state would become a secret society in the near future. As is exhibited by the keen interest of the intelligence community in what we might call the "mind sciences," it would appear that this is exactly what is happening. I would add that the state has never been anything but a secret society, and therein lies the root of its ordained power.

Current scientific advances are merely an extension of the safekeeping and continual propagation of secret knowledge in the hands of the few. The safe haven of this hidden knowledge lies in a caste system, which possesses much more planetary clout than governments and political police. It is a secret society above the law of any land. Some have even called it the Illuminati. In addition, this powerful elite clique has its own police force: the various intelligence tentacles of the US government, such as the CIA, NSA, the Department of Defense, and various military intelligence forces. Such secrets are kept secret under the auspices of "national security." In this sense, Pauwels and Bergier suggest, civilization is a "conspiracy," and "modern life is the silent compact of comfortable folk to keep up pretenses."

Pauwels and Bergier predicted that the secret society will be the future form of government, taking the form of a "cryptocracy." They described in their remarkable 1960 book the following future situation:

> Should war break out, we should no doubt see the regular governments replaced by 'shadow' governments installed, perhaps for the USA in some caves in Virginia, and for the USSR on a floating station in the Arctic. And from that moment it would be treason to disclose the identity of the countries' rulers. Equipped with electronic brains to reduce administrative staff, secret societies would organize the gigantic conflict between the two great blocs of humanity. It is even conceivable that these governments might be situated outside our world, in artificial satellites revolving round the Earth.

The authors did not profess to be proclaiming some "semi-crazy, semi-magical interpretation of facts." They simply believed that, at a certain level, intelligence itself is a kind of secret society, and that its powers are unlimited when it is allowed to develop without boundaries. Thus, it is important to reconsider our conception of a secret society. The authors admitted that this view may seem mad but admonished: "this is because we are saying rapidly and brutally what we have to say, like a man knocking on a sleeper's door when time is running short."

The Kept Secrets of Shamanism

If the time was running short in 1960, the time is now at hand. In particular, the government of the United States, although it has its overt democratic side, has been proven time and again to have a very real but covert 'shadow' side, which, if we accept Pauwels'and Bergier's definition, does truly resemble a secret society. As they so aptly noted, the protection and propagation of scientific knowledge is not much different from the pains taken by secret societies and mainstream religions to co-opt and control arcane knowledge they do not want in the hands and minds of the general populace.

The pre-history of the usurpation and control of ancient shamanistic knowledge is told by Dan Russell in *Shamanism and the Drug Propaganda*. According to Russell, Paleolithic age shamans knew all of the medicinal plants and the means of employing them for various cures. Paleolithic shamans also had a thorough knowledge of midwifery, blood transfusion, organ replacement, anesthesia, vaccination, hypodermic injection and acupuncture. These ancient shamans were also attributed with the gift of being able to see auras. Paleolithic Chinese shamans drew accurate maps of the body points used to this day in acupuncture. As Russell notes, "the intellectual, social and technological contribution of Paleolithic shamanism is immeasurable."

Bronze Age mythology attributes the knowledge of astronomy, mythology, writing and metallurgy to the ancient shamans. Shamans are known to have "encyclopedic genius" with regard to plant medicine and other subjects. Iron Age shamans recited or sang epic stories from memory, and repeated hours and hours of continuous verse. The subject matter in these epic poems would not have survived if they had not been set to memory by generations of singing shamans.

According to Russell, virtually all of the Neolithic drinking vessels that have been discovered display "entheogenic symbolism," and virtually all Neolithic and Bronze Age temples and shrines contain cups, bowls, vases, funnels and ladles which are considered communal drinking vessels. These vases and goblets contain the symbolism of the entheogens, or psychedelic substances, which they contained: psychoactive drugs like mushrooms, barley and opium poppies, and the psychoactive bulbs of lilies, hyacinths and saffron. These images are continuous up until 6500-3500 B.C. Opium was a major crop of Neolithic Europeans and cannabis was grown in Neolithic China. Psychoactive mushrooms were widely used in Neolithic Europe. As Russell writes in *Shamanism and the Drug Propaganda* (p. 148):

> The psychology of archetypal pharmaco-shamanism is basic to Christian theology. It is basic to an understanding of Jesus as *pharmakon*, Eucharist, and basic to an understanding of the demonization of Dionysos, Jesus' Greek alter ego, his Pentheus, as Judas became his Hebrew Pentheus. Jesus' displacement of Dionysos meant, quite literally in the hands of Roman slavers, that Dionysos' sacraments were now illegal....
>
> As power shifted from Greece to Rome, the Greek *mysterion* was replaced by its Roman synonym, *sacramentum*, and the meaning changed from participatory mystery to legal [and military] oath. Thus was the *thyrsos* turned into a billyclub, the fennel stalk into a crooked shepherd's crook, and the sacraments into confused symbols not for consumption.... As totemic groups became more artificial and culture industrialized, mass hypnosis based on the archetypal imagery [emp-

tied of all vital content] replaced participatory shamanism. That is, the rites of imperial municipalities are no longer entheogenic, proprioceptive, transformative, creative; they are symbolized, politicized, standardized, apologetic.

Thus were the dancing snakes of Grandmother Earth turned into Nero's golden idol, barley and poppy into minted metal, a prohibitive substance. Captured rebels were slain in Nero's arena with all the trappings of a *pharmakos* sacrifice of a Greek *polis*, but much more regularly.

As Russell explains, the ancient Greek traditions of imbibing *kannabis*, sacred mushrooms, coca leaf, peyote, and other ancient herbal sacraments are "the most easily accessible doorways to the oracular." As he notes, the last thing the Roman state wanted was to allow their Greek slaves the genuine inspiration discoverable by imbibing the holy mushroom. So, for them, the contents of the holy entheogenic vessels became off bounds. Greek culture was then absorbed and transformed by the Romans into Orthodox Christianity, as Russell calls it: "the mandatory religion of the late Roman slave states, of all medieval European slave states, and the theological underpinning of the Euro-American industrial theocracy." As Russell points out, "we have all become Greek slaves."

In the attempt to keep shamanic power out of the hands of the general populace, the Drug War actually begun by the Romans has continued unabated, and has been quite successful. This Drug War includes the usurpation of ancient knowledge pertaining to the powers that human beings actually have, based upon a dual existence on both material and immaterial levels: the same information which is now being discovered by our newest physical sciences. Yet we have been so successfully duped that we continue to ignore or misconstrue this information. As William Gray writes in *Magical Ritual Methods*:

> The bulk of humanity is quite incapable of effective magical action except as a mass movement. Few minds or souls can extend sufficiently from their average level of existence to exert much influence at other points. Magic is not for the many except concertedly. This is not because most people have not enough power, they have infinitely more than they will ever suspect, and waste more energy in life than is needed to complete a whole evolution.

Most people have been quite successfully duped by the materialist scientific religion of the State, and Christianity has all along been the ally in the propaganda machine. According to Christians, it is heathen to assert that mankind has any power which might be considered for "gods" only. On the contrary, fundamentalist Christians view humans as pathetic creatures born into "original sin." Yet, there is a huge body of ancient knowledge written prior to the New Testament which indicates that the real human potential is something else entirely.

Western science is finally catching up with ancient wisdom. How does it feel to be bitten on the ass? As Pauwels and Bergier note, both the magician and the scientist are archetypes. And as William Gray has noted, "the symbolic tools of magi and mathematician both operate through Inner dimensions to cause Outer effects." But scientists are slow to resolve the disparities becoming evident in Western materialist science. As Thomas Kuhn has noted, normal science seems to be "an attempt to force nature into the preformed and relatively inflexible box that the paradigm supplies." However, a prevailing paradigm can't be overthrown unless there is something there to take its place. What might happen? Societal chaos, disruption of business as usual, big trouble on a small planet? You bet!

As Ouspensky has noted, "the physicist may feel the real worthlessness of both old and new scientific theories, but he is afraid to be left hanging in midair with nothing but a negation." And so, "they shut their eyes to the long series of new facts which threaten to engulf everything in an irresistible flood."

Eventually, however, the dam must break. And when it does, in Dan Smith's words, the "existing conflict between modernity and mystery will be resolved." This paradigm-shattering event will be the event we have all been subconsciously awaiting: the Eschaton. And it will be caused solely by the culture clash of "modernity and mystery" and the final exposure of the true nature of reality: that the world is not an object, but is a 'holomovement' created by its participants.

This book has attempted to illustrate that arcane or Gnostic doctrines actually parallel quantum/post-quantum paradigms in the assertion that reality is shared consensus between individuals. If you put your mind to it, you will no doubt begin to make other observations about reality which will parallel observations which the human mind has deciphered at the akashic level, or drunk at the collective well of Mind-At-Large. This is the great Glass Bead Game of human existence. It is important not to think of magical systems or occult doctrines as necessarily demonic or evil, but something to be treated with reverence and used with responsibility. It's important to embark on your own journey to explore these ideas, and to judge for yourself without fear of 'supernatural' repercussions, as long as you are careful to protect your space with whatever tools you feel are proper.

Incidentally, some Christians consider this a Satanic paradigm conspiracy, asserting that Gnostic traditions are of Satanic origin. What they are doing, in my humble opinion, is turning the human potential for manifesting God's dreams on the material level into a sinful preoccupation. God doesn't mind this game. She/He/It thinks it's lots of fun, and is the reason why creation permeates the manifest level. Christians can't imagine God having fun; they are too busy seeing God as an anthropomorphic tyrant whose words must be followed to the minutest detail. The problem is those 'words' have become jumbled over time, or were purposefully jumbled by patriarchal Church fathers. Why put your faith in such human-tainted dogma as the "King James Bible"? Why not go back to a much more ancient book, the *Bhagavad-gita*, which tells us that any "designated sectarian faith is not eternal," and that eternal service to the Lord Krsna, who is not of human form, is the only unchangeable faith.

RESOURCES AND RECOMMENDED READING

Abram, David, *The Spell of the Sensuous: Perception and Language in a More-Than-Human World*, New York: Vintage, 1997.

Acharya S., *The Christ Conspiracy: The Greatest Story Ever Sold*, (www.truthbeknown.com) Adventures Unlimited, 1999 (815-253-6390).

Alexander, John B., Col., "The New Mental Battlefield: 'Beam Me Up, Spock,'" in *Psychic Warfare: Fact or Fiction?*, (John White, Ed.) 1988.

Anderson, Walter, *The Upstart Spring: Esalen and the American Awakening*, 1983.

Atack, Jon, *A Piece of Blue Sky: Scientology, Dianetics and L. Ron Hubbard Exposed*, NJ: Carol Group, 1990 (out of print but available on line at http://www.cs.cmu.edu/~dst/Library/Shelf/atack/index.html).

Barrow, John D. and Frank J. Tipler, *The Anthropic Cosmological Principle*, UK: Oxford Press, 1988.

Becker, Robert, *The Body Electric: Electromagnetism and the Foundation of Life*, William Morrow, 1987.

Besant, Annie, and C.W. Leadbeater, *Thought-Forms*, IL: Theosophical Publishing House, Wheaton, IL, reprint 1999, Besant, Annie, *Thought-Power: A Brief Occult Survey of the Vast Power Contained in Man's Mental Principle*, IL: Theosophical Publishing House, reprint 1999 (www.insight-books.com).

Blavatsky, Helena, *Isis Unveiled, Secrets of the Ancient Wisdom Tradition*, IL: Theosophical Publishing House, 1997, see also writings in *Devas and Men: A Compilation of Theosophical Studies on the Angelic Kingdom*, Theosophical Publishing House, 1977 (www.insight-books.com).

Bohm, David, *Wholeness and the Implicate Order*, London: Routledge, reissue 1996.

Boylan, Richard, *Labored Journey to the Stars*, (self-published, 2826 "O" Street, Suite 2, Sacramento, CA 95816 or e-mail: drboylan@jps.net.

Brown, Courtney, *Cosmic Voyage: Scientific Discovery of ETs Visiting Earth*, Dutton, 1996.

Budden, Albert, *UFOs, Psychic Close Encounters: The Electromagnetic Indictment*, UK, 1995.

Bullough, Vern, *Sexual Practices & the Medieval Church*, Prometheus Books, Amherst, NY.

Capra, Fritjof, *The Web of Life: A New Scientific Understanding of Living Systems*, NY: Anchor /Doubleday, 1996.

Carter, John, *Sex and Rockets: The Occult World of Jack Parsons*, Feral House, Venice Beach, 1999.

CKLN 88.1 FM Mind Control Radio Series Transcripts, Toronto, Ontario, phone: (416) 595-1477.

Collins, Anne, *In the Sleep Room: The Story of CIA Brainwashing Experiments in Canada*, Key Porter Books, 1998.

Combs, Allan, and Mark Holland, *Synchronicity: Science, Myth and the Trickster*, NY: Marlowe, 1995.

Constable, Trevor James, *Cosmic Pulse of Life: The Revolutionary Biological Power Behind UFOs*, Borderland Sciences, reissue, 1990.

Constantine, Alex, The Constantine Report, (www.redshift.com/~damason/lhreport/articles/const1.html), *Virtual Government: CIA Mind Control Operations in America*, Feral House, 1997, and *Psychic Dictatorship in the U.S.*, Feral House, 1995, (also see articles at www.io.com/~hambone/arch/dames.html)

Cremo, Michael, "City of Nine Gates," http://www.biomindsuperpowers.com/Pages/CityOf9Gates.html, (Bhaktivedanta Institute, 9701 Venice Blvd., Suite 5, Los Angeles, CA 90034 michael.cremo@iskcon.com).

d'Arc, Joan, *Space Travelers and the Genesis of the Human Form*, The Book Tree, CA, 1999, also see, *Paranoid Women Collect Their Thoughts*, Paranoia Publishing, P.O. Box 1041, Providence, RI 02901, $15 ppd.

Devereux, Paul, *Earth Lights Revelation: UFOs and Mystery Lightform Phenomena*.

DeSantillana, Giorgio, *Hamlet's Mill, An Essay Investigating the Origins of Human Knowledge and Its Transmission Through Myth*, Godine, NH, 1977.

Dobbs, Bob, *Phatic Communion*, Bob's homepage is www.posi-tone.com/BOB.html, see also, "Cloning ESP" at www.xenochrony.com. Also see Guffey, Robert.

Doskocil, Engr Ivan, "Coincidental States in Psychotronics," in *First International Congress on Psychotronic Research*, #JPRS L/5022-2, Prague, 1973.

Emmons, Charles, *At the Threshold: UFO's, Science and the New Age*, Wild Flower, NC, 1997.

The Excluded Middle, Greg Bishop, Ed., P.O. Box 481077, Los Angeles, CA90048.

First International Congress on Psychotronic Research, #JPRS L/5022-2, Volume 2, conference proceedings held in Prague in 1973; (available for $58.50 from NTIS at (703) 605-6000). (Previously a government only classified document, Volume 1 of this document (#JPRS L/5022-1) is missing from both the Library of Congress and the NTIS archives, as well as from various Washington DC area university libraries. If anyone has a copy of this, please let me know.)

Fort, Charles, *The Damned Universe of Charles Fort*, Autonomedia, New York, 1993.

Glenn, John (Senator), "Human Research Subject Protection Act," Bill S.193, 105th Congress, 1997, see intro at www.cs.virginia.edu/~alb/glennIntro.html, or entire Bill at http://thomas.loc.gov.

Global Network Against Weapons & Nuclear Power In Space Newsletter, P.O. Box 90083, Gainesville, FL 32607, (352-337-9274), www.globenet.free-online.co.uk.

Goobie, Beth, *The Only-Good Heart*, Pedlar Press, (P.O. Box 26, Station P, Toronto Ontario, M5S 2S6) 1998. (see also, "The Network of Stolen Consciousness," *Paranoia*, Part 1: Issue 24, Part 2: Issue 25), also www.paranoiamagazine.com.

Goswami, Amit, *The Self-Aware Universe: How Consciousness Creates the Material World*, Tarcher, New York, 1995.

Gray, Martin, *Places of Peace and Power*, www.epcnet.com/powerplaces.

Greer, Steven, *Extraterrestrial Contact: The Evidence and Implications*, Crossing Point Pubs., 1999 (see also materials at www.cseti.org).

Grossman, Karl, *The Wrong Stuff: The Space Program's Nuclear Threat to Our Planet*, 1997, Common Courage Press, P.O. Box 702, Monroe, ME 04951.

Guffey, Robert, "Syncronistic Linquistics in The Matrix or How Bob Dobbs Became the Tetrad Manager" in *Paranoia: The Conspiracy Reader*, (Issue 22, P.O. Box 1041, Providence, RI 02901, $7.) (see also at www.paranoiamagazine.com)

Heindel, Max, *The Rosicrucian Cosmo-Conception: Mystic Christ*, Rosicrucian Fellowship, Oceanside, CA, 1997. (see also, Heindel, *Rosicrucian Philosophy in Questions and Answers*, 1990; and *The Rosicrucian Mysteries*, Collected Works, Vol. 12, 1987.)

Herbert, Nick, *Elemental Mind: Human Consciousness and New Physics*, Penguin, NY, 1993.

Hoffman, Michael, II, "Dark Side of a Bad Moon," (see, *Revisionist History*, www.hoffman-info.com)

Huxley, Aldous, *Doors of Perception and Heaven and Hell*, Harper & Row, NY, 1963.

Icke, David, "The Veil of Tears," (www.davidicke.com/icke/articles/veil.html); See also: *Robot's Rebellion: The Story of the Spiritual Renaissance*, Gill & Macmillan, 1994; *And the Truth Shall Set You Free*, Truth Seeker, 1998; *The Biggest Secret: The Book That Will Change the World*, Bridge of Love, 1999.

Jones, Scott, (Ed.) "When Cosmic Cultures Meet," Human Potential Foundation (HPF), Conference, Washington, DC, 1995. (P.O. Box 6, Falls Church, VA 22040)

Jung, Carl, *Flying Saucers: A Modern Myth of Things Seen in the Skies*, 1958, Princeton reissue, 1991, (see also, *Synchronicity: An Acausal Connecting Principle*, Princeton, 1988).

Kasten, Kathy, "Timmy McVeigh was Telling the Truth!" in *Paranoia: The Conspiracy Reader*, (Issue 24, P.O. Box 1041, Providence, RI 02901, $7.)

Kin, L., *Pied Pipers of Heaven, Who Calls the Tune?, From the Bottom to the Top: The Way Out, Scientology, a Handbook for Use*, Volumes 1 and 2, *Scientology: More Than a Cult?* ScienTerra, Wiesbaden, Germany. (Distributed by Art Matrix, POB 880, Ithaca, NY 14851)

Koppang, Randy, Interview with Karla Turner and Melinda Leslie, *Paranoia*, (Issue 24, P.O. Box 1041, Providence, RI 02901, $7)

Kramer, Heinrich and Sprenger, James, *The Malleus Maleficarum: The Notorious Handbook once used to Condemn Witches*, The Book Tree, Escondido, CA, 1 (800) 700-8733, 1999.

Kuhn, Thomas S., *The Structure of Scientific Revolutions*, (3rd.) Chicago, 1996.

Laffoley, Paul, *The Phenomenology of Revelation*, Kent Gallery Inc., 1989 (see amazon.com), see also, Interview, "Paul Explains It All," *Paranoia*, (Issue 5, P.O. Box 1041, Providence, RI 02901, $7)

Lammer, Helmut and Marion, *MILABS: Military Mind Control and Alien Abductions*, IllumiNet Press, Lilburn, GA, 1999. (sincere apologies for leaving this out of Vol. 1 Bibliography)

Little, Gregory, *Grand Illusions: The Spectral Reality Underlying Sexual UFO Abductions*, Eagle Wing, TN, 1994, *People of the Web*, Eagle Wing, 1990, see also, Interview with Remy Chevalier, *Paranoia: The Conspiracy Reader*.

Long, Greg, *Examining the Earthlight Theory: The Yakima UFO Microcosm*, Center for UFO Studies.

Macer-Story, Eugenia, "The Dark Frontier: Master Game Plan of Discarnate Intelligences," in *Paranoid Women Collect Their Thoughts*, (Paranoia Publishing, P.O.B. 1041, Providence, RI 01901, $15 postage paid)

Mandelbaum, W. Adam, *The Psychic Battlefield: A History of the Military-Occult Complex*, St. Martin's Press, NY, 2000.

Mann, Nicholas and Marcia Sutton, *Giants of Gaia*, Brotherhood of Life, 1995.

Mansfield, Victor, *Synchronicity, Science and Soul-Making*, Open Court Press, 1995.

Martin, Graham, *Shadows in the Cave: Mapping the Conscious Universe*.

Maxey, E. Stanton, "The Subject and His Environment," in *First International Congress on Psychotronic Research*, #JPRS L/5022-2, Prague, 1973.

McGowan, Harold, *The Thoughtron Theory of Life and Matter, How it Relates to Scientology and Transcendental Meditation*, Exposition Press, Jericho, NY, 1973.

McMoneagle, Joseph, *The Ultimate Time Machine: A Remote Viewer's Perception of Time and Predictions for the New Millenium*, Hampton Roads, VA, 1998; see also, *Mind Trek*, Hampton Roads, VA, 1997.

McRae, Ronald, M., *Mind Wars: The True Story of Government Research into the Military Potential of Psychic Weapons*, St. Martin's, NY, 1984.

Messinger, Lanny, *The Programming of a Planet*, self-published. (see "The Meaning of Light: A Synopsis of Extra-Terrestrial Intentions and Methods," *Paranoia*, (Spring, 1999, P.O. Box 1041, Providence, RI 02901, $7)

Miklos, Jeno, "A Genetic Hypothesis for Parapsychology: Postulating Psi-Genes," *First International Congress on Psychotronic Research*, #JPRS L/5022-2, Prague, 1973.

Morehouse, David, *Psychic Warrior: Inside the CIA's Stargate Program*, St. Martin's Press, 1998.

Neal, Viola, "Unusual States of Consciousness," in *First International Congress on Psychotronic Research*, #JPRS L/5022-2, Prague, 1973.

Newman, Joseph, *The Energy Machine of Joseph Newman*, (Box 52, Lucedale, MS)

O'Brien, Cathy, *TranceFormation of America*, Reality Marketing, (POB 27740, Las Vegas, NV 89126)

Ostrander, Sheila, and Lynn Schroeder, *Psychic Discoveries Behind the Iron Curtain*, Marlowe, NY, reissued 1997.

Ouspensky, P.D. *Tertium Organum: The Third Canon of Thought*, Vintage Books, New York, 1920, 1982.

Palmer, Trevor, *Catastrophism, Neocatastrophism and Evolution*, (see at http://www.knowledge.co.uk)

Paranoia: The Conspiracy Reader, P.O. Box 1041, Providence, RI 02901, sample issue $7 ppd., indicate Issue # or name of article; or *Paranoid Women Collect Their Thoughts*, $15 ppd.

Pauwels, Louis and Jacques Bergier, *The Dawn of Magic*, Panther, London, 1964.

Pearce, Joseph Chilton, *Crack in the Cosmic Egg: Challenging Constructs of Mind and Reality*, Julian Press, 1988.

Peat, David, *Synchronicity: The Bridge Between Matter and Mind*, Bantam, NY, 1988.

Pinkham, Mark Amaru, *The Return of the Serpents of Wisdom*, Adventures Unlimited, 1997.

Piszkiewicz, Dennis, *The Nazi Rocketeers: Dreams of Space and Crimes of War*, Praeger, CT, 1995.

Puthoff, Harold, "CIA Initiated Remote Viewing at Stanford Research Institute," (www.biomindsuperpowers.com/Pages/CIA-InitiatedRV.html)

Rejdak, Zdenek, "Psychotronics Reveals New Possibilities for Cybernetics," in *First International Congress on Psychotronic Research*, #JPRS L/5022-2, Prague, 1973.

Robertson, Douglas, *The New Renaissance: Computers and the Next Level of Civilization*, Oxford Press, 1998.

Rossman, Michael, "On Some Matters of Concern in Psychic Research," in *Psychic Warfare: Fact or Fiction?*, Aquarian Press, Great Britain, 1988.

Russell, Dan, *Shamanism and the Drug Propaganda: Patriarchy and the Drug War*, Kalyx.com, NY, 1998.

Sarfatti, Jack, "The Starship Builders" (see also "The Parsifal Effect," "Bye, Bye Schrodinger!" (http://stardrive.org/Jack/Synergy.pdf) and other articles at http://www.stardrive.org)

Sartre, Jean-Paul, *Essays in Existentialism*, Citadel Press, 1965, 1993; and *Of Human Freedom*, Philosophical Library Inc., New York, 1966.

Sheldrake, Rupert, *A New Science of Life: The Hypothesis of Morphic Resonance*, Park Street Press, VT, 1995.

Schnabel, Jim, *Remote Viewers: The Secret History of America's Psychic Spies*, Dell, NY, 1997.

Schrader, George A. Jr., Ed., "The Search for Meaning," in *Existential Philosophers*, McGraw-Hill, NY, 1967.

Simpson, Christopher, *Blowback: America's Recruitment of Nazis and its Effect on the Cold War*, Collier, NY, 1988.

Singer, June, *Boundaries of the Soul, The Practice of Jung's Psychology*, Anchor Books, NY, 1973.

Smith, Dan, "The Eschaton" web site, (see writings at www.clark.net/pub/dansmith/), see also Interview with Joan d'Arc, *Paranoia*, at www.paranoiamagazine.com.

Solomon, Robert, *Phenomenology and Existentialism*, University Press of America, NY, 1980.

Stolaroff, Myron, *The Secret Chief: Conversations with a pioneer of the underground psychedelic therapy movement*, Multidisciplinary Approach for Psychedelic Studies (MAPS), 1997, Charlotte, NC www.maps.org/secretchief/

Swann, Ingo, *Penetration: The Question of ET and Human Telepathy*, TwiggsCompany, SD, 1998. (see also other writings at www.biomindsuperpowers.com)

Swann, Ingo, "Scientological Techniques: A Modern Paradigm for the Exploration of Consciousness and Psychic Integration," in *First International Congress on Psychotronic Research*, #JPRS L/5022-2, Prague, 1973.

Tart, Charles, "Six Studies of Out-of-body Experience," *Journal of Near Death Studies* 1997, (also see other papers at www.paradigm-sys.com/cttart)

Talbot, Michael, *The Holographic Universe*, Harper, NY, 1991.

Thompson, Keith, *Angels and Aliens: UFOs and the Mythic Imagination*, Ballantine, NY, 1991.

Thompson, Richard, *Alien Identities: Ancient Insights into Modern UFO Phenomena*, Govardhan Hill, NY, 1995.

Thompson, Richard, *Vedic Cosmography and Astronomy: Celestial Geometry of India.*

Vance, Bruce, *Dreamscape: Voyage in an Alternate Reality*, Theosophical Publishing House, IL, 1989.

Vogel, Marcel, "Man-Plant Communication Experiments," in *First International Congress on Psychotronic Research*, #JPRS L/5022-2, Prague, 1973.

Wall, Judy and Mike Coyle, "Technology to Boggle Your Mind," *Paranoia* (Issue 24), $7. (see also, Judy Wall, "Resonance Newsletter of the Bioelectromagnetics Sig," 684 CR 535, Sumterville, FL33585, and see article in d'Arc, *Paranoid Women Collect Their Thoughts*)

Wertheim, Margaret, *The Pearly Gates of Cyberspace: A History of Space from Dante to the Internet*, W.W. Norton, 2000.

White, John, (ed.), *Psychic Warfare: Fact or Fiction?: An investigation into the use of the mind as a military weapon*, Aquarian Press, Great Britain, 1988.

Wilson, Colin, *Poltergeist: A Study in Destructive Haunting*, Llewellyn, MN, 1993.

Wolf, Fred Alan, *The Dreaming Universe*, Simon & Schuster, NY, 1994.

Index

Space Travelers and the Genesis of the Human Form: Evidence of Intelligent Contact in the Solar System, by Joan d'Arc. Believers in extraterrestrial intelligent life (ETI) have no doubt been confronted with the few standard arguments covered in this book that are pitched by most skeptics. But are they logical and internally consistent? Or are they based on mistaken assumptions, government-media hogwash, and outmoded scientific concepts? Even skeptics may want to explore the logical grounds upon which their staunch protest against the existence of ETI is founded. Can Darwinian evolution actually prove we are alone in the Universe? This book illustrates that Darwinian evolution is actually not an empirically predictable or testable scientific paradigm. Darwinian evolution is a circular argument which serves to keep Earth humans earthbound. This book also shows that ancient artifacts on Mars and the Moon are evidence of "Game Wardens" in our own solar system. Could the Earth be a controlled DNA repository for the ongoing creation and dissemination of life forms, including humans. **(2000) • 208 pages • 6 x 9 • trade paper • illustrated • $18.95 • ISBN 1-58509-127-8**

TRIUMPH OF THE HUMAN SPIRIT: The Greatest Achievements of the Human Soul and How Its Power Can Change Your Life **by Paul Tice.** A triumph of the human spirit happens when we know we are right about something, put our heart into achieving its goal, and then succeed. There is no better feeling. People throughout history have triumphed while fighting for the highest ideal of all – spiritual truth. Some of these people and movements failed, other times they changed the course of history. Those who failed only did so on a physical level, when they were eliminated through violence. Their spirit lives on. This book not only documents the history of spiritual giants, it shows you how you can achieve your own spiritual triumph. Various exercises will strengthen your soul and reveal its hidden power. In today's world we are free to explore the truth without fear of being tortured or executed. As a result, the rewards are great. You will discover your true spiritual power with this work and will be able to tap into it. This is the perfect book for all those who believe in spiritual freedom and have a passion for the truth. **(1999) • 295 pages • 6 x 9 • trade paperback • $19.95 • ISBN 1-885395-57-4**

PAST SHOCK: The Origin of Religion and Its Impact on the Human Soul **by Jack Barranger. Introduction by Paul Tice.** Twenty years ago, Alvin Toffler coined the term "future shock" – a syndrome in which people are overwhelmed by the future. *Past Shock* suggests that events which happened thousands of years ago very strongly impact humanity today. This book reveals incredible observations on our inherited "slave chip" programming and how we've been conditioned to remain spiritually ignorant. Barranger exposes what he calls the "pretender gods," advanced beings who were not divine, but had advanced knowledge of scientific principles which included genetic engineering. Our advanced science of today has unraveled their secrets, and people like Barranger have the knowledge and courage to expose exactly how we were manipulated. Learn about our past conditioning and how to conquer the "slave chip" mentality to begin living life as a spiritually fulfilled being. **(1998) • 126 pages • 6x9 • trade paperback • $12.95 • ISBN 1-885395-08-6**

GOD GAMES: What Do You Do Forever? **by Neil Freer. Introduction by Zecharia Sitchin.** This new book by the author of Breaking the Godspell clearly outlines the entire human evolutionary scenario. While Sitchin has delineated what happened to humankind in the remote past based on ancient texts, Freer outlines the implications for the future. We are all creating the next step we need to take as we evolve from a genetically engineered species into something far beyond what we could ever imagine. We can now play our own "god games." We are convinced that great thinkers in the future will look back on this book, in particular, as being the one which opened the door to a new paradigm now developing. Neil Freer is a brilliant philosopher who recognizes the complete picture today, and is far ahead of all others who wonder what really makes us tick, and where it is that we are going. This book will make readers think in new and different ways. **(1998) • 310 pages • 6 x 9 • trade paperback • $19.95 • ISBN 1-885395-39-6**

OF HEAVEN AND EARTH: Essays Presented at the First Sitchin Studies Day. **Edited by Zecharia Sitchin.** Zecharia Sitchin's previous books have sold millions around the world. This book contains further information on his incredible theories about the origins of mankind and the intervention by intelligences beyond the Earth. This book offers the complete proceedings of the first Sitchin Studies Day. Sitchin's keynote address opens the book, followed by six other prominent speakers whose work has been influenced by Sitchin. The other contributors include two university professors, a clergyman, a UFO expert, a philosopher, and a novelist – who joined Zecharia Sitchin to describe how his findings and conclusions have affected what they teach and preach. They all seem to agree that the myths of ancient peoples were actual events as opposed to being figments of imaginations. Another point of agreement is in Sitchin's work being the early part of a new paradigm – one that is already beginning to shake the very foundations of religion, archaeology and our society in general. **(1996) • 164 pages • 5 1/2 x 8 1/2 • trade paperback • $14.95 • ISBN 1-885395-17-5**

Call for our FREE BOOK TREE CATALOG with over 1000 titles. Order from your favorite bookseller, or we accept Visa, MC, AmEx, or send check or money order (in USD) for the total amount plus 4.50 shipping for 1-3 books (and .50¢ thereafter). The Book Tree • PO Box 724 • Escondido, CA 92033 • (760) 489-5079 • Visit www.thebooktree.com • **Call today (800) 700-TREE**

Of Heaven and Earth: Essays Presented at the First Sitchin Studies Day, edited by Zecharia Sitchin. ISBN 1-885395-17-5 • 164 pages • 5 1/2 x 8 1/2 • trade paper • illustrated • $14.95

God Games: What Do You Do Forever?, by Neil Freer. ISBN 1-885395-39-6 • 312 pages • 6 x 9 • trade paper • $19.95

Past Shock: The Origin of Religion and Its Impact on the Human Soul, by Jack Barranger. ISBN 1-885395-08-6 • 126 pages • 6 x 9 • trade paper • illustrated • $12.95

Triumph of the Human Spirit: The Greatest Achievements of the Human Soul and How Its Power Can Change Your Life, by Paul Tice. ISBN 1-885395-57-4 • 295 pages • 6 x 9 • trade paper • illustrated • $19.95

Space Travelers and the Genesis of the Human Form: Evidence of Intelligent Contact in the Solar System, by Joan d'Arc. ISBN 1-58509-127-8 • 208 pages • 6 x 9 • trade paper • illustrated • $18.95

Mysteries Explored: The Search for Human Origins, UFOs, and Religious Beginnings, by Jack Barranger and Paul Tice. ISBN 1-58509-101-4 • 104 pages • 6 x 9 • trade paper • $12.95

Mushrooms and Mankind: The Impact of Mushrooms on Human Consciousness and Religion, by James Arthur. ISBN 1-58509-151-0 • 103 pages • 6 x 9 • trade paper • $12.95

Vril or Vital Magnetism, with an Introduction by Paul Tice. ISBN 1-58509-030-1 • 124 pages • 5 1/2 x 8 1/2 • trade paper • $12.95

The Odic Force: Letters on Od and Magnetism, by Karl von Reichenbach. ISBN 1-58509-001-8 • 192 pages • 6 x 9 • trade paper • $15.95

The New Revelation: The Coming of a New Spiritual Paradigm, by Arthur Conan Doyle. ISBN 1-58509-220-7 • 124 pages • 6 x 9 • trade paper • $12.95

The Astral World: Its Scenes, Dwellers, and Phenomena, by Swami Panchadasi. ISBN 1-58509-071-9 • 104 pages • 6 x 9 • trade paper • $11.95

Reason and Belief: The Impact of Scientific Discovery on Religious and Spiritual Faith, by Sir Oliver Lodge. ISBN 1-58509-226-6 • 180 pages • 6 x 9 • trade paper • $17.95

William Blake: A Biography, by Basil De Selincourt. ISBN 1-58509-225-8 • 384 pages • 6 x 9 • trade paper • $28.95

The Divine Pymander: And Other Writings of Hermes Trismegistus, translated by John D. Chambers. ISBN 1-58509-046-8 • 196 pages • 6 x 9 • trade paper • $16.95

Theosophy and The Secret Doctrine, by Harriet L. Henderson. Includes *H.P. Blavatsky: An Outline of Her Life,* by Herbert Whyte. ISBN 1-58509-075-1 • 132 pages • 6 x 9 • trade paper • $13.95

The Light of Egypt, Volume One: The Science of the Soul and the Stars, by Thomas H. Burgoyne. ISBN 1-58509-051-4 • 320 pages • 6 x 9 • trade paper • illustrated • $24.95

The Light of Egypt, Volume Two: The Science of the Soul and the Stars, by Thomas H. Burgoyne. ISBN 1-58509-052-2 • 224 pages • 6 x 9 • trade paper • illustrated • $17.95

The Jumping Frog and 18 Other Stories: 19 Unforgettable Mark Twain Stories, by Mark Twain. ISBN 1-58509-200-2 • 128 pages • 6 x 9 • trade paper • $12.95

The Devil's Dictionary: A Guidebook for Cynics, by Ambrose Bierce. ISBN 1-58509-016-6 • 144 pages • 6 x 9 • trade paper • $12.95

The Smoky God: Or The Voyage to the Inner World, by Willis George Emerson. ISBN 1-58509-067-0 • 184 pages • 6 x 9 • trade paper • illustrated • $15.95

A Short History of the World, by H.G. Wells. ISBN 1-58509-211-8 • 320 pages • 6 x 9 • trade paper • $24.95

The Voyages and Discoveries of the Companions of Columbus, by Washington Irving. ISBN 1-58509-500-1 • 352 pages • 6 x 9 • hard cover • $39.95

History of Baalbek, by Michel Alouf. ISBN 1-58509-063-8 • 196 pages • 5 x 8 • trade paper • illustrated • $15.95

Ancient Egyptian Masonry: The Building Craft, by Sommers Clarke and R. Engelback. ISBN 1-58509-059-X • 350 pages • 6 x 9 • trade paper • illustrated • $26.95

That Old Time Religion: The Story of Religious Foundations, by Jordan Maxwell and Paul Tice. ISBN 1-58509-100-6 • 103 pages • 6 x 9 • trade paper • $12.95

The Book of Enoch: A Work of Visionary Revelation and Prophecy, Revealing Divine Secrets and Fantastic Information about Creation, Salvation, Heaven and Hell, translated by R. H. Charles. ISBN 1-58509-019-0 • 152 pages • 5 1/2 x 8 1/2 • trade paper • $13.95

The Book of Enoch: Translated from the Editor's Ethiopic Text and Edited with an Enlarged Introduction, Notes and Indexes, Together with a Reprint of the Greek Fragments, edited by R. H. Charles. ISBN 1-58509-080-8 • 448 pages • 6 x 9 • trade paper • $34.95

The Book of the Secrets of Enoch, translated from the Slavonic by W. R. Morfill. Edited, with Introduction and Notes by R. H. Charles. ISBN 1-58509-020-4 • 148 pages • 5 1/2 x 8 1/2 • trade paper • $13.95

Enuma Elish: The Seven Tablets of Creation, Volume One, by L. W. King. ISBN 1-58509-041-7 • 236 pages • 6 x 9 • trade paper • illustrated • $18.95

Enuma Elish: The Seven Tablets of Creation, Volume Two, by L. W. King. ISBN 1-58509-042-5 • 260 pages • 6 x 9 • trade paper • illustrated • $19.95

Enuma Elish, Volumes One and Two: The Seven Tablets of Creation, by L. W. King. Two volumes from above bound as one. ISBN 1-58509-043-3 • 496 pages • 6 x 9 • trade paper • illustrated • $38.90

The Archko Volume: Documents that Claim Proof to the Life, Death, and Resurrection of Christ, by Drs. McIntosh and Twyman. ISBN 1-58509-082-4 • 248 pages • 6 x 9 • trade paper • $20.95

The Lost Language of Symbolism: An Inquiry into the Origin of Certain Letters, Words, Names, Fairy-Tales, Folklore, and Mythologies, by Harold Bayley. ISBN 1-58509-070-0 • 384 pages • 6 x 9 • trade paper • $27.95

The Book of Jasher: A Suppressed Book that was Removed from the Bible, Referred to in Joshua and Second Samuel, translated by Albinus Alcuin (800 AD). ISBN 1-58509-081-6 • 304 pages • 6 x 9 • trade paper • $24.95

The Bible's Most Embarrassing Moments, with an Introduction by Paul Tice. ISBN 1-58509-025-5 • 172 pages • 5 x 8 • trade paper • $14.95

History of the Cross: The Pagan Origin and Idolatrous Adoption and Worship of the Image, by Henry Dana Ward. ISBN 1-58509-056-5 • 104 pages • 6 x 9 • trade paper • illustrated • $11.95

Was Jesus Influenced by Buddhism? A Comparative Study of the Lives and Thoughts of Gautama and Jesus, by Dwight Goddard. ISBN 1-58509-027-1 • 252 pages • 6 x 9 • trade paper • $19.95

History of the Christian Religion to the Year Two Hundred, by Charles B. Waite. ISBN 1-885395-15-9 • 556 pages. • 6 x 9 • hard cover • $25.00

Symbols, Sex, and the Stars, by Ernest Busenbark. ISBN 1-885395-19-1 • 396 pages • 5 1/2 x 8 1/2 • trade paper • $22.95

History of the First Council of Nice: A World's Christian Convention, A.D. 325, by Dean Dudley. ISBN 1-58509-023-9 • 132 pages • 5 1/2 x 8 1/2 • trade paper • $12.95

The World's Sixteen Crucified Saviors, by Kersey Graves. ISBN 1-58509-018-2 • 436 pages • 5 1/2 x 8 1/2 • trade paper • $29.95

Babylonian Influence on the Bible and Popular Beliefs: A Comparative Study of Genesis I.2, by A. Smythe Palmer. ISBN 1-58509-000-X • 124 pages • 6 x 9 • trade paper • $12.95

Biography of Satan: Exposing the Origins of the Devil, by Kersey Graves. ISBN 1-885395-11-6 • 168 pages • 5 1/2 x 8 1/2 • trade paper • $13.95

The Malleus Maleficarum: The Notorious Handbook Once Used to Condemn and Punish "Witches", by Heinrich Kramer and James Sprenger. ISBN 1-58509-098-0 • 332 pages • 6 x 9 • trade paper • $25.95

Crux Ansata: An Indictment of the Roman Catholic Church, by H. G. Wells. ISBN 1-58509-210-X • 160 pages • 6 x 9 • trade paper • $14.95

Emanuel Swedenborg: The Spiritual Columbus, by U.S.E. (William Spear). ISBN 1-58509-096-4 • 208 pages • 6 x 9 • trade paper • $17.95

Dragons and Dragon Lore, by Ernest Ingersoll. ISBN 1-58509-021-2 • 228 pages • 6 x 9 • trade paper • illustrated • $17.95

The Vision of God, by Nicholas of Cusa. ISBN 1-58509-004-2 • 160 pages • 5 x 8 • trade paper • $13.95

The Historical Jesus and the Mythical Christ: Separating Fact From Fiction, by Gerald Massey. ISBN 1-58509-073-5 • 244 pages • 6 x 9 • trade paper • $18.95

Gog and Magog: The Giants in Guildhall; Their Real and Legendary History, with an Account of Other Giants at Home and Abroad, by F.W. Fairholt. ISBN 1-58509-084-0 • 172 pages • 6 x 9 • trade paper • $16.95

The Origin and Evolution of Religion, by Albert Churchward. ISBN 1-58509-078-6 • 504 pages • 6 x 9 • trade paper • $39.95

The Origin of Biblical Traditions, by Albert T. Clay. ISBN 1-58509-065-4 • 220 pages • 5 1/2 x 8 1/2 • trade paper • $17.95

Aryan Sun Myths, by Sarah Elizabeth Titcomb, Introduction by Charles Morris. ISBN 1-58509-069-7 • 192 pages • 6 x 9 • trade paper • $15.95

The Social Record of Christianity, by Joseph McCabe. Includes *The Lies and Fallacies of the Encyclopedia Britannica*, ISBN 1-58509-215-0 • 204 pages • 6 x 9 • trade paper • $17.95

The History of the Christian Religion and Church During the First Three Centuries, by Dr. Augustus Neander. ISBN 1-58509-077-8 • 112 pages • 6 x 9 • trade paper • $12.95

Ancient Symbol Worship: Influence of the Phallic Idea in the Religions of Antiquity, by Hodder M. Westropp and C. Staniland Wake. ISBN 1-58509-048-4 • 120 pages • 6 x 9 • trade paper • illustrated • $12.95

The Gnosis: Or Ancient Wisdom in the Christian Scriptures, by William Kingsland. ISBN 1-58509-047-6 • 232 pages • 6 x 9 • trade paper • $18.95

The Evolution of the Idea of God: An Inquiry into the Origin of Religions, by Grant Allen. ISBN 1-58509-074-3 • 160 pages • 6 x 9 • trade paper • $14.95

Sun Lore of All Ages: A Survey of Solar Mythology, Folklore, Customs, Worship, Festivals, and Superstition, by William Tyler Olcott. ISBN 1-58509-044-1 • 316 pages • 6 x 9 • trade paper • $24.95

Nature Worship: An Account of Phallic Faiths and Practices Ancient and Modern, by the Author of Phallicism with an Introduction by Tedd St. Rain. ISBN 1-58509-049-2 • 112 pages • 6 x 9 • trade paper • illustrated • $12.95

Life and Religion, by Max Muller. ISBN 1-885395-10-8 • 237 pages • 5 1/2 x 8 1/2 • trade paper • $14.95

Jesus: God, Man, or Myth? An Examination of the Evidence, by Herbert Cutner. ISBN 1-58509-072-7 • 304 pages • 6 x 9 • trade paper • $23.95

Pagan and Christian Creeds: Their Origin and Meaning, by Edward Carpenter. ISBN 1-58509-024-7 • 316 pages • 5 1/2 x 8 1/2 • trade paper • $24.95

The Christ Myth: A Study, by Elizabeth Evans. ISBN 1-58509-037-9 • 136 pages • 6 x 9 • trade paper • $13.95

Popery: Foe of the Church and the Republic, by Joseph F. Van Dyke. ISBN 1-58509-058-1 • 336 pages • 6 x 9 • trade paper • illustrated • $25.95

Career of Religious Ideas, by Hudson Tuttle. ISBN 1-58509-066-2 • 172 pages • 5 x 8 • trade paper • $15.95

Buddhist Suttas: Major Scriptural Writings from Early Buddhism, by T.W. Rhys Davids. ISBN 1-58509-079-4 • 376 pages • 6 x 9 • trade paper • $27.95

Early Buddhism, by T. W. Rhys Davids. Includes *Buddhist Ethics: The Way to Salvation?*, by Paul Tice. ISBN 1-58509-076-X • 112 pages • 6 x 9 • trade paper • $12.95

The Fountain-Head of Religion: A Comparative Study of the Principal Religions of the World and a Manifestation of their Common Origin from the Vedas, by Ganga Prasad. ISBN 1-58509-054-9 • 276 pages • 6 x 9 • trade paper • $22.95

India: What Can It Teach Us?, by Max Muller. ISBN 1-58509-064-6 • 284 pages • 5 1/2 x 8 1/2 • trade paper • $22.95

Matrix of Power: How the World has Been Controlled by Powerful People Without Your Knowledge, by Jordan Maxwell. ISBN 1-58509-120-0 • 104 pages • 6 x 9 • trade paper • $12.95

Cyberculture Counterconspiracy: A Steamshovel Web Reader, Volume One, edited by Kenn Thomas. ISBN 1-58509-125-1 • 180 pages • 6 x 9 • trade paper • illustrated • $16.95

Cyberculture Counterconspiracy: A Steamshovel Web Reader, Volume Two, edited by Kenn Thomas. ISBN 1-58509-126-X • 132 pages • 6 x 9 • trade paper • illustrated • $13.95

Oklahoma City Bombing: The Suppressed Truth, by Jon Rappoport. ISBN 1-885395-22-1 • 112 pages • 5 1/2 x 8 1/2 • trade paper • $12.95

Secret Societies and Subversive Movements, by Nesta H. Webster. ISBN 1-58509-092-1 • 432 pages • 6 x 9 • trade paper • $29.95

The Secret Doctrine of the Rosicrucians, by Magus Incognito. ISBN 1-58509-091-3 • 256 pages • 6 x 9 • trade paper • $20.95

The Origin and Evolution of Freemasonry: Connected with the Origin and Evolution of the Human Race, by Albert Churchward. ISBN 1-58509-029-8 • 240 pages • 6 x 9 • trade paper • $18.95

The Lost Key: An Explanation and Application of Masonic Symbols, by Prentiss Tucker. ISBN 1-58509-050-6 • 192 pages • 6 x 9 • trade paper • illustrated • $15.95

The Character, Claims, and Practical Workings of Freemasonry, by Rev. C.G. Finney. ISBN 1-58509-094-8 • 288 pages • 6 x 9 • trade paper • $22.95

The Secret World Government or "The Hidden Hand": The Unrevealed in History, by Maj.-Gen., Count Cherep-Spiridovich. ISBN 1-58509-093-X • 203 pages • 6 x 9 • trade paper • $17.95

The Magus, Book One: A Complete System of Occult Philosophy, by Francis Barrett. ISBN 1-58509-031-X • 200 pages • 6 x 9 • trade paper • illustrated • $16.95

The Magus, Book Two: A Complete System of Occult Philosophy, by Francis Barrett. ISBN 1-58509-032-8 • 220 pages • 6 x 9 • trade paper • illustrated • $17.95

The Magus, Book One and Two: A Complete System of Occult Philosophy, by Francis Barrett. ISBN 1-58509-033-6 • 420 pages • 6 x 9 • trade paper • illustrated • $34.90

The Key of Solomon The King, by S. Liddell MacGregor Mathers. ISBN 1-58509-022-0 • 152 pages • 6 x 9 • trade paper • illustrated • $12.95

Magic and Mystery in Tibet, by Alexandra David-Neel. ISBN 1-58509-097-2 • 352 pages • 6 x 9 • trade paper • $26.95

The Comte de St. Germain, by I. Cooper Oakley. ISBN 1-58509-068-9 • 280 pages • 6 x 9 • trade paper • illustrated • $22.95

Alchemy Rediscovered and Restored, by A. Cockren. ISBN 1-58509-028-X • 156 pages • 5 1/2 x 8 1/2 • trade paper • $13.95

The 6th and 7th Books of Moses, with an Introduction by Paul Tice. ISBN 1-58509-045-X • 188 pages • 6 x 9 • trade paper • illustrated • $16.95

Printed in the United States
18214LVS00002B/343-363